DOMINICA

PAUL CRASK

www.bradtguides.com

Bradt Guides Ltd, UK
The Globe Pequot Press Inc, USA

Bradt GUIDES
TRAVEL TAKEN SERIOUSLY

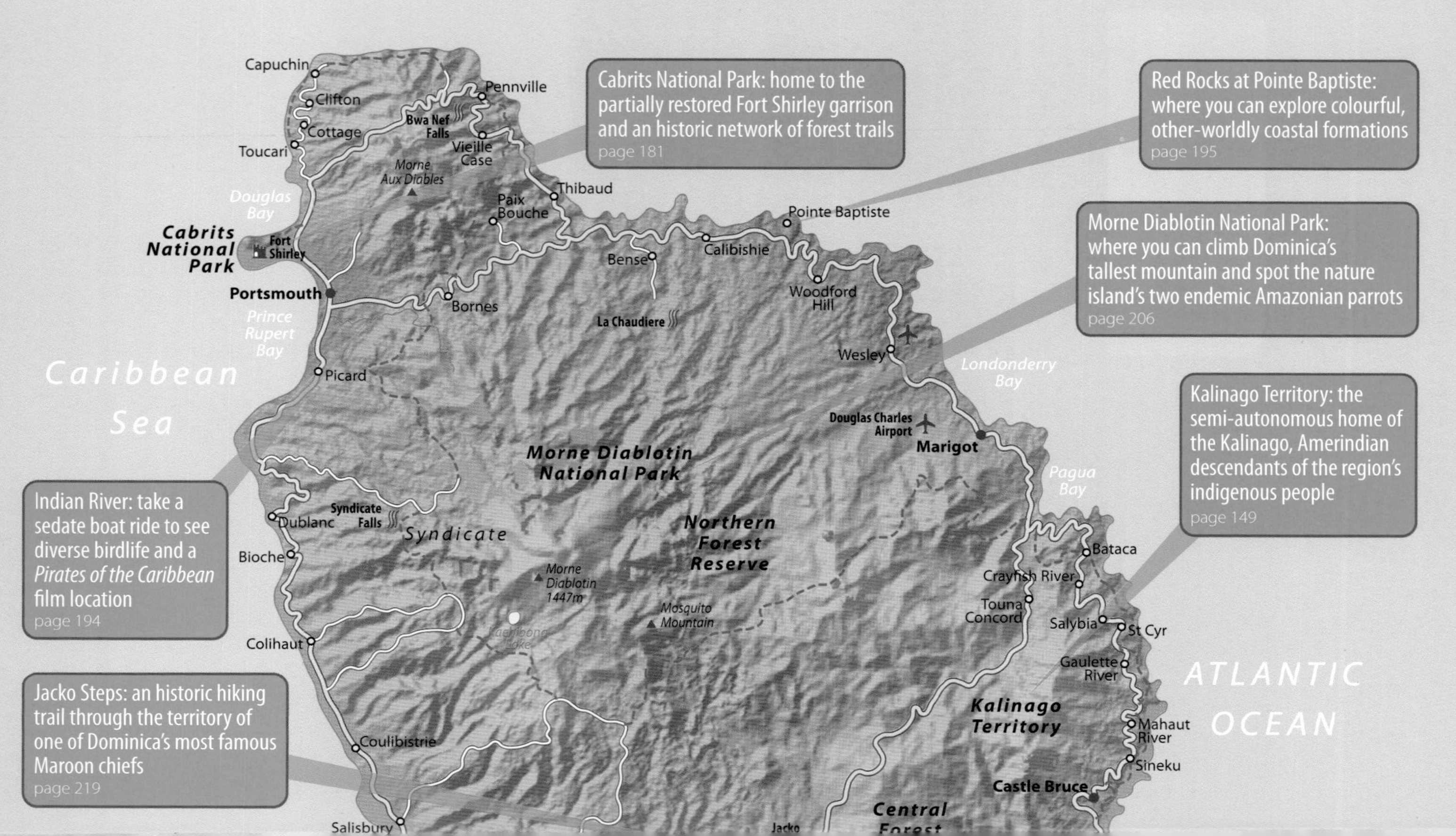

Cabrits National Park: home to the partially restored Fort Shirley garrison and an historic network of forest trails
page 181
Red Rocks at Pointe Baptiste: where you can explore colourful, other-worldly coastal formations
page 195
Morne Diablotin National Park: where you can climb Dominica's tallest mountain and spot the nature island's two endemic Amazonian parrots
page 206
Kalinago Territory: the semi-autonomous home of the Kalinago, Amerindian descendants of the region's indigenous people
page 149
Indian River: take a sedate boat ride to see diverse birdlife and a *Pirates of the Caribbean* film location
page 194
Jacko Steps: an historic hiking trail through the territory of one of Dominica's most famous Maroon chiefs
page 219
Caribbean Sea
ATLANTIC OCEAN
Capuchin
Clifton
Cottage
Toucari
Pennville
Bwa Nef Falls
Vieille Case
Morne Aux Diables
Douglas Bay
Cabrits National Park
Fort Shirley
Portsmouth
Prince Rupert Bay
Picard
Thibaud
Paix Bouche
Bornes
Bense
Calibishie
Pointe Baptiste
Woodford Hill
La Chaudiere
Wesley
Londonderry Bay
Douglas Charles Airport
Marigot
Pagua Bay
Morne Diablotin National Park
Northern Forest Reserve
Syndicate
Syndicate Falls
Dublanc
Bioche
Morne Diablotin 1447m
Mosquito Mountain
Colihaut
Coulibistrie
Salisbury
Jacko
Central Forest
Bataca
Crayfish River
Touna Concord
Salybia
St Cyr
Gaulette River
Kalinago Territory
Mahaut River
Sineku
Castle Bruce

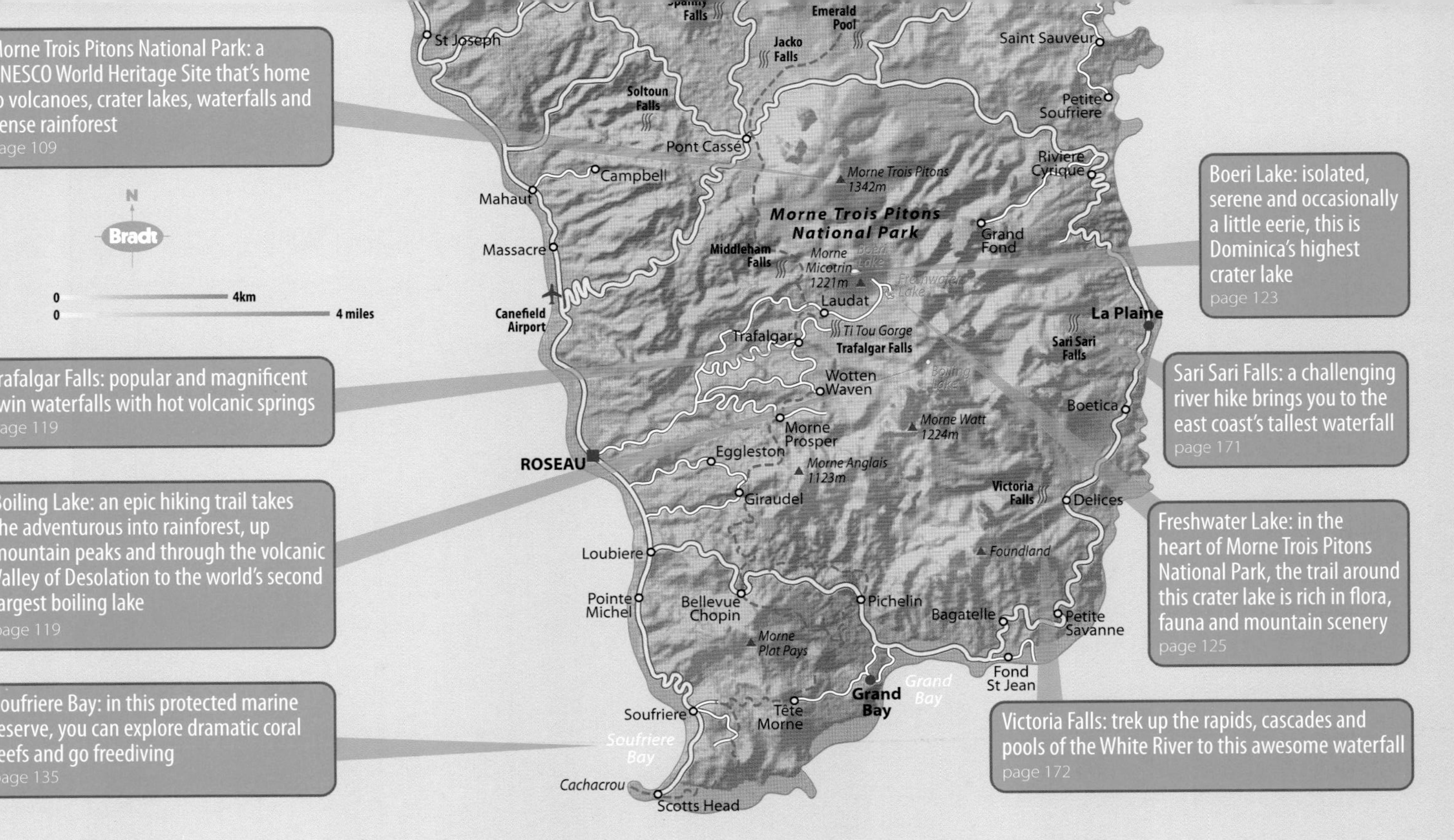
Morne Trois Pitons National Park: a UNESCO World Heritage Site that's home to volcanoes, crater lakes, waterfalls and dense rainforest
page 109
Trafalgar Falls: popular and magnificent twin waterfalls with hot volcanic springs
page 119
Boiling Lake: an epic hiking trail takes the adventurous into rainforest, up mountain peaks and through the volcanic Valley of Desolation to the world's second largest boiling lake
page 119
Soufriere Bay: in this protected marine reserve, you can explore dramatic coral reefs and go freediving
page 135
Boeri Lake: isolated, serene and occasionally a little eerie, this is Dominica's highest crater lake
page 123
Sari Sari Falls: a challenging river hike brings you to the east coast's tallest waterfall
page 171
Freshwater Lake: in the heart of Morne Trois Pitons National Park, the trail around this crater lake is rich in flora, fauna and mountain scenery
page 125
Victoria Falls: trek up the rapids, cascades and pools of the White River to this awesome waterfall
page 172
N
Bradt
0
4km
0
4 miles
St Joseph
Falls
Emerald Pool
Jacko Falls
Saint Sauveur
Soltoun Falls
Petite Soufriere
Pont Casse
Campbell
Riviere Cyrique
Mahaut
Morne Trois Pitons 1342m
Morne Trois Pitons National Park
Grand Fond
Massacre
Middleham Falls
Morne Micotrin 1221m
Boeri Lake
Freshwater Lake
Laudat
Canefield Airport
La Plaine
Sari Sari Falls
Trafalgar
Ti Tou Gorge
Trafalgar Falls
Wotten Waven
Boiling Lake
Boetica
Morne Prosper
Morne Watt 1224m
Eggleston
ROSEAU
Morne Anglais 1123m
Victoria Falls
Giraudel
Delices
Loubiere
Foundland
Pointe Michel
Bellevue Chopin
Pichelin
Bagatelle
Petite Savanne
Morne Plat Pays
Fond St Jean
Grand Bay
Grand Bay
Soufriere
Tête Morne
Soufriere Bay
Cachacrou
Scotts Head

DOMINICA
DON'T MISS...

RIVERS AND WATERFALLS

Dominica is an island with countless rivers and waterfalls, with Victoria Falls one of its most iconic PAGE 172
(DDA)

VOLCANIC LANDSCAPES

The Valley of Desolation on the Boiling Lake Trail is a mystical domain of steaming fumaroles, hot rivers, bubbling mud and vivid colour PAGE 119
(PC)

MOUNTAINS AND RAINFOREST

Dominica's interior is a breathtaking spectacle of imposing mountains and vast swathes of rainforest. Pictured here: Morne Watt in Morne Trois Pitons National Park PAGE 109
(CS)

KALINAGO TERRITORY

This semi-autonomous region is home to descendants of the eastern Caribbean's pre-Colombian people PAGE 149
(PC)

MARINE ENVIRONMENT

Dominica's pristine marine environment is full of life and reflects the dramatic topography of the island itself PAGE 10
(SS)

DOMINICA
IN COLOUR

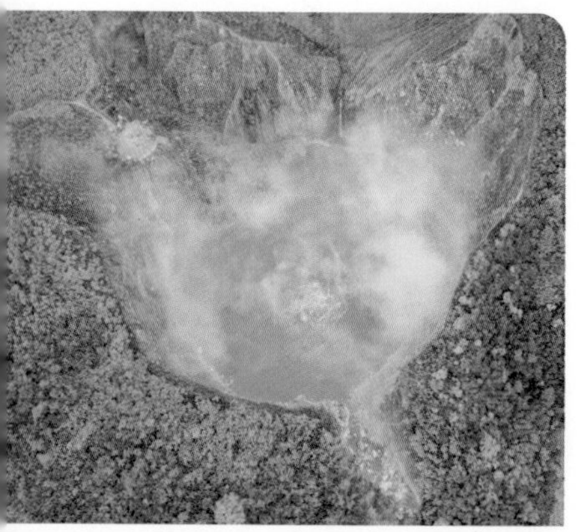

left (JB/S) Boiling Lake is a volcanically active fumarole, said to be the second largest of its kind in the world PAGE 119

below (PC) Red Rocks is a colourful and unusual landscape of weatherworn cliffs PAGE 195

bottom (SB/S) At the head of the Roseau Valley, the magnificent Trafalgar Falls is made up of Mother and Father falls PAGE 119

Often enshrouded in mist, the Freshwater Lake is located in the heart of Morne Trois Pitons National Park PAGE 125 above (PC)

L'Escalier Tete Chien is a legendary coastal formation in the Kalinago Territory PAGE 165 below left (PC)

Batibou is one of several picturesque beaches in the north PAGE 192 below right (DSv/S)

AUTHOR

Paul Crask (Instagram @paulcrask; w anotherdominica.com) grew up in Yorkshire (UK) and, in addition to studying in the former East Germany, graduated from Leeds University in 1988. He then travelled to Japan, working in Yamaguchi prefecture as a language teacher for two years before backpacking from the Far East via North America back to England. After a decade working in London, Paul and his wife Celia embarked on a radical lifestyle change, moving to Celia's native Dominica in 2005. Paul continues to enjoy travel and exploration and knows several islands of the eastern Caribbean inside out. He has written numerous articles for regional and international press, and has authored two Bradt guides: *Dominica* and *Grenada, Carriacou & Petite Martinique*. When not travelling or processing his homegrown coffee, he also photographs, sketches and writes about the more offbeat/less touristy aspects of life on his island home.

AUTHOR'S STORY

My wife, Celia, was born in Dominica and then grew up in England, where I met her in 1991 after living in Japan and backpacking around the world until my money ran out. I spent weekdays commuting by train to London where I worked, and at weekends we would walk the dog, decorate the house, go to the cinema and a restaurant, stroll to the local pub for a drink; the usual stuff. By 2005, we were ready for a change, and we left our jobs, packed up our belongings and moved to the island. They call it 'downshifting', apparently. My friends told me I was going away to 'live the dream' but I suspect they thought I was heading for the beaches of the Dominican Republic. No-one had heard of this place. Surprisingly, many still haven't.

Now, over 18 years later, I find myself writing the fourth edition of this book and the Caribbean's 'nature island' feels as familiar to me as England once did. But there's no routine anymore, for life here seems to change from day to day; few are ever the same.

We've had one or two setbacks – Hurricane Maria in September 2017 being the biggest of them all. Our home survived, many others didn't. When you come here, it will be hard for you to imagine the island with no greenery at all. But nature is amazing and, despite the hardships we all endured at the time and for a year or more afterwards, few of us would ever dream of living anywhere else.

Though not without its own unique set of challenges, life in Dominica offers a freedom and a sense of vitality that reminds me of the carefree tramping around the world of my youth. Perhaps it's the clean air of the rainforest, the freshness of the water, the food I harvest from the fertile soil of my garden, my homegrown and roasted coffee, the opportunities to explore – and get lost – and the people I meet along the way. But writing this guide and the other bits of freelance work that now make up my 'working' life is always a pleasure. Do take all the destination marketing hype with a hefty pinch of salt and travel to Dominica with an open mind, an enthusiasm for nature and the outdoors, and the spirit for adventure, and I think you'll understand what I mean.

Fourth edition published November 2023
First published 2007
Bradt Guides Ltd
31a High Street, Chesham, Buckinghamshire, HP5 1BW, England
www.bradtguides.com
Print edition published in the USA by The Globe Pequot Press Inc,
PO Box 480, Guilford, Connecticut 06437-0480

Project Manager: Elspeth Beidas
Cover research: Paul Crask

ISBN: 9781804691021

British Library Cataloguing in Publication Data
A catalogue record for this book is available from the British Library

Photographs Paul Crask (PC); Pierre Deschamps (PD); Discover Dominica Authority (DDA); Dreamstime.com: 1333809 Ontario Ltd (OL/D); Extreme Dominica (ED); Arun Madisetti/Images Dominica (AM); Shutterstock.com: Amery Butcher (AB/S), Danita Delimont (DD/S), Richard Goldberg (RG/S), Haspil (h/S), JibiBrown (JB/S), Dave Primov (DP/S), Dennis Sabo (DSa/S), Studio Barcelona (SB/S), David Svestka (DSv/S), VeseloInfo (V/S); Celia Sorhaindo (CS); SuperStock (SS); Lu Szumskyj (LS); Waitukubuli Artist Association (WAA)
Front cover Jaco parrot (LS)
Back cover (clockwise from top) Emerald Pool (h/S); hibiscus flower (V/S); spinner dolphins (DD/S)
Title page (clockwise from top left) Scotts Head (SS); Kalinago masks (DDA); Ti Kwen Glo Cho (AB/S)

Maps David McCutcheon FBCart.S; colour map relief base by Nick Rowland FRGS

Typeset by Ian Spick, Bradt Guides and Geethik Technologies, India
Production managed by Jellyfish Print Solutions; printed in India
Digital conversion by www.dataworks.co.in

Acknowledgements

The author would like to thank the following for their contributions to the text:

Stewart Bell is an award-winning Canadian journalist and the author of three non-fiction books, *The Bayou of Pigs*, *The Martyr's Oath*, and *Cold Terror*.

Dr Alan Friedlander is Chief Scientist for National Geographic's Pristine Seas Project and the Director of the Fisheries Ecology Research Lab at the University of Hawaii. He is also a fellow of the Royal Geographic Society.

LIST OF MAPS

Contents

Introduction

When I wrote the third edition of this guidebook, we'd just experienced Tropical Storm Erika, a weather event that dropped so much rain that it washed away two entire villages, ripped out road bridges and scarred numerous mountains with landslides. At the time, many considered it to be one of the island's most destructive storms and its legacy was reflected in the updated descriptions and listings in the book that I wrote back then. Little did any of us know that Erika was nothing compared with what was to come just two years later. Amateur meteorologists who happened to be on the island in September 2017 measured sustained winds of 220mph with even higher gusts. Hurricane Maria (officially a Category 5 storm) wiped out much of the island and left us with mental as well as physical scars. It was indeed a terrible time. You'll note from some of my descriptions that there are still one or two hiking trails and natural attractions that need attention or rehabilitation, but thanks to international assistance and the strength of nature, most of the island has recovered and there's little visual evidence of what transpired. When I look out from my porch now and see the depth of the forest-covered mountainside all the way down to the sea, it's still hard to believe that it ever happened. It's for good reason that Dominica is known as the Caribbean's nature island.

Independent Dominica is a young country that's still figuring out its identity and the direction in which it wishes to travel. Culture reflects the island's historic occupants: ancient Amerindians, Kalinago, European colonists, the enslaved, Maroons and the liberated people of Africa. Although the legacies of enslavement and colonialism are still present, and Dominicans still celebrate all things Creole, many young people are also keen to move on, with the internet and social media now influencing contemporary trends. For some Kalinago, the emphasis is on rediscovering an identity on their own terms, rather than one that has historically been defined by others. Dominica's cultural identity, rather like the style of its popular music, is therefore a *bouyon* of historic and contemporary influences that's regularly shapeshifting.

In terms of travel, Dominica will certainly appeal to nature and culture lovers, hikers and scuba-divers. There's a good selection of easy, intermediate and challenging hiking trails, and the calm and deep inshore waters along the coasts have healthy and topographically dramatic reef systems. There's also a resident sperm whale population. But if you're looking for an offbeat Caribbean destination that hasn't been impacted by more prolific tourism, you'd better come here soon. Resort hotels are being built and an international airport is under construction and scheduled to be operational by 2026. Right now, you can get to Dominica by direct flight from Miami, or indirect flights and connections via Puerto Rico, Sint Maarten, Antigua and Barbados. A high-speed inter-island ferry connects Dominica with Guadeloupe, Martinique and St Lucia (if you must get here indirectly, I highly recommend travelling via one of the French islands – it's a more relaxing journey).

Accommodation is varied. From so-called eco-luxury resorts to off-grid wooden cabins in the thick of the rainforest, there's something for all tastes and budgets. Welcome to beautiful Dominica, the Caribbean's nature island, and a place I'm lucky enough to call home.

KEY TO SYMBOLS

- Airport
- Hospital
- Post office
- Car park
- Castle/fortress
- Historic building
- Tourist information
- Museum
- Statue/monument
- Bank
- Church
- Pharmacy
- Garden
- Cruise ship berth
- Bus stop
- Male/female toilets
- Wall
- Traffic direction arrow
- Steps
- Hiking trail
- Cemetery
- Ruins
- Scenic viewpoint
- Beach
- Waterfall
- Hot spring
- Dive site
- Kayaking
- Mountain peak
- Other attraction
- Stadium
- National park
- Urban park
- Urban market/square etc
- Coral reef
- Swamp
- Relief layers

HOW TO USE THIS GUIDE

AUTHOR'S FAVOURITES Choosing a rewarding hike or finding that unmissable off-the-beaten-track beauty spot can be difficult, so the author has chosen a few of his favourite places throughout the country to point you in the right direction. These 'author's favourites' are marked with a ✷. Accommodation and dining listings are deliberately selective – all recommended by the author.

PRICE CODES Throughout this guide we have used price codes to indicate the cost of those places to stay and eat listed in the guide. For a key to these price codes, see page 56 for accommodation and page 58 for restaurants.

MAPS

Keys and symbols Maps include alphabetical keys covering the locations of those places to stay, eat or drink that are featured in the book. Note that regional maps may not show all hotels and restaurants in the area: other establishments may be located in towns shown on the map.

Grids and grid references The Roseau centre map uses gridlines to allow easy location of sites. Map grid references are listed in square brackets after the name of the place or site of interest in the text, with page number followed by grid number, eg: [93 C3].

FEEDBACK REQUEST

At Bradt Guides we're aware that guidebooks start to go out of date on the day they're published – and that you, our readers, are out there in the field doing research of your own. You'll find out before us when a fine new family-run hotel opens or a favourite restaurant changes hands and goes downhill. So why not tell us about your experiences? Contact us on ☎ 01753 893444 or **e** info@bradtguides.com. We will forward emails to the author who may post updates on the Bradt website at **w** bradtguides.com/updates. Alternatively, you can add a review of the book to Amazon, or share your adventures with us on Facebook, Twitter or Instagram (@BradtGuides).

Part One

GENERAL INFORMATION

DOMINICA AT A GLANCE

Location West Indies at 15°N and 61°W, between Guadeloupe and Martinique
Size Approximately 47km long, 26km wide and 750km² in area
Capital Roseau
Main airport Douglas-Charles (DOM)
Status Parliamentary democracy within the Commonwealth of Nations
Population 70,000 (est)
Languages English and French Creole
Economy Citizenship By Investment (CBI), tourism and agriculture
Main religion Roman Catholic
Currency East Caribbean dollar (EC$)
Exchange rates US$1 = EC$2.7 fixed; £1 = EC$3.5 variable; €1 = EC$3 variable (Aug 2023)
Electricity supply 220–240V, 50Hz. Commonly UK-style 3-pronged outlets.
Time GMT –4 hours
International telephone code +1 767
Flag Cross of yellow, black and white stripes on a green background with a red circle at the centre. Within the circle are ten green stars and a sisserou parrot.
National bird Sisserou parrot (*Amazona imperialis*)

1

Background Information

GEOGRAPHY

Dominica is an independent island nation located in the eastern Caribbean at 15°N and 61°W, between the French islands of Guadeloupe and Martinique. It's the most northerly of the Windward Islands and is approximately 47km long and 26km wide. The island is 750km^2 in area and faces the Atlantic Ocean to the east and the Caribbean Sea to the west. Located on the southwestern coast is the country's capital, Roseau, which is also its main seaport.

The interior of Dominica is one of the youngest and most mountainous landscapes in the region. At the centre of the Lesser Antilles island chain, Dominica's creation is still evident in its nine volcanoes (eight dormant, one active), sulphur deposits, volcanically heated springs and thermal vents (fumaroles) that are found both above and below sea level. Running down the centre of the island is a series of small mountains known as *mornes* (from an old French word), deep valleys, steep ridges and river gorges, all of which are covered in a dense blanket of rainforest, montane thicket and elfin woodland. Dominica's highest mountain is Morne Diablotin, which, at 1,447m, dominates the north of the island and is the second highest in the eastern Caribbean (La Grande Soufriere in Guadeloupe is taller by about 20m).

Rainforest is the most widespread vegetation type, followed by dry coastal woodland. In the higher elevations there are several thousand hectares of montane forest and elfin woodland (also known as cloudforest). Fumarole vegetation can be found in several areas, including the Valley of Desolation (page 109), Cold Soufriere (page 194) and the area around Boiling Lake (page 119).

The coast of Dominica stretches for some 148km and is where most of the population lives. On the Atlantic coastline the inshore waters can be rough and unpredictable, particularly near the mouths of rivers. In stark contrast to this is the west coast, where the Caribbean Sea laps gently along the shore and rough waters and strong currents are rarely experienced. Dominica has a combination of black- and white-sand beaches, though most of its coastline is rocky. In many places steep, rugged cliffs plunge dramatically into deep seas.

CLIMATE

Dominica has a tropical climate with average daytime temperatures typically ranging from around 26°C in January to 32°C or more in June, July and August. Rainfall can be heavy and sustained, especially on the Atlantic coast and in the elevated interior of the island. Average annual rainfall is around 700cm in the interior and 100cm on the west coast. Most of the rain arrives with trade winds from the Atlantic, resulting in showers on the east, or *windward* coast, heavy and persistent rainfall inland over the *mornes*, and lighter showers on the west, or *leeward* coast.

In recent times seasonal weather has been less predictable but, theoretically, the period between July and December is when Dominica is usually at its wettest and is also when it's most vulnerable to tropical depressions, storms and hurricanes. The driest and sunniest months tend to be from January to June (the dry season is known locally as *kawem*) but showers should always be anticipated, and some parts of Dominica can be wet all year round. The combination of sunny, warm weather and intermittent bursts of rainfall can also make the island rather humid at times, especially along the leeward coast where there is less breeze.

Hurricanes and tropical storms that have the potential to impact Dominica and the other islands of the Lesser Antilles tend to develop from tropical depressions in the Atlantic Ocean near the Cape Verde Islands. They are the rains and storms of the African monsoon season that travel all the way across the continent to the west coast and then over the Atlantic Ocean. If sea surface temperatures are warm enough, Sahara dust levels and atmospheric wind shear low, then these disturbances can develop into tropical depressions, storms and hurricanes that track westwards to trouble the Caribbean, Central and North America. Historically, the Atlantic hurricane season is usually at its peak – and most

HURRICANE MARIA

In September 2017, Category 5 Hurricane Maria became the most destructive storm in living memory. Forecast to be either a Category 2 or 3 storm, it rapidly intensified due to conditions created by the warm Atlantic Ocean waters off Dominica's east coast. Unofficial sources measured sustained winds of over 320km/h with gusts of even greater strength. Maria made landfall on Dominica's east coast near the villages of Good Hope and San Sauveur. Instead of continuing a northwest path across the island, the hurricane changed direction and moved on a northerly track before heading out into the Caribbean Sea from the northwest coast. Maria could not have taken a more destructive track and every part of the island was impacted.

According to post-disaster risk assessment conducted by agents of the Government of Dominica, the total damage to the country's housing sector alone amounted to EC$950 million. Almost 5,000 private homes were damaged beyond repair (15% of the country total), and around 24,000 suffered different levels of repairable damage (75% of the country total). Damage was considered to have been amplified by the prevalence of deficient construction practices, poor quality materials and inadequate wind-resilient connections.

In total, Hurricane Maria caused damage amounting to more than EC$3.5 billion – far more than Dominica could ever afford. Thanks to the generous intervention of the international community, as well as the country's regional neighbours, however, Dominica has been able to rebuild and recover.

Hurricane Maria came just two years after Tropical Storm Erika, a weather event that created massive landslides around the island resulting in several deaths and the evacuation and abandonment of two villages in the south: Dubique and Petite Savanne. Due to these experiences, Dominica's government has placed huge emphasis on ensuring 'climate resilience' is factored into all construction projects and that there's a plan in place to enable the island to recover quickly when the next extreme weather event hits.

threatening to the Lesser Antilles – during the months of August and September. The three worst storms to affect Dominica in recent times were Hurricane David in August 1979, Tropical Storm Erika in August 2015 and Hurricane Maria in September 2017.

NATURAL HISTORY AND CONSERVATION

HABITATS Found at the highest elevations, along the mountain tops and the tall ridges of Dominica's interior, is **elfin woodland**, or **cloudforest**. Frequently cloaked in a veil of mist and cloud, the moisture and dampness of this environment provide ideal conditions for mosses, lichens and ferns to thrive. A low-growing regionally endemic tree, known locally as the *kaklen* or *kaklin* (*Clusia mangle*), dominates the terrain, growing in a dense, tangled blanket some 2–3m above the ground. *Kaklen* has thick, ovate leaves, dark-red, hard-skinned fruit, and small white flowers. It's also found in areas of volcanic activity such as Boiling Lake and Cold Soufriere. The *palmiste moutan,* or mountain palm (*Prestoea montana*), occasionally pushes its way through the *kaklen* and other low-growing trees and ferns to reach heights of up to 7m. Other small- to medium-sized palms include the *Geonoma dussiana* and the *Geonoma pinnatifrons*, known locally as the *yanga*. Also commonly found at these higher elevations is the *kwé kwé wouj* (*Charianthus alpinus*), which is a low-growing tree with small clusters of red flowers with yellow stamens. The flowers and shrubs of the elfin forest typically bear their fruit in these small clusters and include two endemic species of thoroughworts: *Chromolaena impetiolaris* and *Chromolaena macrodon*. Two other endemics are *Inga dominicensis* and *Bealeria peteolaris*; they are more usually found growing in the heights of Morne Diablotin National Park (page 206).

Located at a slightly lower elevation is a layer of **montane forest**, or montane thicket. This is a habitat of transition that includes mosses and lichens, such as the endemic *Parmelia cryptochlora*, that are also found in elfin woodland. Common trees of the montane forest include the *bwa bandé* (*Richeria grandis*) of the Euphorbiaceae family and the *resinier montagne* (*Podocarpus coriacius*), which is a variety of yew.

Below the montane forest is Dominica's expansive **rainforest**. In this area of more modest rainfall, with deeper, well-drained soil, you'll come across magnificent trees such as the *gommier* (*Dacryodes excelsa*), also known regionally as the *tabonuco* or *candlewood* because of the flammable gum-like sap that oozes from its bark. These trees tower upwards of 30 or 40m and provide food and shelter for Dominica's endemic parrots (page 7). The rainforest is also the habitat of several species of *chatanier* (*Sloanea dentate*, *Sloanea caribaea* and *Sloanea berteriana*), both large- and small-leaf varieties, which have huge buttress roots that stretch far out across the forest floor. Other trees known locally as the *mang blanc* (*Symphonia globulifera*), *mang wouj* and *bwa kanno* (*Cecropia peltata*, or the trumpet tree) have prop roots and are also common in this habitat. The *karapit* (*Amanoa caribaea*) produces both buttress and prop roots and is one of the most abundant species of large tree growing in the rainforest. Together with the *balata* (*Manilkara bidentata*), also known as *bulletwood*, these two trees are often used in local construction because of their (anecdotal) durability and resistance to rain.

Along the unsheltered east coast of Dominica, you'll see **littoral woodland**. The vegetation here tends to have thick leaves to withstand the wind and salt spray. Shaped by strong Atlantic trade winds, the trees and shrubs along this coast visibly reflect the effects of the weather. Common trees include white cedar, sea grape, almond and coconut.

On the west coast of Dominica, usually sheltered from the severest weather, there is dry **coastal woodland**. The west coast has less rainfall than the rest of the island and this is reflected in the type of vegetation found here. Many of the trees are semi-deciduous and they shed leaves during excessively dry periods to conserve moisture and nutrients. Common species such as the *kampech* (*Haematoxylum campechianum*, or logwood) also have sharp thorns.

Growing in the volcanically active areas of the island, such as the Valley of Desolation, Boiling Lake, Wotten Waven, Galion, Cold Soufriere and the Soufriere Sulphur Springs, are examples of **fumarole vegetation**. The plants found here can withstand both steam and sulphur-laden gases.

PLANTS AND FLOWERS Close to 200 different species of fern have been recorded in Dominica, as well as around 20 species of bromeliads, 75 species of orchids and a dozen or more other endemic plant species. The tree fern (*Cyathea arborea*), known locally as *fougère* or *fwigè*, is widespread and can be found both within the heart of the rainforest as well as on its more deciduous margins. It's also grown ornamentally in some domestic gardens. On forest trails look out for the *pawasol agouti* (*Selaginella*), a low-growing fern that covers the forest floor and provides a hiding place for the elusive agouti (page 8). The *z'ailes mouches* (*Caludovica insignis*) is a common rainforest plant with palm-like leaves that split into two lobes. It's one of several plants that were traditionally used by the indigenous Kalinago for roof thatching and waterproofing baskets. Bromeliads include both epiphytes (plants that grow on top of other plants in a non-parasitical manner, deriving nutrients from air and rainfall) as well as terrestrial varieties. *Ananas grand bois* (*Glomeropitcairnia pendulifera*) is the largest bromeliad found in Dominica and is often seen on the branches of trees in rainforest, montane thicket and elfin woodland habitats. The high ridge of the Morne Anglais Trail (page 143) is a good place to see them.

Dominica's **national flower** is the *bwa kwaib* (*Sabinea carinalis*). It's an arboreal blossom that grows in dry coastal areas and, when in bloom, displays bright red flowers. Good examples can be seen in the Botanic Gardens in Roseau (page 105), at the top of Morne Espagnol (page 207) and within the garrison at Fort Shirley in Cabrits National Park (page 182).

Throughout Dominica, both in the wild and in lovingly tended gardens, it's common to see many varieties of tropical flowers and plants such as allamanda (*Allamanda cathartica*), angel's trumpet (*Brugmansia candida*), anthurium (*Anthurium andraeanum*), bird of paradise flower (*Strelitzia reginae*), bougainvillea

ROUCOU

Roucou (*Bixa orellana*), also known as *annatto* and *uruku*, is a fruiting tree that grows to around 5m in height and produces prickly, heart-shaped pods, each containing around 50 seeds. These seeds are coated in a reddish pigment that produces a vibrant dye. According to European accounts, Dominica's indigenous Amerindian people, the Kalinago, used this dye as a body paint. For centuries it has also been used as a medicinal plant that is thought to be useful for treating skin problems, fevers, dysentery, liver disease and even hepatitis. The leaves are used to calm the stomach and also as an antiseptic. Today, roucou is still used worldwide as a food colouring – often as an alternative to saffron – as well as a herbal remedy and an ingredient in skin- and hair-care products.

(*Bougainvillea*), ginger (*Zingiberaceae*), hibiscus (*Hibiscus*), heliconia (*Heliconia*) and ixora (*Ixora*). Flowering trees such as the flamboyant *Delonix regia* are usually seen growing along the drier west coast and are very bright and colourful when in full bloom.

Dominica also has many interesting and delicious types of vegetables and fruits. Dominicans often tend a family garden where they grow vegetables and traditional crops such as yams, dasheen, sweet potatoes or tannias. These *provisions* are traditional staples of the Dominican diet (page 57).

The *calabash* is a large round gourd that is cultivated on vines and harvested for use as a functional container or eating bowl. It's also dried and ornately decorated by local artisans (page 33) and makes for a unique and attractive souvenir (the roadside craft shops in the Kalinago Territory are the best places to look).

Medicinal plants play an important role in Dominican life. Rastafarians, Kalinago and predominantly the older generation of Dominicans retain the knowledge of their forebears and 'bush teas' and other herbal remedies are still in common use. What may seem like a weed to many could in fact be *verveine* (*Stachytarpheta jamaicensis*) or *tabac zombie* (*Pluchea symphytifolia*), plants that are often used to make tea infusions for colds, fevers and other such ailments. Take a walk in the forest or a cultivated garden with someone who knows about the subject, and you may be surprised by the extent and variety of ordinary-looking plants that are still regularly used for their medicinal properties.

BIRDS Almost 200 species of bird have been recorded in Dominica, including island and regional endemics. Most are migratory, of course, and it's thought that only around 60 of the recorded species are actually resident on the island. Dominica's endemic birds include the imperial Amazon parrot (*Amazona imperialis*), locally known as the **sisserou**. The large and colourful yet extremely elusive sisserou is a highly endangered species and is usually only observed in the elevated mature rainforest of the island's highest mountain, Morne Diablotin. Dominica's second endemic parrot is the **jaco** (*Amazona arausiaca*), which is smaller than the sisserou, greater in number and usually sighted at slightly lower elevations throughout the island's forested interior. To date, nine regionally endemic bird species have been recorded: the Lesser Antillean swift (*Chaetura martinica*), the blue-headed hummingbird (*Cyanophaia bicolor*), the Lesser Antillean flycatcher (*Myiarchus oberi*), the Lesser Antillean peewee (*Contopus latirostris*), the forest thrush (*Cichlerminia lherminieri*), the scaly-breasted thrasher (*Margarops fuscus*), the trembler (*Cinclocerthia rufcauda*), the plumbeous warbler (*Dendroica plumbea*) and the Lesser Antillean bullfinch (*Loxigilla noctis*).

Dominica has four recorded species of **hummingbird**: the purple-throated Carib (*Eulampis jugularis*), the green-throated Carib (*Sericotes holosericeus*), the Antillean crested hummingbird (*Orythorhyncus cristatus*) and the regionally endemic blue-headed hummingbird (*Cyanophaia bicolor*).

Along Dominica's inshore waters, especially in the Scotts Head and Soufriere Bay area, you can see magnificent frigatebirds (*Fregata magnificens*) circling and occasionally fighting with other seabirds for their catch. Other coastal birds include brown pelicans (*Pelecanus occidentalis*), brown boobies (*Sula leucogaster*) and occasionally the neotropic cormorant (*Phalacrocorax brasilianus*). The red-billed tropicbird (*Phaethon aethereus*), the white-tailed tropicbird (*Phaethon lepturus*) and several species of petrel and tern may also be observed.

Sandy shorelines, freshwater lakes and rivers provide a habitat for the belted kingfisher (*Ceryle alcyon*), the ringed kingfisher (*Ceryle torquatus*), the cattle egret

(*Bubulcus ibis*), the green heron (*Butorides virescens*), and a variety of plovers and sandpipers. Along the swampy and brackish margins of the Indian River (page 194) you're likely to see the common moorhen (*Gallinula chloropus*) and the Caribbean coot (*Fulica caribaea*). If you're lucky you may also catch sight of a white ibis (*Eudocimus albus*) and several species of teal and duck.

Dominica's forest habitats are home to a variety of bird species. The mangrove cuckoo (*Coccyzus minor*) and the rufous-throated solitaire (*Myadestes genibarbis*), commonly known as the **mountain whistler**, or *siffleur montagne*, are particularly vocal. The unmistakable call of the solitary mountain whistler sounds rather like a squeaky bicycle wheel and accompanies hikers throughout Dominica's elevated rainforest interior. The ground dove (*Columbina passerina*), the bananaquit (*Coereba flaveola*), the Lesser Antillean saltator (*Saltator albicollis*), over 20 species of warbler and around five species of flycatcher can also be seen and heard in the island's vast tracts of forest and woodland.

Birds of prey observed in Dominica include the northern harrier (*Circus cyaneus*), the broad-winged hawk (*Buteo platypterus*), the merlin (*Falco columbarius*), the American kestrel (*Falco sparverius*), the barn owl (*Tyto alba*) and the peregrine falcon (*Falco peregrinus*).

MAMMALS The **agouti** (*Dasyprocta leporina*) is a wild land rodent species that's thought to have been introduced by Amerindians as a food source and is still common in the forests of South America. Roughly the size of a rabbit, it's a ground-dwelling rodent that's related to the guinea pig. It has coarse, dark-brown hair and pink ears and is built for running at speed. A herbivore that eats fallen fruits and tubers, the agouti's penchant for digging up root crops makes it unpopular with farmers though its main habitat is the rainforest. If you happen to see one on a trail, then stand still to observe it otherwise it will sprint off into the cover and safety of the undergrowth.

The **manicou** (*Didelphys marsupialis insularis*) is a tree-dwelling opossum that's thought to have been introduced at the beginning of the 19th century, either by Amerindian travellers or by accident. Though widespread in the Americas, and common in Dominica, it's nocturnal and therefore rarely encountered. **Wild pigs** (*Sus scrofa*) are considered to be one of the widest-ranging mammals in the world and are common but elusive in Dominica. Described as invasive 'ecosystem disruptors', they live in the depths of Dominica's interior, particularly in the southern and eastern foothills of Morne Diablotin, where local hunters have reportedly come across some large and defensively aggressive specimens. Unless you're hiking in the deep bush, it's extremely unlikely your paths will ever cross. In all my years of hiking Dominica's trails, I've never seen one, though I have come across evidence of their digging around tree roots along WNT Segment 8. Pig hunting is allowed all year though fewer and fewer people seem to do it these days. There's no reliable information regarding the size of Dominica's wild pig population.

Twelve species of **bat** have been recorded on the island, of which four are endemic to the region: the Lesser Antillean long-tongued bat (*Monohyllus plethodon*), the Lesser Antillean tree bat (*Ardops nichollsi*), the Antillean cave bat (*Brachyphylla cavernarum*) and the mouse-eared bat (*Myotis dominicensis*), which is only found in Dominica and neighbouring Guadeloupe. Dominica's largest species is the fisherman bat (*Noctilio leporinus*), which is rufous-coloured and predominantly lives in sea caves. Bats are most common in the forest though many can be seen emerging from the corrugated gaps of galvanised-steel rooftops at dusk.

WILD DOMINIQUE

WildDominique is a non-government organisation (NGO) that was founded by Dominican Jeanelle Brisbane – at the time of writing, Dominica's only qualified ecologist (a surprising fact for a country that calls itself 'nature island'!). The organisation undertakes several activities in a loose partnership with Dominica's Forestry, Wildlife and Parks Division, in particular monitoring and recording wildlife, and working with schools to develop an appreciation of the island's diverse natural environment. 'We market and speak about Dominica as a nature island, but in addition to a disconnect between people and nature, there's also a big disparity between sustainable tourism and true ecological conservation,' says Jeanelle. 'Although I do sometimes feel somewhat alone, I really want to help to transform Dominica into a more meaningful "nature island" and help to develop a framework for better education and opportunities for employment in this field.' To learn more about and support WildDominique go to **w** wilddominique.org.

REPTILES AND AMPHIBIANS The **zandoli** (*Anolis oculatus*), or tree lizard, is endemic to Dominica. Small and well camouflaged, they inhabit woodlands and gardens throughout the island, though they are more prominent in the forested interior. The adult male has an orange and yellow throat fan that he extends to attract females. A recent arrival to the island is the Puerto Rican crested anole lizard (*Anolis cristatellus*), which is an invasive and aggressive species that competes with the native zandoli. The **abòlò** (*Ameiva fuscata*), or ground lizard, is also endemic to Dominica. It's common in low-lying dry habitats and is much larger than the zandoli. It's often seen and heard in coastal woodland and gardens – you'll see lots on the Cabrits National Park trails (page 197). The house **gecko** and tree gecko are lizards that usually appear at night, on the prowl for moths. They are both known locally as the *mabouya*, the Kalinago name for an evil spirit. The Lesser Antillean **iguana** (*Iguana delicatissima*) is also commonly seen, particularly on the island's drier west coast which is a habitat they prefer. You may also come across an invasive species, the striped-tailed iguana (*Iguana iguana*), also on the west coast.

Of the four species of snake recorded on the island, none is venomous. The largest is the **Dominican boa** (*Boa nebulosa*), or *tête chien*, which can grow to 3.5m (8ft) and is particularly unusual because it doesn't lay eggs like most reptiles, but instead gives birth to live young. The *kouwès nwé* (*Alsophis sibonius*) is a racer snake that's endemic to Dominica and the *kouwès jenga* (*Erythrolamprus juliae*) is a ground snake that's endemic to Dominica and Guadeloupe. Both snakes are usually found in drier coastal woodlands, though they can also be found in semi-deciduous woodland and rainforest margins.

The largest frog found on the island is known locally as the **mountain chicken** (*Leptodactyllus fallax*), or *crapaud*, and is endemic to both Dominica and Montserrat. Mountain chicken used to be considered the national dish, though the chytrid fungus disease that has plagued and devastated amphibians around the world also reached Dominica, sparing the *crapaud* from the restaurant menu but seriously reducing its number to near extinction. Dominica responded to the threat of this disease by banning amphibian imports, protecting the *crapaud* from hunting, and by establishing a captive breeding facility at the Botanic Gardens under the Darwin Initiative Project, with assistance from the Zoological Society of London. Sadly, this facility was destroyed by Hurricane Maria in 2017 and has not been replaced. Though working very closely with their colleagues on the island of Montserrat in an attempt to protect and save the mountain chicken, experts fear the future remains uncertain for this species which is now rarely observed (often, if discovered, its location is kept secret in order to protect it from hunters). Recent evidence suggests that the surviving populations of mountain chicken may have begun to develop resistance to the chytrid fungus, though it's still too early to know for sure.

Far more common than the mountain chicken is the **tree frog**, also known as the *tink frog*. This frog can be found in wet habitats throughout Dominica, from the depths of the rainforest to an upturned plant pot in an urban garden. Together with crickets and grasshoppers, the tree frog is part of the chorus of song you hear from the forest at nightfall or on rainy days.

BUTTERFLIES AND OTHER INSECTS Over 50 species of **butterfly** have been recorded in Dominica, two of which are endemic to the island. They are the Dominican Snout (*Libytheana fulvescens*) and the Dominican hairstreak (*Electrostrymon dominicana*). Both are usually found in dry areas, particularly along the west coast. To date, seven of the recorded species are considered regionally endemic. They are the St Lucia mestra (*Mestra cana*), the lesser whirlabout (*Polites dictynna*), the sub-tailed skipper (*Urbanus obscurus*), Godman's leaf (*Memphis dominicana*), Godman's hairstreak (*Allosmaitia piplea*), the bronze hairstreak (*Electrostrymon angerona*) and the broken dash skipper (*Wallengrenia ophites*).

Dominica is home to over 60 endemic beetle species, including one of the largest in the world, the Hercules beetle (*Dynastes hercules*). Other notable insects include moths, fireflies, stick insects, grasshoppers, crickets, whip tailed scorpions, centipedes and millipedes.

FRESHWATER FISH AND CRUSTACEANS Dominica's many rivers are home to several species of fish, the most common of which is the mountain mullet (*Agonostomus monticola*). There are over ten recorded species of freshwater shrimp, crayfish and other edible shellfish. Within Morne Trois Pitons National Park, Freshwater Lake (page 125) is home to a species of tilapia (*Tilapia mossambica*) that was deliberately introduced to this natural reservoir.

There are around 20 recorded species of river and land crab in Dominica. The cyrique (*Guinotia dentata*) is usually seen in wet places, around rivers and pools, and is sometimes cooked for food. The black crab (*Gegarcinus ruricola*) is usually found in dry forest areas along Dominica's west coast and is the primary ingredient of *crab back*, a traditional dish that's eaten during the Creole and Independence season (page 57).

Titiwi is the Kalinago name that is still used today for a type of goby (*Sicydium punctatum*) that hatches in fresh water, develops in the sea, and then returns to the rivers to spawn. Usually in September, at night-time and accompanied by seasonal storms that are known locally as 'titiwi lightning', coastal villagers catch nets full of these small fish at river mouths and traditionally cook them as an *ackra*, a small fritter that's fried in oil (page 57). The mouth of the Layou River on the west coast is a good place to see this, though you have to be there at either dusk or dawn.

MARINE ENVIRONMENT In the usually calm Caribbean Sea along Dominica's west coast it's possible to see whales and dolphins all year round, and the underwater environment has a reputation for some of the best scuba-diving in the region. Beneath the surface there are steep drop-offs descending into the abyss, sea pinnacles rising from the seabed, expansive coral reefs, volcanic fumaroles and an exuberance of aquatic life. Reflecting the dramatic topography above the water, Dominica's pristine marine environment is a spectacular fusion of life, colour and depth.

Coral reefs Dominica's coral reefs have a foundation of granite cliffs and large boulders. Reef topography is varied, though many consist of steep walls and pinnacles. Shallow reefs tend to run quickly away into deeper waters or occupy narrow ledges above precipitous drop-offs. The waters around the reefs are usually clear due to their depth and the fact that silt in water-borne run-off from the island's heavy deluges tends to dissipate very quickly. Like all coral reefs around the world, they are susceptible to the effects of climate change and global warming but the cold water rising from the depths offers a degree of protection. Although coral bleaching has been seen here, it's an uncommon occurrence. Stony coral tissue loss disease (SCTLD) is present, however (page 142). Hard and soft corals adorn Dominica's reefs. Common gorgonians include sea fans and sea whips. Stony coral varieties include finger coral, star coral, sheet coral and brain coral. Azure vase sponges, tube sponges and giant barrel sponges are also in abundance.

Fish Large numbers of fish live in and around the reefs and occasionally migratory pelagics can be seen passing by in the deep blue beyond the formations. The abundance of fish life, and in particular large numbers of juveniles, is testament to the relatively unspoilt nature of the marine environment. The reefs are nursing grounds to many species including damselfish, butterflyfish, angelfish and surgeonfish. Large shoals of yellow- and blue-striped grunts hover along the margins of reef edges, groups of soldierfish may be observed suspended beneath overhangs or in the shadows of arches or small caverns, and goby, blenny, jawfish and flounder find a home in patches of sand. Parrotfish, cowfish, trunkfish, trumpetfish and spotted drum are just some of the many common varieties inhabiting an already colourful reef system, where in every nook and cranny a moray, octopus, lobster or sharptail eel may also be making a home.

Sharks are rarely seen along the west coast. The most observed species is the nurse shark, which can sometimes be seen resting on the sand beneath plate coral. Whale sharks have been recorded here, as have hammerheads and reef sharks. Rays provide more regular sightings and include the stingray and the spotted eagle ray. Barracuda are also present, often in large numbers (especially around the Cachacrou isthmus at Scotts Head), as are large schools of predatory jacks and mackerel.

Some of the more unusual species of fish are interesting to recreational divers and marine photographers. The longlure frogfish (*Antennarius multiocellatus*) is one such example. Using camouflage, the frogfish is able to make itself look like part of the sponge or coral it's inhabiting. The first spine of its dorsal fin is highly modified and acts as a lure to fish that swim by. The frogfish then makes a movement that's thought to be one of the fastest of all animals alive: in around one-sixth of a second it extends its mouth and sucks in prey that can be even larger than itself. The frogfish has a voracious appetite and is also cannibalistic. If fishing is bad in one area, it simply takes its rod and lure and moves to the next. In addition to the frogfish, Dominica's reefs are home to a variety of other interesting species such as seahorses, scorpionfish, pipefish, batfish and flying gurnards.

Other marine creatures Along the east coast of Dominica endangered **giant leatherbacks** (*Dermochelys coriacea*), the largest of all living sea turtles, return annually to lay their clusters of eggs in the sand (page 166). The giant leatherback is one of four species of turtle observed in the waters around Dominica. The hawksbill turtle (*Eretmochelys imbriocota*) is easily the most common. The green turtle (*Chelonia mydas*) and the loggerhead turtle (*Caretta caretta*) may also be seen, though more rarely.

Dominica's waters are home to several echinoderms including the aptly named donkey dung sea cucumber, long-spined urchins and a variety of colourful crinoids. Octopus and squid are also evident and there are several varieties of crab, lobster and shrimp. Fanworms, fireworms, feather duster worms and Christmas tree worms are widespread.

Whales and dolphins Several species of whale routinely visit the deep coastal waters of Dominica. The most prevalent is the sperm whale (*Physeter macrocephallus*), which is here all year round. Other species of whale that may be sighted include short-finned pilot whales (*Globicephala melaena*), humpback whales (*Megaptera novaeangliae*) and false killer whales (*Pseudorca crassidens*).

Pods of dolphins are often spotted along the west coast, occasionally even from the shore. The most common are spinner dolphins (*Stenella longirostris*) though other frequently observed species include bottlenose dolphins (*Tursiops truncatus*), Atlantic spotted dolphins (*Stenella frontalis*) and Fraser's dolphins (*Lagenodelphis hosei*).

NATIONAL GEOGRAPHIC PRISTINE SEAS

National Geographic's Pristine Seas project explored Dominica's marine environment from its nearshore coral reefs to some of its deepest depths from November to December 2022. Using a wide range of tools and methods, the team of explorers, scientists and filmmakers documented the rich marine life surrounding Dominica from the smallest microbial organisms all the way up to sperm whales, one of the largest, loudest and deepest-diving animals in the ocean.

During the expedition, Pristine Seas surveyed around the entire island, including the calm Caribbean west coast, the rough and rugged Atlantic east coast, Macouba Bank located 35km southwest of the island, and open ocean offshore waters, all with the aim of painting a comprehensive picture of the breadth of Dominica's entire marine ecosystem. This expedition was conducted in partnership with the Government of Dominica and included young Dominican explorers who shared their knowledge and passion for this special place they call home.

The nearshore marine ecosystem was highly diverse with corals, gorgonians, sponges, seagrass beds and even bubbling geothermal reefs, which provided habitat for a wide range of fishes and invertebrates. Observations of the critically endangered elkhorn coral, which was once common throughout the Caribbean but now rare, is a hopeful sign for the recovery of this ecologically important species. Over 70 species of sponges were documented, along with 150 species of fishes and myriad other species.

The Soufriere Scott's Head Marine Reserve had the highest diversity and abundance of large fishes around Dominica. The dive teams were surrounded by huge groups of large and curious barracudas up in the water column, while schools of snappers and grunts swarmed around the coral-covered bottom. These large fishes are important for replenishing fish stocks outside of this protected area and show the benefits that greater protection from overfishing could achieve elsewhere locally. At many locations around the island, large parrotfishes can be seen, grazing among the corals and keeping them free from destructive overgrowth of algae.

CONSERVATION Reflecting the need to protect and preserve its rich natural environment, both above and below sea level, Dominica has several national parks, and forest and marine reserves.

National parks In 1997, the 7,000ha **Morne Trois Pitons National Park** became a UNESCO World Heritage Site. According to UNESCO,

> 'Luxuriant natural tropical forest blends with scenic volcanic features of great scientific interest in this national park centred on the 1,342m-high volcano known as Morne Trois Pitons. With its precipitous slopes and deeply incised valleys, 50 fumaroles, hot springs, three freshwater lakes, a "boiling lake" and five volcanoes, located on the park's nearly 7,000 ha, together with the richest biodiversity in the Lesser Antilles, Morne Trois Pitons National Park presents a rare combination of natural features of World Heritage value.'

The word *morne* is an Old French word meaning 'small mountain' and usually precedes the name of Dominica's peaks. Morne Micotrin, also known as Morne Macaque, is 1,221m tall and is located a short distance to the south of Morne Trois Pitons. Nestled within a circular crater between these two mountains is the 2ha **Boeri Lake**. At an elevation of 853m, it's the highest mountain lake on the island.

Specially constructed deep-sea cameras were deployed to depths of more than 1,000m, revealing previously unexplored unique and diverse ecosystems. An extraordinary encounter with a 4m-long sixgill shark at 500m depth surprised the team when it investigated the bait attached to the camera, biting straight through the mooring line and ultimately releasing the camera from its anchor, causing a late-night boat chase for its recovery – 20km away!

Globally and throughout the Caribbean, threats to coral reefs are many – among them overfishing, sedimentation due to poor land-use practices and coastal development, invasive species, disease and climate change. Dominica is not immune to some of these threats, and its reefs may be at a tipping point due to local and global threats.

However, renewed interest in more effective marine management and better sustainable land use practices could be the best defence from these threats so as not to suffer the same fate as other Caribbean coral reefs. A healthy marine environment is important to the people of Dominica for food security, cultural practices, protection from storms and the intrinsic value of this unique ecosystem. Dominica can be an example of how to sustainably manage its environment in a rapidly changing world.

Pristine Seas' outputs from the expedition include the production of a scientific report detailing the research findings and a documentary film. Together, the scientific report and documentary film aim to serve as tools for Dominica to help inform its future planning so its environment and people will be protected and remain resilient. For more information about Pristine Seas, see w nationalgeographic.org/pristine-seas.

***Dr Alan Friedlander** is Chief Scientist for National Geographic's Pristine Seas project and the Director of the Fisheries Ecology Research Lab at the University of Hawaii. He is also a fellow of the Royal Geographic Society.*

A short distance to the east of Morne Micotrin is the 4ha **Freshwater Lake**, at an elevation of 762m.

A high ridge runs southwards from Morne Micotrin until it reaches the pointed and weather-beaten summit of Morne Watt at 1,224m. To the east of this imposing mountain is the **Valley of Desolation**, an active volcanic landscape of steaming gas vents, heated rivers and cascades, bubbling mud and a crust of colourful, sulphur-stained rock. The Valley of Desolation caldera is categorised as an active volcano. Located at the northern end of the valley is **Boiling Lake**, a flooded fumarole some 66m in diameter. It's one of the largest of its kind in the world, second only, it's said, to Frying Pan Lake and the interconnected Inferno Crater Lake in Waimangu Volcanic Rift Valley, New Zealand. The lake's nebulous, boiling hot waters spill over a cleft on its eastern margins and create the White River, which runs down a deep valley beneath the Grand Soufriere Hills, passing over several waterfalls, including Victoria Falls near Delices (page 172), until it joins the Pointe Mulâtre River and, finally, the Atlantic Ocean. At the park's southern tip is Morne Anglais, which rises to 1,123m above Dominica's west coast.

In January 2000 the 3,335ha **Morne Diablotin National Park** was established. The park contains rainforest, montane forest and elfin woodland habitats and has some of the densest and least explored terrain in all of Dominica. At the heart of the park is Dominica's highest peak, Morne Diablotin, which rises to 1,447m and dominates the landscape in the north. This park was created primarily to protect the habitat of Dominica's two endemic and endangered Amazon parrots, the sisserou and the jaco (page 7), but is also home to many other bird species, as well as a population of wild pigs (page 8).

The 525ha **Cabrits National Park** was established in 1986. It's located to the north of Portsmouth, on a peninsula formed by two volcanic peaks: East Cabrit at 140m and West Cabrit at 171m. Within the park, and its most prominent feature, are the semi-restored ruins of the 18th-century Fort Shirley garrison (page 182). The park contains dry coastal woodland and is connected to the mainland by the island's largest swamp and wetland area. Around the coastline is 421ha of marine environment that has been designated the Cabrits Marine Reserve.

Forest reserves When it was formed in 1977, the **Northern Forest Reserve** covered 8,900ha, but it ceded land to the formation of Morne Diablotin National Park in January 2000. Located in the north of Dominica, it's a vast tract of montane and rainforest habitats and contains some of the island's largest tree species.

Extending down from the Northern Forest Reserve to the valleys of the Layou and Pagua rivers are further high ridges and areas of dense forest. The Layou is Dominica's longest river, and the area to the north and east of the Layou River valley is the 410ha **Central Forest Reserve**, Dominica's oldest forest reserve, which was established in 1952.

Soufriere Scotts Head Marine Reserve (SSMR) The SSMR is in the southwest of Dominica and contains some of the island's most visited and well-known dive sites. The ambition of the reserve was to protect the marine environment at the same time as providing structure and balance to the demands of both tourism and the traditional fishing heritage of the villages in this region. The jury is out on whether this happens in practice. The reserve runs from the isthmus of Cachacrou to the Champagne Reef system south of the coastal community of Pointe Michel and is comprised of priority zones for fishing, scuba-diving and marine nurseries. Within the reserve, dive sites such as L'Abym, La Sorciere, Danglebens Pinnacles and Scotts Head Drop-off provide visiting scuba-divers with a spectacular combination of life, colour and dramatic reef formations. The waters here are extremely deep, and the reefs largely bereft of sand, so turbidity is rarely a problem and thus visibility is usually excellent all year round. Scuba-diving and snorkelling in the SSMR draws a US$2 fee per snorkeller or scuba diver, which is supposed to go towards its management, much in the same way that the site pass system is designed to support designated 'eco' attractions on land. With two large resorts, a dive shop, a watersports centre, a freediving operation and two fishing villages all located around Soufriere Bay, the conservation principles of the SSMR are likely to be tested in the years ahead.

HISTORY

EARLY SETTLERS Stone tools discovered at archaeological sites along the Antilles archipelago suggest that Dominica's first arrivals would have been hunter gatherers from the Orinoco River Delta who made their way up the island chain from South America some 5,000 years ago. Material culture (the durable stuff that's made and discarded by humans) in the form of remnants of stoneware, ceramics and structures gives anthropologists and archaeologists clues as to who these people were and how they might have lived and travelled around the islands, but much of the story remains speculative because there are so many gaps in the evidence so far discovered. To go beyond the material culture of these people, we must consider the written accounts of others, namely Europeans, who observed, interpreted and formed their own opinions. Experts in this subject differ in their interpretation of material culture, and in their view of how migration and occupation of the islands was enacted from Central and South America, but most do agree that waves of different people arrived at, settled on, and travelled between islands over many generations. It's likely that the rather simplistic picture of **Taino** in the north and **Kalinago** (also referred to as *Caribs*) in the south was, in fact, a far more confused, transient and perhaps turbulent affair by the time Europeans arrived in the region. The indigenous people they met in Dominica and surrounding islands of the Lesser Antilles did refer to themselves as Kalinago, however, and most of their surviving contemporary descendants in Dominica (known by them as ***Wai'tukubuli*** – roughly translated to 'tall is her body') now occupy a semi-autonomous territory on the island's east coast (page 155). It's also worth bearing in mind that any historic records of the Kalinago would have been penned by Europeans with personal perspectives, values, prejudices and interpretations that may have been based on fleeting encounters with only a handful of indigenous people.

The first Amerindian settlers on these islands are often referred to as **Arawaks**. This is a little misleading as the term refers to people who spoke in variants of the Arawakan language. It's thought that the first migratory hunter gatherers were eventually displaced by an Arawakan-speaking people known as the **Igneri** who settled on the islands. Like the Taino of the Greater Antilles, the Igneri were probably animists who worshipped nature spirits and lived in harmony with, and had a good understanding of, their environment. Most scholars believe that although the Taino and the Igneri were Arawakan-speaking peoples, the Igneri spoke a slightly different version of Arawakan that was unique to them.

Archaeologists, historians and anthropologists have suggested the Igneri probably engaged in inter-island/community trade; they also farmed, built thatched houses, made pottery (referred to as Saladoid and Cayo, depending on the era), wove cotton and crafted ocean-going canoes. They are believed to have lived on the island for around 1,000 years before the arrival of another Arawakan-speaking people: the Kalinago.

Often considered by archaeologists and anthropologists to have been a more warrior-like Amerindian tribe, the Kalinago had probably displaced or subsumed the Igneri by around the end of the 14th century, just a hundred years before the arrival of Columbus and the first Europeans to the region. The Kalinago are thought to have adopted the language spoken by the Igneri, explaining why their vocabulary has Arawakan origin rather than Cariban or Lokono, which was spoken in the region of South America where the Kalinago were from.

Like their predecessors, the Kalinago worshipped ancestors and nature spirits in the form of iconic *zemi stones*, and they also excelled at boatbuilding and fishing. These are traditions that live on among the present-day Kalinago who try to preserve their cultural heritage. Carved out of the trunks of *gommier* trees, their larger boats, called *canoua* (source of the word *Canoe*), were said to be up to 15m long and capable of travelling long distances across open seas. Smaller craft included the *couliana*, also carved out of whole tree trunks, and *pwi pwi*, a very simple raft that was probably used more for inshore fishing (you'll often see modern versions of *pwi pwi* along the shoreline at Soufriere and Scotts Head). These vessels would carry Kalinago men on hunting trips for fish, lobster and other shellfish and conch, as well as on trading and perhaps raiding parties to neighbouring islands or even attacking European ships. Kalinago women would likely have had a more domestic role, taking care of the children, cooking, running the farms, weaving hammocks and making baskets from the dried outer bark of the *larouma* reed (page 163).

NEW ARRIVALS On 3 November 1493 Columbus's fleet sighted the island the Kalinago had called **Wai'tukubuli**. He decided to call it Dominica.

Through enslavement, murder and disease, it's said to have taken just 30 years of Spanish occupation to eradicate the Taino people of the Greater Antilles and, as enslaved labour consequently became a scarce commodity, the Spanish turned their attention to capturing the Amerindian people of the Lesser Antilles. Incredibly, the Kalinago steadfastly resisted. The so-called 'discovery' of the New World attracted fortune seekers and colonists from other seafaring nations such as France, Britain and the Netherlands, who all competed in the Caribbean region. Dominica was a tough nut to crack, however. Though it was seen as a prize, the topography of the island with its mountains and inaccessible forests, together with a large population of fighting Kalinago, made incursions dangerous and often deadly. Trade with the indigenous people for food and water was usually carried out from the safety of the ship, rather than stepping ashore.

Despite its inhospitable nature, in 1635, France claimed Dominica as its own and in 1642 French missionaries arrived on the island for the first time. The Kalinago continued to hold the French and later the British in check, however, and in 1686 both countries signed a treaty stating that Dominica would be a neutral island belonging to the indigenous people.

Despite the treaty, French timber merchants established small logging camps on Dominica's south coast in the Grand Bay area, where they also grew *ground provisions* and eventually coffee and sugarcane that they transported by boat to Martinique. These settlements grew into large estates which began to use enslaved African labour.

The French fought with the British over 'ownership' of the island and by the turn of the 19th century Dominica was in British hands. The encroachment of European colonists had impacted the indigenous Kalinago who had now retreated to the island's rugged and less accessible east and northeast. Although there are no records of either the French or the British enslaving Kalinago, it's clear the European presence impacted the Kalinago population. Yet they somehow held on. The British carved up the island into estates that were often purchased as investments by absent owners who never set foot on the island. Instead, their businesses were run by managers who were expected to fulfil production quotas of sugar, molasses, coffee, rum and so on. This drove the demand for enslaved labour.

The British were brutal colonisers and the flogging, torture and execution of their enslaved workforce was common practice. Many of the enslaved managed to escape captivity by running away into the dense forest and forming small settlements in remote mountain locations. Plantation owners in the Caribbean region referred to these bands of 'runaways' as **Maroons**. Towards the end of the 18th century Dominica's Maroon population had grown significantly in number and encampments were widespread. As time went by, Dominica's fighting Maroons became well armed and organised and launched successful and sometimes violent raids on estates, plundering food, setting fire to buildings and, on occasion, killing estate managers.

In 1813, Major General George Robert Ainslie became Governor of Dominica. He was a violent, oppressive, perhaps even psychopathic man, and his brutality against the Maroons and those who helped or harboured them is captured in the public and military trial transcripts of Polly Pattullo's *Your Time is Done Now. Slavery, Resistance and Defeat: the Maroon Trials of Dominica: (1813–1814)* (Papillote Press, 2015). With scant regard for British 'slave laws', and pressured into action by the British ruling classes, he set about 'eradicating the evil' of Dominica's Maroons.

Ainslie created a legion of 500 men to deal with the Maroons, and those captured were often tortured and executed in public at the Sunday Market in Roseau (page 209). Their heads were cut off and put on stakes on the estates from which they had escaped or on roads into the town to serve as a very visual warning to others. On 12 July 1814, Chief Jacko, one of the island's most famous Maroon leaders, was shot and killed by John LeVilloux in a bloody battle with the Loyal Dominica Rangers – a militia of 'trusty slaves' who were offered the reward of freedom in exchange for killing a Maroon chief. According to witness testimony, Jacko had killed two Rangers, wounded a third and was preparing to fire on another when LeVilloux's musket delivered a fatal blow to the head. According to Ainslie, Jacko had been a Maroon for 'upwards of 40 years'. His death brought about the end to what are referred to by historians as the Second Maroon Wars.

Dominica became an island of isolated village communities and small plantation estates that grew sugar, coffee, limes and coconuts. Even though it was under British rule, Dominica's main influences still came from the neighbouring French colonies of Martinique and Guadeloupe. When British landowners were forced either to abandon or sell off failing estates, it was often the increasing number of free people of colour or *mulattos* (now considered a derogatory term) arriving from Martinique and Guadeloupe who took over and tried to make them viable again. And they in turn became slave owners. The enslaved Africans thus absorbed more of the language and culture of France than of Britain, and so it was not long before Creole, a combination of French vocabulary and strong African dialect and syntax, was spoken as a first language (it's still spoken today and is commonly referred to as patois). A new Creole culture was born out of enslavement which, in addition to language, was also reflected in dance, games, music, instruments and modes of dress (page 30).

INDEPENDENT PEOPLE In 1838, following the full abolition of slavery, Dominica became the first and only British Caribbean colony to have a legislature that

LA SOYE: THE TOWN BENEATH THE SAND

Several days after Hurricane Maria ravaged Dominica in 2017, local historian Dr Lennox Honychurch was strolling along the beach near his home at Woodford Hill in the northeast of the island, when he made an interesting discovery. Exposed by the effects of the extreme weather event, including beach erosion caused by high tidal surges, were pottery fragments from the past. Intriguingly, they were not, it seemed, from the same origin or era. Some of the ceramics were Amerindian – possibly Cayo – and the others were European, possibly French or Dutch. Honychurch contacted Mark Hauser, Associate Professor of Anthropology at Northwestern University. Hauser had been visiting Dominica for around ten years on various field seasons to study colonial estate sites at Bois Cotlette, Sugarloaf and Morne Patates. Keen to understand the effects of the hurricane on Dominica's historical legacies, he was more than happy to investigate Honychurch's discovery. What Hauser learned on that first exploratory trip was enough for him to organise a small team of experts to return to Dominica to examine the location in more detail.

The area first appears on an anonymous map of 1760 as a settlement called La Soye, but no known historic records shed any light on who may have lived there, for how long, why it was so named (La Soye is French for silk) and why it was eventually abandoned. Because of an inhospitable and largely inaccessible environment of mountains and thick forest, and its occupation by a formidable population of Kalinago, Dominica was the last island in the eastern Caribbean to be colonised by Europeans seeking their fortunes. The first recorded European settlement was in the early 1700s, when French lumbermen from Martinique arrived and set up camp on the south coast in an area now known as Grand Bay. Given the lack of information about the La Soye community, the only way to understand its story would be through archaeology.

The first test excavation holes at the La Soye site on Woodford Hill Beach certainly caused a stir. Not really knowing what they might find, Hauser's team unearthed a wealth of diverse artefacts from a very small sample area. It included glassware, clay pipes, ceramics of Amerindian and European legacy, trade items such as trinkets and beads, ironware such as nails and a tool for making musket shot, and even a perfect little sewing thimble. It felt as if they had chanced on a storeroom or warehouse, but what real meaning could be learned from these relics?

The first real surprise was the date. The discovery of scores of Dutch Delft blue pottery fragments suggested the early 1600s – a century before the first records of any kind of European occupation of Dominica. This was later verified by carbon dating charcoal fragments (related to cooking or blacksmithing) from the same soil strata. The trinkets, beads and Cayo pottery fragments suggested contact, interaction and probably trade between the island's indigenous people and the newcomers.

We know that expeditions had called at the island during this period. Sir Francis Drake's logs state that, with the help of Kalinago, he had provisioned his ship in Prince Rupert's Bay on the island's west coast as early as 1565. It's also known that, for a time, Europeans traded with the Kalinago of other eastern Caribbean

was not controlled by the white planter class. However, it was not to last. The planters began lobbying for greater British rule and in 1871 Dominica became part of the Leeward Island Federation. In 1896 Crown Colony government was established.

islands, seeking tobacco and cotton which were valuable commodities in Europe. This was an era and a region of fortune seekers, pirates, and privateers. It was also a time when the indigenous Kalinago and the island resources they had long depended upon came under serious threat. There's evidence of numerous Kalinago settlements along Dominica's northeastern coastline, and the island of Marie-Galante, an important foraging ground that would soon be taken by the French, is located directly across the water. Should La Soye reveal itself as an early trading outpost, it would be a new entry in Dominica's historical record.

With his interest peaked, Hauser and his colleagues managed to secure funding for additional studies (interrupted only by the global Covid-19 pandemic) with the ambition of further developing the curious story of La Soye. In July 2022, supported by the National Science Foundation, several specialist teams collaborated, blending different areas of expertise and technologies that included soil and botanical sampling, lidar, and magnetronomy. The application of these specialisms resulted in a rough map of the coastal land that suggested around a dozen stone buildings and a couple of stone roads had once existed there. Hauser speculated that the settlement may well have extended from the beach into the bay, with rising water levels perhaps eventually covering as much as half of it.

With a theoretical plan of the settlement on their laptops, the team set about excavating small test pits to verify what the technology was indicating – a procedure that's known as ground truthing. The excavations did indeed reveal the stone foundations of buildings and road, but they also surprised the team with evidence of wooden post holes, something the technology didn't capture. Wooden post holes would have supported framed structures, possibly belonging to an earlier Kalinago presence. One building on top of another suggested succession or displacement.

So far, the story of La Soye seems to begin with an Amerindian settlement that was certainly Kalinago but may have existed even earlier. In the late 1500s and early 1600s, European vessels arrived in the bay, probably at the end of their transatlantic voyage, perhaps to undertake essential careenage and provisioning. We can imagine first contact with the island's indigenous Kalinago may have included basic trade for fresh water and food that developed into a more commercial (though unrecorded) exchange dealing in tobacco and cotton. At some point in time, that outpost became a village, and that village eventually displaced the indigenous people who had been there before (it's thought by some experts that the Kalinago were already beginning to move to higher ground from coastal margins). And then at an unknown later date, the village was entirely abandoned.

Although the picture is becoming clearer, many questions remain unanswered. Was La Soye the domain of pirates and privateers, or perhaps the trading outpost of a French settlement in nearby Marie-Galante? Why the name La Soye? And what predicament resulted in its abandonment? Hopefully, further field seasons will help us learn more about this enigmatic town beneath the sand.

Dominica's first Crown Colony administrator was a man called Hesketh Bell. In a six-year period from 1899 to 1905 he constructed Dominica's first highway, the Imperial Road, which ran from Roseau to Bells; he connected Portsmouth to Roseau by telephone; he initiated the first electricity service; he designed the Public

Library for which he had secured funding from the famous philanthropist, Andrew Carnegie; he opened a new jetty at Roseau; and he made proposals to set aside some 1,530ha for the island's indigenous Kalinago. Over the next 60 years, Dominica's population increased and its infrastructure and social institutions slowly developed to support it. In 1967 Dominica achieved Associated Statehood, giving the island total self-governance, and on 3 November 1978, exactly 485 years to the day after Columbus had first sighted the island, Dominica gained full independence from Britain.

A few years before independence, following a series of incidents and complaints by influential members of the community, Prime Minister Patrick John and his Labour Party passed the Prohibited and Unlawful Societies and Associations Act, also known as the **Dread Act**. This law stated that Rastafarians wearing their hair in dreadlocks were subject to arrest without warrant, were not permitted bail, and could be held without charges for at least 48 hours. Moreover, the act prohibited the prosecution of any individual who injured or killed a 'Dread'. In practice, this meant – and resulted in – the assault and murder of Rastafarians by law enforcement officers who were immune from prosecution. Many Rastafarians or Dreads who were not already living in Dominica's forests soon fled to them, becoming akin to modern day Maroons. While most Rastafarians and Dreads were peace-loving people and activists following the lead of the Black Power movement

A TIME OF DREAD

In 2018, I interviewed Moses James, a Rastafarian who was a victim of the Dread Act. These are his words.

There was a sad story in Dominica in the seventies. Can you imagine how a government could pass a law against dreadlocks? At that time there were not many people in Dominica with dreadlocks, but there were some who used to go in people's gardens and claim them, steal produce and so on. And then there were criminal attacks and at least one murder. But, you know, if there's a group of bad men doing these kinds of things, you go after them, arrest them for their crimes. No-one would have a problem with that. It's normal. But you don't pass a law that makes it legal to shoot and kill anyone who has dreadlocks. You don't do that. But that's what they did. The 1974 Prohibited and Unlawful Societies and Associations Act, known as the Dread Act. This was wrong. It was against our fundamental human rights. And that law changed my life.

I was 24 years old, and I already lived in the mountains with some other people where we made our gardens in swamps because of the natural nutrients in them. Swamp dasheen is the best dasheen! We had all kinds of food growing in abundance, probably more than most, so we had no need to go stealing or claiming other people's gardens. No need at all. In fact, people used to come to us for food. But the police came after us anyway. Sadly, some of those police just wanted to shoot the Rasta. There was a lot of prejudice.

My friends and I were living up in the mountains when the Dread Act was passed, and we knew nothing about it until one day when two men came up to see us. They brought a copy of the Act telling us it was very serious and that we should leave the mountain and go back down home. One of the men had a pair of scissors to show us how serious it was. Two guys from Roseau who were living up there with us let him cut their locks. They cried when he did it. I refused to allow my locks to be cut. This turned out to be one of the most difficult decisions of my life because it had so many implications and repercussions. The men left, leaving just two of us in the mountain.

of the time, there were of course exceptions, and the Dread Act provided the more extreme and criminal elements of society with a reason to act outside the law. In 1981, under the government of Eugenia Charles, the Dominica House of Assembly passed the Prevention of Terrorism Temporary Provisions Act. Section 18 of this new legislation repealed the Dread Act.

The birth of the new **Commonwealth of Dominica** was testing. On 29 August 1979 Hurricane David hit the island, causing widespread devastation, and in 1981, a very odd incident took place. A group of North American mercenaries and former Dominica Defence Force officers attempted an overthrow of the government of Eugenia Charles. The mercenaries were made up of Canadian and US right-wing extremists, gangsters, former soldiers and even Ku Klux Klan Grand Wizard Don Black. This bizarre operation, code-named **Red Dog**, was meant to restore former Dominica premier Patrick John to power in a kind of puppet regime, which would allow this group to exploit the island and turn it into a form of criminal paradise that would launder money and manufacture and export illicit drugs. For countless bizarre reasons, the coup attempt was a disaster and failed before it left the shores of the United States. In Dominica, Patrick John faced trial and was found to have been a supporter of the attempted coup – a charge he consistently rejected. Eugenia Charles, the Caribbean's first female prime minister, went on to lead Dominica for 15 years.

Early one morning I came down to the village to bring some vegetables to my mother. When I reached the house, she also told me how serious things were and advised me to cut my locks. But I refused to do that. While I was by the well in her garden bringing water for her, I saw soldiers out on the road, and I quickly hid in the bush. I could see that they had already arrested one man. They came to my mother's house to question her and when they left, I came out of the bush where I was hiding to go back to fetch water. But there were three soldiers waiting in ambush. They tied and beat me, then they brought me down here to where my shack was in the valley and burned it down in front of me. They made me stand there and watch, tied up and bleeding. I loved that shack. It was real Kalinago style.

They had arrested three of us altogether. Tied and beaten, our locks cut off with a blunt machete, they paraded us through the village. Two big trucks arrived, and they threw us in like animals. I was in prison for six months, but they had to release me on a technicality. For a while afterwards, things seemed to have calmed down a bit and Rastas began growing their locks again.

One Sunday morning I went to the village with a couple of friends to buy some calabash. On the way back I heard a gunshot and felt a bullet hit my leg. The other two men ran, and I heard someone shout 'Don't move!'. But I ran too. I saw the policeman, and I knew him. He had a reputation for hunting down Rastas. He told me not to run and came after me with his gun, but I ran again. Don't forget, it was still legal for him to shoot me dead. He fired and hit me in the leg again. Then he fired and hit me in the side of my stomach; the bullet passing right through. But I kept on running and he shot me a third time in the leg. Three bullets I had in it. My friends helped me, and we escaped by crossing the White River. We climbed up the mountain and hid in a ravine on the other side. My friends tried to take the bullets out of my leg with a penknife, but they made it worse, and I suffered bitterly. Those bullets stayed there for seven years before I had them removed, but the damage had been done. Now I limp and must walk with the aid of a stick. But I've never stopped living a Rasta way of life. It's my way of life, and nature has so much to offer. I like to share this way of living and my knowledge of plants and herbs with other people who visit me here. All are welcome.

RESEARCHING *BAYOU OF PIGS*

The mercenaries who decided to invade Dominica in 1981 were an unlikely alliance of misfits – Vietnam vets, Ku Klux Klansmen, militant Rastafarians, disgruntled Dominican soldiers, the ex-prime minister and a gun-loving mobster from Toronto. Dominica was having a tough time back then. Hurricanes had battered the island, the economy was struggling and the government had all but collapsed. The American and Canadian mercenaries who decided to take advantage of Dominica's troubles had a simple plan: invade Roseau by sea, overthrow Prime Minister Eugenia Charles and get rich. Financed by US investors, they were going to strip the island of its resources and open casinos, drug labs and arms depots. What could go wrong?

When I began investigating this little-known piece of Caribbean history for my book, *Bayou of Pigs*, I soon realised this was the strangest story I had ever come across in two decades of journalism. Nobody could make up a tale this bizarre. To find out what had happened, I tracked down the members of the conspiracy one by one. I soon found that some were dead. One had been murdered in Canada, another was executed by hanging, and a financier had killed himself with a shotgun. The leader of the coup, Mike Perdue of Houston, had died of AIDS in prison. Even those still alive weren't easy to find. One had changed his name and was living in a Colorado trailer park. Another was in a Canadian prison, serving time for gun trafficking. When I told him I wanted to put his mugshot in the book, he told me not to. He said he had better photos. A week later an envelope arrived in the mail. Inside were a half-dozen pictures showing him posing with machine guns and ammunition belts. One of the group had undergone a sex change. She suggested we meet in person so that, following the interview, we could 'have a little shag on the couch'. Let's stick to phone interviews, I said. A few people would not talk to me but most did. In fact, some of them still had papers from the plot – photographs taken during reconnaissance missions to Dominica, even plane tickets and hotel and car rental receipts. I was also able to get copies of the invasion plans, which diagrammed how the mercenaries would land at Rockaway Beach and storm the police headquarters in Roseau.

When I began to read the US government's file on the coup, I was confused at first. The memos contained a lot of references to GOD, which isn't usually something you find in FBI correspondence. It puzzled me until I figured out that

More recently, two storms (Tropical Storm Erika in 2015 and Hurricane Maria in 2017) caused widespread devastation to Dominica's infrastructure and natural environment (page 4). Thanks to international assistance, Dominica has largely recovered from these severe weather events, though the south coast villages of Dubique and Petite Savanne have been officially abandoned and are considered too dangerous for habitation. Some former residents have, however, returned.

GOVERNMENT AND POLITICS

Dominica is a parliamentary democracy within the Commonwealth of Nations. The head of state is the president who is appointed by parliament for a five-year term and is required to be politically independent. The president and prime minister make up Dominica's executive branch. Dominica's legislative branch, or parliament, is the House of Assembly, of which 21 are ministers elected by popular

GOD was Washington shorthand for the Government of Dominica. So I guess you could say that Dominica is GOD's paradise. When I began visiting the island, hiking to waterfalls and walking the beaches, I quickly realised that was true, even if it almost became a crooks' paradise. In the weeks before the coup, the conspirators met in Toronto, Louisiana and Antigua. They plotted. They recruited. They raised money and bought guns. And they carefully mapped out how they would remove Prime Minister Charles from office and install Patrick John in her place. 'Imagine what you could do if you owned your own country,' said Wolfgang Droege, the Canadian KKK boss who was deputy-leader of the plot. The problem was, the conspirators were not only ambitious, they were also imbeciles. The ship they hired to transport them and their guns to Dominica was immediately infiltrated by US agents. The ship's captain, Mike Howell, had tipped off the Bureau of Alcohol, Tobacco and Firearms. Special Agents John Osburg and Wiley Lloyd Grafton posed as crewmen on the ship as they secretly tape-recorded the conspirators. The ATF called its investigation Bayou of Pigs – a Louisiana take on the infamous Bay of Pigs invasion of Cuba. Canadian police also found out. The mercenaries wanted to bring a news reporter along with them to document their invasion for posterity, so they 'embedded' a Toronto radio reporter named Gord Sivell. Once he found out that lives would be lost, Sivell went to the police. Police on Dominica got wind of the plot as well, through their own inquiries. The FBI knew, the US State Department knew. The Royal Canadian Mounted Police knew. The Dominica coup may have been one of the worst kept secrets in the history of mercenaries. On 27 April 1981, as the soldiers of fortune were about to set sail from New Orleans, police moved in and made the arrests. They seized guns, ammunition, inflatable rafts, Tennessee whiskey and Nazi flags. More than two dozen people were arrested and ultimately convicted in the US, Canada and Dominica. 'It was an exercise in stupidity,' Bob Prichard, an army veteran who was convicted for his role in the plot, told me. 'The worst part was, I was stupid enough to go along with it.'

Stewart Bell is an award-winning Canadian journalist and the author of three non-fiction books, The Bayou of Pigs, The Martyr's Oath *and* Cold Terror. *He is currently an investigative journalist for* **w** *globalnews.ca.*

vote in single-seat constituencies; five senators are appointed by the president on the advice of the prime minister and four on the advice of the leader of the opposition. There is no upper house.

At the time of writing, Roosevelt Skerrit of the Dominica Labour Party (DLP; colour: red) is the longest serving prime minister of Dominica. He was elected in 2004. The main opposition is the United Workers Party (UWP; colour: blue), though as they refused to contest the 2022 snap election, independents – at the time of writing – occupy opposition seats in parliament. Due to the inability of any form of opposition to gain substantial ground in the political arena, Dominica has, in effect, operated as a single-party state since 2004. Dominicans nonetheless love to debate politics and are usually either staunchly red or blue. Partisan politics impacts radio stations and newspapers, and certain constituencies rarely change colour, regardless of the effectiveness or ineffectiveness of their parliamentary representative.

Dominica's foreign policy is, to a large extent, influenced by the willingness of other nations to establish partnerships, invest, or provide grants, loans and technical expertise. For this reason, the People's Republic of China, Cuba and Venezuela have become close political and economic partners in recent years, along with several other nations. The People's Republic of China has provided funding and labour for several infrastructure projects such as Windsor Park Stadium and the Dominica–China Friendship Hospital (formerly Princess Margaret Hospital) in Goodwill, near Roseau, and Dominica subscribes to the One China policy. Cuba provides medical expertise and was also helpful in the clear-up after Hurricane Maria. Venezuela provides financial assistance as well as fuel in the form of petroleum products and LPG gas which is used by most of the population for cooking. The European Union has also been a substantial provider of grant and development finance to Dominica in the context of large infrastructure projects that have included agriculture, health, access roads, waste management, irrigation and water supply. Funding from the EU also paid for the development of the Wai'tukubuli National Trail and initial testing for geothermal energy.

Dominica has ten administrative divisions, or parishes. They are St Andrew, St David, St George, St John, St Joseph, St Luke, St Mark, St Patrick, St Paul and St Peter. The Ministry of Kalinago Affairs represents the interests of the Kalinago population and the affairs of the Kalinago Territory, together with the Kalinago Council and the Kalinago Chief. Dominica's village councils are elected by popular vote and are responsible for local amenities, services and sanitation.

LAW Dominica's judiciary is independent of both executive and legislative branches and its legal system is based on English common law. Dominica's law upholds freedom of speech and freedom of religion, and it prohibits discrimination based on race, gender, place of origin, colour and creed. The island's only security force is the Dominica Police Force, which is overseen by the prime minister's office. Dominica's law prohibits arbitrary arrest and it does not detain political prisoners.

ECONOMY

Dominica is a member of the Organisation of Eastern Caribbean States (OECS) and is committed to an agreement to allow the free movement of goods and labour across OECS-participating countries. The OECS is in turn committed to the CARICOM (Caribbean Community) ambition to develop the Caribbean Single Market Economy (CSME). Dominica is also a member of ALBA (Alianza Bolivariana para los Pueblos de Nuestra América – the Bolivarian Alliance for the Peoples of our America). The aim of ALBA is to attempt economic integration of member nations of South America and the Caribbean based on a premise of social welfare, bartering and mutual financial assistance.

Prime Minister Skerrit's legacy may well be the introduction and development of the **Citizenship by Investment (CBI)** programme as the nation's primary source of overseas income. Selling nationhood and passports to fund the construction of low-cost housing, hotel developments and other projects has been controversial due largely to the alleged opaque nature of the programme's finances and no obvious limits to the number of citizenships to be sold. Yet it has also been effective in providing finance to social development projects such as housing for the poor and displaced that the country would scarcely be able to afford without it. At the time of writing, Dominica's international airport project is also being funded by the CBI programme, as are several luxury hotel resorts.

Having been dependent on monoculture for more than half a century, Dominica's agriculture sector has never properly recovered from the end of the 'banana boom' in the 1980s and 90s. Plenty of money has been invested in agriculture programmes – mostly by outside agencies such as the European Union – but a lack of long-term strategy as well as easy access to profitable markets have hindered any kind of sustainable resurgence. The apparent low rate of return on hard physical labour puts off many young Dominicans when it comes to large-scale farming, and thus the traditional demographic has become an aging one. Given the fertility of its soil, the increasing need to be less reliant on food imports, and a proven track record in coffee, cocoa, bananas and other crops, it's surprising that the agriculture sector has floundered for so long after the banana bubble burst.

Like most Caribbean islands these days, tourism has a higher economic priority than agriculture. Unlike other Caribbean islands, however, Dominica cannot boast the idyllic white-sand beaches and turquoise seas of the tourism brochures, and nor does it yet have an airport big enough for large passenger jets (though, as I write, one is being constructed near Wesley in the northeast and is scheduled to be operational by 2026). Access for European travellers is currently indirect and expensive. Given most people associate the Caribbean with sea, sand and sailboats rather than rainforest, waterfalls and hiking, it's also a challenge for Dominica to compete. And people still confuse Dominica with the Dominican Republic.

Dominica's economic welfare is also underpinned by remittances from its diaspora – Dominicans living and working overseas. These remittances – often referred to as the 'barrel economy' as personal items used to be shipped in oil drums – are significant and a major source of external funding and benefits in kind for individuals and families living here.

AGRICULTURE Before CBI and tourism, agriculture was the traditional mainstay of the Dominican economy. In recent times, however, Dominica's agriculture sector has contracted. The farming of bananas for export to Britain and other EU countries was struck a severe blow by successive changes to world trade rules, removing subsidy support for small island growers and pitting them against the economies of scale that are enjoyed by mass producers. A second blow came with black sigatoka leaf spot disease, which meant that bananas could no longer survive the two-week transatlantic voyage on container ships. Many Dominican farmers have not been able to survive these events and have left the industry altogether, sometimes preferring to sell their land to real-estate developers and speculators. Many farms have simply been abandoned and left to nature. Those who remain in the sector have had to change the way they manage and operate their businesses, producing for and selling to specialist markets both at home and neighbouring islands via ferry, small boats and hucksters. The decline in profitability and poor access to markets has adversely affected the image and the attraction of farming for young Dominicans, with many no longer considering it an attractive or worthwhile occupation. As a consequence, the farmer demographic is growing older and many fieldhands are now low-paid migrant workers from troubled Haiti. Many small 'gardens' still exist and thrive in rural villages around Dominica. These are private plots that feed families and provide a small income by selling to local shops or Saturday markets. One problem with this is a lack of diversity because people will not risk growing crops that they don't know will sell. Travellers will therefore notice that fresh local produce in shops and on market stalls tends to be the same rather limited selection of vegetables, fruits and *ground provisions*. Anything different tends to be imported. There have

CUTLASS AND MACHETE

The weapon of choice for sailors and pirates in the 17th and 18th centuries was the cutlass. It is a short sabre with a broad, curved blade and was useful for close combat on ship and shore, as well as for cutting through rope and wood. On land it was also used as an agricultural tool, particularly effective for cutting through rainforest and harvesting sugarcane.

Also used both as a weapon and an agricultural tool was the machete. Very similar in shape and length to a cutlass, the machete has a broad blade with a very thin, sharp cutting edge. It is, however, much less elegant in design than the naval cutlass, and is sometimes called the 'poor man's sword'. Variations of the machete exist in many countries across the world. The *parang*, *golok* and *bolo* are similar long knives used in Malaysia, Indonesia and the Philippines. In Nepal it is the *kukri* and in China the *dao*.

In Dominica today the machete continues to be used as an agricultural tool for cutting overgrown bushes, trees and weeds, and for harvesting crops, and the household that does not possess at least one is very much in the minority. Commonly referred to as a cutlass, the tool is in fact a simple machete, rather than its upmarket relative. Visitors to Dominica may see both men and women walking along the roadside carrying one. This should not cause alarm, although it almost certainly will at first.

been attempts to revitalise the sector by focusing on historic crops such as coffee and cocoa, as well as others such as pineapples and passionfruits, but these tend to be short-lived initiatives that fade away when the funding for them (often from grant aid) runs out. It feels like there is no long-term vision for the sector and that initiatives come and go with the availability of overseas financial assistance.

In recent times, however, a few small-scale, specialist farms have sprung up, often established and run by young people, that focus on high-quality, niche products and innovative farming methods that incorporate organic growing, permaculture, soil composition management and so on. Using social media, they're also influencing others. This is an encouraging development that seems to be gaining traction. Several of these farms are open to visitors to help them generate additional income (page 74).

There's also a small group of entrepreneurial Dominicans who have developed a range of **agri-products**. Although they are cottage industries at most, their products are natural and often of high quality. These products include soaps and shampoos, herbal teas, honey, coffee, cocoa tea, cassava and farine flour, coconut oil, bay oil and bay rum, plantain chips and more. A good place to find such products is in a small shop in the covered section of the Old Market in Roseau called **Zeb Kweyol – House of Herbs** (f ZebKweyol; ⏲ 09.00–16.00 Mon–Fri, 09.00–14.00 Sat).

FISHERIES Fishing is a traditional occupation in Dominica and every coastal village has its community of fishermen. Colourful wooden boats as well as modern fibreglass vessels can be seen pulled up on the beach or moored close to the shore, and there's usually a regular spot where daily catches are sold. Many fishermen sell directly to hotels, restaurants and supermarkets (often by mobile phone before they even reach land), some sell at established fish markets in Roseau, Marigot and Portsmouth, and others simply meander around village communities either in a pick-up truck or pushing a barrow, blowing a conch shell to let people know there's fish for sale.

You'll also see fishermen selling by the roadside on makeshift benches or cable drums. (Be careful when you do as cars and buses tend to pull over and stop without any kind of warning.)

Migratory pelagics such as marlin, tuna and dorado (mahi-mahi, also known locally as *dolphin*) are usually caught from small boats using long hand lines and homemade artificial lures. This takes place several miles offshore using fish-attracting devices (FADs) that are usually floats made from an assortment of tree branches or palm fronds. Small fish are drawn to these floating structures, creating a concentrated food source for larger predators.

Inshore fishermen use basketware or chicken-wire traps and seine nets to catch mackerel, ballyhoo, jacks, sprats and even small tuna. Almost all lobsters that are caught are sold directly to hotels and restaurants, and you will rarely see them for sale elsewhere. Unlike most of the eastern Caribbean, conch (also known locally as *lambie*) is uncommon as the sea around Dominica's coastline gets deep very quickly. A visit to one of the fish markets or roadside stalls is worthwhile – even if just to watch large fish being chopped into steaks with machetes.

TOURISM Because of its dramatic and largely unspoiled natural environment, Dominica is rightly promoted as a destination for nature lovers and its marketing tagline is 'Nature Island of the Caribbean'. In addition to hikers, scuba-divers, researchers, backpackers, birdwatchers and other nature enthusiasts, Dominica receives 200 or more cruise ships each year. For independent travellers, this means planning your activities to take account of crowded sites as well as roads (especially in the Roseau Valley) that may be congested with tour buses. Despite the environmental damage caused by cruise ships – a factor that would seem to run counter to the notion of 'nature island' – it's clear that the tourism authorities are working to increase their number and provide more attractions, such as a cable car to Boiling Lake, to the thousands of day visitors that arrive on cruise ships each year.

Although it's essentially rather a contradiction in terms, 'ecotourism' is usually used to describe Dominica's tourism industry, particularly in the context of the stayover market. The Ministry of Tourism (**w** tourism.gov.dm) provides the political direction and operational management of the sector, and the Discover Dominica Authority (DDA; **w** discoverdominica.com) is responsible for creating and implementing destination marketing strategies, social media content and so on. Additionally, the Dominica Hotel and Tourism Association (**w** dhta.org) represents the interests of its paying members and works with DDA to promote the destination.

According to official statistics, the number of annual pre-pandemic stayover visitors was around 62,000. In 2021, this figure fell to 15,000 but by 2022 it rose sharply to 60,000. Major stayover markets are the French West Indies (Guadeloupe and Martinique), France, Canada, Germany, UK, and USA (source: DDA).

PEOPLE

It's a sweeping statement, of course, but by and large Dominicans are friendly and helpful towards travellers. Sometimes serious outward expressions can be a little off-putting, but if you persist beyond such first impressions you're usually greeted with warm and memorable encounters with the people of Dominica.

Dominicans are usually keen to talk about the natural beauty of their country and will offer plenty of information, help and advice. Politics and social commentary are always hot topics here (you may want to steer clear of these discussions), though Dominicans will willingly offer you an opinion on absolutely any subject at all, from world affairs to how best to park your car. If you make the effort to engage with Dominicans beyond those working in your hotel and on your tour bus, you are usually rewarded with an interesting insight into island life.

POPULATION Dominica's population is estimated at somewhere between 65,000 and 70,000, with some 20% or so living in or around the capital, Roseau. The population declined following Hurricane Maria in 2017, when many people left and didn't return, but has remained fairly unchanged in recent years (migration to other islands in search of work is common, as is using the US Virgin Islands as a stepping-stone to a Green Card). Dominica's large overseas diaspora predominantly lives in the US, UK and Canada.

ETHNICITY The majority of Dominicans are descendants of enslaved Africans brought to the island by the French and British in the 18th and 19th centuries. Many are also descendants of free people of colour who migrated from the French islands of Guadeloupe and Martinique. Dominica is the only island in the eastern Caribbean that is still home to a people who were here before the arrival of Columbus in 1493. The Kalinago are of Amerindian descent and number between 2,500 and 3,000, the majority of whom live on the east coast in or around the 1,530ha Kalinago Territory (page 155). There's a small population of people from the Middle East whose ancestors came to the Caribbean as merchants, a growing number of working Chinese and Haitians, as well as Europeans and Americans who have either retired or established tourism businesses here.

LANGUAGE

Dominica's official language is English, which is spoken by everyone. There's a second language that's known as *patois* or French Creole (also *kwéyòl*) and is a legacy of colonialism and enslavement. Patois is still commonly used, especially in rural areas and in communities such as Grand Bay where cultural traditions

KWÉYÒL

Some examples of French Creole, or *patois*, from Marcel D'jamala Fontaine's *Dominica's Diksyonnè* (2003):

Good day	*Bon jou*
Good afternoon	*Bon apwé midi*
Good evening	*Bon swé*
How are you?	*Sa ka fete?*
My name is Paul	*Non mwen sé Paul*
I love Dominica	*Mwen enmé Domnik*
It is a beautiful day	*Jòdi sé yon bèl jou*
It is raining	*Lapli ka tonbé*
I am thirsty	*Mon swèf*
I am hungry	*Mon fen*
I would like a drink	*Mon vlé on bwè*
How much is it?	*Konmen ou sa?*

remain strong. As with all Creole languages, patois has a mixture of influences: in this case, France and Africa. Often regarded as a rural or peasant language, patois is enjoying something of a revival and has strong associations with Dominica's cultural heritage.

The Arawakan variation spoken by the Kalinago is no longer a living language in Dominica, though this too is more commonly seen and heard in recent times as the Kalinago try to revive and promote their own cultural heritage. Many villages and rivers around Dominica still retain their 'Kalinago' names (eg: Colihaut, Coulibistrie, Calibishie, Sari Sari and so on).

RELIGION

From the moment Columbus arrived on his second voyage in 1493, the *zemi* stones and ancestral spirit worship of the Amerindian tribes across the region were brutally replaced by the crucifix and the Roman Catholic Church. Vieille Case (or Itassi as it was known to the Kalinago) was the site of the island's first Roman Catholic Mass in 1646, and in the early 18th century French Jesuits erected the first Roman Catholic church in Roseau. Today, with around 80% of the population as followers, Roman Catholicism is by far the dominant religion. Faith in all Christian denominations present on the island – including Methodists, Pentecostals, Seventh Day Adventists, Baptists and Jehovah's Witnesses – is very strong and deeply woven into the fabric of modern Dominican society. Other minority religions include Islam, Baha'i and Rastafarianism. Dominica's constitution provides for religious freedom of all faiths.

Although religion is strong and most Dominicans have very conservative beliefs, Dominica has many social issues such as the abuse of women and children, teenage pregnancies, alcoholism, and having children outside of marriage.

EDUCATION

Primary school education is mandatory in Dominica. It lasts for seven years and ends with the common entrance exam. Secondary education was made universal in 2005 and lasts for five years. It's completed by pupils sitting examinations for the Caribbean Examinations Council Secondary Education Certificate, known as GCE O-levels. There are also several non-governmental primary and secondary schools operating on the island.

Dominica's State College opened its doors in September 2002. Its formation amalgamated several disparate tertiary education establishments under one roof with the aim of better organising standards, policies and opportunities. The college offers further education in traditional as well as vocational subjects such as hospitality and tourism, nursing, agriculture and teaching. The college was badly damaged by Hurricane Maria and, controversially, has never been properly repaired, even though it's still open to study.

The University of the West Indies (UWI) Open Campus offers Dominicans the opportunity to enrol in some degree programmes that may take place entirely within Dominica or may be split between the Dominica school and the main UWI campus in Jamaica.

Dominica's tertiary education system receives small but welcome boosts through scholarships that are awarded by individuals, organisations or governments. It is through such scholarships that talented Dominicans of all backgrounds can pursue further education in institutions abroad that, under normal circumstances, would be well beyond the reach of most pockets. The downside of this is that not all overseas students return.

CULTURE

Following the decline and forced retreat of the Kalinago population to the northeast of the island, it was the European colonists and their enslaved workforce who fashioned a new cultural identity in Dominica. Of the Europeans it was the French rather than the British who made the greatest impression, due largely to the proximity of Guadeloupe and Martinique, and the movement of traders and free people of colour between the islands. African tribal traditions including dance, dress and belief systems merged with the culture of France, from the dances and festivals of its royal courts to the language, music and fashions of its Caribbean island settlers. And so it was that the emergent **French Creole** dominated the cultural landscape of Dominica from the 19th century onwards.

Today, Creole is one of the key ingredients of Dominica's cultural landscape and, together with a fresh movement in 'Kalinago consciousness' history and tradition, the revival of African roots and heritage, and the inevitable influence of contemporary American culture, past merges with present to create a multicultural fusion of sound, colour and language that's continuously shapeshifting.

TRADITIONAL DRESS Commonly worn by women from the 1800s to the 1960s, the ***wob dwiyet*** is now only seen at national festivals such as the Creole and Independence celebrations that take place during October and November each year. You may also see it at Carnival. Starting life as a dress worn on Sundays or feast days when enslaved women were permitted to discard their drab uniforms and dress up in the kind of colours to which they were more accustomed, the traditional Creole *wob dwiyet* dress was born. Over the years the style has been modified and accessories have been added to develop this attire, but the combination of bright skirt over white chemise, with lace adornments, coloured headscarf and kerchief is in essence the same as the national dress that is worn today.

The wearer of the *wob dwiyet* is known as the *matador* and for formal occasions she may choose to wear a headpiece, or *tête en l'air*, made of a square piece of **madras**. This square of Indian cotton, made by the Kalabari in the vicinity of Chennai (formerly Madras), was known as the *mouchoir madras* and became popular with Creole women towards the end of the 18th century. French, English and Portuguese merchants were involved in the trade of madras, or *injiri*, as it's known in India, around 400 years ago. It's thought these merchants brought the material to West Africa where it was worn by the Igbo people in southern Nigeria. Traditionally madras was made with vegetable dyes which ran, or 'bled', each time the material was washed, becoming blurred over time. Today most madras is still made in India but with chemical dyes. It's usually associated with all things Creole.

MUSIC AND DANCE Traditional music and dance finds its roots in the island's history. From the enslaved workers from West Africa and the influences of their British and French oppressors, songs, music and dance emerged that are still enjoyed today. The goatskin drum, or *la peau cabwit*, provides a traditional beat that has echoes of Africa, whereas lyrics are often sung by women in an enchanting French Creole.

The ***bélé*** is a Creole dance of African origin. The *tambou twavail* or *tambou bélé* drum is the centrepiece and the dance moves reflect the courtship between the man and the woman as they move in turn towards the drum and its resonating rhythm. By the time the dance reaches its conclusion, the drum is booming loudly and the man and woman are dancing together with quick steps and vigorous body movements, symbolising their union.

The **quadrille** is a more formal square dance that originates in the French courts of the 19th century. Four couples traditionally dance together. The ladies, known as the *dam*, dance in *wob dwiyet* costume, with the men, known as the *kavalyé*, leading. Often referred to as 'heel and toe', the quadrille's style is aristocratic, graceful and elegant, and today it's a key part of Dominica's Independence celebrations. Its traditional accompaniment is a **jing ping** band. This is usually a four-instrument ensemble that comprises a tambourine (*tambal*), a long boom pipe (*boumboum*), a rattle or scraper (*shak-shak*, or *gwage*) and an accordion, which replaced the original bamboo flute.

Dominica's popular music scene really began in the 1960s with **calypso** and **steelpan** music. These genres are still popular and the Swinging Stars calypso band that was formed in Roseau in 1959 still performs to packed houses today, though the line-up has changed somewhat. In the 1970s a new Dominican music style called **cadence-lypso** became fashionable across the Caribbean. This music combined calypso with *kompa*, a Creole music genre from Haiti. **Zouk** music from Martinique and **soca** from Trinidad arrived in Dominica in the 1980s and eclipsed the cadence-lypso scene. Zouk takes its influences from reggae and salsa, and soca is a fusion of calypso and Trinidad's Indian music, sometimes called *chutney* music. One of Dominica's most popular bands, Windward Caribbean Kulture (WCK), combined cadence-lypso with jing ping to produce **bouyon** music, which has also become a very popular genre in Dominica, Martinique and Guadeloupe. Most contemporary Dominican bands play a form of bouyon music. Other popular music forms are reggae, dancehall and rap.

CARNIVAL The pre-Lenten festival of Carnival (also called *Mas Domnik* and *Real Mas*) that takes place on the Monday and Tuesday before Ash Wednesday each year, is a time when Dominicans party hard, 'jump up', 'free up' and let their hair down (though they also seem to do this with increasing frequency at various *fetes* throughout the year). Although today the music is a modern combination of calypso, steelpan and bouyon, usually transported in electronic format with huge amplifiers and speakers crammed on to flat-bed trucks, the colourful costumes and the spirit of dancing are still, occasionally, tantalising reflections of the past. French settlers may have brought the festival of *masquerade* to Dominica, but it was the enslaved Africans who added a raw rhythm, vibrancy and just a hint of rebellion. It's that colour, spirit and edge that is still in evidence in today's Carnival, despite it being continuously reshaped and revamped under the tourism umbrella.

The calypsos that are sung in competitions prior to Carnival hark back to the *chante-mas*, a tradition of song and satire that evolved as part of the preparations for Carnival. The female *chanteulles* would sing short, cutting ballads that ridiculed administrators or perpetrators of bad deeds. Today calypso songs are much longer, though the lyrics still contain a large dose of irony or political and social commentary.

Carnival costumes were originally little different from those worn in African tribal festivals. Most notable is the ***sensay*** costume, which has now become associated with Dominica's *Old Mas* Carnival parades – its fierce mask and horned headpiece with ruffles of cloth strips completely cover the wearer and cascade in layers from the head down to the ground. Although one or two of these original themes survive, today costumes are of modern materials and design, and in more recent years have become far more mainstream – lots of bikinis and feathers – a trend that's bemoaned by traditionalists.

ARCHITECTURE Many of the small wooden houses that can be seen in villages across Dominica are based on a simple design that goes back to the thatched huts of the indigenous Kalinago people who were here when the Europeans arrived. These small houses, called *ti kai* or *kai kwéyòl*, typically have a half-hip shingle roof designed for hurricanes, quick water run-off, and to enable air circulation. They have a small veranda, jalousie-style windows with strong hurricane shutters and are sometimes raised on piles or pillars. Today the roofs are often made of modern galvanised steel. Although ti kai are often viewed as poor people's houses and are gradually being replaced by far less attractive concrete blocks, their traditional design has stood the test of time.

Elements of Caribbean colonial style are evident in some of the older buildings across Dominica, but especially in the French Quarter in Roseau. King George V Street still provides surviving examples of traditional verandas, jalousie windows, wooden shutters and ornate and intricately designed fretwork beneath the eaves of the upper floors.

Indigenous architectural styles can be seen at the Kalinago Barana Auté in the community of Crayfish River in the Kalinago Territory, which was designed as a model village depicting indigenous buildings such as thatched *karbets* and *ajoupas* (page 162).

ARTISTS Everyday island life, culture and the natural environment have been inspiring artists since colonialism in the 1700s (I'd like to say since the earliest settlers, but so far only one very tiny petroglyph has been discovered). Indeed, these days there are many young people creating impressive work in what is a poorly supported arts scene. Here's a taster of some of the island's most notable artists.

Born in Rome in 1730, **Agostino Brunias** was hired by Sir William Young, governor of Dominica in 1771, as his personal artist. Brunias fell in love with the island and stayed there until his death in 1796. During his life he painted many scenes of Dominica: detailed images of enslaved workers in the fields, washing, cooking and dancing that offer an interesting insight into the Dominica of the day. There are examples of his work in the Dominica Museum (page 103).

For travellers interested in the contemporary art scene, **The Waitukubuli Artist Association (WAA)** (w kubuliarts.com) is a group of Dominican and Dominica-based overseas artists who, as well as creating individual artworks, also come together on public projects – often in the form of commissioned street art and sculpture. The Dominica sign on the Roseau Bay Front is an example of their work. WAA organises exhibitions throughout the year (usually, though not always at the Old Mill Cultural Centre). Check their Facebook page (f kubuliarts) for upcoming events and community-based art projects.

Earl Etienne was one of Dominica's most noted contemporary artists. Sadly, he died in 2022. Though his artistic style changed throughout his life, he was perhaps best known for his technique of *bouzzaille*, which incorporated smoke and soot patterns from which images of Dominican folk life emerge. His paintings of traditional *bélé* are also excellent and extremely collectible. A larger than life figure, Earl would often create elaborate carnival costumes for himself and walk around in his trademark painted jeans. His work is displayed at the Old Mill Cultural Centre.

Pauline Marcelle (w paulinemarcelle.com) is a Dominican artist who lives and works in Vienna. She has received international acclaim and has exhibited her work all around the world. Pauline is my favourite Dominican artist and I recommend a visit to her website.

Other artisans Dominica is home to some creative and talented craftspeople who fashion ornaments, batiks, calabash bowls and bags, jewellery, masks and so on. Unfortunately, it's often difficult to find their work as they don't have many outlets. You should note that most items on sale at the stalls and souvenir stands you see at Roseau's Old Market and popular visitor sites are mass-produced Chinese imports and – except for some Kalinago baskets – are hardly ever locally made. Local artisans receive very little effective and sustainable support from the authorities. A good place to find some local crafts is the **Zeb Kweyol** shop in the covered section of the Old Market. A handful of the island's larger hotels (notably Jungle Bay and Coulibri Ridge) have souvenir shops or boutiques that stock locally made products.

WRITERS, POETS AND STORYTELLERS Dominica's two most famous literary icons, Jean Rhys and Phyllis Shand Allfrey, lived around the same time and were daughters of British settlers. In more recent times, several homegrown writers and poets have also achieved recognition for their work.

Jean Rhys was born in Cork Street, Roseau in 1890. Her father was a Welsh doctor and her mother a member of the Lockhart family who owned the Geneva Estate at Grand Bay. Rhys left Dominica at the age of 16 for schooling in England, during which time the Geneva Estate house was razed to the ground by arsonists. In 1936 she made a last trip to Dominica, which included a visit to the remains of Geneva, and it was the attacks on this family estate that were reflected in the burning of 'Coulibri' in her acclaimed 1966 novel, *Wide Sargasso Sea*, which imagines the early life of Bertha Mason from Charlotte Brontë's *Jane Eyre*. Jean Rhys died in 1979.

Phyllis Shand Allfrey was born in 1908, a year after Jean Rhys left Dominica for England. Her only novel, *The Orchid House*, was published in 1953. It's a largely biographical story of the three daughters of a once-wealthy but now impoverished white family, told through the eyes of Lally, a black nurse. The book received praise and was even made into a film for British television. A grass-roots activist and Fabian socialist, in 1954 Allfrey founded the Dominica Labour Party, the country's first political party. Phyllis Shand Allfrey died in 1986.

Elma Napier was born in Scotland in 1892 but settled in Dominica in 1932 where she spent the remainder of her life. She lived with her husband at Pointe Baptiste and became the first woman to be elected to a Caribbean legislature. She loved exploring the island and wrote an autobiography of her life in Dominica called *Black and White Sands*. Napier died in 1973 and was buried next to her husband 'in a quiet place under trees' on the Pointe Baptiste Estate.

Lennox Honychurch is a national treasure. Dominica's only historian and archivist, he is the author of a number of non-fiction works including *The Dominica Story – A History of the Island*, first published in 1975 and still Dominica's definitive historical reference, and *Negre Mawon: The Fighting Maroons of Dominica*, published in 2014. He has also written several other educational reference books. A Doctor of Philosophy and an anthropologist, Dominica-born Honychurch is also an artist, poet and conservationist. He oversaw the restoration of the Fort Shirley garrison in Cabrits National Park (page 182) and was actively involved in the recent archaeology work at La Soye (page 18).

Alwin Bully was a renowned playwright, artist, theatrical director and film maker. His contribution to the arts in the Caribbean has been immense. He was also the author of *The Cocoa Dancer*, a short story collection. Sadly, Alwin died in March 2023.

Giftus John is a storyteller and poet. His book *Mesyé Kwik! Kwak!* is a collection of short stories set against the backdrop of the west coast village of St Joseph where he grew up. He has also written a collection of poems called *The Island Man Sings His Song*.

Alick Lazare is a writer and poet. His popular novel *Pharcel* tells the story of a Maroon in colonial Dominica.

Celia A Sorhaindo is a contemporary writer whose published poetry collections include *Guabancex* and *Radical Normalisation*.

If you're interested in fiction and non-fiction from Dominica and the wider Caribbean, two publishers that are worth checking out are Papillote Press (**w** papillotepress.co.uk) and Peepal Tree Press (**w** peepaltreepress.com).

FOLKLORE Dominican culture is embellished with several colourful myths and legends that have their origins in the spirit tales, practices and beliefs of West African tribes as well as in later Creole folkloric influences. For some Dominicans this lore extends beyond simple superstition and is still to be found lurking in the shadows of the island's more contemporary practices and belief systems.

Obeah, a kind of magic or witchcraft, is rumoured to still be practised by local shamans. Based on a belief in supernatural forces that can forge or quell evil spirits, Obeah men or Obeah women may be engaged to cast spells or create potions. Until recently, there was even one who advertised in one of the local newspapers.

There are two night spirits the unassuming visitor may wish to look out for. The ***soucouyan*** of West African origin sheds her skin and flies through the forest in a ball of flames on the lookout for the blood of people and animals. If her skin happens to be found it can be rubbed with salt to make it difficult and painful for her to put back on, or alternatively a calabash of peas can be placed next to it which she must count before she is able to transform herself back into a human. Successful escape from a *soucouyan* may just place you in the hands of **La Diablesse**, however, which is altogether bad news. This beautiful woman walking through the forest by the light of the moon lures men deeper and deeper into the woods, where she transforms herself into a wild old crone who causes her victims to either go mad or die. Avoiding the *soucouyan* and La Diablesse doesn't mean you are out of those deep woods just yet, however. Go for a swim in a river and you may come across **Mama Glo**, a female spirit of lakes and rivers who also takes on the appearance of a beautiful woman or even a mermaid. She may command you to undertake a series of menial tasks with a promise of reward, but if you choose to disobey, she may turn very nasty indeed. Take a nap on the forest floor and you may be visited by a ***jombie***, or evil spirit. If it finds you sleeping, the *jombie* could destroy your health or bring you a lifetime of bad luck. Fortunately, there is a remedy for its curse. Unfortunately, it requires the help of Obeah…

Background Information CULTURE

1

2

Practical Information

WHEN TO VISIT

Because Dominica's attractions and accommodation options are spread around the island rather than concentrated in one area or around beaches, it never feels overrun by tourists. The 'busiest' time of year is during the **cruise ship season** which usually starts at the beginning of November and finishes by the end of April. During this period around 200 or more cruise ships will call at Roseau and occasionally at Portsmouth. On some days there may be no ships at all, on others there may be two or three, offloading at the Roseau Bay Front, the ferry terminal or the Woodbridge Bay port. Convoys of buses and taxis taking these day-visitors on tours to accessible attractions means that some roads become congested – especially up and down the Roseau Valley – and sites such as Emerald Pool, Trafalgar Falls and Ti Tou Gorge become rather crowded. It's also more difficult to catch a public bus at this time as some drivers will drop their routes in favour of the more lucrative cruise ship business, meaning you'll often see schoolchildren enduring long treks home or people laden with shopping bags or low-pressure gas bottles trying to hitch a ride by the roadside. Roseau becomes a little more crowded with meandering, often disorientated tourists looking for something interesting to photograph, free Wi-Fi, cheap beer, designer boutiques or the Botanic Gardens, and walking along the middle of the road oblivious to all the traffic. It's a lively time of year on the island and, despite the obvious environmental issues that run counter to the whole 'nature island' ethos, many Dominicans depend on the short-but-busy cruise ship season for a living.

Creole Week and **Independence celebrations** take place in the latter half of October and the beginning of November. At this time, there are several cultural events culminating in the World Creole Music Festival. Creole Week (usually the last week in October) is especially busy with lots of visitors arriving by ferry from the neighbouring French islands of Guadeloupe and Martinique. If you plan on coming to Dominica at this time of year then consider booking well in advance as flights, ferries and accommodation usually fill up quickly.

Carnival preparations and events start in early January with numerous fringe parties and Calypso elimination competitions (known as tents) and reach their peak on the Monday and Tuesday before Ash Wednesday. On an island of seemingly endless parties and fetes, Dominicans and visitors can enjoy uninterrupted days of around-the-clock festivities during the Carnival period. Many Dominicans love and look forward to absolutely any reason to 'fete' and Carnival is the biggest excuse of all. There's much to enjoy and experience during Carnival, even if you're not a rum drinker: street parades, Carnival Queen and Calypso Monarch competitions, live music, dancing and plenty of barbecue street food. Though it's certainly not on a par with Rio or Trinidad, and some of the more traditional features are certainly being lost to modern trends, Dominica's singular version of Carnival is an entertaining and lively time to be on the island.

Climate-wise, the **weather** from January to June grows steadily hotter and the rains eventually peter out during the dry season. April, May and June are great months for hiking the interior and climbing the high peaks as cloud cover is usually minimal and views across the island are often unrestricted. Trails, though in places wet all year round, become a little less so at this time of the year and rivers and waterfalls are more predictable. As the cruise ship season has usually wound down by the end of April, the more popular and accessible sites are also far less crowded.

The Atlantic hurricane season starts in July and ends in November, though it usually peaks in the Lesser and Greater Antilles during the months of August and September. Hurricanes begin life as African monsoons that move from the west coast of Africa into the Atlantic and make their way westwards towards the Caribbean and the Gulf of Mexico. Whether tropical depressions become tropical storms and then develop into hurricanes is down to sea temperatures, Sahara dust and wind shear. Due to Dominica's vulnerability during this period, August and September tend to be very quiet months and some hotels and tour operators choose to close and take a holiday themselves – especially in September. Often, accommodation prices are discounted, and most tourists are visitors from the neighbouring islands of Guadeloupe and Martinique. Contrary to popular belief, hurricanes don't usually roll in one after another. August and September can actually be pleasant months – though usually hot – and a good time to explore. But there's a risk, of course. September 2017 saw the worst storm in living memory when Category 5 Hurricane Maria tore up the island in just a matter of hours (page 4).

From October to December the weather is usually changeable, and often rainy with heavy downpours. Mornings of clear skies and sunshine can be followed by dark clouds and squall. It's unpredictable. But whatever time of the year you decide to visit, you should always prepare to get wet – unless you're not planning to move far from the hotel bar and pool, of course. Tour operators like to refer to the rain as 'liquid sunshine' but make no mistake, it is rain, and it can be heavy. Dominica's mountainous, rainforest-covered interior is lush and green for a reason. Several years ago, one of Dominica's destination marketing campaigns used the slogan 'It rains here'. It was short-lived but apt.

My recommendation, unless you are coming especially for one of the festival periods, is to come in May or June. The cruise ships have gone, and the weather is usually great.

HIGHLIGHTS

Unless you thought you were going to a beach in the Dominican Republic, most travellers come to Dominica to experience nature and spend a week or two in the great outdoors.

TRAILS, LAKES AND WATERFALLS Dominica has a wealth of walking tracks. Its signature hike (and my favourite) is the Boiling Lake Trail (page 119) that begins in Laudat and crosses the active Valley of Desolation caldera. Also within Morne Trois Pitons National Park (UNESCO World Heritage Site) are two further lake trails: Freshwater Lake (page 125) and Boeri Lake (page 123). Both are short and can be completed back to back in half a day. My favourite mountain hike in this national park is the Morne Anglais trail (page 143) that starts in the village of Giraudel. I think this peak enjoys the best views of all Dominica's climbable *mornes*. There are three tall waterfalls that are worth their relatively short, though occasionally tricky trails: Middleham Falls (page 126), Victoria Falls (page 172) and Sari Sari Falls (page 171). Find time to journey up the Roseau Valley to Trafalgar Falls (page 119) and the hot springs at Wotten Waven (page 117).

UNDERWATER WORLD The dive sites in the Soufriere Scotts Head Marine Reserve (page 14) and along the Atlantic side of the Cachacrou isthmus are exceptional in their health and diversity. Even if you're not a certified diver, a try-dive or even a four-day certification course are great options here as waters within the reserve are sheltered and there's lots of interesting marine life to see. Snorkellers will enjoy the volcanic activity on Champagne Reef (page 142) and on shallow formations atop steep drop-offs such as La Sorciere and L'Abym.

Given sperm whales are present in Dominica's coastal waters all year round, a whale- and dolphin-watching boat trip (page 85) is usually worthwhile.

CULTURE AND HERITAGE The Kalinago Territory (page 155) is a must-visit for anyone interested in the culture, history and heritage of Dominica's indigenous people. I especially like to walk the Horseback Ridge and village loop (page 169) with its fabulous views and opportunities to engage with locals. Visit the Kalinago Barana Auté (page 162), engage a Kalinago guide and buy some authentic basketware.

For colonial history, explore the Fort Shirley garrison and walking trails in Cabrits National Park (page 181). The jungle ruins are especially interesting and the view from the gun battery atop East Cabrit is certainly worth the short hike (page 197).

One of the most interesting hiking trails in Dominica is Jacko Steps (page 219), which is an atmospheric, as well as beautifully natural walk in the footsteps of the enslaved people who liberated themselves and lived in camps in Dominica's hard-

MY TOP TEN

I'm an outdoors person and I like to walk, so my top ten things to do reflects that.

1. The Boiling Lake Trail
2. The Morne Anglais Trail
3. Scuba-diving (a try-dive if you're not certified)
4. The Jacko Steps Trail
5. The Horseback Ridge and Kalinago villages walk
6. Fort Shirley and the Cabrits National Park trails
7. Trafalgar Falls
8. The Victoria Falls Trail
9. Small-scale, specialist farms and gardens
10. Canyoning

Even if you're not a hiker or a scuba diver, I think the most important thing you can do is get out of your car and take a walk – especially through a country or Kalinago village; it's hands down the best way to get to know Dominica as well as meet its people.

to-reach places. The steps were carved into a cliffside by Chief Jacko's group and provided them with access to and from the Layou River.

Festivities that take place during the Carnival (page 31) and Creole Week (page 62) periods are modern takes on heritage that grew out of colonial Dominica and – in the form of traditional costume, music and dance – are colourful and entertaining examples of an African-Caribbean culture that has one foot in the past and another planted firmly in the present.

SUGGESTED ITINERARIES

GREAT DAYS OUT If you're here for more than a week, I think it's a good idea to split up your accommodation rather than stay in one place for the entire duration. It cuts down on the driving around and you can see more of the island at a relaxed pace. If you've arrived here by plane, then start in the south and work your way back up north to the airport. If you're renting a car, pick a company that will let you pick up and drop off at the airport when you leave.

If you're mostly hiking, start on the signature trails in the south (Boiling Lake, Morne Anglais, Freshwater Lake, Boeri Lake, Middleham Falls), then head up north for some of the easier walks (Cabrits trails, Syndicate Trail and waterfall, Horseback Ridge) and the beaches.

If you're mostly **scuba-diving**, again start in the south in the Soufriere Scotts Head Marine Reserve, and then head up to the Cabrits for a few dives.

Assuming you plan on leaving the sun lounger and doing a little exploring, here are some ideas for great days out.

The south

- Hike the Boiling Lake Trail, follow it with a swim up Ti Tou Gorge and then a hot sulphur bath under the stars at one of the hot springs in Wotten Waven.
- Walk the Galion Loop Trail in the morning and have lunch in Scotts Head or Soufriere. Go swimming, snorkelling or kayaking in the afternoon.
- Hike the Freshwater Lake Trail and Boeri Lake Trail back to back (or the Middleham Falls Trail). Visit Trafalgar Falls and a Wotten Waven hot spring in the afternoon and evening.
- Hike to the top of Morne Anglais and then spend the afternoon snorkelling on Champagne Reef
- Walk the Victoria Falls Trail in the morning and explore some of the more accessible waterfalls of the Heart of Dominica in the afternoon (Emerald Pool, Spanny Falls, Jacko Falls).

The north

- Explore Fort Shirley then walk the East Cabrit Trail. Afterwards take a boat trip up the Indian River.
- Walk the Syndicate Nature Trail and the Syndicate Falls Trail (consider a guided birdwatching walk). Spend some time on the beach at Purple Turtle.
- Spend the day on the Horseback Ridge and Kalinago villages walk. Call in at Kalinago Barana Auté.
- Walk the Jacko Steps Trail then head to Mero beach via the scenic Warner road.
- Drive a loop through the Morne Aux Diables volcano from Portsmouth or Calibishie. Include Cold Soufriere, enjoy the stunning coastal views on the road around Pennville, and hike the short trail to Bwa Nef Falls. Finish with lunch or dinner at Toucari or Calibishie.

TOUR OPERATORS

There are few international tour operators offering Dominica as a holiday destination and, when they do, it almost always includes the same handful of upmarket accommodation options (Secret Bay, Jungle Bay, Fort Young and so on). The more flexible, though time-consuming, way to plan and book your Dominica trip is to do it yourself.

For accommodation, as well as using this book, it's worth browsing the plentiful options on **w** airbnb.com and **w** booking.com. There's also an on-island offering (**w** bookingdominica.com) – a public-private collaboration that includes the Discover Dominica Authority (DDA) and Dominica Hotel and Tourism Association (DHTA).

INTERNATIONAL OPERATORS These international operators offer packages to Dominica.

Caradonna Dive Adventures w caradonna.com
Caribtours w caribtours.co.uk
Kenwood Travel w kenwoodtravel.co.uk
Kuoni w kuoni.co.uk
Responsible Travel w responsibletravel.com

ALL-INCLUSIVES Some of the bigger hotels (those mentioned above) have started to offer all-inclusive (or 'island-inclusive') holiday packages, which may be of interest to you. These usually include accommodation, meals, and a fixed daily menu of tours. Wanderlust Caribbean (**w** wanderlustcaribbean.com) is a great option if you want to get stuck into the great outdoors. It's a small boutique hotel near Calibishie and it offers a wide range of all-inclusive adventure packages (page 178).

TOURIST OFFICES

For up-to-date details of Dominica's tourism representatives in Europe and North America, check the contact page of the Discover Dominica Authority's (DDA) website (**w** discoverdominica.com). Their office on the island is located at 5–7 Great Marlborough Street, Roseau (767 448 2045; **e** tourism@dominica.dm). Please note that DDA is primarily a marketing agency and may disappoint if you are looking for specific information about activities such as hiking trails or scuba-diving.

RED TAPE

ENTRY REQUIREMENTS All visitors to Dominica require a valid passport. You may also be asked to show either a return or an onward ticket, though this rarely happens. You must be able to provide details of your hotel or the address of family, friends, etc, so be sure to have this written down somewhere.

At the time of writing, there were no longer any restrictions or pre-travel requirements regarding Covid-19. If you are unsure, or the situation changes, the DDA website usually carries the latest information in this context. Also at the time of writing, an online landing card was being launched. The website for this is **w** edcard.dominica.gov.dm.

CUSTOMS It's common practice for customs officers to randomly ask travellers to open their luggage for inspection at ports of entry in Dominica, so don't think you are being singled out in any way. Arriving passengers must complete a customs declaration form and hand it to a customs officer prior to inspection (this may change with the introduction of the online landing card; see opposite). Usually, the customs officer will ask you where you are staying, whether you are here on business or vacation, whether you are bringing any food items and so on. Just answer honestly, be polite and smile – even though you may be hot, tired, delayed, grumpy and ready for a rum punch and a shower. You're in the Caribbean now. Everything moves at a different pace.

DEPARTURE Usually, departure taxes are included in the cost of your ticket (though at the time of writing, you must still go to a departures booth to get a stamp before going to the immigration desk, but this may change). You'll be asked to complete a departure form, which you hand in to immigration officials prior to security scans and so on (this may also change with the advent of the online landing card project; see opposite).

It's worth having a flights app on your phone so that you can check for yourself what's going on. The arrivals and departures board seems to display what should theoretically be happening, rather than what actually is, and ground staff often seem reluctant to share bad news. I use Flightradar24, a free app, though I'm sure there are other options. There's free Wi-Fi at Douglas-Charles Airport.

MARRIAGE REQUIREMENTS If you're planning on tying the knot in Dominica there's a bit of red tape, but authorities have streamlined the process to market the island as a wedding destination. Assuming your wedding is being organised by your hotel, they will help you with it all as part of their service. Ask your wedding organiser or the Discover Dominica Authority (**w** discoverdominica.com/en/weddings) for the latest legal requirements and a list of the documents you must bring with you.

CONSULATES AND EMBASSIES

For a full list of embassies and consulates in Dominica, go to **w** embassypages.com/dominica.

GETTING THERE AND AWAY

BY AIR At the time of writing, Dominica has two airports, both too small for large commercial passenger jets. Construction of a new international airport has begun with a view to it being operational in 2026. Its location is near Wesley in the northeast (it hasn't been named yet). In the meantime, for long-haul journeys you must fly to another Caribbean island and then transfer to an inter-island air service. The most popular air hubs are Puerto Rico, Antigua, Sint Maarten and Barbados. At the time of writing, there's a direct service between Dominica and Miami with American Eagle.

Dominica's main airport is **Douglas-Charles Airport (DOM)** (formerly known as Melville Hall Airport, which is still used on some websites). Located a little to the north of Marigot, it's a small and attractive airport with a river and tropical gardens. Landing here can be interesting (or terrifying, depending on your perspective) as aircraft bank low over trees and ridges to the west, bringing farms and farmers often rather more sharply into focus than you may like.

From the US and Canada to Caribbean hubs

The following airlines fly to Caribbean hubs where there are connecting inter-island services to Dominica. It's worth bearing in mind that airlines may review these routes periodically & adjust frequency & schedules depending on demand & profitability.

Air Canada w aircanada.com. Connections via Antigua & Barbados.
American Airlines w aa.com. Connections via Antigua, Barbados, Puerto Rico & St Lucia.
Delta w delta.com. Connections via Puerto Rico & St Lucia.
Frontier w flyfrontier.com. Connections via Puerto Rico.
JetBlue w jetblue.com. Connections via Antigua, Barbados, Puerto Rico & St Lucia.
Southwest Airlines w southwest.com. Connections via Puerto Rico.
Spirit Airlines w spirit.com. Connections via Puerto Rico.

From the US mainland direct to Dominica

American Eagle w aa.com

From the UK and mainland Europe to Carribbean hubs

Aer Lingus w aerlingus.com. UK to & from Barbados.
British Airways w britishairways.com. UK to & from Antigua, Barbados, Grenada & St Lucia.
KLM w klm.nl. Netherlands (Amsterdam) to & from Barbados.
Lufthansa w lufthansa.com. Germany (Frankfurt) to & from Barbados.
Virgin Atlantic w virgin-atlantic.com. UK to & from Antigua, Barbados, Grenada & St Lucia.

To Dominica via the French Caribbean

An alternative way to fly to Dominica is to combine flight with ferry by heading to either of Dominica's French neighbours, Guadeloupe or Martinique. This is worth considering as an option, especially if you like the idea of spending a couple of nights in the French Caribbean either side of your Dominica stay.

Air Canada w aircanada.com. To & from Montreal.
Air Caraïbes w aircaraibes.com. To & from Paris.
Air France w airfrance.com. To & from Miami & Paris.
Corsair w flycorsair.com. To & from Paris.
JetBlue w jetblue.com. To & from New York.

Inter-island connecting flights

The most common way to get to & from Dominica by air is via one of the Caribbean island hubs. Some inter-island airlines have long had a reputation for unreliable services & sadly this is still quite true.

INCLUDING THE FRENCH CARIBBEAN

Perhaps an odd suggestion at first sight but think about including Guadeloupe or Martinique in your schedule. Why? Well, inter-island flights are expensive and can be unreliable. Also, it's not always easy making same-day connections and trying to do so creates exactly the kind of anxiety you're probably trying to get away from for a couple of weeks. This may change, of course, when Dominica's international airport becomes operational. One idea that I've increasingly come to like is to fly to Guadeloupe or Martinique, spend a couple of days relaxing on the beach, drinking wine and eating fabulous food, and then catch the high-speed ferry to Dominica. You can fly to either one of the islands from the US and France, and I know a few Brits who have chosen to take the train to Paris and get to Dominica this way – and they've found it cheaper than flights from London and then Barbados. The inter-island ferry calls at Roseau and sometimes Portsmouth. Do some research – you may find you like the idea.

Last-minute changes, delays & cancellations do happen, especially if the weather is bad. Consider travel insurance.

Air Antilles w airantilles.com. Connections via Guadeloupe, Martinique & Sint Maarten.

Caribbean Airlines w caribbeanairlines.com. Connections via Barbados & Trinidad.

Intercaribbean Airways w intercaribbean.com. Connections via Barbados & St Lucia.

Liat w liat.com. Connections via Antigua.

Silver Airways w silverairways.com. Connections via Puerto Rico.

Douglas-Charles Airport Though its days are clearly limited (theoretically, by 2026), Douglas-Charles Airport is actually rather picturesque, located alongside the Melville Hall River and beautified with colourfully landscaped gardens. Functionally, it has a small restaurant, ATM, taxi and car rental services (located in the car park beyond the main terminal). If you need one, you'll be relieved to read that the airport also has a VIP Lounge.

Taxi fares from the airport to destinations around the island are fixed and drivers operating to and from the airport have special licences to do so. You will get asked if you'd like a taxi when you emerge from the arrival hall, but it's usually orderly and respectful, and there's no need to worry or be on the defensive. There isn't a public bus service to and from the airport (though you can stand outside the airport gates and flag one down).

Baggage Please check airline websites for up-to-date information on baggage allowances and restrictions. If you're connecting, there are three things to check: whether you can check your bags all the way through to Dominica, whether you must pick them up and re-check them, and whether the inter-island airline has baggage limits that are lower that your international carrier.

Make sure your checked bags are properly tagged with your name and address. Should your bags not turn up at Douglas-Charles with you (sadly, this does happen), make your way to the airline check-in desk in the departure hall and complete the requisite forms. Usually, baggage delays are short, and you can normally expect your luggage to arrive the following day. Your hotel may well deal with this for you but fill in the forms anyway.

BY FERRY **L'Express des Iles** (w express-des-iles.com) and **Val'ferry** (w valferry.fr) operate a high-speed ferry service between the islands of Guadeloupe (including Les Saintes and Marie-Galante), Dominica, Martinique and St Lucia. The ferries arrive at and depart from the terminal on Roseau's Bay Front and – on some days – the Cabrits near Portsmouth. For schedules, pricing and reservations, see their websites. It's a great service – I recommend it – though do be prepared for a bit of a scrum at the ferry terminals! Hang back and wait is my advice.

BY PRIVATE YACHT Visitors to Dominica arriving by private or charter vessel should contact the Dominica Port Authority on VHF channel 16. Customs clearance is mandatory before anchoring. Two copies of the crew and passenger list are required, and you must pay an environmental levy. Ports of entry are in Portsmouth on the northwest coast, Roseau on the west coast and Anse Du Mai on the east coast. While there's no properly established marina in Dominica, popular anchorages are at Prince Rupert Bay on the northwest coast and Castle Comfort in the southwest. The Soufriere Scotts Head Marine Reserve on the southern tip of Dominica is out of bounds as an anchorage.

BEFORE YOU GO There are no immunisation requirements for visitors to Dominica except proof of vaccination against **yellow fever** for those over one year of age if coming from a yellow fever endemic area (eg: certain countries in sub-Saharan Africa and South America) or anyone transiting for more than 12 hours in a yellow fever endemic area. If the vaccine has been deemed unsuitable for you, you should obtain an exemption certificate from a registered yellow fever centre (eg: some primary care doctors and most travel clinics). If you are unsure whether this applies to you, then check with a doctor ideally before you leave home and at least ten days before entering Dominica. There is no endemic malaria but there are other mosquito-borne diseases to avoid, including dengue fever and Zika virus. Dominica's water is safe to drink though travellers who have particularly sensitive stomachs may wish to use a re-usable filter bottle or bottled water as an alternative. Even if the water is clean the different mineral content can lead to an upset stomach. It is recommended that standard vaccinations such as tetanus are up to date. **Tetanus** vaccine is usually combined with **diphtheria** and **polio** and/or **pertussis** (whooping cough) in an all-in-one vaccine: this protects for ten years. Travellers should also consider protecting themselves from **hepatitis A.**

Visitors requiring health care in Dominica are required to pay up front for treatment. Medical insurance is strongly recommended, particularly if participating in activities such as hiking or scuba-diving. Ensure that your policy covers you for the activities you wish to enjoy. Vaccination against **hepatitis B** is recommended for long stays and for those working with children or in a medical setting. Carriage of the virus in the local population is estimated at 2–10%. The course comprises three doses of vaccine given over a minimum of 21 days for those aged 16 or over. For those under 16 the minimum time to complete three doses is two months. Both these schedules require a booster dose in one year to give longer-lasting protection. Wherever possible, the longer course of 0, 1, and 6 months is preferred for more sustained protection.

Prolonged immobility on long-haul flights can result in deep-vein thrombosis (DVT), which can be dangerous if the clot travels to the lungs to cause pulmonary embolus. The risk increases with age, and is higher in obese or pregnant travellers, heavy smokers, those at the extremes of height, and anybody with a history of clots, recent major operation or varicose veins surgery, cancer, a stroke or heart disease. If any of these criteria apply, consult a doctor before you travel.

TRAVEL CLINICS AND HEALTH INFORMATION A full list of current travel clinic websites worldwide is available on w istm.org. For other journey preparation information, consult w travelhealthpro.org.uk (UK) or w wwwnc.cdc.gov/travel (USA). All advice found online should be used in conjunction with expert advice received prior to or during travel.

INSECT BITES

Mosquitoes and sand flies

Although there's no risk of malaria in Dominica, mosquito bites can still spoil your trip. You should bring insect repellent and ensure you apply it both day and night when you are out and about. Scratching bites can result in open wounds and infections so try to resist. Most hotels in Dominica will have mosquito screens and/or bed nets. Failing this, air conditioning and electric standing or ceiling fans usually work well as a night-time deterrent.

Dengue fever occurs throughout the Caribbean. This virus is transmitted by a day-biting mosquito (Aedes aegypti), which is why it is important to use DEET-based insect repellents during the day. Acceptable alternatives to DEET include icaridin, p-menthane diol or 3-ethlyaminopropionate (IR3535). Use your sunscreen first and the insect repellent second. If you are in forested areas then you would be advised also to wear long-sleeved cotton clothing and trousers for added protection. There are four types of dengue fever for which there is currently no cure. Dengue is rarely fatal if you have not had it before. However, even a primary infection can be unpleasant and causes a fever, with a headache, joint and muscle pains and sometimes a rash. Repeated infections with different strains can lead to a more serious haemorrhagic form of the disease, which can result in death. It is important, therefore, to avoid mosquito bites whenever possible.

Chikungunya is also a virus that is transmitted by the daytime biting Aedes mosquito. Its symptoms are similar to those of dengue – headache, muscle pain, joint swelling or a rash – and there is no vaccine or medicine to prevent chikungunya infection. To protect against chikungunya, follow the advice above.

In March 2016, the first case of **Zika virus disease** was reported in Dominica. Symptoms of Zika virus occur in about 25% of patients. These include itchy red eyes, an itchy rash and sometimes fever and muscle aches; symptoms are mostly short-lived. However, there are implications for women who are pregnant and travelling in risk areas, and for those who are planning pregnancy. Up-to-date guidance can be found at w travelhealthpro.org.uk/news/635/zika-virus-disease-reminder-for-travellers-and-health-professionals. Although the 2016 outbreak subsided, the virus continues to circulate at low levels and could erupt again. Like dengue and chikungunya, Zika is spread by day-biting Aedes mosquitoes so the same precautions taken to prevent those infections apply.

Sand flies are members of the subfamily Phlebotominae and are tiny blood-sucking insects. They are attracted to warm-blooded animals, such as humans, and can sometimes be a nuisance on beaches and in areas of mangrove. As with the mosquito, the small bites of the female can irritate and become inflamed if you rub or scratch them. Insect repellent will help.

Chiggers (*Trombicula alfreddugesi*) Chiggers are known locally as *bête wouj* and are the parasitic larvae of the harvest mite that move to the tips of leaves and grasses. When you brush against them, they migrate to your body and then seek out a protected warm spot (often beneath the waistband of underwear or in other places you would rather they not venture) where they pierce your skin and suck up the tissue. An irritating rash appears which is caused by an allergic reaction to the salivary secretions of the larvae, which drop off the skin once they have had their fill. They leave you with the rash as a memento of their visit, however, which can develop into severe welts if you scratch them a lot or if you're particularly sensitive to having insects partying in your nether regions. Insect repellents containing DEET help to prevent them hopping aboard your body in the first place, as do Vaseline and coconut oil.

Biting ants These little – and occasionally rather large – critters can catch you by surprise. Bites are usually the result of either standing and pausing on a nest or brushing against or holding on to branches or foliage where ants are going about their business. Small ants can be all over you in seconds and their bites are like needles. Take care where you put your feet and hands and, if you have rested clothes or shoes anywhere, give them a good shake before putting them on again.

The larger carpenter worker ants (known locally as *tac-tacs*) bite hard, sometimes breaking the skin and spraying formic acid. This can result in a painful swelling that may last a couple of days.

Ticks In the Caribbean, tick-borne diseases frequently affect pets and livestock, but are rarely reported in humans. This may in part be due to limited surveillance and under-reporting. Hikers are nonetheless advised to take precautions against tick bites by wearing trousers and long sleeves.

TRAVELLERS' DIARRHOEA Around 50% of travellers will get a bout of diarrhoea, which can spoil a good holiday so it is always wise to take basic precautions. Piped tap water in Dominica is generally safe to drink. Those who have concerns about local water quality or who are susceptible to infection may wish to use a re-usable filter bottle (such as aquapure traveller) or bottled water. Avoid food that has been left around or looks like it has been reheated – buffet meals are often the worst culprits. Food should be thoroughly cooked and served piping hot. Remember to wash your hands before eating. If you do get diarrhoea, in most cases it will settle down after 24 hours with rest, drinking plenty of fluids and taking rehydration salts (eg: Electrolade or Dioralyte). Imodium (loperamide) can be helpful to slow down bowel movements, but should not be used in severe diarrhoea with abdominal pain, fever, or blood in the stools. A minority of high-risk travellers may be prescribed 'standby' antibiotics (such as azithromycin) to treat the infection early. If the diarrhoea comes with a fever and/or blood and/or slime then you should seek medical help immediately as it is important to get the correct diagnosis and if necessary the appropriate antibiotics. That said, by taking sensible precautions you can minimise your chances of getting diarrhoea while still being able to eat and enjoy local foods.

PRICKLY HEAT A very itchy red skin rash known as *miliaria*, or prickly heat, is caused by sweating in humid weather conditions. This can be a common problem for visitors who are not used to tropical climates. Dead skin cells and bacteria block sweat glands and the skin becomes inflamed. Air conditioning, cold showers, calamine lotion or, in severe cases, steroid creams can bring relief. Aloe vera may also help. If you find you're suffering from heat rash, try to avoid exerting yourself for a couple of days to reduce sweating and give your skin a chance to recover. Cool shaded rivers and easily accessible waterfall pools are alternative outings, as is a nice shady bar with a fresh juice or a cold beer, of course.

DEHYDRATION, HEAT EXHAUSTION AND HEATSTROKE High temperatures, humidity, exertion and a lack of adequate fluids will inevitably result in dehydration, heat exhaustion and possibly heatstroke. It's incredibly easy to become dehydrated in a tropical climate. Most people don't even realise that their irritability, weariness and dizziness may be due to a lack of water. When out walking take as much water as you can carry. Drink plenty of water before hiking and drink at regular intervals during your outing.

Dominica's rivers are usually clean and the water safe to drink – if they are upstream from urban areas and farms. Rainforest hiking usually means a ready supply of water is on hand and many people drink it with no ill effect. If you're concerned about it, or have a sensitive stomach, then there are many good portable water filters on the market these days and it's worth having one in your backpack.

Heat exhaustion occurs when the body's cooling system hits overdrive. Profuse sweating, pale clammy skin, fast shallow breathing, nausea, headaches, rapid weak pulse and stomach cramps are all signs of heat exhaustion. It's important to counter this quickly by trying to cool the body down. Sit in the shade, take a dip in a river or pool, drink plenty of water and relax.

Heatstroke can be fatal. This occurs when the body's cooling system has collapsed completely. Skin becomes hot and red, breathing slows and confusion and dizziness lead to unconsciousness. Cooling the body down is paramount and immediate medical assistance is essential.

SUN DAMAGE In a very short period the hot Caribbean sun will redden and burn your skin. Try to stay in the shade as much as you can, wear a hat, consider protecting sensitive skin with a sunscreen (at least SPF 30) and wear good-quality sunglasses to protect your eyes. Sun reflecting on the water can be especially damaging if you're exposed to it for too long without adequate protection. If your skin is not used to the sun, limit direct exposure as much as possible. Wearing a T-shirt to protect your back when snorkelling is also a good idea. Sunbathing is not recommended, but if you do, try to limit direct exposure to no more than 20 minutes and stay out of the sun during the hottest part of the day. Sunburn is not only harmful to your skin, it's painful and can spoil your holiday. Wearing light-coloured, loose shirts, skirts and trousers made from cotton or moisture-wicking fabrics is a good option.

SCUBA-DIVING INJURIES Certified scuba-divers should always dive conservatively and within recreational dive limits. Diving Dominica's reefs is not especially challenging, though wall diving means you're exposed to very deep waters. It's therefore important to maintain good buoyancy and check your depth and no-decompression limits.

Decompression sickness can be avoided by diving conservative profiles, ascending slowly and making safety stops at 5m. Signs and symptoms of decompression sickness include tingling or numbness in extremities, aching joints, rashes, headaches, dizziness and nausea. If affected, request 100% pure oxygen and seek medical assistance. Decompression sickness can be fatal and while the most severe symptoms become apparent within the first 2 hours of surfacing, problems can emerge up to 24 hours after diving. Allow dive crew to help and advise you. They are trained in managing dive emergencies.

At the time of writing, there's no functioning hyperbaric chamber in Dominica. This may change, of course, so you may wish to check with your preferred dive operator. In any event, it's a sensible precaution to take out dive insurance to cover the cost of any evacuation and emergency recompression treatments that may be required.

AQUATIC LIFE INJURIES Whether scuba-diving, snorkelling or just having fun in the sea, it's always possible to pick up an injury from aquatic life. Dominica's seas are relatively safe and aquatic life injuries tend to come from contact with sea urchins or small jellyfish. Sea urchins are bottom dwellers, usually found around rocks. They have sharp spines that can pierce the skin of your feet if you stand on them. Typically, the tips of the spines break off and embed themselves under the skin. This can be painful and if not treated may cause an infection. It's prudent to seek medical assistance. A local remedy for the removal of sea urchin spines is to heat up some soft wax (a special soft wax that can be bought at a pharmacy), place the hot wax over the affected area and cover with a bandage. Leave it on overnight and the spines usually disappear.

Contact with small jellyfish can result in a small but painful sting. Rubbing makes it worse. If possible, remove any visible traces of tentacles with tweezers (not with your fingers, as the tentacles still retain their sting) and douse the affected area with white vinegar. Most dive boats and operators will carry a bottle of white vinegar in their first aid kit especially for this type of injury.

You should also avoid contact with fireworms. They look a little like hairy caterpillars and you may see them crawling over rocks or reef formations in both deep and shallow water. Touching them causes the bristles to embed into your skin, resulting in irritation and a rash.

The most environmentally friendly way of scuba-diving and snorkelling is not to touch anything.

SEXUALLY TRANSMITTED DISEASES Unprotected sex is risky in any part of the world and Dominica is no exception. The official incidence of HIV infection is relatively low, however discrimination and the stigma attached to the disease may mean that reported cases do not reflect the true picture. Common sense and caution is the best advice. If you must indulge, use condoms or femidoms, which help reduce the risk of transmission – these are best brought from home to ensure their quality. If you notice any genital ulcers or discharge, get treatment promptly since these increase the risk of acquiring HIV. If you do have unprotected sex, visit a clinic as soon as possible; this should be within 24 hours, or no later than 72 hours, for post-exposure prophylaxis.

USEFUL CONTACTS

Emergencies 911
Dominica–China Friendship Hospital Roseau; 767 266 2000
Marigot Hospital 767 266 2800
Portsmouth Hospital 767 266 5605

SAFETY

Dominica is a relatively safe country for visitors, but you should not take anything for granted. Precautions here are no different from those you would take anywhere else in the world. There are relatively few reported incidents of visitors experiencing crime, particularly violent crime, but it does happen and fear of bad publicity for the island means that such incidents don't always make the news. Travellers should take common-sense precautions such as dressing conservatively, avoiding conflict and not flaunting wealth openly. If approached by people asking for money, either give them a few dollars or politely decline and walk on.

WOMEN TRAVELLERS

Women travelling alone are likely to attract attention from local men, but it's far more likely to be flirtatious rather than anything threatening. Common sense applies, and I'm sure most women travellers know how to handle themselves. If you can, try to avoid going to remote places alone, both by day and by night, try to dress as conservatively as your taste in fashion will allow, and don't bathe topless (it's illegal in any case). Also bear in mind the fact that some of the beaches in the northeast now have security guards because of problems that have occurred in the past. If you do attract unwanted attention from local men, just be as polite and good-humoured as possible in the way you express your wish to be left alone. Avoid conflict, resist becoming angry and don't try to humiliate or belittle anyone. Some recommend wearing dark sunglasses as this helps you avoid eye contact and may also enhance your confidence.

TRAVELLERS WITH A DISABILITY

Dominica is not an easy place for travellers with disabilities to navigate and you'll find Roseau a near impossible challenge. Many pavements are either broken, have vehicles parked on them, or have semi-permanent stalls blocking access. Even without disability, it's a challenging obstacle course. Crossing roads often means negotiating open rain gutters as well as trying to avoid traffic.

Some hotels have better access and facilities than others, but you must contact them before booking rather than assume that all will be well. In terms of sightseeing, most natural attractions other than beaches have steps (this includes the more accessible sites such as Trafalgar Falls and Emerald Pool). Dive operators such as Dive Dominica (and thus Fort Young) and Nature Island Dive are accustomed to taking out divers with disabilities, though you may wish to confirm with them in advance. A whale- and dolphin-watching trip is an option, and some of the hot springs at Wotten Waven (Tia's, for example) have very accessible pools.

TRAVELLING WITH CHILDREN

Dominica is a great place to explore with children – they can enjoy a sense of freedom and adventure in a natural environment that may not be possible at home. Family-friendly walking trails and natural attractions that spring to mind are: Trafalgar Falls, Emerald Pool, Spanny Falls, Syndicate Nature Trail and Syndicate Falls, Fort Shirley garrison and the East Cabrit Trail, Middleham Falls, and Freshwater Lake. Activities could also include whale and dolphin watching, and an Indian River boat ride. Good beaches and easy bathing can be found at Purple Turtle Beach, Mero and Hodges Bay.

LGBTQIA+ TRAVELLERS

Majority views on LGBTQIA+ relationships are in accord with conservative church doctrine, especially among the older generation; among younger people, this is far less so. Like some other Caribbean islands, Dominica has not decriminalised homosexuality – though this seems likely to change in 2023 on human rights grounds. Members of Dominica's LGBTQIA+ community are therefore currently forced to maintain a low profile and are unable to express their sexuality openly and without prejudice. As a visitor, how you choose to deal with this is your choice, of course. But you should be aware that overt displays of your sexuality will certainly draw attention, and responses will be unpredictable in nature.

Minority Rights Dominica (MiRiDom; e miridom@gmail.com) is an equal rights pressure group that's trying to change legislation as well as social attitudes towards Dominica's LGBTQIA+ community. To find out more about the situation in Dominica, or support its activities, please get in touch.

WHAT TO TAKE

In terms of clothing, you must prepare for a hot and humid climate with the possibility of heavy downpours, depending on the time of year you visit. If you're going to be doing some hiking you must bring footwear that can handle river crossings, slippery rocks and mud. I wear cross-trail shoes rather than heavy hiking boots – they're lighter, they dry quickly and they usually have good, flexible soles that work well on wet surfaces. But if you've been wearing the same tried-and-tested footwear for years, stick to what you know and prefer. A hiking pole is handy on difficult ground and for river crossings, as is a waterproof bag for cameras and other valuables. Bring a hat and sunglasses to protect your eyes.

Depending on where you're staying, you may wish to have lightweight trousers to give your legs and ankles some protection from mosquitoes when the sun goes down. If you're staying somewhere elevated during the winter months, then also come prepared for cool evenings.

If you're taking prescription medicine, bring an adequate supply. Dominica's pharmacies are generally well stocked, but you shouldn't depend on them having what you need. Make sure to also take out adequate health insurance that will get you home in the event something serious occurs. Dominica's hospitals shouldn't be on your must-visit list.

Regarding charging phones, laptops and so on, the default supply is 220V with UK-style three-pin socket. It's worth checking with your hotel to see if they have a dual UK and US supply.

MONEY AND BUDGETING

CURRENCY Dominica's currency is the Eastern Caribbean dollar (commonly written EC$ though officially XCD) and it has been fixed to the US dollar at a rate of US$1 = EC$2.7 since 1979. Notes come in denominations of EC$100, EC$50, EC$20, EC$10 and EC$5. Coins come in denominations of EC$1, and then 50, 25, 10 and 5 cents. The Eastern Caribbean dollar is also the official currency of Anguilla, Antigua and Barbuda, Grenada, St Kitts and Nevis, St Lucia, Montserrat and St Vincent. It's issued by the Eastern Caribbean Central Bank which is based in St Kitts and Nevis.

US dollars are widely accepted across the island, and you'll usually be quoted prices in both EC and US dollars. Euros are also accepted – especially by souvenir vendors – though not as commonly as the US dollar. Please be aware that the euro to EC dollar rate is not fixed. It's uncommon for shops and street vendors to accept UK pounds sterling.

There are ATMs in Roseau, Portsmouth, Calibishie and Marigot as well as at Douglas-Charles Airport. Most shops and hotels accept all major **credit cards**, though many don't accept American Express.

BANKS Banking hours are usually 08.00–14.00 Monday–Thursday and 08.00–16.00 Friday, but some banks and branches have a slight variation on this. Expect queues.

National Bank of Dominica 767 255 2300; **e** customersupport@nbd.dm; **w** nbdominica.com. Has 2 branches in Roseau – 1 on Hillsborough St & 1 on Dame Eugenia Charles Bd (Bay Front) – as well as branches in Canefield (Imperial Rd) & Portsmouth (Bay St).

Republic Bank Hillsborough St, Roseau; 767 448 5800; **e** republicbank.dm@rfhl.com; **w** republicbankdominica.com

MONEY TRANSFERS There are **Western Union** and **Moneygram** agents in Roseau, Portsmouth and several village locations around the island.

BUDGETING Dominica, like the rest of the Caribbean, isn't a cheap destination. In fact, I think it's getting ever more expensive. By the time you add up flights, ferries, accommodation, taxis, tour guides, eating out and a bag full of local souvenirs, it can add up to be a pricey holiday. Nevertheless, if you're prepared to forgo a bit of luxury, there are ways to keep costs down once you've made it to the island.

SHOPPING LIST

If it helps, here are some sample prices (in US$) at the time of writing.

1.5 litre bottle of spring water $2.00
Bottle of beer $2.25
0.75 litre bottle of low-quality wine $10
Loaf of bread $1.75
1 litre UHT carton milk $2.25
0.5kg fresh fish $4.50
Tube of toothpaste $4.50
Bar of soap $1.25
Souvenir T-shirt $15
Street snack (bake or fried chicken piece) $1
1 litre petrol $1.30

One important thing to consider is the time of year. It's less expensive to holiday in Dominica in the months of July through September – you just have to roll the dice with tropical storms and hurricanes (but hey, you should try living here). Occasional natural disasters aside, it's actually a nice time to come. There are no cruise ships, nowhere is crowded and most visitors tend to be island neighbours from Guadeloupe and Martinique.

Budget travellers Flights during the low season can cost as little as half those at busier times of year. UK and European travellers should look into flights between Paris and Guadeloupe – they can be cheaper than connections via Barbados (page 42). There are genuine eco lodges and rustic cabins all around the island as well as inexpensive B&Bs (check w airbnb.com and w booking.com). Some can be rather basic; others have a few creature comforts. Sharing facilities also makes accommodation cheaper. Overnight prices can be as low as US$50. A good way to keep food prices down is to eat at snackettes – often, you'll find them cheaper than self-catering and buying food from supermarkets. A local lunch (page 56) is filling and can cost as little as EC$15. Getting around by public bus is the cheapest option, but there are a few downsides: most tend to run at 'rush hour' times in the morning and late afternoon (depending on your route, you can have a long wait at other times of day); they won't take you all the way to natural attractions – you'll have to get off at the closest point and then walk; and they tend to operate at breakneck speeds, overtake into oncoming traffic and around blind corners, so there's a safety factor to consider. You can also try thumbing a ride. Local people do it – often to save money on bus fares because they earn minimum wage – so there's no reason why you shouldn't give it a go.

There are plenty of activities in Dominica that have no access fee though some of them do require a site pass. A weekly site pass is the most economical. Also, there are several trails described in this book that can be easily managed without forking out for a hiking guide – but please don't take any financial shortcuts with the more challenging or offbeat trails.

Average budget The choice of mid-priced accommodation is wide and varied with rates falling somewhere between US$75 and US$175 per night. It's a nice idea to stay in at least two different places if you can. This cuts down travelling time to sites and gives you a little more variety and local colour. It will also work out cheaper with less travel. Car rental rates work out at about US$60–80 per day for a standard 4x4 jeep (discounts for longer periods). It costs in the region of US$50 to fill up with fuel. If you're unable to splash out too much, consider renting a car for half your stay and using public buses or hitchhiking to more accessible places on other days. Private tours can be reasonably priced – ask your hotel for recommendations (often they will have their own local guides). Buy a weekly site pass and try to eat locally. Give yourself an occasional dining treat at one of the fancier restaurants where a main course costs around US$20–40.

'Eco-luxury' Dominica's so-called 'eco-luxury' market is on the rise, and you can spend as much as US$3,000 a night if exclusivity is your thing. For this, you'll get luxurious furnishings, amazing views and lots of other high-class and private 'eco-chic' treats that you had no idea you needed. The high-end hotels and resorts usually have their own guides and tour itineraries.

GETTING AROUND

The best way to get around Dominica is by car, but you may well find the roads and local driving practices more than a little challenging. Depending on your experience of driving on holiday, Dominica's roads can be quite stressful to navigate. Having said that, a bus ride can also be a seat-of-your-pants affair that may leave you with a renewed lust for life by the time you get off. Organised tours and private

CATCHING A BUS

Here are the locations of bus stops in Roseau and Portsmouth, together with routes and a selection of fares.

ROSEAU BUS STOPS

Kennedy Avenue (near the Arawak House of Culture) Buses to Rosalie, Riviere Cyrique, La Plaine, Morne Jaune and Boetica.

King George V Street (opposite Jolly's Pharmacy) Buses to Newtown, Castle Comfort, Loubiere and Pointe Michel.

Old Street (near the Old Market) Buses to Soufriere and Scotts Head.

Old Street (next to Whitchurch supermarket) Buses to Eggleston and Giraudel.

Corner of Castle Street and Cross Street Buses to Stowe, Bagatelle, Fond St Jean and Petite Savanne.

River Bank, along from the New Market (outbound traffic bridge) Buses to Portsmouth and villages along the west coast highway, Castle Bruce, Kalinago Territory, Marigot, Wesley, Calibishie (via Portsmouth) and Vieille Case (via Portsmouth).

River Bank, between Independence Street and Great George Street (inbound traffic bridge) Buses to Goodwill, Canefield, St Aroment, Massacre, Mahaut and St Joseph.

Cross Street Buses to Morne Bruce and Kings Hill.

Hanover Street (Old Market end) Buses to Bellevue Chopin, Pichelin, Grand Bay and Tête Morne.

Hanover Street (New Market end) Buses that go all the way to Delices and Boetica.

King George V Street (near Astaphans) **and Valley Road** (just over the junction with King George V St – look for 'Keep Clear' markings on the road) Buses to Trafalgar, Wotten Waven, Shawford, Morne Prosper and Laudat.

taxis usually go at a more sedate pace, though they will be a more expensive option unless there are several of you to share the cost.

BUSES Roseau, Portsmouth and – to a lesser extent – Marigot are the main hubs for public bus transport. There is, however, no central terminus in Roseau and there are no numbered bus routes around the island. Local people are accustomed to knowing where all the different bus stops are in the capital, but as a visitor you may find it somewhat confusing. Buses to different parts of the island depart from bus stops located on different streets and at no fixed times. They tend to leave when the driver is satisfied that they have enough passengers (buses can be crammed full before they leave), or when they have finished eating their lunch, chatting with their friends, done their shopping and so on. On some routes, such as the west coast highway between Portsmouth and Roseau, and the Imperial Road between the capital and Marigot, buses usually run frequently. On other routes, buses tend to run mostly at 'rush hour' times in the morning and late afternoon. This can mean long waits.

Dominica's buses are small minivans and can be identified by the letters 'H', 'HA' or 'HB' on the licence plate. Many bus drivers also decorate the windscreen of their vehicles with a name or a slogan so that they become recognisable along the routes they drive. This doesn't help visitors, of course. In addition to designated bus stops, simply flagging down a bus along the roadside is common practice.

Note that most buses stop running in the evening and there are reduced numbers on Sundays.

PORTSMOUTH BUS STOPS

By the mini roundabout on the southern end of Bay Street Buses to Roseau and villages along the west coast.

Along the south side of Benjamin's Park (right at the mini roundabout above) Buses to Calibishie, Vieille Case, Wesley and Marigot.

Bay Street (near the market) Buses to Pennville, Toucari, Cottage, Clifton and Capuchin.

BUS FARES Bus fares are inexpensive – between EC$2 and EC$12.50 on individual routes. Prices are fixed and regulated by the government. The only time you would ever negotiate a fare is if you're commissioning a private taxi service (some drivers may offer you a private outing if things are slow, but they must have a permit to do this). Here's an example of some public bus fares:

Roseau to Portsmouth: EC$10
Roseau to the Kalinago Territory: EC$12.50
Roseau to Laudat: EC$4.50
Roseau to Trafalgar: EC$4
Roseau to Scotts Head: EC$4.50
Roseau to La Plaine: EC$11.50
Roseau to Marigot: EC$12.50
Portsmouth to Capuchin: EC$4
Portsmouth to Calibishie: EC$5
Portsmouth to Marigot: EC$8

Ask the driver to let you know when you get to your destination and pay either when you get on or off. Try to have coins or small note denominations. To stop the bus, call out 'Stopping!'.

TAXIS Dominica's taxi drivers are licensed by the government and should always display their official credentials. There are no standard rates for private taxi hire, so it's down to the individual driver and a little negotiation on your part. Most taxi drivers offer island tours, but they must have additional credentials as tour guides to show you around sites or take you hiking. Some taxi drivers have this dual licensing, and others work in partnership with tour guides.

CAR HIRE There are lots of car rental companies in Dominica, some of which are tiny operations with just a handful of vehicles, while others are much bigger with larger and varied fleets. The most common rental cars are 4x4 jeeps. Prices vary but you should expect to pay about US$60–80 per day depending on the vehicle, with discounted rates usually offered for longer rental periods. Collision damage waiver is normally an additional cost. Some rental companies offer free drop-off and pick-up at airports and hotels.

The government requires that you buy a visitor's temporary driving licence. This costs US$12 for a one-month licence (this is the minimum) and is usually obtained from the car hire company itself. Visitor licences can also be purchased in Roseau from the Inland Revenue building, which is located on the street to the side of the House of Assembly. To rent a car and purchase a visitor licence, you must be able to present either your domestic or international driving licence, so make sure you bring it.

It's worth contacting car hire companies for quotes and bookings prior to arrival, especially at busy periods such as Carnival and Creole. Also check to see if it's possible to collect the car and drop it off at the airport (some companies have an office at Douglas-Charles Airport). By no means comprehensive, here's a selection of local rental agencies.

Courtesy Car Rental 767 448 7763; e courtesyrental@cwdom.dm; w dominicacarrentals.com
Happy Car Rentals 767 276 4659; e happycarrentals@gmail.com; w happycardominica.com
Island Car Rentals 767 255 6844; e reservations@islandcar.dm; w islandcar.dm
QB Vehicle Rentals 767 265 3654; e bookings@qbvehicles.com; w qbvehicles.com
Valley Car Rental 767 275 1310; e valley@cwdom.dm; w valleyrentacar.com
Yadah Car Rental 767 225 6923; e yadahcarrental@gmail.com; w yadahcarrentals.com

Check the car over carefully prior to signing any documentation and paying. Look for scratches and bumps, test lights and brakes, and examine tyre tread. Make sure any bodywork defects are properly recorded on the rental agreement and take photos or a video with your phone. If the vehicle has poor tyre tread, request a replacement. If the car handles poorly when you first take it out, return it and request a replacement straight away. Do not settle. Dominica has some unforgiving, tricky and remote roads. If you have a breakdown, don't try to fix the car (or let anyone else try). The onus is on the rental company to meet you and provide you with a replacement vehicle. Call them, explain the situation and your location. If you have to leave the car, ensure it is parked safely and locked up. Take photos of it.

It will cost around EC$100–150 to fill up your car. There are filling stations all around the island, but it's always prudent to ensure that you have a full tank before setting off. One thing you should note is that not all filling stations accept debit or credit card payment, so don't depend on it. Carry cash (US dollars are accepted) and ask about card payment before you fill up.

DRIVING IN DOMINICA Driving in Dominica can be quite a stressful experience for visitors. It is, however, the most convenient way of getting around, especially if your stay is a short one and you want to see and do as much as possible.

Driving is on the left, though it may not seem like it sometimes. Local driving can be somewhat unpredictable, and safety and etiquette are not always evident. Expect high-speed driving, overtaking into oncoming traffic and on blind corners, stopping or pulling out without warning and (my particular favourite) indicating in one direction and turning in another. Some roads are narrow with hairpin corners and steep precipices. In urban areas especially, there can be hard-to-see drainage gutters on the passenger side. This can be tricky when driving in the dark or against oncoming traffic. Drive slowly. Don't feel pressured into driving at a speed that makes you uncomfortable. If there's a vehicle on your rear bumper, let it pass – pull over if necessary. Whenever you approach a blind corner, hit your horn several times to let anyone coming the other way know you're there. Don't be shy about this. The louder the better. And blow your horn if you suspect someone is going to pull out in front of you. You'll find bus drivers to be some of the faster and more aggressive road users – especially during 'rush hour' periods when they're trying to maximise their revenue. Keep a watchful eye out for this. In Roseau, keep a watchful eye out for young guys weaving in and out of traffic on motor scooters – they may well be overtaking you on the inside. Also, look out for pot-holes. Most of the main roads have good surfaces but heavy rains quickly erode poorly laid tarmac and wash away makeshift repairs.

HITCHING Hitching or *riding* is common in Dominica. It's often possible to wave down a pick-up truck and jump on the back for a free ride. Conversely, when driving, expect to see people asking for a ride along the main highways or on the outskirts of villages. Hitching a ride is quite an effective way to get around, though it may involve long waits, sometimes in heavy downpours. It's also a nice way to meet Dominicans and experience a side to the island that's not possible in other circumstances. If you do sit in the back of a pick-up truck, be careful where you sit and ensure you have something to hold on to.

If you're visiting the Syndicate area, or you're on remote farm access roads, bear in mind that fieldhands may wish to get a ride down to the main road. It's nice to help them out.

ACCOMMODATION

There's a complete range of accommodation options in Dominica that will suit all tastes and budgets. At the top end, there are so-called 'eco-luxury' hotels and resorts – upmarket boutique accommodation that suits those looking for exclusivity, comfort and ease. Mid-range accommodation is plentiful, mostly in the form of small hotels, lodges and self-catering cottages and villas. For budget travellers there are B&Bs, private rooms, rustic cabins and some limited camping. Volunteering or working holidays are not as common as they were after Hurricane Maria in 2017, but they do still exist.

CHARGES AND RATINGS Hotel accommodation charges are subject to a 10% government tax (VAT). Some hotels will also add an additional 10–15% service charge. Check quoted rates prior to booking to avoid unpleasant surprises.

Note The accommodation listed in this guide is deliberately selective and by no means comprehensive. There's far more online, especially via booking sites such

ACCOMMODATION PRICE CODES

Codes are used to accompany accommodation listings in this guide. They are meant to give a basic indication of price based on a double room per night in the high season. Please check websites or call ahead of booking to confirm exact rates. Most hotels on Dominica quote their prices in US$ rather than EC$.

$$$$$	US$350+
$$$$	US$250–350
$$$	US$150–250
$$	US$100–150
$	<US$100

as **w** airbnb.com and **w** booking.com, where many hotels and villas may also offer discounted rates. I recommend spending some time browsing all the options – especially by location and cost. Price codes used in this guide are current at the time of writing and are based on double occupancy per room per night during the peak season, or roughly the equivalent for self-catering accommodation with weekly rates, unless stated otherwise. Please be aware that price codes are meant as guides only and are subject to change.

CAMPING Opportunities to camp are limited in Dominica. It's illegal to camp on beaches or in any other public places, but it's fine to camp on private land so long as you have the owner's permission. Camping out on the Wai'tukubuli National Trail is accepted if you're through-hiking and have a trail pass, but you must minimise your impact on the environment. You can find organised camping at 3 Rivers (page 153), D-Smart Farm (page 215) and Rodney's Wellness Retreat (page 133).

EATING AND DRINKING

When Amerindians arrived at the island they called Wai'tukubuli, it was probably a combination of seafood and cassava that formed the basis of their diet. As agricultural practices developed on the island, root crops such as yams, sweet potatoes and tannias were cultivated for food. Among other things, European settlers introduced crops such as bananas, breadfruit, mangoes, plantain, coffee and sugar. Enslaved Africans working Dominica's coffee and sugar plantations would have grown and eaten root crops, or *provisions* (from 'provision grounds' – designated areas the enslaved were allocated to grow food to eat and sell), which they spiced up with seasonings such as peppers, bay leaves, parsley, celery and thyme, adopting some of the influences of the French and mixing them with their own heritage. Following the abolition of slavery, these Caribbean Creole culinary practices continued to develop, particularly with the arrival of liberated people from the French islands, and remain the foundation for the traditional dishes served in many of Dominica's homes, snackettes and Creole restaurants today.

LUNCH There's no grabbing a quick sandwich to eat at your desk while you work here. Dominicans have always taken lunch seriously – it's the main meal of the day for most people and is traditionally one that's designed to fill you up. Lunch consists of meat or fish that's accompanied by an assortment of *ground provisions*, rice, *fig* (boiled green banana), plantain, beans, salad and sometimes a thick wedge of macaroni cheese. A local eatery will therefore advertise 'pork lunch' (usually stewed pork), 'chicken lunch' (usually stewed or fried chicken) or 'fish lunch' (usually tuna or mahi-mahi – also known locally as dolphin – steak, though occasionally reef fish). These days, some restaurants serve contemporary variations of lunch, but a local snackette will pile it up on a plate and only charge you in the region of EC$15–20.

LOCAL DISHES There are many traditional dishes for you to try and, if you've travelled to other Caribbean islands, it's interesting to see local variations of similar themes. Perhaps one of the oldest and most basic is the one-pot dish, or *braf*. One-pot cooking simply means placing all the ingredients you have, whatever they may be, in one large pot, cooking them up in water and seasoning to create a nutritious broth. This dish tends to be eaten in homes rather than in restaurants, though some local eateries do serve it, especially on Friday nights (fish *braf*) and Saturday mornings (pig's and cow's foot *braf*). Braf is also a traditional picnic dish, and you may come across local people having a weekend cook-up on a beach or riverbank.

Most local dishes are rich in *provisions*, vegetables and seasonings. You may find meat and fish dishes a little overcooked for your liking. This is a legacy of the past, and a lack of proper refrigeration. Dominicans – especially the older generation – have become accustomed to eating meat dishes in this way. Larger restaurants are more likely to prepare meat and seafood in a more 'international' manner and may ask you how you would like your meat cooked, though this is not a given. **Hot pepper sauce**, made from scotch bonnet peppers, is often used to spice up dishes. Be careful with it: just a few drops can transform a dish, and maybe not in the way you want!

Callaloo* soup** is a traditional dish made from young *dasheen* leaves (a *ground provision*), and occasionally spinach. It's a thick green soup that's often served with dumplings and (during the Creole season) a species of land crab. Other popular soup dishes are pumpkin soup, **goat water**, which is a goat meat stew, and ***chatou* water**, a soup made with octopus. ***Sancoche is a traditional dish made from coconut milk, *provisions* and usually codfish. ***Ackra*** is a kind of seasoned and fried fritter, often made from codfish, breadfruit, tannia and, from September to November, in the days after the moon's last quarter, ***titiwi***, which is a juvenile goby caught in fine nets at the mouths of rivers. ***Crab back*** is a delicious savoury dish that's only available during the Creole season. The land crab's flesh is mixed with a secret combination of spices and seasonings and then stuffed back into the shell, sprinkled with breadcrumbs and baked in a hot oven. Every crab back tastes slightly different,

PROVISIONS

When eating out or shopping for food, you'll come across *provisions*, also known as *ground provisions*. This term refers to any one of a collection of root crops such as varieties of yam, eddoe, dasheen, sweet potato or tannia. The term is occasionally stretched to include breadfruit, plantain and green bananas (rather confusingly known as *figs*) though purists will contest this inclusion. *Provisions* are usually boiled and served with a main meat dish. They also appear prominently in traditional soups or one-pot *brafs* (broths). *Provisions* are very filling and are high in carbohydrates. Historically grown and eaten by enslaved labourers on plantations and estates, they remain a staple food across the Caribbean, especially for those whose work involves a lot of physical activity.

RESTAURANT PRICE CODES

The following codes are used in this guide to indicate the average price for a main course in a restaurant or local eatery. Typically, the most expensive thing you can eat in a restaurant is lobster, which may run to EC$100 or so. One of the cheapest dishes is probably *roti*, which costs around EC$10–15. Excluded are prices for roadside snacks such as barbecue chicken, plantain, bakes and so on, which cost less than EC$10.

$$$ EC$80+
$$ EC$50–80
$ EC$15–50

Please remember that some menu prices, especially in hotel restaurants, may exclude local tax (VAT of 15%) and service charge (usually 10%). This can make quite a difference to your bill, so do check.

and cooks often keep their recipe a closely guarded secret. **Curried goat** is a popular spicy meat dish (and yes, it is goat), usually served with rice. Less often seen these days – and only during the hunting season (usually October–December) – **stewed agouti** is another traditional dish. A common staple is a heavily seasoned rice dish called ***pelau***, usually a lunch dish served as chicken *pelau*.

Vegetarians should have few problems finding good food in Dominica. With a preponderance of fresh fruit and vegetables, the choice is varied. *Tannia ackra*, rice and peas, fried plantain, breadfruit puffs, *provisions*, vegetable *sancoche* and macaroni cheese are all staple foods and common dishes. What you may find, however, is that there are no specific vegetarian dishes mentioned on a menu – so you may have to work with the restaurant on concocting one (eg: a stewed pork lunch without the stewed pork, and so on). Vegan food is rather more specialised, and you'll probably need to seek out Ital eateries. Ital is a term commonly used by Rastafarians to mean wholesome, natural food. It's always vegetarian and often vegan.

If you happen to hear the distinctive sound of a **conch shell** being blown, then it means a fisherman is selling his catch. The fish caught locally and used in Dominican cooking will typically include tuna, marlin, jacks, snapper and dorado (mahi-mahi, also known locally as *dowad* or *dolphin*).

Popular roadside snacks include ***bakes***, a fried flour-and-water dough that's usually stuffed with seasoned saltfish, tuna or cheese. You'll also see people selling fried or barbecue chicken, corn and plantain. Unfortunately, Dominica doesn't have a great variety of street food, which is a real shame as the ingredients are there. It's mostly just barbecue or worse – hot dog sausage on a stick.

A filling snack is ***roti***, a flatbread most commonly stuffed with either curried vegetables or chicken. It's of Trinidadian origin and is an inexpensive dish that's filling and great if you're on a tight budget. Less common, but try it if you see it, is doubles – another Trinidadian dish that's made of a light bread stuffed with curried chickpeas. It's messy but fabulous.

LOCAL DRINKS

Non-alcoholic Although sugary fizzy drinks dominate, freshly made juices are usually available, the selection being determined by what's in season. Lime squash and freshly made ginger beer are particularly refreshing drinks on hot days.

Passionfruit, pineapple, orange and grapefruit juices are also commonly served. Less familiar fruit drinks may include cherry juice, barbadine punch, soursop and carambola. All of them are worth trying if available. ***Sorrel***, known in some parts of the Caribbean as hibiscus tea, is a delicious drink, usually available around the festive season. It's made from the sepals of the sorrel flower (*Hibiscus sabdariffa*) and is fruity and fragrant. It's also served as a warm, spiced tea or as a wine, and tastes rather like a European Christmas mulled wine. **Coconut water** extracted from unripe *jelly* coconuts is an acquired taste, though it's very refreshing, especially directly from a coconut. Always drink coconut water and/or fresh fruit juice in moderation. Too much may have the effect of a laxative.

When thirsty, drink water. Tap water is clean and safe to drink. Bottled spring water is available but, given Dominica has no means of recycling plastic, you may prefer to bring a re-usable flask and stick to tap water.

Arabica coffee is cultivated on a small scale in the heights of Dominica's interior (mostly in the Syndicate area) and you may find artisanal versions of it in the shops. There are also several blends of **cocoa tea** available, which are made from locally grown cocoa and mixed with a variety of spices to make a delicious hot beverage. You should also try local **bush tea**. These teas are made from an assortment of herbs and are believed to have medicinal properties for many conditions from colds, headaches and fevers to stomach aches and even insomnia.

Alcoholic drinks Dominica has two main rum producers. The Belfast Estate produces blends called Soca rum, Red Cap rum and Bois Bandé rum, and the Shillingford Estate produces dark and light Macoucheri rum. Dominicans will further decant rums from these distilleries into bottles as a basis for their own individual blends of **rum punch** and **bush rum**, the latter usually being white cask rum with an infusion of herbs, spices or tree bark. Some simply make their own from molasses in backyard sheds. One of the island's most famous blends of bush rum is ***bois bandé***, which is said to have a tumescent effect upon male drinkers. Locals – especially tour guides – will often refer to it as a 'natural Viagra'. Stripping pieces of the bois bandé tree's much sought-after bark is common practice, though illegal in the national parks where it's mostly found. Other popular bush rum blends are *spice,* which has cinnamon added, *pueve* with pepper, *nannie* with rosemary and *l'absent* with aniseed. Bush rums are usually sold in village rum shops and bars, though you may also find them in more upmarket bars and restaurants. Try Islet View Restaurant near Castle Bruce (page 154) for just about the widest selection of bush rums on the island.

Rum punch is usually a little smoother than bush rum blends. Popular varieties are those made from lime and from passionfruit. Take care when drinking rum punches as their mild flavour masks what is often a high alcohol content.

SEA MOSS

Sea moss is the name given to a red algal genus called *Gracilaria*, which is cultivated in many parts of the world for its *agar*, a gelatinous polymer that's used as a preservative jelly, a culture medium, a laxative, a clarifying agent in brewing, a thickening agent in baking and cooking, and in the Caribbean as the basis for a thickened milk drink or dessert. In Dominica, sea moss comes in several flavours. The drink is said to be vitamin-rich and a useful tonic for a variety of medical conditions.

FRUITS AND VEGETABLES

Some of the less familiar fresh fruits and vegetables you may come across in Dominica are:

Ackee Related to the lychee, toxic when immature or overripe, commonly grown and eaten in Jamaica, usually fried with salt fish.
Barbadine Large fruit grown on a vine, eaten as a fruit or cooked and served as a vegetable when unripe. Sometimes combined with lemon and sugar as a juice.
Breadfruit Large round fruit with white flesh that's sometimes fried in butter or served in a salad – or with codfish at Creole time.
Canep Small round fruit with thin green skin and soft, tart flesh. Often sold in bunches by the roadside.
Carambola Also called star fruit, eaten as a fruit or blended as a juice.
Christophene A pear-like green-skinned squash, usually eaten boiled or fried as a vegetable.
Custard apple Heart-shaped fruit with sweet, custard-like flesh. Usually eaten as a dessert.
Dasheen A small, starchy tuber, usually eaten like a potato.
Green banana Confusingly referred to as *figs*, actually unripe bananas, usually boiled and eaten as a *provision*.
Guava Original Arawakan name for this scented fruit, which is eaten raw, turned into jam or blended as a juice.
Mangosteen A reddish-purple fruit when ripe with sweet and creamy white flesh.
Noni Fruit with a pungent odour when ripe (hence the name *vomit fruit* in some countries). Considered medicinal, it's either eaten as a fruit or blended as a drink.

For many years Dominica's national beer has been **Kubuli,** which used to be brewed using natural spring water by the Dominica Brewery at Snug Corner near the southern village of Loubiere. The brewery was destroyed by a storm, however, and Kubuli is now brewed in St Vincent rather than in Dominica, making its claim as the national beer somewhat flimsy these days.

PUBLIC HOLIDAYS AND EVENTS

JANUARY New Year's Day (1 Jan) is a public holiday. Calypso tents (knockout heats) take place at various venues during January in the build-up to the Calypso Monarch Final that's held at Carnival time in February/March.

FEBRUARY/MARCH Dominica's Carnival (also known as *Mas Domnik* and *Real Mas*) takes place on the Monday and Tuesday before Ash Wednesday. These two days are also public holidays. The Carnival season runs throughout the month and includes: the Carnival Queen Show, the Calypso Monarch competition, Pan by the Bay (steel pan drumming on Roseau's Bay Front), costume parades, T-shirt band parades, street jams and 'jump-ups', and traditional *la peau cabwit* drumming. There are also numerous fringe party events in the run-up to Carnival.

Tewé Vaval is the symbolic burial, or sacrificial burning, of the spirit of Carnival that takes place on Ash Wednesday. Formerly a fairly sombre ceremony at which

Okra Long, crisp green pods, often used as a flavouring for stews and soups. Also eaten parboiled and fried.
Passionfruit Round yellow fruit with soft, sweet pulp. Usually blended for juice.
Pawpaw Also called papaya, with an elongated shape, yellow when ripe and eaten as a fruit. Green, unripe pawpaw is often used in salads or pickles.
Plantain A type of banana that is either fried or boiled and eaten as a *provision*. Also seen as fried plantain chips, a popular snack.
Pommerac Large fruit with bright red skin, often used to make jam.
Sapodilla Round fruit with reddish brown skin. Fleshy pulp is often used to make custard or ice cream.
Sorrel Member of the hibiscus family, a plant with edible flowers, fruits and leaves. Usually brewed as a tea or blended for juice. Also used as a natural medication and traditionally consumed at Christmas.
Soursop Large green ovoid fruit with soft spines. Tart white flesh is sweetened to make a delicious juice or ice cream.
Sugar apple Similar to a custard apple but with sweet white flesh. Usually eaten as a dessert.
Sweet potato Not a yam, and not a potato. Actually belonging to the bindweed family, this elongated vegetable has a sweet flavour. It's often boiled, roasted or mashed.
Tamarind Segmented pod with a reddish-brown shell. The inner pulp is mixed with sugar to make tamarind balls, a popular confectionery.
Tannia A small, starchy tuber, usually eaten like a potato.
Taro Also called eddoe, a small potato-like tuber. Usually eaten like a potato.
Yam Large tuber that is boiled, fried or roasted as a staple *provision*.

people dressed in funeral attire and carried a coffin with an effigy of Carnival to a funeral pyre, this traditional event, like several others in Dominica, has morphed into a fete or 'jump-up' and an excuse to extend the partying by an extra day. Visitors can experience Tewé Vaval at Bataca in the Kalinago Territory and in the west coast village of Dublanc. I'd advise against combining alcohol with jumping over the fires as some do – your travel insurance may not cover it.

APRIL Good Friday and Easter Monday are public holidays.

MAY Labour Day on 1 May is a public holiday. The **Dominica Festival of Arts** (**DOMFESTA**) takes place throughout the month of May. DOMFESTA is designed to promote and celebrate the arts in Dominica. Look out for a schedule of events and entertainment – most likely on Facebook, but call in at the Old Mill in Canefield if you're on the island. The biggest splash either at the end of April or beginning of May is the annual Jazz 'n Creole festival that takes place at the Fort Shirley garrison in Cabrits National Park. There are numerous fringe parties and events in the build-up to the main event. May is usually the month for Dominica's **Hike Fest** at which a series of hikes are organised by the Dominica Hotel and Tourism Association. The Giraudel and Eggleston village **flower show** also usually takes place in May.

JUNE Whit Monday is a public holiday.

JULY Dominica's annual **Dive Fest** takes place over one week in July. This event is organised by the Dominica Watersports Association and includes introductory pool and ocean scuba-diving experiences, children's events, Kalinago canoe racing, evening cruises and parties. The aim of Dive Fest is to promote diving and watersports in Dominica, especially to local people. It's also another excuse to party and the best attended event is usually the final day at Soufriere.

AUGUST Dominica celebrates Emancipation Day in August, which is also a public holiday. It's often accompanied by the annual Emancipation Hike.

SEPTEMBER Look out for Kalinago cultural celebrations taking place during September.

OCTOBER October is the month for Creole and Independence celebrations. Look out for published events such as traditional dancing, music and singing. It's also a great time to eat traditional Creole food; be sure to try the *crab back* (page 57).

Creole Week takes place during the last week of October and includes several events culminating in the three-night **World Creole Music Festival**, which is held at Windsor Park Sports Stadium in Roseau.

NOVEMBER 3 November is **Independence Day**, and the following day is the **National Day of Community Service**, both of which are public holidays.

DECEMBER Christmas Day and Boxing Day, 25 and 26 December, are public holidays.

SHOPPING

Shopping for food, drink and toiletry items is rarely a problem in Dominica though prices may take you by surprise. Imported food items and hygiene products are expensive. In Roseau the larger supermarkets are usually well stocked, and throughout the island there are numerous small shops, minimarts and the ubiquitous 'variety stores' that sell basic items. The major shops and pharmacies carry a good stock of baby foods, nappies and cleaning and sanitary products. If you're visiting from the US, you'll recognise many of the brands.

Markets and roadside vendors sell fresh locally grown fruit and vegetables. The best time to go to the Roseau New Market is on Friday afternoon and evening or early Saturday morning, though it's set up all week. One downside is that most stalls sell pretty much the same thing and at the same prices – it's an odd market in that respect, and there's not much variety beyond the same staples. You'll also discover that a great number of the vendors are Haitian women, just as many farm labourers are Haitian men. Dominica welcomes economic migrants from Haiti, where there's a humanitarian crisis, and many of them work for minimum wage as farm labourers or market hucksters. (You'll often see lines of Haitians at Western Union and Moneygram offices, sending money to their families back home.)

Most villages will have some form of Saturday market, though they are much smaller affairs than the Roseau market. There's a good Saturday morning market in Portsmouth. If you pass through interior farming villages such as Bells, for example, look out for people selling fresh produce along the roadside. If you see people selling jelly coconuts, do stop and treat yourself to a refreshing drink.

You can buy fresh fish from the fish markets at Roseau, Marigot and Portsmouth, from fishing villages such as Fond St Jean, Saint Sauveur and Scotts Head (to name just a few), and from wherever you hear the distinctive sound of a conch shell being blown. It's mostly tuna, mahi-mahi or jacks. Snapper and lobster never seem to make it to the fish markets – they go straight to the restaurants, sold via mobile phones by fishermen before they even reach the shore.

Most shops open from around 08.30 and close between 16.00 and 17.30. Some stay open longer. The majority close from around 14.00 on Saturdays and are, with a few exceptions, closed all day on Sundays.

If you're looking for shopping malls and designer boutiques, you're going to be disappointed. Dominica has a smattering of duty-free shops around the Roseau Bay Front, but that's about it. Except for a few Kalinago baskets, the souvenir stalls tend to sell mass-produced imported items rather than anything local or unique to Dominica. They're fine for T-shirts, though. Seek out Zeb Kweyol in the covered section of Roseau's Old Market for exclusively local products.

ARTS AND ENTERTAINMENT

CONTEMPORARY MUSIC Dominica's music scene is dominated by bouyon artists, but you'll also hear cadence, zouk, soca, calypso and reggae. Live concerts take place at various locations throughout the year. The main live music event is the **World Creole Music Festival** that takes place during the last week of October each year. This three-night event falls within Creole Week, which is part of Dominica's Independence celebrations. Although the week is a celebration of Creole culture and tradition, the music festival does not appear to limit itself to a particular genre and there are usually reggae and dancehall performers.

Fort Shirley is the venue for the annual Jazz 'n Creole music event that's usually held in May. Jazz afficionados should be aware that the word is used very loosely indeed, and the event has morphed into more of a chic social gathering for lovers of fashion and Instagram rather than for lovers of jazz (I saw a promo poster for a Jazz 'n Creole warm-up event that said, 'dress jazzy', so you get the idea). Nevertheless, there have been some notable artists from home and abroad in the past and so it's always worth checking the event information (the Discover Dominica Authority or Dominica Festivals Facebook pages are usually best for this).

PERFORMING ARTS The **Dominica Festival of Arts (DOMFESTA)** takes place each May. The festival is designed to promote and celebrate the arts in Dominica and is usually a good time to catch a cultural event. If you're here during this period, call in at the Old Mill Cultural Centre in Canefield (page 95) to find out what's happening.

Theatre performances are rare these days, though they occasionally take place at the Arawak House of Culture in Roseau. There's also a live poetry and music event called Lyrics Under the Stars that's worth looking out for. Again, check with the Cultural Division at the Old Mill.

The **Alliance Française** also hosts occasional art, film and book events and it's worth calling in to find out if there's anything interesting going on during your stay. It is located outside the eastern boundary of the Botanic Gardens, just next to the Bath Estate bridge on the Roseau Valley road (see map, page 91).

OPENING TIMES

Business hours vary, although most will open their doors at 08.00–08.30. In the morning, expect traffic to be heavy entering the capital from 07.30 onwards. Most

ISLAND TIME

You may have heard the phrase 'island time' – well, it's a real concept. Many things generally happen when they're good and ready regardless of what the hour and minute hand may say. Snackettes and bars usually have no fixed opening hours, or breakfast, lunch or dinner times. Food is just ready when it's ready. Or it's not ready at all. Maybe the owner has had to close for a few hours and go to town to pay bills, or perhaps it's just a late start or inclement weather.

The food and drink listings in this guide will have opening days and times where they're generally applied. In some cases, I'll describe a looser breakfast (08.00–10.00), lunch (noon–15.00), or dinner (18.00–21.00) opening period rather than specific times. And when it comes to bars, rum shops and snackettes, I won't usually include times at all. Simply assume all day into the evening unless stated otherwise.

Island time (you may hear people refer to 'Dominica time') is present in many aspects of life. Some doctors and dentists, for example, give all their patients the same 08.00 appointment time, and you'll hardly ever see a starting time advertised for events such as concerts – even World Creole Music Festival. If you're waiting for a bus to leave Roseau or Portsmouth, asking when it will depart may result in replies such as 'soon', 'in a while' or (my favourite) 'just now' – but you'll rarely be given an actual time. And if you are, don't take it too seriously. The bus will leave when the driver is ready, when they've finished chatting with friends, when it's crammed full with passengers or when shopping bags have been loaded for someone elderly or infirm in a village on the bus route.

If you're used to fixed times and a fast lifestyle, island time may be a challenge to you. When you've lived here for 20 years, however, you tend to leave your watch at home.

businesses will end their working day between 16.00 and 17.30 so it is also busy on the roads at that time. A five-day week is standard though more and more businesses also open on Saturday mornings. Government offices are open Monday–Friday.

See also *Island Time* above.

MEDIA AND COMMUNICATIONS

MEDIA Dominica has two national newspapers, ***The Chronicle*** and ***The Sun***, each published once a week in English. Both have political bias. TV shows, including films and sports, are purchased and broadcast by Digicel and Flow. Local TV programming is almost non-existent. The main radio stations broadcasting in Dominica are **DBS Radio** (88.1FM), **Q95FM** (95FM), **Vibes Radio** (99.5FM) and **Kairi FM** (107.9FM, 93.1FM and 88.7FM). It's radio and social media that most Dominicans turn to for news and events. Radio stations also tend to have a political bias. Online, there's w dominicanewsonline.com and w emonewsdm.com.

If you're interested in what social media has to offer, then you could check the Facebook pages for Discover Dominica and Dominica Festivals – though do be prepared for rather a lot of hyperbole.

POSTAL SERVICE The main branch of Dominica's post office (🕘 08.00–16.00 Mon–Fri) is located on Bay Front/Dame Eugenia Charles Boulevard opposite the

Roseau ferry terminal. Postal delivery times between Dominica and the US and Europe fluctuate wildly and it's become an unreliable means of communication. Courier companies include Fedex and DHL, both of whom have offices in downtown Roseau.

If you actually do receive packages from abroad you must collect them from the parcels office on the ground floor of the main post office and open them in the presence of a customs official, who will determine the level of duty that you must pay. Proof of identification is required when collecting packages, along with a bagful of patience. The parcels office closes for lunch between 13.00 and 14.00.

TELEPHONE The international dialling code for Dominica is +1 767 followed by a number consisting of seven digits.

Mobile phones Mobile-phone operators with outlets in Dominica include Flow and Digicel. If you don't have your own mobile phone or other handheld device with roaming services, it's possible to purchase a prepaid phone from one of these suppliers. All you need is identification. If you're planning on hiking or renting a car, you should carry a phone with you, just in case. Add your hotel and car rental company to contacts.

INTERNET Dominica has good high-speed internet services, and most hotels and restaurants offer free Wi-Fi connections to their guests and patrons. There's also free Wi-Fi at Douglas-Charles Airport.

COURIERS Private international courier services offer a quick, reliable alternative to Dominica's unreliable postal system.

DHL Agents: HHV Whitchurch Travel Agency Ltd, cnr Hanover St & Kennedy Av, Roseau; ☎767 255 1140

Fedex Agents: Express Courier, cnr Cork St & Old St, Roseau; ☎767 448 0992

CULTURAL ETIQUETTE

DRESS When walking around Roseau, or any other town or village for that matter, please wear a top. You'll certainly cause offence if you are under-dressed in public and places of business. Women should also bear in mind that sunbathing topless is illegal in Dominica. If you're a churchgoer, dress conservatively for services.

DRUGS AND ALCOHOL Confine your consumption to bars and don't walk around the streets drinking alcohol – unless it is Carnival, of course! The possession of 28 grams or 1 ounce of cannabis has been decriminalised. The aroma of marijuana is therefore common – especially at events and festivals. Further legislation regarding cannabis is expected. Be aware that drugs such as cocaine are illegal.

PEOPLE EXPERIENCING HOMELESSNESS At some point during your trip you're likely to be asked by someone living rough for money – especially in Roseau. Dominica has no safety net for people who have either fallen on tough times or who are addicts. 'Gimme a dollar' is something you may hear, though it's never threatening. Many of the people living on the streets of Roseau have been doing so for years and, if you live here, you get to learn all their names and interact with them as you would with anyone else. They are not professional beggars – they just need a bit of help to get by.

TAKING PHOTOGRAPHS OF PEOPLE Many Dominicans are sensitive to tourists taking photographs of them. You must always ask for permission first. Not doing so may result in an unpleasant confrontation. Some people may ask for money in exchange for a photograph. Clearly things are different at festival times such as Carnival and there's no problem with you taking photos of street parades.

BUSINESS Working practices in some organisations, particularly those associated with government departments, can appear somewhat dated by modern standards. Completing one task may require several trips back and forth between different people with different roles and in different buildings – it's a legacy of colonialism that hasn't been updated. If you're lucky, the people you must deal with will all be available and located in the same place, but don't count on it. If you're in a hurry or if you tend to be an impatient person, you may well become frustrated by what are often very time-consuming processes, especially in the unforgiving heat of downtown Roseau.

Service standards are not great, in fact they are often far from it. It all depends on the person and situation – and a lot is also down to you and how you interact. It's worth bearing in mind that many people don't earn very much at all and are not always valued by their employers. Smile and be friendly. Don't lecture – remember you know nothing about what's going on in the life of the person serving you. Of course, there are always exceptions, and you may well find that your holiday is replete with pleasant, happy, smiling faces and attentive people. Whatever the situation, don't let it spoil your day.

TRAVELLING POSITIVELY

Throughout this guide you'll be encouraged to look out for and support local businesses, farmers, artists and so on. Dominica also has many practical problems that several NGOs and local groups of volunteers try to resolve or improve upon. Dominicans living abroad are continually a great source of assistance to these organisations by sending materials and helping with fundraising. Visitors to Dominica can also make a big difference. Think about contacting one of these organisations before or during your visit and asking how you might be able to help.

Abilities Unlimited – Workshop for the Blind Federation Dr, Roseau; 767 448 2203. This is a craft workshop & store selling straw bags, baskets, mats & other items created by blind artisans. It's well signposted near the traffic island at the Dominica–China Friendship Hospital. Please call in & support them.

Alpha Centre Goodwill, Roseau; 767 448 6509. A voluntary school for children & adults with intellectual disabilities & sensory, physical & communication disorders. The centre provides education, parental skills training & support.

Dominica Dementia Foundation Picard; 767 245 8372; w dominicadementiafoundation.org. Founded by an 18-year-old Dominican student during her gap year, now successfully providing support to families to improve the lives of those with dementia.

Dominica Infirmary Home for the Aged Independence St, Roseau; 767 448 2636. Provides institutional care for the destitute, aged & infirm. Also provides a day-care centre for the elderly.

3

Activities and Special Interests

There are many ways to enjoy Dominica. A healthy interest in the great outdoors, natural history and cultural heritage will help you to get the most out of your stay on this offbeat and naturally beautiful Caribbean island.

TOUR OPERATORS AND PRIVATE GUIDES

Licensed tour guides are trained and certified by the Discover Dominica Authority and should be able to present an official and current photo identification card upon request. The training they receive is generally focused on cruise ship tourism and bus tours, rather than on other activities. All are trained in emergency first aid. The best hiking guides are those who have learned the trails first-hand, specialise in trails around where they live, walk them often, and have genuine enthusiasm for the environment. Scuba guides (divemasters and instructors) are usually PADI certified.

You are likely to be approached by taxi drivers offering you tours, especially in Roseau when cruise ships are in. You may also be approached by people at popular trailheads such as Boiling Lake. It's your call on whether you wish to engage someone, but it's highly likely that the best guides are those who don't have to hang around on the off chance or try to hustle you. The best advice I can give is to do as much forward planning as you can so you're not forced to make spur-of-the-moment decisions that you may feel uncomfortable with or even regret later. You're probably only here once – so, if you want a guide, work on getting a good one.

Depending on what you're hoping to do, first decide whether you need a guide or not, and then try to book one in advance. I've listed some guides and tour operators in this chapter, but hoteliers are also a good source of information as they usually have working relations with reliable guides. Be sure to agree the cost of the activity before you begin – including the currency. Don't engage a guide who seems to avoid giving you a price or who asks you to say how much you think you should pay.

SITE FEES AND PASSES

The **Ecotourist Site User Fee Programme** was established in 1997 to generate revenues from non-residents for the maintenance and upkeep of some of the island's most popular natural attractions. It's rather illogical and in need of an update.

At the time of writing, the user fee programme covers only 12 designated ecotourism sites: Emerald Pool, Boiling Lake, Freshwater Lake, Boeri Lake, Middleham Falls, Cabrits National Park, Syndicate Nature Trail, Indian River, Trafalgar Falls, Morne Trois Pitons, Morne Diablotin and Soufriere Sulphur Springs. The Botanic Gardens is also a designated ecotourism site, but the fee is not collected. For some reason the programme doesn't cover places such as Morne Anglais, Sari Sari Falls, Victoria Falls, Jacko Steps, Chemin L'Etang and others.

WELLNESS

Wellness is a term that's used a lot in Dominica's destination marketing material, on hotel websites and so on. It's also part of the island's tourism strategy. The context is the island itself: its natural environment, clean river water, fresh air and especially its forests. It builds on the theory that being close to nature is good for you and, as Dominica is the Caribbean's nature island, this is the best place in the region for you to come and experience a heightened sense of improved rejuvenation of body and mind – especially if you live a busy life in a town or city. Given most high-end resorts can offer wellness in the form of spa treatments, different types of massage, yoga and so on, what makes Dominica different is its wild places. In other words, you must step outdoors and immerse yourself in the island's forests, rivers and seas for the magic to really happen; to experience nature up close and personal. Beyond all the hyperbole, there's certainly something to it. I can testify that I feel fabulous when I'm on a forest trail or picking coffee in my mountain garden. The same goes for bird and whale watching, hanging neutrally buoyant over a coral reef formation, soaking in a volcanically heated spring, tasting fruit you've never eaten before, 'freeing up' at a festival, or swimming in a waterfall pool. This, in essence, is what's meant by wellness in the context of Dominica.

Permits can be purchased directly at Emerald Pool, Cabrits National Park, Trafalgar Falls, the Syndicate Nature Trail (don't count on this reception centre being open outside the cruise ship season though, so consider buying a pass elsewhere) and the Forestry Division office near the Botanic Gardens and Alliance Française. Permits can also be purchased from independent vendors – look for signs – and from tour operators and some hotels.

At present, two types of permits are available. A **site pass** costs US$5 and is valid for one site for one day only. A **week pass** costs US$12 and is valid for all sites for one week. Clearly, the single site pass option makes little sense.

Just to confuse you even further, there's a separate fee programme for the **Wai'tukubuli National Trail** (WNT). It costs US$12 per day on the trail or US$40 for 15 days of WNT hiking. You can buy tickets from some of the same vendors as the Ecotourist site passes and from the Forestry Division office. A simple pass for everything – rather like the visitor driving licence – would make a lot more sense and I'm hoping the pass system may soon be updated and streamlined accordingly.

Scuba-divers and snorkellers wishing to enjoy the sights of the Soufriere Scotts Head Marine Reserve must pay a **marine reserve fee** of US$2 per person. This fee is usually collected by dive and snorkelling operators as part of their charge.

BEACHES AND BAYS

Although Dominica isn't really known for its beaches, it does have some very nice ones. Here's a selection.

Antrizle Page 150. An offbeat beach, but a lovely one, in the elevated village of Antrizle, between Atkinson & Hatton Garden. Access to the bay is via a narrow road from the heart of this tiny village.

Batibou Page 190. Access to this sheltered & beautiful bay & beach is via private land & there's an access fee. Find it on the outskirts of Calibishie. There's beach security here.

Bell Hall, Douglas Bay Page 184. This is a lovely sliver of a beach on a gorgeously serene bay near the InterContinental Cabrits Resort & Spa.

Champagne Page 130. Noted for its volcanically active reef system, the beach is a mixture of smooth pebbles & sand. It's good for swimming & snorkelling. On the cruise ship itinerary, so busy busy.

Coconut Beach Page 184. Skirting the whole of Picard, this is a long & beautiful beach with its very own shipwreck.

Hampstead Page 190. A *Pirates of the Caribbean* film location, Hampstead is an expansive beach & bay that occasionally has high surf. Access is through private land, so there's a small fee.

Hodges Bay Page 190. This is a narrow strip of sand around a large crescent-shaped bay & with an accessible islet. Good for kids.

Mero Page 212. A long stretch of black-sand beach with several bars & local eateries. Sun loungers are available to rent. On the cruise ship itinerary.

Pointe Baptiste Page 190. Access to this beach is via a track from the village. It's a rare white-sand beach on the margins of a rocky bay near the Red Rocks.

Purple Turtle Page 184. This is a long stretch of beach along the margins of Prince Rupert Bay in the Lagoon area of Portsmouth. With sailboats at anchor & the Cabrits isthmus nearby, it's a scenic location with several bars & eateries. Sheltered & shallow waters means it's good for kids.

Salisbury Page 212. An offbeat but beautiful beach, Salisbury shouldn't be overlooked by anyone staying in central & west Dominica. Discover it down a rough track from the main coastal road, opposite the charming Roman Catholic church.

Sandy Bay Page 188. Hidden away behind the sprawling hillside village of Marigot is a lovely white-sand beach & bay.

Secret Beach Page 184. Only accessible by water, this is a lovely white-sand beach that has shallow reef formations that are great for snorkelling.

Turtle Point Page 190. Easy to miss, this is a lovely white-sand beach located in a small bay near Woodford Hill.

Woodford Hill Page 190. This is a lovely white-sand beach in a large bay that occasionally has a strong undertow. It's the location of the La Soye archaeology site (page 18) & usually has beach security.

BIRDWATCHING

Usually, organised birdwatching tours will take place on or around the **Syndicate Nature Trail** in Morne Diablotin National Park (page 219) or part of WNT Segment 10 which is nearby (page 224). This accessible forest region is the primary habitat of the endangered **sisserou** parrot (page 7) but you'll also see the **jaco** parrot and a variety of other bird species here too. The gently undulating Syndicate Nature Trail passes through a lush rainforest habitat and there's a great lookout point across the Dublanc River valley with expansive views over the forest.

Dominica's hiking trails are all opportunities to encounter birdlife, especially those within the three national parks. The Layou River and the Indian River are especially good for observing water birds.

MOUNTAIN WHISTLER, THE HIKER'S COMPANION

The mountain whistler (in Creole, *siffleur montagne*; Scientific name rufous-throated solitaire) is my favourite bird. A loner whose habitat is the wilderness of Dominica, the mountain whistler's unmistakable call is what you hear when you're hiking Dominica's dense forests and paying close attention to what's around you. A plaintive, almost sorrowful cry that speaks to profound solitude, the mountain whistler's call is the soundtrack to hiking in the nature island. And as soon as I hear it, I feel at home.

A BIRDER'S CHECKLIST

Here's a taster of some of the bird species in Dominica:

Antillean-crested hummingbird (*Orthorhyncus cristatus*)
Antillean euphonia (*Chlorophonia musica*)
Bananaquit (*Coereba flaveola*)
Belted kingfisher (*Megaceryle alcyon*)
Blue-headed hummingbird (*Cyanophaia bicolor*)
Broad-winged hawk (*Buteo platypterus*)
Brown trembler (*Cinclocerthia ruficauda*)
Carib grackle (*Quiscalus lugubris*)
Caribbean martin (*Progne dominicensis*)
Cattle egret (*Bubulcus ibis*)
Forest thrush (*Turdus lherminieri*)
Green heron (*Butorides virescens*)
Green-throated Carib (*Eulampis holosericeus*)
Grey kingbird (*Tyrannus dominicensis*)
Imperial parrot (*Amazona imperialis*)
Lesser Antillean bullfinch (*Loxigilla noctis*)
Lesser Antillean flycatcher (*Myiarchus oberi*)
Lesser Antillean saltator (*Saltator albicollis*)
Lesser Antillean swift (*Chaetura martinica*)
Magnificent frigatebird (*Fregata magnificens*)
Mangrove cuckoo (*Coccyzus minor grenadensis*)
Pearly-eyed thrasher (*Margarops fuscatus*)
Plumbeous warbler (*Setophaga plumbea*)
Purple-throated Carib (*Eulampis jugularis*)
Red-necked parrot (*Amazona arausiaca*)
Ringed kingfisher (*Megaceryle torquatus*)
Rufous-throated solitaire (*Myadestes genibarbis*)
Scaly-breasted thrasher (*Allenia fusca*)
Smooth-billed ani (*Crotophaga ani*)
Yellow-throated vireo (*Vireo flavifrons*)
Zenaida dove (*Zenaida aurita*)

Bertrand Jno Baptiste 767 245 4768; **e** drbirdy2@cwdom.dm. Nicknamed 'Birdy', Bertrand Jno Baptiste is Dominica's best-known birdwatching expert & guide. He offers tours for birders of all levels of interest & will also help you to find the specific birds you are interested in observing & photographing. Birdy is not only very knowledgeable, he's also great company & highly recommended.

Elvis Stedman (E Voyage Dominica) 767 225 1971; **e** elvistourguide@gmail.com. Elvis combines a love of hiking with an extensive knowledge of Dominica's tropical flora & fauna. He's a popular choice of guide with visiting student groups & academics & has a good knowledge of the island's birdlife.

KHATTS Tours 767 448 1660, 767 235 3517; **e** info@khatts.com; **w** khattstours.com. Long established tour operator offering a range of experiences in the hinterlands of Dominica. Birdwatching tours usually take place on the Syndicate Nature Trail.

BOAT TOURS

Some of the main dive, whale-watching and fishing operators also offer boat trips along the west coast. You can also charter local river boat operators in the

Portsmouth area, notably from Purple Turtle Beach and the Indian River visitor centre (page 194). Here are some suggestions.

Caribbean Deep Sea Fishing Newtown, Roseau; 767 616 3500. Coastal cruises on the Ocean Villa run out of Newtown near Roseau. This operator also offers whale watching & fishing.
Dominica Water Tours Scotts Head; 767 245 5480; w dominicawatertours.com. This operator offers private small boat charters that include coastal tours, whale watching, fishing & snorkelling.
Eddison Tours & Yacht Services 767 225 3626; e info@eddisontours.dm; w eddisontours.dm. With years of experience, Eddison is a Portsmouth-based tour operator offering boat trips in the north that can include fishing & the Indian River.
Island Style Fishing Fortune, Roseau; 767 265 0518; e islandstylefishing@gmail.com; w islandstylefishing.com. With many years of experience, Captain Jerry offers chartered boat tours, whale watching & fishing trips.
Waitukubuli Adventure Tour Co Roseau; 767 440 4660; e info@waitukubulitours.com; w waitukubulitours.com. Chartered coastal cruises, whale watching & fishing trips are offered by this experienced tour company.

BUS AND JEEP TOURS

If the thought of self-driving Dominica's roads fills you with dread, then bus and jeep tours are good alternatives. In addition to the selective list below, you should check with your hotel to see if they run their own sightseeing tours or whether they recommend an operator. During the peak season (November to May) many sightseeing guides are occupied with cruise ship tours. Here's a selection:

Ali Auguiste 767 265 2699; e firstnation365@gmail.com. Ali is an experienced Kalinago guide who specialises in Kalinago Territory tours as well as sightseeing around the island.
DG Tours 767 317 7238; e devongreenaway123@gmail.com. Devon Greenaway is an experienced guide who offers a range of half- & full-day tours around the island, as well as general taxi services. He's also happy for you to create your own tour.
Dominica Untouchable Tours 767 316 7702, 767 245 3089; e untouchabletours@yahoo.com; w dominicauntouchabletours.com. Based in Calibishie, experienced guide Wendy Marcellin offers island-wide full- & half-day tours incorporating hiking trails, waterfalls & cultural sights.
Eddison Tours & Yacht Services 767 225 3626; e info@eddisontours.dm; w eddisontours.dm. With years of experience, Portsmouth-based Eddison offers a selection of island-wide sightseeing trips, hiking & Indian River boat tours.
Jenn Tours 767 276 4659; e happycarrentals@gmail.com. Jenner Robinson is an experienced sightseeing & hiking guide who also has his own car rental company.
Just Go Dominica 767 245 4328; e justgodominica@gmail.com; w justgodominica.com. Experienced tour & hiking guide Nahjie & his team offer a wide selection of island tours, from sightseeing to hiking & canyoning.
KHATTS Tours 767 448 1660, 767 235 3517; e info@khatts.com; w khattstours.com. Long established tour operator offering a raft of travel experiences including sightseeing tours.
Mr Nature Tours 767 276 3957; e gussiekenneth@yahoo.com. Portsmouth-based guide & taxi driver Kenneth Gussie offers island sightseeing tours & Indian River boat trips. Speciality tours include Portsmouth cultural tours & outdoor barbecues.
Petra Tours 767 285 5550; w petra-tours-dominica.com. Petra is an experienced English- & German-speaking tour guide offering island-wide sightseeing tours & short hikes.

CANYONING

Canyoning, or canyoneering, involves making your way through a canyon from a start to a finish point. Usually, the canyon has a river in it, and often there are waterfalls and cascades. In order to progress through the canyon and along the river, you must rappel down any waterfalls you meet and jump off the cascades into pools. Equipment includes a rappelling device, ropes, hard hat, wetsuit and buoyancy jacket. All you need is a swimsuit and either strong surf shoes or an old pair of sneakers (sandals are not recommended for this).

Most canyoning takes place within the river canyon below Ti Tou Gorge, though there are several other exciting and challenging routes for the more experienced (including down the father falls at Trafalgar). The standard trip through Ti Tou Canyon usually takes up to 4 hours, depending on group numbers. The waterfalls, pools and rock formations here are spectacular and Cathedral Canyon, the last you reach, is one of the most naturally beautiful places on the island. I highly recommend a canyoning trip, and the best thing is that no prior experience is necessary – you're given training and all the equipment you need before you set off.

Canyoning-Dominica 767 616 7118; e email@canyoning-dominica.com; w canyoning-dominica.com. Experienced canyoneer Nathalie Dalboussières aka Ti Nath Kanion leads French- & English-speaking canyoning trips for both complete beginners & those with experience. Training is on the fly before you set off & wetsuit, helmet & harness are provided.

Extreme Dominica 767 285 9136, 767 245 4328; e info@extremedominica.com; w extremedominica.com. Extreme Dominica offers a wide range of canyoning trips depending on your experience; from Ti Tou Gorge to the Breakfast River & Trafalgar Falls – even canyoning at night. All equipment, training (on a purpose-built wall) & transportation to & from the canyon is included in the price & advanced training courses & trips are available. Guides are trained & certified by the American Canyoneering Association & a 3-way safety system keeps you safe when rappelling.

CRUISE SHIP DAY VISITORS

If Dominica is on your cruise itinerary, the best piece of advice I can give you is to get out of Roseau. You'll be disappointed if you hang around the capital. Roseau doesn't have shopping malls, designer boutiques, a cruise ship village or a handy boardwalk with bars and restaurants close to the ship. Walking around the capital isn't easy either. The pavements are often crowded with stalls or parked vehicles and there are large drainage gutters to negotiate. So, take an excursion – either via the cruise ship or with one of the many private tour bus drivers that you'll see touting for business near the Roseau jetty or the Woodbridge Bay port.

Bus tours are fairly standard and private operators are regulated. Popular excursions will usually include Emerald Pool (page 215) and Trafalgar Falls (page 119) – both of which you should try to see. Other places worth visiting and usually offered on a half-day tour are Spanny Falls (page 217), Ti Tou Gorge (page 118) and the Hot Springs at Wotten Waven (page 117). Short and manageable hikes worth considering include Middleham Falls (page 126), Freshwater Lake (page 125), Boeri Lake (page 123) and the Galion Loop (page 144). Canyoning, whale watching and scuba-diving (all described in this chapter) are usually available as shore excursions, all of which are certainly worthwhile.

You should note that not all private bus drivers are also certified guides. In other words, if you go to Trafalgar Falls, for example, your bus driver may not have the requisite certification to guide you once you get there. So, before you commit, do ask your driver if they are also a certified guide. All private operators should display their credentials – on the bus and in the form of an ID. If your driver is elusive regarding the cost of a tour or asks you to pay what you think it's worth, then find another one. Agree the price and currency up front.

FISHING

Although specialist sportfishing operators are few compared to other destinations in the region, it's possible to go deep-sea and inshore fishing off the island's west coast. Deep-sea fishing offers a chance to catch bonito, mahi-mahi and marlin (note, Dominica hasn't implemented a tagging/catch-and-release system of sportfishing). Inshore, you can catch jacks, snapper and kingfish. Freshwater river fishing is restricted to residents with permits at certain times of the year.

Caribbean Deep Sea Fishing Newtown, Roseau; \ 767 616 3500. Sportfishing trips on the *Ocean Villa* run out of Newtown near Roseau. This operator also offers whale watching & coastal cruises.

Dominica Water Tours Scotts Head; \ 767 245 5480; w dominicawatertours.com. This operator offers private small boat charters that include fishing trips. You can also combine fishing with other activities such as whale watching, snorkelling or coastal tours.

Eddison Tours & Yacht Services \ 767 225 3626; e info@eddisontours.dm; w eddisontours.dm. Eddison is an experienced & knowledgeable Portsmouth-based tour operator offering a selection of island-wide sightseeing trips, hiking & Indian River boat tours. He also offers short inshore fishing trips (hand-lining & bottom fishing) in Prince Rupert Bay.

Island Style Fishing Fortune, Roseau; \ 767 265 0518; e islandstylefishing@gmail.com; w islandstylefishing.com. Experienced Captain Jerry Daway offers 4-, 6-, & 8hr fishing charters on his fully rigged Bertram sportfishing boat, *Southern Cross*. Jerry has an interesting story & is a knowledgeable & friendly guy. He has great reviews & has even taken out celebs. Jerry also runs whale-watching, snorkelling & coastal sightseeing trips.

Keepin It Real Toucari; \ 767 225 7657. Keepin It Real is a bayside restaurant (a very good one!) in the pretty northern village of Toucari. But if you ask, owner Derrick Augustine can also organise an inshore fishing trip for you. If you don't catch anything for him to cook, don't worry – the lobster is fabulous.

Waitukubuli Adventure Tour Co Newtown, Roseau; \ 767 440 4660; e info@waitukubulitours.com; w waitukubulitours.com. This family-run tour operator has 2 sportfishing boats & offers 4–8hr sportfishing trips out of Roseau. Other boating activities are also available.

FREEDIVING

Freediving is a watersport that involves swimming underwater while holding your breath. The practice goes back to ancient times and there are still fishermen, sponge- and pearl-divers in places such as Japan and the Philippines who harvest from the seabed while holding their breath. In 1976, Frenchman Jacques Mayol became the first known freediver to descend to 100m. His life and achievements were the inspiration for the 1988 Luc Besson film *The Big Blue*, which itself inspired the growth in popularity of freediving. Mayol's philosophy was for him to achieve a state of mind akin to that achieved by relaxation, meditation, yoga and so on. These activities continue to be closely associated with freediving. If you've seen the film, you'll know that Mayol had an affinity for and attachment to dolphins, and his book *The Dolphin Within Man* discusses how humans might reawaken dormant mental and physical faculties to rediscover the kind of relationship with water that dolphins enjoy.

There are several competitive 'apnea' disciplines in the sport, some of which use large single fins, and others of which use a descent rope. It's a specialist activity that requires both mental, technical and physical skills, as well as training and practice. Every year, there are freediving competitions around the world where limits are frequently exceeded, and new world record holders are crowned. In Dominica, freediving is centred around Soufriere Bay, which is deep and enjoys calm, protected waters all year round.

Blue Element Freediving Soufriere; **w** blueelementfreediving.com. Set up by freedivers Sofia Gómez Uribe & Jonathan Sunnex, Blue Element offers courses & training for beginner & experienced freedivers. It also hosts an annual competition. Book freediving experiences & get more information via the website.

Deep Dominica Soufriere; **w** deepdominica.com. Year-round freediving as well as training courses are offered by this popular Soufriere-based freediving operation. As well as beginner, intermediate & advance courses, Deep Dominica hosts an AIDA & CMAS sanctioned freediving competition.

GARDENS, FARMS AND FOOD

For travellers interested in tropical gardens, farming and cooking, there are several interesting options. It's also worth noting that if you're here in May, there might be a Flower Show in Giraudel or Eggleston. It's hard to find out about these things if you don't use social media, so get in touch with Discover Dominica Authority (767 448 2045; **e** tourism@dominica.dm) for more information.

Dominica is a place where people who want to get close to nature, and to innovate and live alternative, healthier lifestyles, attempt to do something a little different. Although the realities of living and trying to make a living in Dominica can be a challenge – whether you're from here or from overseas – those who persist often create wonderful things. Recently, a number of local people – many of them quite young – have created small farmsteads where they specialise in certain types of horticulture, for example exotic fruits and heirloom species. I sense a trend emerging, and I'm hopeful about it. So, if this is your thing too, here are some farms, gardens and cooking experiences that are certainly worth checking out.

Blackbird Farm Bellevue Chopin; **w** blackbirdfarms.com. This is a women-owned & managed organic livestock, fruit & vegetable farm on the high hillsides of Bellevue Chopin (page 141). At the time of writing, the farm was planning to open for tours but had not done so yet. But, if this is of interest, keep it on your radar & contact them when you get here.

Botanic Gardens Roseau. Dominica's Botanic Gardens has been around since the 1890s (page 105). It's experienced several destructive weather events in its time & has never had the expertise or attention needed to return it to its former glory, but it's still really worth spending some time there – especially when the flamboyant, cannonball & yellow poui trees are blossoming. Be careful of traffic – the Botanic Gardens has become a busy thoroughfare & it can also get crowded with cruise ship buses in peak season. There's a small plant nursery next to the Ministry of Agriculture buildings that's worth a look, as is the sisserou parrot aviary. Also follow the signs & take the track up Jack's Walk & enjoy the views from Morne Bruce if there are no cruise crowds about (page 106).

Cocoa Valley Eco Farms Touna Concord; 767 276 1234; 24hr advance notice required. Kenny & his young & enthusiastic family offer a fascinating tour of their 'all-natural' farm in the Kalinago Territory near Touna Concord. Afterwards enjoy an outdoor cook-up & taste some of the produce they grow (page 162). The farm is well signposted on the main road in Concord. Note, you must make a shallow river crossing to get there.

Cooking with Daria Giraudel; 767 616 5187; **e** daria.eugene@gmail.com; **w** cookingwithdaria.com. Daria Eugene offers Creole cooking classes for groups & individuals in her garden kitchen at her home in Gommier near Giraudel. Learn about Caribbean ingredients, how they are used & then cook yourself something tasty to eat. This is a popular experience & on the cruise itinerary – so book well in advance.

D-Smart Farm Corona, Pont Cassé; 767 315 5128; e d-smartfarm@hotmail.com. The lovely Dawn Francis heads up this family-run permaculture farm just off the main road near Pont Cassé. Popular as an educational school outing, the farm also has an A-frame wooden cabin & tents for rent in a forested camping ground (page 215).

Free Up Farm Syndicate; 767 614 3153; e freeupfarm@gmail.com; w freeupfarm.com. This 3ha permaculture farm is in the elevated heights of Syndicate – traditionally a farming area for citrus & coffee. It's owned & managed by Aubrey & Lulu who have created a project that includes the cultivation of a wide variety of trees, plants & food using permaculture methods. Visitors are welcome (it's prudent to contact them before showing up). It's an evolving initiative that also welcomes skilled permaculture experts & volunteers (page 216).

Papillote Tropical Gardens Trafalgar; 767 448 2287; e papillote@cwdom.dm; w papillote.dm. For many years, Papillote has been one of Dominica's most renowned private gardens. Take a self-guided or an accompanied hillside walk through 2ha of tropical trees & plants, where you can also enjoy waterfalls & volcanically heated springs (page 118).

Paradise Valley Bornes; 767 277 4671. Paradise Valley is a large botanical garden & plant nursery in the northern village of Bornes. Forever evolving, it's the eye-catching creation of Dominica's foremost contemporary landscape gardener, Dian Douglas. The diverse & colourful gardens are enjoyed via a series of tracks & trails. Open daily, guided & self-guided tours are available. Paradise Valley is also becoming a popular setting for weddings & events. Rental cottages will be available soon (page 195).

Pointe Baptiste Estate Pointe Baptiste, Calibishie; 767 225 5378; e manager@pointebaptiste.com; w pointebaptiste.com. Historic Pointe Baptiste Estate is home to a family-run chocolate factory where visitors are welcome to learn about cocoa & the chocolate-making process as well as sample & buy some of their products (page 195).

Soma Garden Pagua; 767 277 6062; e somagardens767@gmail.com; contact 24hrs in advance. Vaughan Green is an enthusiastic young farmer who describes himself as a 'fruit fiend'. Indeed, his expansive farm along the Pagua River is full of fruit trees – over 50 different varieties. His fascinating tours are geared towards small groups & include fruit tasting. There's also great access to Pagua River pools if you feel like bathing after your farm tour (page 166).

HIKING

Dominica has a vast network of trails and tracks. Many are historic, cut by Amerindians, enslaved estate workers or Maroons. Some are functional, linking villages and providing access to farmlands or traces for hunters. And others are recreational, leading to lakes, rivers, mountaintops and waterfalls. If you enjoy walking in nature, then Dominica should provide satisfaction in bucketloads.

Frustrating, however, is the fact that insufficient resources and expertise are made available to ensure the island's walking trails are managed and regularly maintained to a high standard. This means that, from time to time, trails can be overgrown and hard to follow. At the time of writing, it's only the Wai'tukubuli National Trail segments that have ever had blazes marking the route – others have nothing more than a trailhead sign at most. Fortunately for visiting hiking enthusiasts, except for damage from extreme weather events, the well-beaten paths you're likely to walk on the island tend to look after themselves or are cleared by hiking guides and hoteliers. There's no doubt that if Dominica's hiking trails were properly managed and developed, they would be world-class.

Tropical Storm Erika in 2015 and Hurricane Maria in 2017 caused their fair share of damage to several trails that, at the time of writing, have not yet been restored or cleared properly. Some of the more obscure trails you may have heard of – such as Bolive Falls and Perdu Temps – are also too difficult for me to recommend right now. The trails described in this book are therefore deliberately selective rather than comprehensive. I summarise the difficulties you'll encounter and whether a guide is recommended or optional.

At the time of writing, very little up-to-date information is published by the authorities about the condition of hiking trails. I suggest consulting the following:

Dominica Forestry & Parks Division ☎ 767 266 5852; e forestry@dominica.gov.dm, nationalparks@dominica.gov.dm. For trail information.

Dominica Ministry of Tourism ☎ 767 266 3497; e tourism@dominica.gov.dm. For feedback on your hiking experience.

Walking in Dominica's rainforest can often mean getting wet and dirty. A towel and a change of clothes either to take along or to leave in your car at the trailhead is something you'll appreciate when you return. If you take a change of clothes with you on the hike, be sure to put them in a waterproof or plastic bag.

TRAIL DESCRIPTIONS

In previous editions of this book, I came up with a detailed analysis of trail difficulty. I think it was maybe a little more than anyone really needed and, because everyone is different, generalisations on difficulty levels don't really work either. So, for this edition I've simply gone with an introductory overview highlighting the main challenges as well as the rough duration of the hike. I hope it's still helpful. I've also rewritten the descriptions to remove some of the detail. I know this sounds a bit counterintuitive, but I've learned from experience that weather events, climate change, landslides and erosion all combine to change the landscape over time, demonstrating an impermanence and natural transformation that render descriptions like 'turn left at the large boulder', 'turn right at the chatanier tree' and so on, all potentially unhelpful or misleading. Even though the subtleties of the landscape may change, the trail route itself rarely differs, so that's my new focus, along with highlights such as viewpoints, natural history and cultural heritage. The Wai'tukubuli National Trail (WNT) segments are still (at the time of writing) the only trails that have directional blazes (blue and yellow). If they're regularly refreshed (the forest habitat tends to make them fade quickly) then the routes should – theoretically – be easy to follow. (I'm not sure if this will take off, but some of us are now preparing to use a 'universal trail symbol' that we came up with, and maybe you'll come across it on some of the less beaten paths. It's a symbol that represents a *tête chien* (boa constrictor) snake (page 9) with its head as an arrow.)

There's also an interesting change that you'd probably only notice if you've been living here. Although Hurricane Maria's destruction of the forest has largely been repaired by nature herself, the canopy is not as dense as it was before. GPS tracking apps and devices that were sketchy before the hurricane now work quite well. I use one if I'm walking somewhere new and, even if it's not completely accurate, I find it does help. So, if you're coming here with the aim of doing a lot of hiking, I think an app on your phone is a useful companion to my broad trail descriptions and any other references you may use for your Dominica hiking adventures.

Generally speaking, it's a bad idea to hike to waterfalls or cross rivers if there has been heavy rain, or if heavy rain is forecast. Flash flooding does happen and you should avoid any hike that involves significant river crossings or river hiking. Use common sense and a reasonable degree of caution when deciding where to go in inclement weather. If local people advise against a hike due to heavy rainfall or swollen rivers, take heed and go somewhere else instead.

WAI'TUKUBULI NATIONAL TRAIL The Wai'tukubuli National Trail (WNT) runs from the south of the island at Cachacrou to the northwest where it comes to an end at Cabrits National Park. It's about 200km in length and is split into 14 connected segments. Each segment has its own unique set of challenges as well as areas of historic, cultural and natural interest.

Although the trail has been in existence for several years now, it has not been developed to reach its full potential. All the segments were impacted by both Tropical Storm Erika and Hurricane Maria. At the time of writing, all are 'clear', but many need proper rehabilitation.

Camping, in theory, is not allowed, but the authorities acknowledge that it would be impossible to through-hike the trail without pitching a tent or a hammock on some of the segments. So, if you must overnight, please keep your impact on the environment to a minimum and stick to the trail. You may find it difficult to find flat and even ground. I've used a Hennessy Hammock (w hennessyhammock.com) when through-hiking, which I've found to be very flexible, lightweight and with minimal environmental impact. If you're through-hiking, please be aware that this is a tough trail with some steep and muddy ups and downs, some narrow ledges, and plenty of river crossings. And if it still hasn't been properly rehabilitated when you hike it, there's certainly a chance of getting lost – especially on segments 8 and 9 (I urge you to hire a guide for these two). Try to keep your backpack as light as possible to better manage those places where you must climb and/or need good balance.

Trail signage takes the form of signposts, information boards (if they're still standing) and yellow-and-blue painted blazes (which are often faded). In some areas signage and blazes are inadequate, so don't walk for too long with your head down! Always be sure you can see a blaze, or at least remember where the last one was. In the descriptions, I've noted areas where you can bail out of the segment if completion isn't an option.

I'm informed by the authorities that there are indeed plans to rehabilitate the WNT and to have a dedicated trail management unit, but wheels turn slowly here and, so far, hiking trail management and development has never been a priority – despite all the destination marketing hyperbole. Trail clearing has largely been down to private individuals and hiking guides. I think it's worth you sending your hiking feedback to the Ministry of Tourism and the Forestry and Parks Division (page 27) because sometimes external voices can be more impactful.

HIKING GUIDES Good hiking guides know which way to go when routes become unclear, are usually trained in first aid, and can provide interesting information about the cultural and natural history of the trail. Hiring guides provides a source of income to local people and, by extension, their families and communities. Local knowledge will enhance your Dominica experience and the reassurance a good guide can provide when a trail is new to you is also invaluable.

Most hotels and guesthouses will be happy to arrange hiking tours for their guests using local tour operators or independent guides. It's always worth asking for recommendations. Some may employ their own guides. If you decide to hire

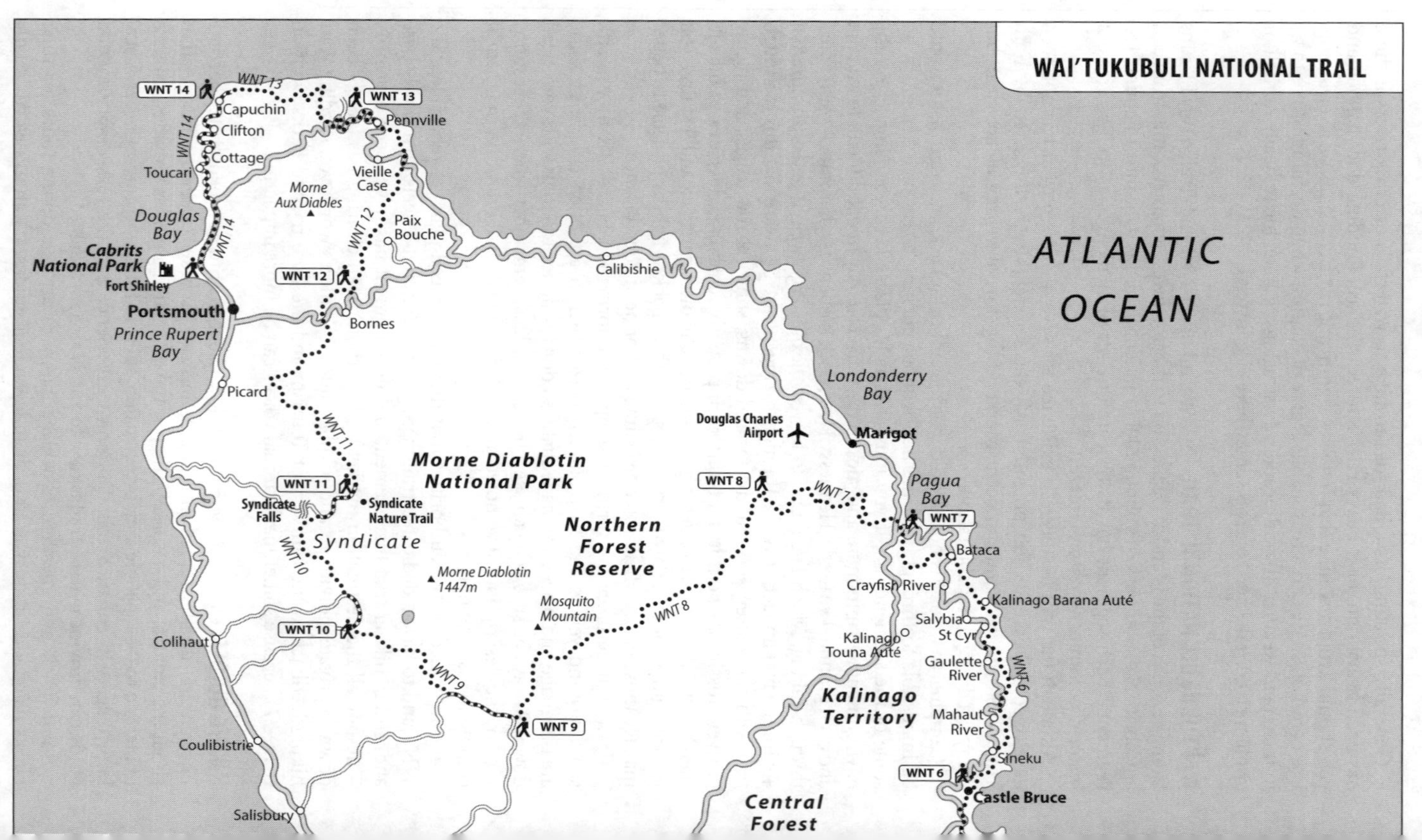

WAI'TUKUBULI NATIONAL TRAIL
ATLANTIC
OCEAN
WNT 14
WNT 13
Capuchin
Clifton
Cottage
Toucari
Pennville
Vieille
Case
Morne
Aux Diables
Paix
Bouche
Douglas
Bay
Cabrits
National Park
Fort Shirley
WNT 12
Portsmouth
Bornes
Prince Rupert
Bay
Calibishie
Picard
WNT 11
Londonderry
Bay
Douglas Charles
Airport
Marigot
Morne Diablotin
National Park
WNT 11
Syndicate
Falls
Syndicate
Nature Trail
Syndicate
WNT 10
Northern
Forest
Reserve
WNT 8
WNT 7
Pagua
Bay
WNT 7
Bataca
Morne Diablotin
1447m
Mosquito
Mountain
Crayfish River
Kalinago Barana Auté
WNT 8
Salybia
St Cyr
Kalinago
Touna Auté
WNT 10
Colihaut
WNT 9
Gaulette
River
WNT 6
Kalinago
Territory
Mahaut
River
WNT 9
Coulibistrie
Sineku
WNT 6
Castle Bruce
Salisbury
Central
Forest

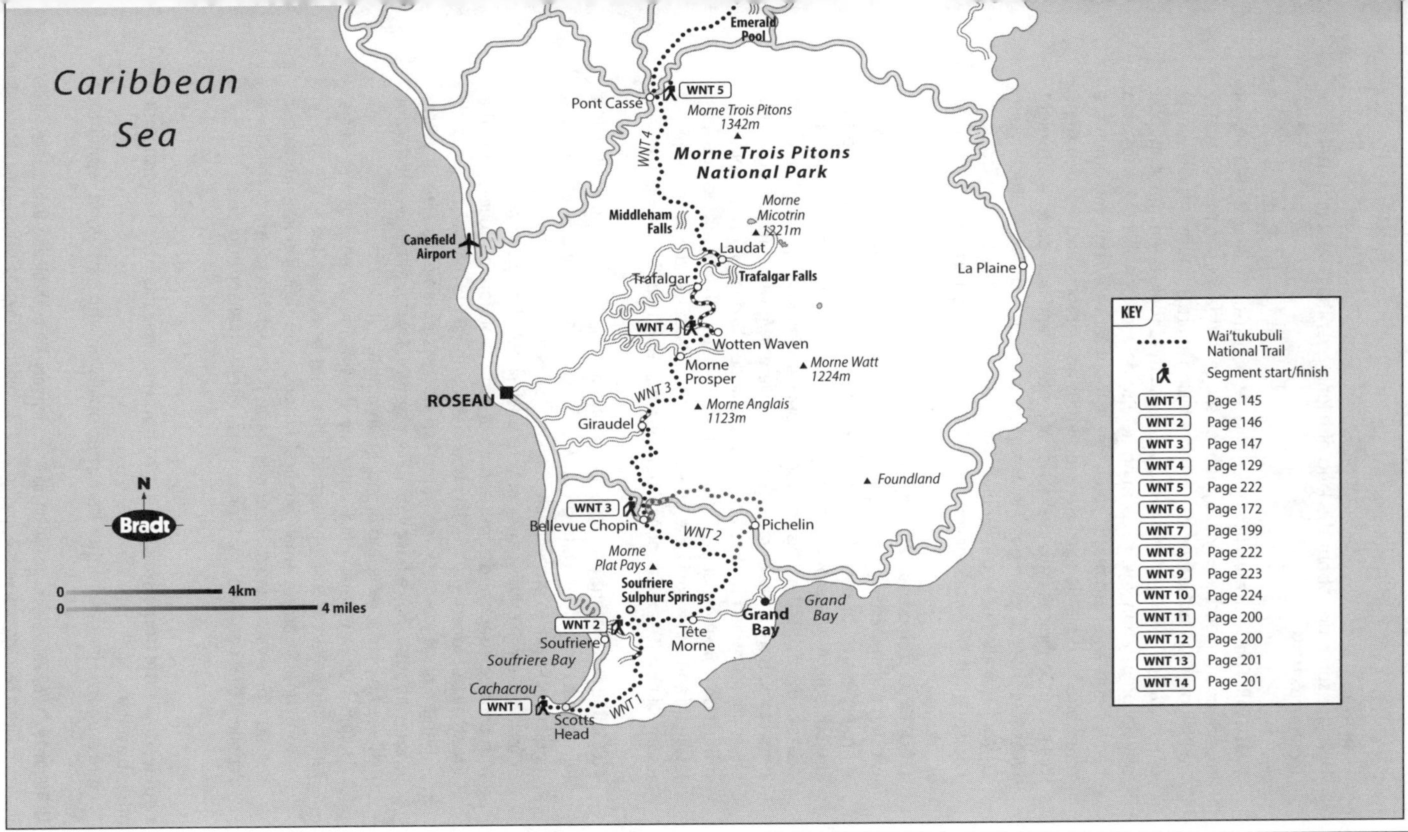

Caribbean Sea

Emerald Pool
Pont Cassé
WNT 5
Morne Trois Pitons 1342m
Morne Trois Pitons National Park
WNT 4
Middleham Falls
Morne Micotrin 1221m
Canefield Airport
Laudat
Trafalgar
Trafalgar Falls
La Plaine
WNT 4
Wotten Waven
Morne Prosper
Morne Watt 1224m
WNT 3
ROSEAU
Morne Anglais 1123m
Giraudel
Foundland
N
Bradt
WNT 3
Bellevue Chopin
Pichelin
WNT 2
Morne Plat Pays
Soufriere Sulphur Springs
0 4km
0 4 miles
Grand Bay
Grand Bay
WNT 2
Soufriere
Tête Morne
Soufriere Bay
Cachacrou
WNT 1
WNT 1
Scotts Head

KEY

....	Wai'tukubuli National Trail
(hiker symbol)	Segment start/finish
WNT 1	Page 145
WNT 2	Page 146
WNT 3	Page 147
WNT 4	Page 129
WNT 5	Page 222
WNT 6	Page 172
WNT 7	Page 199
WNT 8	Page 222
WNT 9	Page 223
WNT 10	Page 224
WNT 11	Page 200
WNT 12	Page 200
WNT 13	Page 201
WNT 14	Page 201

HIKING GEAR

Here are some tips about the kind of hiking gear that I've found useful for Dominica's trails.

FOOTWEAR Footwear must fit well, be able to stand up to challenging terrain, get muddy and wet and keep you upright on slippery surfaces, and then be able to do it all over again the next day without falling apart. Because of the diversity of terrain, Dominica is tough on footwear, and this should be an important part of your preparation if you're coming here to do a lot of walking. Try to avoid heavy boots and hard plastic soles. Heavy footwear will weigh you down too much and hard plastic soles are treacherous on wet rocks and wooden steps. I've hiked Dominica's trails in all kinds of footwear and now prefer lightweight cross-trail shoes. They're good in water and on slippery surfaces, and they also dry out quickly. But you may have your favourite tried-and-tested boots, of course, and if they work for you then stick with what you're comfortable with.

CLOTHING Clothing should be lightweight. T-shirts are just fine but moisture-wicking hiking shirts with UV and mosquito protection are the better, though more expensive, options. Lightweight shorts that you can swim in and that dry out quickly are also optimal. If you plan on climbing some of Dominica's peaks or more obscure trails, then you should also bring long hiking trousers to protect you from areas of razor grass and overgrown vegetation. Long-sleeve shirts are also good for this and have the added benefit of giving you more protection from mosquitoes, chiggers and ant bites. A hat to protect you from both rain and sun is advisable, as is a pair of sunglasses. And bring a rain jacket – sorry, I know it's the Caribbean, but you'll probably need it at some point.

ACCESSORIES A waterproof daypack (or one with a cover) is a good idea, but failing that bring along waterproof or ziplock bags that you can carry inside a regular backpack to protect valuables and sensitive items from the rain and/or falling during a river crossing. Your pack should be comfortable to wear, with padded straps and some degree of protection for your back. Keep the size small but functional – unless you're through-hiking the WNT.

Bring a re-usable flask for water. Tap water is potable here but if you're worried about it, buy a flask with a filter system. Try not to buy bottled water – there's no plastic recycling facility in Dominica.

I find walking poles help on tricky terrain and when crossing rivers. Telescopic poles can also be stashed when they're not needed.

You should carry a small medical kit with you that includes antiseptic solution or swabs, gauze, bandage, tape and painkillers. Bring mosquito repellent that contains DEET (or a natural alternative) and sunscreen.

a guide, do a little homework and try to find one who has been recommended by other travellers.

Here are some guides I either know personally or who have good reputations.

Ali Auguiste 767 265 2699; e firstnation365@gmail.com. Ali is a Kalinago with years of guiding experience. He's a great guide for the Kalinago Territory, Morne Diablotin & Boiling Lake. Amiable & good company, Ali also has a good knowledge of Kalinago cultural heritage as well as plants & birds.

Ashton Prosper ☎ 767 245 1443. Ashton has been guiding for over 40 years. He's usually hanging out at Trafalgar visitor centre & will take you up the boulders to the 'Father Falls'. He's also an option for the Boiling Lake Trail.

Bevin Lewis (Rodney's Wellness Retreat) ☎ 767 235 3417; e relax@rodneyswellness.com; w rodneyswellness.com. Bevin is an experienced guide. In addition to the trails around Rodney's Wellness Retreat in the southwest, he's also a regular Boiling Lake hiker.

David Victorin ☎ 767 225 0006. David is based out of Crescent Moon Cabins in the Heart of Dominica & has been hiking the island's forest trails for many years. He's a great choice for Boiling Lake, Middleham Falls (including from Sylvania & Cochrane) & many more.

Devon Greenaway (DG Tours) ☎ 767 317 7238; e dg_tours@hotmail.com. Devon offers a range of tours & experiences all around the island including hiking the main lake & waterfall trails.

Elvis Stedman (E Voyage Dominica) ☎ 767 225 1971; e elvistourguide@gmail.com. Elvis combines a love of hiking with an extensive knowledge of Dominica's tropical flora. He's a popular choice of guide with visiting student groups & academics.

Jenner Robinson (Jenn Tours) ☎ 767 276 4659; e happycarrentals@gmail.com. Jenner is an experienced sightseeing & hiking guide. Although he's based in Marigot, he knows many hiking trails all around the island.

KHATTS ☎ 767 448 1660, 767 235 3517; e info@khatts.com; w khattstours.com. Ken & his team are long-established tour operators offering a raft of travel experiences including guided hiking on many trails island-wide.

Marshee Tours ☎ 767 613 8961; e deshaunralph767@gmail.com. This group of Laudat-based guides can usually be found at Ti Tou Gorge renting out buoyancy jackets & tubes. They also offer guided hiking on the popular trails of Morne Trois Pitons National Park.

Michael Eugene (Experiences Caribbean) ☎ 767 616 5827; e jtasexperience@gmail.com. Mike is an experienced hiking guide & has good knowledge of WNT segments & other trails, especially in Morne Trois Pitons National Park & the south.

Nahjie Laflouf (Just Go Dominica) ☎ 767 245 4328; e justgodominica@gmail.com; w justgodominica.com. Nahjie & his hand-picked team of guides are extremely knowledgeable & experienced as well as good company. Morne Trois Pitons National Park is their back garden, & they are Boiling Lake Trail experts, but they'll happily take you anywhere.

Nigel George ☎ 767 285 3179. Nigel is a popular hiking guide. He'll walk pretty much anywhere with you & his trail knowledge is extensive. He's a good choice for Jacko Steps, Sari Sari Falls, Morne Diablotin, WNT segments & others.

Peter Green (Bushman Tours) ☎ 767 235 2270; e pgbushmantours@gmail.com. Peter is best known as a Boiling Lake guide though he also offers guided services on other trails in Morne Trois Pitons National Park.

Wendy Marcellin (Dominica Untouchable Tours) ☎ 767 245 3089; e untouchabletours@yahoo.com; w dominicauntouchabletours.com. Based in Calibishie, Wendy is a great choice for hiking & exploring in the north. As well as Dominica's main hiking trails, he's also got a locker full of other creative walks along the northern coastline.

HORSERIDING

Horseriding in Dominica is an engaging activity that offers a completely different perspective of the island's tracks and trails. It's an option for experienced riders as well as those who have never been on a horse before. Horseriding tours usually begin with a short training session for beginners and include all the equipment you need. They are fully guided and can last from 30 minutes to 4 hours. Horseriding lessons on the flat and over jumps are also available. There are two stables offering horseriding tours and lessons, both in the north near Portsmouth.

Brandy Manor Riding Center Brandy, Bornes; ☎ 767 235 4871, 767 612 0978; e brandymanor@ymail.com, brandymanorridingcenter@gmail.com; w brandymanor.wix.com/riding-center. Whether you're a novice or a seasoned rider, Yasmin & Linton offer guided horse rides through semi-deciduous woodland & rainforest around Brandy Estate, WNT Segment 11 & around Sugarloaf Mountain, where you can enjoy superb views of Prince Rupert Bay & Morne Diablotin National Park. Trail rides are between 30mins & 4hrs. Flatwork & jumping lessons are also available.

Rainforest Riding Bell Hall, Portsmouth; ☎ 767 445 3619, 767 265 7386; **e** rainforestriding@yahoo.com; **w** rainforestriding.com. Canadian & long-time Dominica resident Valerie Francis offers accompanied horseriding around the Cabrits National Park trails, on part of WNT Segment 14, & along Purple Turtle Beach. She will also teach you how to ride & has a training ring at her Bell Hall farm near Douglas Bay.

KAYAKING

If you're a pro kayaker, you may be interested in touching base with the **Dominica Canoeing & Kayaking Association** (☎ 767 245 9894; **e** president.dcka@gmail.com). If you're a regular kayaker or enthusiastic amateur, you should get in touch with the **Soufriere Outdoor Center** (☎ 767 616 4848; **e** soufriereoutdoorcenter@gmail.com). Based on the waterfront in Soufriere (page 141), this specialist operator offers guided kayaking, rentals and kayaking lessons. You could also consider participating in their scheduled trips on the 60km **Waitukubuli Sea Trail** they devised.

Although they're primarily geared up for cruise visitors, **Wacky Rollers** (**w** wackyrollers.com) offers river-to-ocean kayaking tours along the Layou River. Kayaking is also possible on Freshwater Lake. You can just turn up at the **Freshwater Lake Facility**, or you could call ahead (☎ 767 245 7061). Otherwise, check with your hotel (some west coast hotels have kayaks) or ask your nearest dive operator (page 85).

RIVER TUBING

River tubing is a popular activity for people visiting Dominica by cruise ship. Stayover visitors may have to either form or join a group – check with the operators. Sit in a large inflatable tube, shoot gentle rapids and drift sedately along a river through Dominica's forest. Life jackets are provided and trained guides are on hand to tell you about the area and to assist in case of difficulties. Operators have vehicles to take you to the entry point and collect you at the exit.

Antours River Tubing ☎ 767 276 5168; **e** antours@yahoo.com; **w** dominicarivertubing.com. This operator offers river tubing to cruise & stayover travellers. Combination packages offer river tubing with other excursions to Emerald Pool, Mero Beach, Trafalgar Falls & more. Age & health restrictions apply. Contact for details & minimum group sizes.

Hibiscus Valley Inn Tours ☎ 767 276 3694; **e** hibiscusvalleyinn@gmail.com; **w** hibiscusvalley.com. Located in Concord along the Pagua River, Hibiscus Valley Inn has its own tour company. A river tubing trip takes around 1–2hrs & you can combine it with a guided rainforest hike & riverside 'cook-up'. This operator offers river tubing to cruise & stayover travellers.

Wacky Rollers ☎ 767 616 8276; **e** wackyrollers@gmail.com; **w** wackyrollers.com. Also firmly established as a cruise ship tour operator, Wacky Rollers offers guided river tubing trips of around 90mins on the Layou River. Age & health restrictions apply. Contact for minimum group sizes.

SCUBA-DIVING

Dominica has a reputation for excellent scuba-diving and is a popular destination for marine biologists, oceanographers and underwater photographers. Conditions in the leeward waters – for example, in the Soufriere Scotts Head Marine Reserve – are usually unchallenging, with little or no current and rarely any surface chop. Visibility is normally excellent and divers can see lots of small marine creatures, fishes and hard and soft corals, as well as spectacular underwater topography. Reef formations are healthy and transform to abyssal drop-offs close to the shoreline. Move into the more exposed water of the channels and conditions are a little tougher, but the rewards are worth it, especially on harder-to-reach sites such as Mountain Top.

Calm inshore conditions also make Dominica a great place to take a certification course or to do an accompanied try-dive. Most dive shops have in-house professional instructors offering a range of recreational and speciality dive courses. All scuba-diving in Dominica must be undertaken via one of the island's dive operators and is usually from a boat. You cannot independently rent tanks and drive yourself to a dive spot as you can in some other Caribbean destinations.

Certified divers must present their certification card. Few operators will ask to see logbooks given the relatively easy diving conditions and the lack of diveable wrecks. If it's been a while since your last dive trip, do the sensible thing and take a short refresher and local orientation dive with an instructor before stepping off a boat. Being able to properly maintain buoyancy is critical given the amount of wall diving here.

Typically, a two-tank boat dive will cost around US$100–120 plus marine reserve fees, if applicable, which are US$2 per diver. A diver refresher usually costs around US$40 and full equipment rental is around US$25 per day.

DIVE SITES

Southern dive sites On the south coast of Dominica there are several dive sites that require either intermediate or advanced diving skills or experience. This is because conditions in the Atlantic can sometimes be a little rough and strong currents occasionally pick up during the dive. Interesting sites along this coast include **Suburbs**, a wall dive that drops to a shelf at around 40m before dropping again into the abyss; **Village**, another dramatic wall dive; and **Condo**, which is a huge volcanic boulder at a depth of 18m. These sites tend to attract larger fish and the occasional migratory pelagic. Visibility is usually excellent here. **Des Fous**, **Mountain Top** and **Lost Horizons** are advanced sites that are only visited by special request due to both location and degree of difficulty.

At the tip of Scotts Head there are some excellent dive sites. **Swiss Cheese** and **Scotts Head Pinnacle** are favourites, with a spectacular swim-through archway at 14m where you will come across lots of blackbar soldierfish. These two sites are part of the same formation and can be combined to make a great first or second dive. At the heart of the Soufriere Scotts Head Marine Reserve is a vast underwater volcanic crater. On the western edge of this crater is a wonderful wall dive called **Cachacrou**, the Kalinago name for the isthmus off Scotts Head village, and just beyond this site is a beautiful wall dive called **Scotts Head Point**. This site starts shallow above a large patch of sand and reef before dropping spectacularly into the crater. Myriads of fish, in particular Creole wrasse, can fill your entire field of vision. On the northern edge of Scotts Head, within the shelter of Soufriere Bay, is the popular **Scotts Head Drop-Off**. This site stretches to the east and west of the mooring and so can be experienced in two different ways. It is a nice, sheltered site that combines the spectacular topography of Dominica's reefs with a wide variety of corals, sponges, fish and many other sea creatures. You'll often see large barracuda patrolling their territory here. The three sea mounts of **Soufriere Pinnacles** on the north of the crater, within sight of the beautiful Soufriere Church, is a nice pinnacle dive where you'll often encounter juvenile hawksbill turtles.

La Sorciere, or Witches Point, lies directly below a tall cliff to the north of Soufriere and is a great wall dive. Turtle sightings are almost guaranteed, both along the wall as well as on the shallow reef above. A short distance to the north of La Sorciere is **L'Abym**, or The Abyss, a dramatic wall dive located very close to the steep cliffs of the shoreline and dropping into the depths of the volcano. There is an interesting dive along the cliff face between La Sorciere and L'Abym; ask your divemaster about it. **Danglebens Pinnacles** is a series of beautiful sea mounts on the northern edge of the Soufriere crater. The site drops to around 40m and is alive with a variety of corals and fish. Hawksbill turtle sightings are also common here. **Danglebens North** is a broad expanse of reef that runs from the shore until it ends in a steep wall. It is a nice dive site with plenty to see in both the shallow areas close to the shore and along the deeper formation to the west.

Coral Gardens is a large flat reef system at a depth of around 15m that connects both Danglebens sites. Nurse sharks are occasionally seen resting on the sand beneath coral shelves around the western edge of this reef formation. **Pointe Guignard** is a small site that runs around a rocky headland. It has some caves and a fun swim-through on the way back to the mooring. To the north of Pointe Guignard is **Champagne Reef**, a large flat formation that extends from the shore until it reaches a drop-off. This site regularly features in destination marketing and has become best known for the submerged fumaroles located close to the shoreline that blow a constant stream of bubbles from the sea floor. To the southwest of the bubbles lie some encrusted cannons and chains, and to the east of the reef system are two small shipwrecks. Operators in the south also tend to visit Champagne Reef as a night dive. **Solomon Reef** is an unusual and rarely visited site located rather incongruously beneath the very ugly quarry face between Loubiere and Pointe Michel. Despite its location, this reef formation is interesting and teeming with a rich variety of marine life.

Central dive sites Central dive site topography is a little less dramatic than in the south, yet there are expansive coral reefs, steep vertical walls and a comparable diversity of marine life. Longshore currents do occasionally come into play as the waters are less protected, but often these dives will suit beginner and intermediate divers alike. Just south of the coastal village of Tarou is **Rodney's Rock**, a volcanic outcrop with a shallow reef at a depth of about 15m. Off the beach at Mero are two sites: **Maggie's Point**, a series of thin coral formations and sand patches, and **Castaways Reef**, a flat expanse of reef formations and sand that goes down to 24m. Both sites are suitable for novices. A little further out is **Barry's Dream**, a nice wall dive that descends to around 35m. Close to the village of Salisbury, off the coast of Grand Savanne, are six dive sites, including four wall dives. **Lauro Reef** is a wall dive that drops quickly to 35m close to the shore; **Brain Coral Reef**, **Nose Reef** and **Whale Shark Reef** are stunning walls that are adorned with barrel sponges, hard and soft corals, and a variety of marine life including seahorses, rays and the occasional nurse shark. North of Grand Savanne is **Coral Gardens North**, a flat reef that starts shallow close to the shore and descends gradually to around 35m.

Northern dive sites The **Nadine** is a wreck site that's accessible to less experienced divers. Sitting upright at around 25m, it's usually good for spotting rays. **Volcano** is a site for advanced divers on the southern edge of Douglas Bay. It's an active volcanic site with fumaroles venting from the seabed. **Shark's Mouth** is a series of large boulders encrusted with corals and huge barrel sponges. The site extends from the shoreline to a depth of 40m. **Anchor Point** is also made up of boulders and extends from the shore. On the western tip of the peninsula is the boulder reef of **One Finger Rock** and to the north of this site, **Five Finger Rock**. On the northern edge of Douglas Bay is the steeply sloping reef of **Douglas Bay Point**. Around the corner in Toucari Bay are the twin sites of **Toucari Bay Point** and **Toucari Caves**, which are often explored as a single dive. Toucari Caves is a series of caverns and swim-throughs at a depth of around 12m. It's an extremely photogenic site with an abundance of coral and fish life. There's also a submerged fumarole. At the tip of the island is **Point Break**, a spectacular though rarely visited wall dive with very strong currents, and only for advanced, experienced divers.

Dive shops

Cabrits Dive Center Picard, Portsmouth; ☎767 276 5373; e info.cabrits@gmail.com; w cabritsdive.com. A French-owned & operated PADI 5-Star Center, Cabrits Dive offers boat diving & certification courses. Enriched air (Nitrox) diving is also available.

Dive Dominica Castle Comfort, Roseau; ☎767 448 2188; e dive@divedominica.com; w divedominica.com. Long-established dive operator offering daily 2-tank boat diving for small & large groups. Also offered are certification courses & enriched air (Nitrox) diving. At the time of writing, Dive Dominica is the service provider for the dive shop at Fort Young Hotel.

Island Dive Operation Purple Turtle Beach; ☎767 277 5673. This small scuba-diving operator offers daily boat diving at the Cabrits & Toucari Bay sites, as well as try-dives & tuition off the beach. Find the office near the PAYS centre on Purple Turtle Beach.

JC Ocean Adventures Cabrits National Park; ☎767 295 0757; w jcoceanadventures.com. Located within Cabrits National Park near the main reception building, JC Ocean Adventures offers boat diving, snorkelling, PADI dive tuition & whale-watching excursions.

Nature Island Dive Soufriere; ☎767 245 6505; e natureislanddive@gmail.com; w natureislanddive.com. This is an experienced & established operator offering daily boat diving & certification courses. It's known for its personal, small group diving, underwater photography & reef conservation.

Sunset Bay Club Coulibistrie; ☎767 446 6522; e sunset@cwdom.dm; w sunsetbayclubhotel.com. Sunset Bay Club operates a PADI dive shop & 2 small boats each capable of carrying up to 10 divers. Equipment rental, dive training & snorkelling trips are also available.

SNORKELLING

There are several accessible reefs around the coast that are good for snorkelling. Shallow formations are alive with hard and soft corals and an abundance of colourful fish. Conditions along the west coast are usually calm with little surface chop, especially in sheltered bays such as those at Soufriere and Toucari. Snorkelling can be undertaken independently from the shore or from a boat with most of the island's scuba-diving operators. Snorkelling with a dive shop is a good idea for first-timers and the inexperienced. Popular sites accessible from the shore include the sheltered drop-off at **Scotts Head**, **Soufriere Pinnacles** and the shallow fumaroles at **Champagne Reef** to the south of Pointe Michel. Snorkelling is good around the **Cabrits** and in **Toucari Bay**. If you charter a water taxi from the Indian River or Purple Turtle Beach, you could head to **Secret Beach** where there is great snorkelling on shallow reef formations. On the east coast, you could try the shallow inshore reef at **Calibishie** (locals often forage for sea urchins and octopus here) and the leeward side of the islet at **Hodges Bay**.

WHALE AND DOLPHIN WATCHING

Sperm whales breed in the waters around Dominica and therefore sightings of these magnificent creatures are common year-round. Pilot and humpback whales are also frequently encountered, as are large playful pods of spinner, Atlantic spotted and bottlenose dolphins. Though dolphins can sometimes be seen from the shore, a boat excursion increases the likelihood of sightings, and close encounters with dolphins and whales are experiences treasured by many. Nevertheless, before opting for a whale-watching trip, you should be aware that there are absolutely no guarantees when it comes to sightings. Operators reasonably claim success rates of over 80% but it's possible for a whale-watching excursion to become a rather pleasant, though perhaps disappointing, boat ride. Be ready for this. Your boat captain and their crew will do their best, but if whales are not around or are travelling fast, it may just be one of those days. Excursions usually take 3–4 hours and include refreshments. Sea conditions along the west coast are usually calm.

An increasing number of operators and luxury resorts are now offering in-water swimming with Dominica's sperm whales. It's a legal requirement to have a government-issued permit to do this (currently, the numbers issued are restricted and expensive), which your tour operator or resort will include in the cost of the trip. Because of this requirement, you must book well in advance. If you feel comfortable with this kind of tour and it's something that you want to do, be sure to confirm prices in advance and check that a government permit has been purchased (ask to see it). If considering such an outing, please bear in mind that we don't know what kind of impact an increase in such tours may have on the whales' wellbeing and behaviour.

Caribbean Deep Sea Fishing Newtown, Roseau; ☎ 767 616 3500. Whale-watching trips on the *Ocean Villa* run out of Newtown near Roseau. This operator also offers coastal cruises & fishing.

Dive Dominica Castle Comfort, Roseau; ☎ 767 448 2188; e dive@divedominica.com; w divedominica.com. Dive Dominica offers scheduled & chartered whale-watching tours. Check the website or call in at the office for the latest schedule. Boats depart at 14.00, tours are 3–4hrs (subject to change).

Dominica Water Tours Scotts Head; ☎ 767 245 5480; w dominicawatertours.com. This operator offers private small boat charters that include whale watching. You can also combine whale watching with other activities such as fishing, snorkelling or coastal tours.

Island Style Fishing Fortune, Roseau; ☎ 767 265 0518; e islandstylefishing@gmail.com; w islandstylefishing.com. With many years of experience, Captain Jerry offers chartered whale-watching tours.

Waitukubuli Adventure Tour Co Roseau; ☎ 767 440 4660; e info@waitukubulitours.com; w waitukubulitours.com. Whale-watching tours are offered by this family-run tour operator. Contact for schedules & charters.

WORK AND STUDY

During the pandemic, the Dominica government devised and launched a programme called **Work In Nature** (w windominica.gov.dm) that was an extended visa programme for people who wanted to get away from populous areas. This programme continues and is an opportunity for digital nomads to work remotely from Dominica for up to 18 months. The programme is available to individuals, families and business teams, and children are permitted to attend local schools during the visa period. Other attractions include an income tax waiver and a duty-free allowance on the importation of personal items. For more information and to apply, check the website.

Dominica attracts academics and research groups from overseas institutions and organisations specialising in natural sciences and anthropology. There's not too much to offer in terms of dedicated facilities, though at the time of writing the **Archbold Tropical Research & Education Centre** at Springfield is being repaired and rehabilitated following the 2017 hurricane. Another option is the **University of the West Indies Open Campus**, located near the Botanic Gardens in Roseau. There's also good dormitory accommodation and meeting facilities at the restored **Fort Shirley garrison** in Cabrits National Park. To find out more and book it, you must contact the Forestry, Wildlife and Parks Division (767 266 5855, 767 266 5852; e nationalparks@dominica.gov.dm).

Part Two

THE GUIDE

4

Roseau and Environs

Roseau is Dominica's capital and its main seaport. It's located on the southwest coast of the island at the foot of a broad river valley (Roseau Valley). The commercial and administrative district of Roseau is to the south of the river, and the predominantly residential neighbourhoods of Pottersville, Goodwill and St Aroment are to the north. At the southern edge of the central district is the old French Quarter, where the original European settlement was built (the Kalinago were already here). To its south is the coastal road to Soufriere and Scotts Head, passing through the crowded neighbourhoods of Newtown and Citronniere. Along the eastern edge of Roseau are the Botanic Gardens and the main road that runs through the Roseau Valley to Laudat, Trafalgar and Wotten Waven.

First impressions of Roseau are generally mixed. It's a small town that, due to space restrictions, is beginning to grow upwards in a rather nebulous architectural style of concrete blocks, moulded columns and balustrades. Although Caribbean colonial architecture certainly carries its share of historical baggage, the prettier older buildings of the capital with their porticoes, fretwork, louvres, verandas and hip roofs are unfortunately diminishing in number. Pavements that are not occupied by parked vehicles and semi-permanent market stalls are in short supply, and on several streets there are large open drainage gutters to negotiate. Recently, it seems that the whole of Roseau is turning into a market, with stalls occupying many pavements (you must walk through them or pass by on the road) selling everything from souvenirs and clothes to perfume and cleaning products. Walk with your head down, dodging vehicles, trying not to fall through gaping holes in the pavement, and the town can certainly feel rather ugly and oppressive. But take your time, walk slowly, look up at the jalousie windows, the ornate fretwork verandas and the mountainous backdrop, and – admittedly, with a little effort – it can be a different town altogether. Roseau needs time to grow on you, however, and travellers are not here long enough to appreciate some of its harder-to-find charm and nuances. But whatever you make of it, Roseau is really not a place for travellers to linger; for the beauty, intrigue and natural attractions of this Caribbean island all lie beyond its pocket-sized and often sweltering capital.

A BRIEF HISTORY OF ROSEAU

Chief Ukale's Kalinago settlement on the flat lands around the river mouth was called **Sairi**. We don't know how long it was there before the Europeans turned up, but we can assume it probably predates the Kalinago (page 15). During their occupation of Dominica in the early 1700s, the French renamed the settlement Roseau after the preponderance of tall river reeds (*Arundo saccharoides*) that still grow wild in the Roseau Valley, especially in the

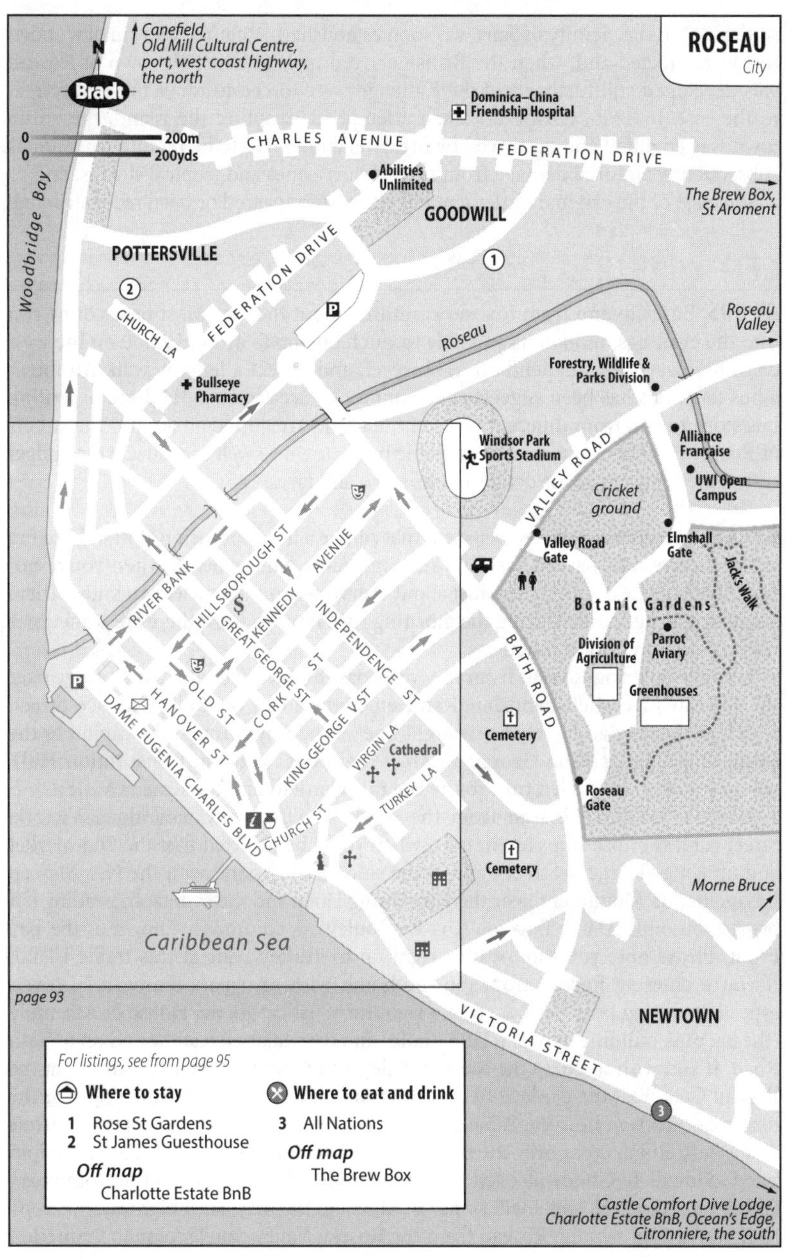

area between Wotten Waven and Trafalgar. The town almost had to endure a third name change during the British occupation when King George III decided to call it Charlotteville after his wife, but unfortunately for the royal couple the name didn't stick and the town reverted to Roseau. Sairi, it seems, was lost forever.

Foresters from Martinique arrived on Dominica's south coast and began building houses alongside the Kalinago in the early 18th century, and a French settlement in the vicinity of Sairi was soon established. A church and small wooden fort were erected and, when the British arrived in 1761, the new town of Roseau was developed still further and the Kalinago were forced to move out and retreat to the east. In 1805, during a French attempt to recapture the island, the entire town was engulfed and destroyed by fire. Everything had to be rebuilt. Roseau has subsequently endured damage from several hurricanes and tropical storms, and so a large part of the original settlement has either disappeared or been reconstructed.

GETTING THERE AND AWAY

BY BUS Buses to and from Roseau run throughout the day. Most buses don't run into the evenings, though it's possible to catch one up to around 21.00 on the west coast highway. Don't depend on it, however, and expect a lengthy wait. Although a bus terminus has been suggested on numerous occasions, at the time of writing bus stops to and from different parts of the island are dotted all around the streets of Roseau, which results in a lot of traffic in the town as well as a puzzle for budget travellers. See page 52 for details of bus stops and fares.

BY CAR Roseau has a one-way system that can be a little confusing at first. Looking at the direction of parked cars and moving traffic will help you when you're not sure. If you make a wrong turn, just about everyone around will let you know. There are no traffic lights, but during the morning rush hour to work there are sometimes traffic police on duty at junctions.

If you're entering Roseau from the west coast highway you'll cross a bridge over the Roseau River (left-hand lane) and enter the town on Independence Street, which is one-way and goes in a straight line all the way through the capital to the south. It will cross King George V Street (before it heads up Constitution Hill), where you can make a left turn to the Botanic Gardens and the Roseau Valley.

If you're entering Roseau from the south, you'll usually pass along Victoria Street (unless cruise ships are in port, when you'll be diverted past the Old Market and up King George V Street), and at the small traffic island with the Neg Mawon Emancipation Monument near the Fort Young Hotel and the cenotaph, heading left brings you on to Dame Eugenia Charles Boulevard, commonly known as the Bay Front. Please note you cannot turn right on to Turkey Lane at this traffic island. If you're entering Roseau from the south and wish to bypass the heart of town, especially during busy periods, take a right turn just before the House of Assembly (the big pink building opposite DBS Radio) and then take a left at the end on to Bath Road. If you wish to go up the Roseau Valley, head into the Botanic Gardens at the Roseau Gate. Exit the gardens to the left at the Elmshall Gate and turn right at the next road junction near the Alliance Française. If you wish to head north, continue along Bath Road, cross over the bridge, take a right at the traffic island and go up into Goodwill. In Goodwill, a left turn at the traffic island in front of the Dominica–China Friendship Hospital will bring you down to the west coast highway.

If you're approaching Roseau from the Roseau Valley, you'll come to a junction just over the Roseau River bridge. Left will take you past the Alliance Française and UWI Campus into the Botanic Gardens via the Elmshall Gate, where you can bypass Roseau for the south (this is also a good way of getting back to Fort Young – just take a right when you see the DBS Radio station on Victoria Street). A right turn will take you past the Forestry, Wildlife and Parks Division office and around the back of Windsor Park Stadium to the bridge that leads up to Goodwill. This is a good way of bypassing the heart of the capital if you're heading north along the west coast highway. Straight on at the initial Valley Road junction brings you to the top of King George V Street (you should see the Police Headquarters) where you must turn right on to Bath Road.

Great George Street is one-way and runs northwest out of town over the Roseau River. Once across the bridge, an immediate left turn will get you on to the west coast highway and straight on will take you to Federation Drive, Goodwill, the hospital and St Aroment. A fourth bridge, often referred to as the 'Chinese Bridge',

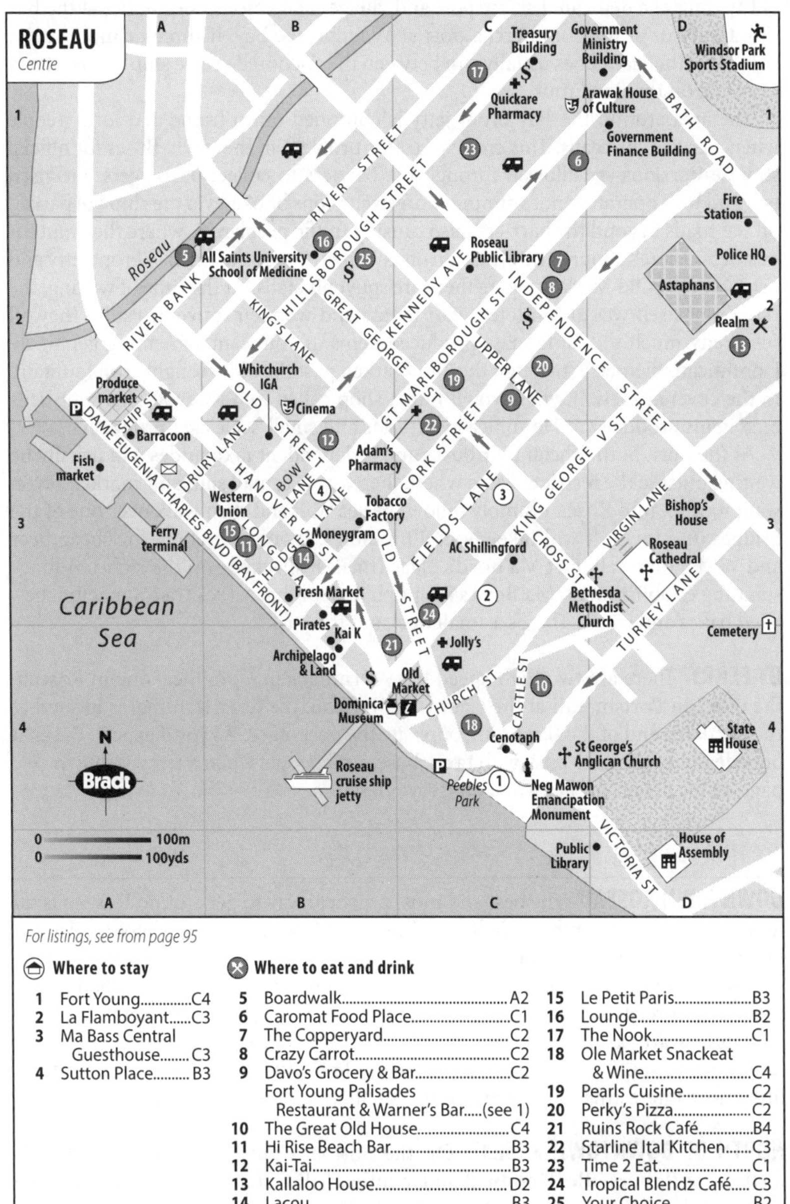

crosses the Roseau River at the northern end of Hanover Street by the New Market. You can cross it from Roseau, heading north, and you'll be on the west coast highway. You can also cross it from the north, but the one-way system will send you up along River Bank and around in circles unless you know the back streets, where it's possible to get through to the Bay Front.

BY CRUISE SHIP Roseau is currently Dominica's main cruise ship port (there's always talk of a dedicated cruise port and village) and vessels dock either at the Bay Front jetty or at the commercial port at Woodbridge Bay. If three or more cruise ships call, then launches usually run between the anchored cruise ship and the ferry terminal on the Bay Front.

The area around the Bay Front jetty is cordoned off to traffic and local people when a cruise ship calls. This creates a traffic problem in the town. Buses for official shore excursions are allowed through the barriers to collect passengers. Licensed taxi and tour operators not running shore excursions booked via the ship are parked on the roads beyond the barriers (also causing traffic problems), where they tout for business. There's a tourist information office directly opposite the Bay Front jetty and behind it, the Old Market, where there are souvenir stalls. At the time of writing, the Bay Front itself was also littered with tented and wooden souvenir stalls. They all sell pretty much the same mass-produced items. If you want something genuinely Dominican, then walk through the Old Market, past the old wrought-iron fountain, to the covered section where you'll find a shop called Zeb Kweyol. This shop sells only items produced in Dominica by artisans and small-scale agri-producers.

At the port, both official tour buses and independent taxi guides will usually be waiting outside the restricted area where there's also a small souvenir market. If you want to walk into Roseau, simply follow the sea wall and then walk over one of the bridges into town. It will take about 20 minutes. If you're looking for cheap beer and Wi-Fi, then call in at Ma Boyd's place (the last snackette on the right). A long-standing establishment, Ma Boyd's is a popular spot that serves traditional lunches, fried bakes and so on. There's a small deck out the back.

BY FERRY There are two high-speed ferry terminals in Dominica: one in Roseau, the other in Portsmouth at the Cabrits. In Roseau, the ferry terminal is located at the northern end of the Bay Front, opposite the post office. As you'd expect, the area outside the terminal is busy with taxis, buses and people when a ferry is due in. See page 43 for details of the two main ferry operators.

ORIENTATION AND GETTING AROUND

DOWNTOWN ROSEAU The best and most practical way to get around Roseau is on foot, but even that can be a challenge. The town is small and nowhere is very far, but a lack of proper footpaths, holes, extended porticoes and open gutters make walking quite troublesome, and it's important to watch out for traffic when you're inevitably forced on to the roads. Finding your way around the central area is straightforward, as the layout is a grid system with all roads running in a straight line north to south or east to west. In the old French Quarter, the road layout is a little more interesting, but the area is too small for you to get seriously lost.

NORTH OF DOWNTOWN ROSEAU On the northern outskirts of Roseau are the districts of **Pottersville**, **Goodwill** and, a little further along the coast, beyond the port and the cliffs, **Canefield**. Above Goodwill, at the end of Federation Drive, is

St Aroment. These areas are mostly residential, interspersed with small businesses and the occasional guesthouse. The Dominica–China Friendship Hospital is on Federation Drive in Goodwill.

Canefield used to be one of the largest sugar-and-lime producing estates on the island. Some of the original buildings were restored, and in 1988 the **Old Mill Cultural Centre** was opened, housing the offices of Dominica's Cultural Division. The centre hosts a theatre, art gallery and dance studio. It's a good place to call in and find out about events that may be taking place during your stay.

SOUTH OF DOWNTOWN ROSEAU To the south of Roseau along the coastal road are the residential communities of **Newtown** and **Citronniere**. Life in Newtown seems to revolve around the main thoroughfare, Victoria Street, which can be a lively place, especially in the evenings when locals can be seen sitting out on their stoops, discussing local affairs, listening to music, braiding hair, spilling drunkenly into the road, or just watching the world go by and shouting out to people they recognise in passing vehicles. The playing field on the northern edge of the two joined-up communities is Newtown Savannah, where football matches are played and live music events are occasionally hosted.

WHERE TO STAY

If you're keen on staying in or around Roseau, options are rather limited. On online booking sites, you'll find quite a lot of budget accommodation in Roseau – rooms and apartments mostly – and in the more affluent areas such as Morne Daniel near Canefield, there are villas to rent. It all depends on your preference and what you're in Dominica to do, of course, but if you're looking at Roseau, you could also consider accommodation in the Roseau Valley and the southern villages.

Fort Young Hotel [93 C4] (100 rooms) Victoria St; 767 448 5000; e sales@fortyounghotel.com; w fortyounghotel.com. For many years Dominica's best-known resort & business hotel, & still a very popular place to stay on the island, Fort Young has stylish oceanfront rooms & suites, all with AC, en-suite bathrooms, veranda, telephone, TV & Wi-Fi. Suites also have living areas & kitchenettes. The hotel has 2 restaurants & bars, there's a spa, gym, duty-free shopping, private jetty, infinity pool, sun terrace & jacuzzi. The hotel also has an activities desk & fully kitted-out dive shop (scuba-diving in partnership with Dive Dominica). All-inclusive packages are available (Fort Young's tagline is 'island-included resort'). At the time of writing, the hotel was undergoing refurbishment & development with new rooms coming online (the total will be 100). **$$$$–$$$$$**

Charlotte Estate BnB [map, page 91] (5 rooms) Newtown; 767 317 1343; e charlotteestatebnb@gmail.com; w charlotteestatebnb.com. Incongruously located behind the hustle & bustle of the Newtown main drag, this fully refurbished former estate house is an interesting place to stay. The 3 rooms in the main house are stylish & modern in design but also retain traditional colonial architectural features. They have large private bathrooms, AC, ceiling fans & mosquito nets. The 2 detached cottage rooms are more modern & have private bathrooms. There's a large communal room, veranda & extensive gardens containing former estate ruins. **$$$**

Sutton Place Hotel [93 B3] (8 rooms) Old St; 767 449 8700; e sutton2@cwdom.dm. Aimed primarily at the business traveller though suitable for anyone looking for a base in Roseau, Sutton Place is an historic hotel in the heart of the capital with 5 standard rooms & 3 suites. All rooms have en-suite bathrooms, AC, TV & Wi-Fi. Rooms are traditionally decorated, some with 4-poster beds. Suites have a living area, dining table & kitchenette. B/fast is usually included in the price. The hotel is well managed & is a pleasant place to stay if you want to be downtown. **$$$**

La Flamboyant Hotel [93 C3] (16 rooms) 22 King George V St; 767 440 7190, 767

TIMBO'S

At the time of writing, there's a proposed CBI-funded hotel development project on Victoria Street between downtown Roseau and Newtown. The description is that of a high-rise luxury hotel aimed at the business and leisure market. Known as Timbo's, it currently doesn't have a website, but it may be worth a Google if this is of interest to you.

245 1040; e laflamboyanthotel@gmail.com; w laflamboyanthotel.dm. La Flamboyant is a colourful business-style hotel located in downtown Roseau. Its standard rooms have en-suite bathroom, AC, TV & Wi-Fi. Its executive rooms also have fridge & business facilities. There's a bar & restaurant serving both traditional Creole & international food, & in the basement there's a conference room. If you're coming for Carnival, book a balcony room – it's a great location to watch the street parade. Unfussy & somewhat rudimentary, La Flamboyant is a clean & tidy place to stay for travellers on a budget, especially during the festive seasons. **$$**

Rose St Gardens [map, page 91] (4 rooms, 1 suite) Rose St, Goodwill; ☎ 767 316 6000; w rosestreetgardens.com. This is charming & artistic accommodation in the Roseau suburb of Goodwill. Rooms have AC, private bathroom, Wi-Fi & TV. There's a delightful garden terrace with views over Roseau. **$–$$**

St James Guesthouse [map, page 91] (14 rooms) Church Ln, Goodwill; ☎ 767 448 7170; e stjamesguesthouse@hotmail.com; w stjamesdominica.com. Owned & managed by the lovely Carol & Phil, this is a great budget accommodation choice within easy walking distance of downtown Roseau. All rooms have AC, private bathroom, TV & Wi-Fi. Some rooms also have a mini fridge, night safe & kettle. There's a restaurant & bar where guests can enjoy continental b/fast (included) & dinner by reservation. Tours, airport & ferry shuttles can be organised. **$–$$**

Ma Bass Central Guesthouse [93 C3] (12 rooms) Fields Ln; ☎ 767 448 2999, 767 275 1997. A basic but clean & long-established guesthouse down a quiet lane just off Independence St. Most rooms have fans, shared bathroom & kitchen facilities. Verandas overlook the rooftops of the town with nice views of mountains & sea. This is a decent option for travellers on a limited budget who don't mind sharing facilities. **$**

WHERE TO EAT AND DRINK

CREOLE AND INTERNATIONAL DINING

The Great Old House [93 C4] Castle St; ☎ 767 440 7549; ⏲ 18.00–22.00 Mon–Sat. A favourite with locals & visitors, The Great Old House combines a high standard of traditional Caribbean cooking with international influences. Fish & seafood dishes are usually very good. **$$–$$$**

Lacou [93 B3] Hodges Ln; ☎ 767 613 3017; ⏲ noon–21.00 Wed–Sat. Lacou is a fine-dining restaurant within the restored Melrose House, an historic 18th-century stone building in the heart of Roseau. Showcasing local producers, dishes are a fusion of Dominica, France & Italy. Try the ceviche with daikon & watermelon radish, or the cooked-overnight goat shoulder. **$$–$$$**

Fort Young Palisades Restaurant & Warner's Bar [93 C4] Bay Front; ☎ 767 448 5000; ⏲ Palisades: for b/fast & lunch daily, dinner Wed–Sat; Warner's: for b/fast, lunch & dinner daily. Fort Young's stylish Palisades Restaurant is deck-style with sea views. Cuisine is a combination of Creole & international dishes – including vegetarian & vegan options. The less formal Warner's Bar is also sea-facing & offers a good selection of affordable b/fast, lunch/bites & dinner dishes that include salads, burgers, roti & pizza. Palisades **$$–$$$**, Warner's **$–$$**

The Copperyard [93 C2] Great Marlborough St; ☎ 767 245 1947; ⏲ 10.00–18.00 Mon–Sat. A great place for lunch in the capital, The Copperyard serves a modern take on traditional Creole lunches. Try the stewed chicken with coconut ginger sauce or the fish roti. It's all very good here. **$**

Le Petit Paris [93 B3] Bay Front; ☎ 767 275 7777; ⏲ 08.30–18.00 Mon–Wed, 08.30–21.00 Thu–Fri, 08.30-17.00 Sat. Located at the northern end of the Bay Front, near the ferry terminal, Le Petit Paris is a French café & restaurant as well as a bakery & take-out. From coffee, croissants, quiche & croque monsieur to pizza, burger, fish & chips & pasta, there's a lot of good stuff here & it's stood the test of time. Vegetarian options are available & there are some dreamy desserts. $

CARIBBEAN LUNCHES

If you fancy tackling a full-on traditional Caribbean lunch (page 56), these places are worth a try.

Kallaloo House [93 D2] King George V St; 767 615 7549; lunchtime only Mon–Sat. Hearty, high-quality traditional Caribbean lunches can be enjoyed out on the veranda or pre-ordered as a take-out. Meat or fish with large helpings of rice & *provisions*; roti is also a speciality. Come hungry. $

Pearls Cuisine [93 C2] Great Marlborough St; 767 613 8707; 08.00–15.00 Mon–Sat. Long-established restaurant & caterer offering good local b/fast & lunch. $

Time 2 Eat [93 C1] Hillsborough St; 767 285 0744; 08.00–16.00 Mon–Fri. Serving traditional b/fast & lunches, with specialities such as goat water & *souse* (pickled pig trotter). $

Your Choice Restaurant [93 B2] Hillsborough St; 767 614 1167; b/fast & lunch Mon–Sat. Large helpings of traditional Caribbean food. Come hungry. $

VEGETARIAN AND VEGAN

Starline Ital Kitchen [93 C3] Cork St; 767 265 3683; f; 08.00–16.00 Mon–Sat. Describing itself as a plant-based restaurant, Starline serves b/fast, snacks & lunch with fresh fruit juices, bush teas, cocoa teas & coffee. Ackras, stuffed bakes, veggie wraps & sandwiches, lunches & stews are just some of the offerings at this popular eatery. Check the Facebook page for occasional live music events. $

NOTEWORTHY BARS, CAFÉS AND SNACKETTES

Roseau's bars & snackettes come & go but, at the time of writing, here are several that I like. Some offer simple b/fasts while most usually focus on traditional lunches. All of it is inexpensive. Just turn up & see what's cooking – though note that by 14.00 lunches are usually sold out. Some bars are popular hangouts, especially on Fri nights & at the end of the month when people get paid. Opening times are fluid. Most are generally open all day and into the evening – unless stated otherwise. Roseau isn't a dangerous place at night, but it's prudent not to be out drinking alone.

All Nations [map, page 91] Victoria St, Newtown; eves only, usually from 18.00, earlier on Sat. Good for fish & chips. Located near Newtown Savannah.

Boardwalk [93 A2] River Bank. A covered arcade by the Portsmouth bus stop with several small snackettes selling a range of cheap eats.

The Brew Box [map, page 91] Federation Dr, Goodwill; 11.00–eve Tue–Sat. Located above BloomBox Garden Centre, this popular bistro-style bar offers drinks, paninis, salads & occasional live music. Nice views of Roseau.

Caromat Food Place [93 C1] Kennedy Av. Great stuffed bakes & usually a selection of fresh juices. Also good for lunch. Located near the Gov Finance Building.

Crazy Carrot [93 C2]Independence St. Serves a wide selection of healthy fruit juices & smoothies to order.

Davo's Grocery & Bar [93 C2] Upper Ln. An established & popular downtown bar, especially on Fri after work when most people spill on to the street. Snacks & BBQ available. Davo's is also a grocery selling essentials.

Hi Rise Beach Bar [93 B3] Bay Front. Located near Le Petit Paris & overlooking the Bay Front, this

REALM

As this book went to press, a swanky new bar and restaurant (at least that's how the promo material portrayed it) was being constructed on King George V Street, opposite the Astaphans department store. Called Realm, it certainly looks like one to keep an eye out for when you visit.

beach-themed bar & eatery is popular with cruise ship visitors.
Kai-Tai [93 B3] Old St. Located opposite Courts department store, this is a popular music & party venue, also serving food.
Lounge [93 B2] Hillsborough St; 🕘 eves only. Hard to spot (the sign is tiny), Lounge is a courtyard bar located behind buildings on Hillsborough St between Gt George St & Independence St.
The Nook [93 C1] Hillsborough St. Café & wine bar serving drinks, pastries, soups & other snacks.
Ole Market Snackeat & Wine [93 C4] Old St. Hole-in-the-wall bar & snackette near the Old Market serving b/fast, traditional lunches & sandwiches. The stuffed bakes are great.
Perky's Pizza [93 C2] Cork St. Yep, pizza! & pretty good.
Ruins Rock Café [93 B4] King George V St. Popular with the cruise ship crowd as it's close to the jetty, this colourful & lively bar also sells fast food-style eats.
Tropical Blendz Café [93 C3] Old St. Serving b/fast & lunch, including wraps, salads, coffee, cocoa & herbal teas, local juices & smoothies. Hard to spot. Look for the blackboard outside, head up the stairs & through the clothing boutique!

SHOPPING

Much to the chagrin of many day-trippers, Roseau has no air-conditioned malls stuffed with designer boutiques and tech stores. It's not really a place you go shopping for pleasure, it's where you look to buy what you need, do business and banking, deal with red tape and pay bills. Instead of malls, Roseau's small shops are spread all around and in every corner of the town – and, with a bit of luck and the moon in the right phase, some of them may even have what you're looking for. But you should never count on it!

On every street, it seems, there are Chinese-owned shops selling everything from cheap shoes, clothes and bags to kitchenware, children's toys and plant pots. There's also an abundance of beauty salons, barber shops, bakeries, bars and snackettes. Several supermarkets sell a decent range of foodstuffs – much of it imported – and the produce market is good for fruits and vegetables (Friday afternoons and Saturday mornings are best). Pharmacies are usually well stocked, and there are some small hardware, electronics, computer and phone shops that cover the basics. Effective and efficient shopping requires good knowledge of the town – something that can take years – a lot of walking and even more patience. Here are some suggestions.

SUPERMARKETS

AC Shillingford [93 C3] King George V St. Supermarket located inside a traditional old building on the cnr of King George V St & Cross St. Basic food items & household essentials.
Astaphans [93 D2] King George V St. Department store upstairs, supermarket downstairs. There's a dedicated car park that you get to via the final left-hand turn off Independence St before you reach King George V St.
Fresh Market [93 B3] Cnr Bay Front & Cork St. Supermarket downstairs, pharmacy upstairs.
S Mart Goodwill. Supermarket located on the west coast highway between downtown Roseau & the port. Parking.
Whitchurch IGA [93 B3] Old St. Supermarket with popular deli & cakes counter.

LOCAL PRODUCTS

Abilities Unlimited [map, page 91] Federation Dr. Workshop for the blind selling a range of basketware. Located near the Dominica–China Friendship Hospital.
Zeb Kweyol [93 C4] Old Market (covered section). Only stocks items made in Dominica. The focus is on agri-products but there's also a selection of crafts.

BOUTIQUES, ALCOHOL AND DUTY FREE

Archipelago & Land [93 B4] Bay Front. Sharing the same building with access from the Bay Front. Land sells leatherwares, Archipelago sells wines, spirits & other duty-free items.
Jewellers International [93 C4] Fort Young Hotel. Duty-free jeweller.

LOCAL PRODUCTS

Try to support Dominica's cottage industries and buy local products if you can (you'll have to search beyond the souvenir stalls). By no means a comprehensive list, here is a selection that's worth looking out for when you go shopping. You'll find some of these and other products at the big supermarkets and souvenir or duty-free shops. One place worth seeking out is **Zeb Kweyol**, which is in the covered section of the Old Market.

Aunty's Agro Processing Hot pepper sauce & seasoning pepper sauce.
Bee Natural Infused beeswax balms & deodorants.
Belfast Estate Blended rum including popular brands such as Soca, Bois Bandé (BB) & Red Cap.
Busy's Pure Honey Honey made near the village of Colihaut.
Café Local Arabica coffee from the village of Giraudel.
Coal Pot Products Soaps, shampoo, massage oils, pepper sauce & coffee from Grand Bay.
Hey Mama Products Wildcrafted (foraged) sea moss.
Jaydees Naturals Natural skin & hair products.
Lapawi Farms Cassava flour, toloma, cocoa sticks & more.
Macoucherie Rum Distillery Blended Macoucherie Rum.
Natural Botanicals Soaps & shampoo made from natural products.
Nature Blends Essential oils.
Nature Farms Moringa leaf, turmeric & *bois bandé* powder.
Nibco Rum punch & pepper sauce.
Wellzone Natural handmade soaps & other personal hygiene products.

Kai K [93 B4] Bay Front. Clothes boutique with an upmarket selection.

Pirates [93 B3] Long Ln. Good range of wines & spirits plus a selection of standard duty-free items.

OTHER PRACTICALITIES

MONEY AND BANKS Most shops and vendors will also accept US dollars. Additionally, most shops and restaurants in town will accept debit and credit cards but do check first; far fewer will accept American Express cards. If you pay in US dollars, your change will usually be in local currency.

Banks usually open between **08.00 and 14.00 Monday–Thursday** and **08.00–16.00 Friday**. All have ATMs that you can use to get local currency only (Eastern Caribbean dollars). Banks will also exchange currency inside.

National Bank of Dominica [93 C1] Hillsborough St. There are also branches on Bay Front in Roseau [93 B4] & Imperial Rd in Canefield. Additional ATMs are on King George V St & Old St (outside Whitchurch IGA).

Republic Bank [93 B2] Hillsborough St

MEDICAL The **Dominica–China Friendship Hospital** is the island's main medical facility and is located on Federation Drive in Goodwill. The hospital has a 24-hour casualty unit. For assistance: 767 266 2000.

Roseau's **pharmacies** are usually well stocked and are open six days a week 08.00–17.00 Monday–Friday and (usually) 08.00–14.30 Saturday. For help on Sundays, you must contact or visit the hospital. If you're taking medication, it's a good idea to bring enough of it with you. Here are some good pharmacies in Roseau.

Adam's Pharmacy [93 C2] Gt Marlborough St
Bullseye Pharmacy [map, page 91] Federation Dr, Goodwill
Jolly's [93 C4] King George V St
Quickare Pharmacy [93 C1] Hillsborough St

SAFETY Roseau is small and generally safe. You may get asked for money but it's never with malice.

Walking the streets of Roseau late at night is when you're most likely to encounter any kind of threat, though it's uncommon. If it does happen, focus on getting through it rather than fighting back. Report the incident to your hotel (get them to contact the police immediately). It's very important that you report incidents otherwise the problem goes unrecorded and someone else may become a victim. Don't expect to see uniformed policemen on the beat at night. It simply doesn't happen here.

POST OFFICE The main post office [93 A3] is at the northern end of the Bay Front (Dame Eugenia Charles Boulevard), opposite the Roseau ferry terminal, and is open 08.00–17.00 Monday, 08.00–16.00 Tuesday–Friday. The postal service is unreliable. Post can take weeks, even months, or it simply doesn't turn up at all. If you must send something important either from or to Dominica, use one of the courier companies instead.

PUBLIC TOILETS There are two public toilets in Roseau. One is located at the side of the tourist information building on the Bay Front [93 C4], just near the Old Market. The other is located just inside the Valley Road gate of the Botanic Gardens. You'll need EC$1.

WHAT TO SEE AND DO

CENTRAL ROSEAU Along the riverbank, at the northern tip of the Bay Front, is the main **produce market** [93 A2]. Here, vendors sell fresh fruit and vegetables, *ground provisions*, flowers, seasonings, meat and poultry. The market is open every day except Sunday, but most farmers and hucksters arrive to sell their goods on Friday and Saturday. From early in the morning, the Saturday market in Roseau is a lively affair, in fact almost a social occasion, where people buy and sell and meet up and chat with friends. Around the margins of the market, Haitian women sell produce in boxes and crates, and along the riverbank you can often buy fish, jelly coconuts and even barbecue coals. In the covered areas you'll find flowers, clothing, local produce, occasionally crafts, a meat market and a smattering of bars and simple eateries. During the Creole and Independence period in October, stallholders usually wear traditional madras (page 30).

It's the largest market in Dominica and it's worth a visit. The variety of produce isn't especially diverse and vendors tend to sell the same things at the same prices. If you want to take photos, make sure you ask for permission first. Market vendors are sensitive about photography and if you don't ask permission, verbal altercations can ensue.

Located on the western edge of the New Market along the Bay Front is the Roseau **fish market** [93 A3]. It's busiest on Saturdays though if there's an excess of fish being caught, it can be busy all week. You tend to see the same fish here: tuna, mahi-mahi,

A WALK AROUND HISTORIC ROSEAU

This route will take between 2 and 3 hours at a leisurely pace. Take plenty of water – Roseau is hot.

Start in front of the Roseau cruise ship jetty facing the old post office building, now home to the tourist information centre and Dominica Museum. Take the road between the museum and the National Bank of Dominica and head northeast away from the sea up King George V Street. To your right is the Old Market. Continue straight on up King George V Street, taking note of the traditional architecture of the upper floors. At the junction with Great George Street, on your left, is Norwood House, one of the last surviving 19th-century town houses built almost entirely of wood. Continue along King George V Street right up to the junction with Bath Road. The Police Headquarters building will be on your left.

Straight ahead is Valley Road, gateway to the Roseau Valley. A short distance up this road on the right is an entrance to the Botanic Gardens (Valley Road Gate). Enter the gardens and walk alongside the cricket ground, which should be on your left. At the intersection, go left and then look for the sign to Jack's Walk, which will be on your right. Climb the steep footpath to the top of Morne Bruce and look out across the town from the viewpoint. Return down Jack's Walk. At the bottom, take a left and then a right down the steps. The path emerges by the parrot aviary where, despite the fencing and restricted views, it's possible to see sisserou parrots.

From the aviary, head left at the junction and follow the path past the fallen giant baobab tree and the crushed school bus, and then exit the gardens through the Roseau Gate. Walk straight ahead at the road junction. Be careful because there's no footpath here. The Catholic cemetery is on your left. Take the second road on the left. This is Virgin Lane and it runs past the Bishop's House and main entrance of Roseau Cathedral. Continue along Virgin Lane to the junction. The Bethesda Methodist Church is on your left. Turn left and then take the second right along Turkey Lane and walk to the end. At the junction with the small traffic island, turn left. The ruined St George's Anglican Church is on your left-hand side followed by the grounds of the State House and then the House of Assembly. Cross the road and turn full circle, heading back towards town. The Public Library is on your left followed by the Fort Young Hotel. On the north side of Fort Young is Peebles Park with its flamboyant trees and bandstand. Cross the road to the cenotaph. On the far side of the cenotaph is the pretty Fort Lane. Walk down this old, cobbled street. At the bottom of Fort Lane turn left on Church Street and head back to the Old Market and the Bay Front, where your walk began.

occasionally marlin, and sometimes small reef fish. You'll hardly ever see lobster – it's usually sold directly to hotels and restaurants – and even inshore fish such as snapper are uncommon at the market. Regardless of the variety, it's always interesting to see fish being chopped up with a wooden mallet and large machete!

A little further along the Bay Front is the Roseau **ferry terminal** [93 A3] where you can catch the high-speed catamaran service that operates between Guadeloupe, Dominica, Martinique and St Lucia (page 43). The Roseau City Council buildings, located opposite the fisheries complex and the ferry terminal, are some of the oldest still standing in the town. This structure was once the town's **barracoon** [93 A3], where enslaved Africans were temporarily barracked before being auctioned in the small courtyard beyond the archway on the south side of the building. The style of the barracoon is similar to those constructed on the West African coast to house the enslaved prior to boarding ships for the West Indies. At the time of writing, the front of the barracoon building is in a rather dilapidated state of repair.

To the south of the Roseau City Council buildings and across from the ferry terminal is the main **post office** [93 A3]. From here the Bay Front (officially, Dame Eugenia Charles Boulevard) runs along the shore to the Fort Young Hotel at its southern tip. Along the Bay Front there are a couple of bars and cafés, boutiques, a supermarket and duty-free shops, the tourist information building and the Dominica Museum. In the centre of the Bay Front is the Registry and Court House. The Bay Front is also the location of the Roseau **cruise ship jetty** [93 B4].

From the Bay Front, Roseau moves inland in blocks of shops, eateries, banks and other businesses. Most shops are quite small and functional with little to attract visitors who are accustomed to large shopping malls and a plentiful supply of just about everything. There is an increasing number of cheap Chinese import shops, all of which seem to sell pretty much the same items.

Windsor Park Sports Stadium [93 D1] is located on Bath Road at the end of Kennedy Avenue. It was funded by the People's Republic of China and constructed around the clock by an imported workforce in 2008. With a capacity of around 12,000 spectators, the stadium hosts occasional football and cricket matches as well as cultural and music events in the forecourt. The annual World Creole Music Festival takes place here.

KING GEORGE V STREET AND THE FRENCH QUARTER King George V Street runs in a straight line from the Bay Front right across the town to the entrance of the Roseau Valley. South of King George V Street is the area where French settlers developed a small village in the early 18th century. Referred to these days as the French Quarter, this area retains the character of a more historic Roseau which, despite the impact of hurricanes and conflagration, is still palpable when walking its meandering streets.

King George V Street is one of Roseau's busier thoroughfares. It can be tricky to negotiate as a combination of parked vehicles and street vendors clog the pavements, often forcing you into the road. At varying times of the day it's busy with either traffic, shoppers, street vendors or schoolchildren, and at lunchtimes all of them at once. The eastern end is dominated by the Astaphans department store and the rather foreboding battleship-grey Police Headquarters building. To the west of the junction with Independence Street there are several small shops, restaurants, snackettes and bars located in old buildings of stone and wood and displaying some enduring examples of Caribbean colonial architecture. Upper-floor jalousie-style windows are framed by heavy wooden shutters and iron and wooden verandas are decorated with ornate fretwork. To appreciate this street from an architectural perspective you must walk it looking up, rather than down, for that is where you will see these interesting features and get a better feel for the colonial history of the island's capital.

At the western end of King George V Street is the **Old Market** [93 C4]. This used to be a place where produce and other wares were traded, where the enslaved were auctioned, and where public executions of captured runaways were carried out, particularly during the early 1800s under the tyrannical governorship of

SHAPE

The Society for Historic Architectural Preservation and Enhancement is a non-profit group whose aim is to highlight the importance of the island's historic buildings and the application of time-honoured architectural styles and building methods. Many of the island's older wooden buildings, known as *ti kai*, survived the 2017 hurricane. Their simple architectural style is based on a long history of learning that goes back to the island's Amerindian settlers. Developing methods to construct shelters that could withstand tropical storms and hurricanes yet allow breezes to flow through to keep occupants cool, has formed the basis of traditional architectural design. Some of that knowledge, as well as the cultural design aspects of historic buildings, is being lost. SHAPE has a Facebook and Instagram page. You can also email them for more information or to offer support at e shapedomnik@gmail.com. Also, there's an interesting book on Dominica's *ti kai* published by Papillote Press (w papillotepress.co.uk).

Major General Robert Ainslie (page 17). Today, in rather stark contrast, it hosts a souvenir market that's predominantly patronised by cruise ship tourists. I can't help thinking that this historic market square could be better utilised. It's interesting to note how the old streets laid by the French settlers radiate out from this central point. King George V Street goes straight up to the Roseau Valley, Hanover Street goes in a straight line to the Roseau River and Church Street leads to Roseau Cathedral. Located within the Old Market Square is a cast-iron fountain where a well once stood, and the Dawbiney hucksters shelter which is still used today. The well was abandoned when the water was believed to have been tainted by the blood of so many of the island's captured Maroons who were executed here. Between the Old Market and the Bay Front is the town's former post office building, constructed in 1810. Today it houses the **tourist information** office [93 C4] (🕘 08.00–16.00 Mon–Fri, & at w/ends for cruise ships) on the ground floor and the **Dominica Museum** above (🕘 09.00–16.00 Mon–Fri; entrance fee US$3). The entrance to the museum is up a flight of steps on the Bay Front side of the building. The museum is a rather claustrophobic space with interesting artefacts and artworks. Although the content is engaging, the museum would certainly benefit from an experienced curator to improve its displays. Nevertheless, it's worth popping in (note, there's also a small museum at the Old Mill Cultural Centre in Canefield; page 95).

At the southern tip of Bay Front is **Fort Young** [93 C4]. On a slightly elevated position above the original French settlement, a small wooden fort was constructed in 1720 to protect Roseau's inhabitants from attack. A sturdier stone structure was built in 1770 by Sir William Young, the first British governor of Dominica. Between 1778 and 1805 the French attempted to recapture the island from the British and the fort was the scene of much fighting. It was as a direct result of this warfare that in 1805 the settlement of Roseau caught fire and was razed to the ground. From the 1850s the fort was used as a police station and a hundred years later, in 1964, it was converted into a hotel. The hotel had to be rebuilt following Hurricane David 15 years later and, at the time of writing, is undergoing further reconstruction and development following Hurricane Maria in 2017. The original battlements and ramparts of the fort can still be seen beneath and around its modern additions.

Next to the Fort Young Hotel is **Peebles Park** [93 C4] which, with its bandstand, trees and benches, is an historic and important little oasis of greenery in a town where real estate is at a premium. The space used to be a pasture for horses and donkeys when people came to market and was laid out as a park in 1928. A children's playground has recently been added. On the small enclosed triangular

ROSEAU CATHEDRAL

In all likelihood the first Catholic church in Roseau was an open-sided wooden hut with a roof made of river reeds, and it would have been in such an inauspicious setting that Bishop Dom Gervaise administered the sacrament of confirmation to French foresters in 1727. French settlers arriving from Martinique established themselves along the south coast and began to concentrate in the Kalinago village of Sairi. In 1730 Father Guillaume Martel arrived and began work on a solid timber church for his growing congregation. The new church had a stone floor and was approximately 12m long by 5m wide. Located in the same area as the present cathedral, this timber structure survived for almost a hundred years until it was destroyed by a hurricane in 1816. It was not until 24 years later that a replacement was completed, only for everyone to decide it was far too small. Emancipation meant that former enslaved estate workers were now also free to worship in Roseau's church, and so a programme of enlargement began that didn't reach its conclusion until around a hundred years later.

In 1855 the main steeple was erected and in 1865 the Kalinago offered a hand by cutting and transporting timber from the *simaruba* tree, from the northeast down to Roseau. For around three months, the Kalinago camped on the edge of town at night and installed a wooden ceiling in the cathedral by day. Around that time a huge stone pulpit carved by prisoners in the notorious Devil's Island penal colony arrived in Roseau from Cayenne in French Guiana. In 1873 the Chapel of St Joseph was constructed on the southeast corner with a crypt beneath it for deceased bishops and priests, and in 1878 Father Auguste Fort extended the aisles and had the east steeple built. Another hurricane inflicted considerable damage in 1883, but in its aftermath, funds were collected to repair it along with other damaged churches around the island. It was during this period that the stained-glass windows were added. In 1902 new stone pillars were installed and new pews carved, and in 1916 the west steeple was added, the stones for which came from the old church at Pointe Michel. This balanced the external appearance of the cathedral. In 1925 the cathedral was consecrated by Bishop James Morris.

There have been few changes since 1925, though one or two small, modern additions such as electric lighting, a clock and an address system have been installed. Originally named L'Eglise de Notre Dame du Bon Port du Mouillage de Roseau, the cathedral has developed its presence and stands majestically overlooking the town today as Our Lady of Fair Haven. Its size is deceptive. From the outside it seems quite small, but once inside it feels very spacious, light and airy thanks to the stained glass and the open windows that run along both east and west walls from the main entrance to the altar.

For many years now, the cathedral has been off limits while it has its roof renovated (raising funds has been challenging). At the time of writing there was no published deadline for completion of this work.

lawn opposite the park is the **cenotaph** [93 C4], a memorial to Dominicans who lost their lives fighting in World Wars I and II. The smaller memorial next to the cenotaph is in honour of the Free French who came to Dominica in 1940 from Martinique and Guadeloupe following the fall of France to Germany. Those islands supported the Vichy regime until US naval blockades forced them to switch their allegiance to the Free French. Near the cenotaph, sited on a small traffic island, is the **Neg Mawon Emancipation Monument** [93 C4]. This is a memorial to the fighting Maroons of Dominica (page 209) as well as to the emancipation of the island's enslaved.

On the southern side of Fort Young is the **Public Library** [93 D5]. Designed by Dominica's first Crown Colony administrator, Hesketh Bell, and funded by philanthropist Andrew Carnegie, the library was constructed in 1906. At the time of writing, it's in a state of disrepair following Hurricane Maria in 2017 and a couple of fires thereafter. Clearly, it hasn't been a priority and there's much speculation about its future. In its prime, it was a lovely old building with a Georgian-style veranda around the south side overlooking a small lawned garden and the sea.

Across Victoria Street, opposite the library, is the gated entrance to the grounds of the **State House** [93 D4]. The old state house is the building on the left; the new, much larger and unconscionably expensive replacement is the one taking centre stage on the right. When it was built, the State House was an extremely controversial and divisive construction project, with many saying the country had other, more urgent priorities. Next door is the colourful **House of Assembly** [93 D5], Dominica's parliament building. It was originally constructed in 1811, but in 1979 it was destroyed by arsonists and had to be rebuilt.

On the corner of Victoria Street, opposite the cenotaph and Fort Young, is the ruin of **St George's Anglican Church** [93 C4] of the Diocese of the North Eastern Caribbean and Aruba. Built in the 1820s, the church was yet another victim of Hurricane David in 1979 and had to be reconstructed. In September 2017, Hurricane Maria badly damaged it yet again and it's now standing roofless and in partial ruin.

The quaint Fort Lane, between the cenotaph and Church Street, is a good example of how Roseau perhaps once appeared – the cream-and-red painted house on the corner is typical of the town's historic vernacular architecture. On the corner of Cross Street and Virgin Lane is the **Bethesda Methodist Church** [93 D3] which is situated near **Roseau Cathedral** [93 D3]. To the east of the cathedral is the **Bishop's House** [93 D3], which was constructed in the late 1800s.

THE BOTANIC GARDENS The Botanic Gardens are on the east of town along the Valley Road. Planting of the 16ha land, formerly a sugar plantation, began in 1890. The original idea for the gardens was an economic one, propagating crop seedlings for the island's farmers. The ornamental gardens that survive in part today are the result of the lifelong work of Joseph Jones, who managed their development from 1892. Botanists from Kew Gardens in England supplied a wealth of tropical species that they had collected from all over the world, thereby transforming the gardens from a purely functional nursery to an attractive urban landscape of exotic trees and flowering shrubs. Ornately decorated wrought-iron gates were erected, ponds were created, and over 80 species of palm were also added. Part of the gardens was later lawned and set aside for a cricket ground and small pavilion.

Hurricane David wrought havoc on the gardens in 1979 and much was lost. With a strong resolve, however, the gardens were cleared of debris and some species were replanted. Hurricane Maria in 2017 downed several more trees and, though still a pleasant and scenic oasis with many interesting tree species, it feels like it's transitioning from botanic gardens to park.

The garden retains an economic section where Division of Agriculture, veterinary and laboratory buildings are located, along with greenhouses for plant propagation. There's also a sisserou parrot aviary. In front of the Agricultural Division buildings are the crushed remains of a school bus. A giant African baobab tree fell on the empty bus during Hurricane David, and it was left there, exactly as it fell, in memory of the storm. The tree was cut but lateral off-shoots grew and produced the tree you see today.

The Botanic Gardens is a nice place to spend a couple of hours, perhaps with a picnic. The Forestry, Wildlife and Parks Division, located just off Valley Road, opposite the Alliance Française, sells *An Illustrated Guide to Dominica's Botanic Gardens* which is a good source of information if you are interested in the local and exotic plants and trees that were planted here.

Highlights of the gardens include: the *bwa kwaib* (*Sabinea carinalis*), Dominica's national flower (look for it between the Roseau Gate and the crushed bus); the Cannonball tree (*Couropita guianensis*), a South American species with unusual round fruits; Colville's glory (*Colvillea racemosa*), a beautiful tree when in bloom; the golden shower tree (*Cassia fistula*), with fragrant golden flowers when in bloom; the velvet tamarind (*Dialium indum*), an evergreen with a tangy edible fruit; and the roucou (*Bixa orellana*), whose seeds were used as a food colouring and a dye for Kalinago body painting. There are also several species of palm including: the sago palm (*Cycadaceae*), the bottle palm (*Mascarena lagenicaulis*), the gouglou palm (*Acrocomia aculeate*), and the scheelea palm (*Attalea butyracea*).

In addition to cricket matches, the gardens are used for a range of activities including music festivals and casual sports. You may see people practising stilt-walking (*bwa bwa*) here in the weeks before Carnival, or groups of children out with their teachers on a walk (*belle marché*) and a picnic. During the cruise season the gardens can get a bit crowded with tourists and buses, or even a rather bizarre little train (you'll know it when you see it), especially in the mornings.

The Botanic Gardens are within easy walking distance of downtown Roseau. Simply walk up to the end of King George V Street from the Bay Front and, at the junction with Valley Road and Bath Road (by the Police Headquarters), go straight on. The Valley Road Gate is just a couple of hundred metres on the right.

MORNE BRUCE AND JACK'S WALK Located on the eastern edge of the Botanic Gardens is the steep pinnacle of Morne Bruce. From the summit of this low peak there are expansive views of the town and the sea beyond. Named after James Bruce, a captain of the Royal Engineers who designed many of the island's original fortifications in the 18th century, the site was selected by the British as the location for a military garrison. Today there's still a cannon overlooking the town, as well as what's left of the original barracks and officers' quarters. The buildings on the summit are now used by the government and the police. The giant cross was erected in the 1920s.

There are two ways to reach the summit of Morne Bruce. One is by road, taking the first turning on the left after the Anglican cemetery on Bath Road – simply follow the road all the way up to the top. The more adventurous may wish to take a 20-minute walk to the top up a footpath called **Jack's Walk**, located on the northeastern side of the Botanic Gardens near the Elmshall Gate. The footpath is signposted. It's a short but steep climb and some of the steps are a little tricky. The views of Roseau from the top are certainly worth it, though.

During the height of the cruise ship season, it can get quite crowded at the viewing point on Morne Bruce as it's a popular stop-off for bus tours. There are also several souvenir vendors here at this time of the year (selling the same things as the vendors on the Bay Front and in the Old Market!). A nice time to go is later in the afternoon, say around 17.00, when the heat of the day is waning and the sun is thinking about setting over the Caribbean. If you go by road rather than via Jack's Walk, look out for **Top Bar**, a small and colourful place set back from the apex of a bend (you may only see it on the way up). It's a nice place to have a drink, enjoy the views and watch the sun go down on a lovely Dominica day.

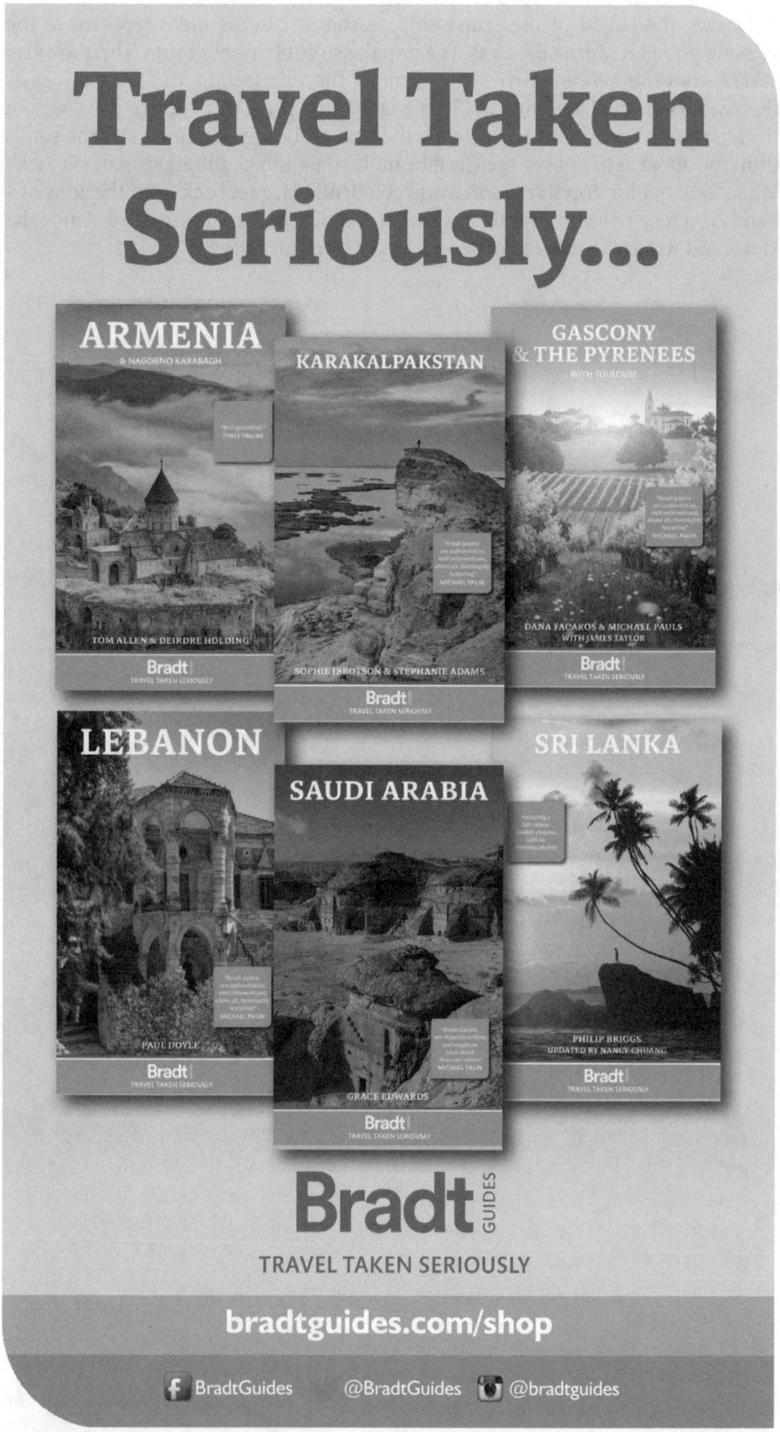
Travel Taken Seriously...
ARMENIA
& NAGORNO KARABAGH
TOM ALLEN & DEIRDRE HOLDING
Bradt
TRAVEL TAKEN SERIOUSLY
KARAKALPAKSTAN
SOPHIE IBBOTSON & STEPHANIE ADAMS
Bradt
TRAVEL TAKEN SERIOUSLY
GASCONY
& THE PYRENEES
WITH TOULOUSE
DANA FACAROS & MICHAEL PAULS
WITH JAMES TAYLOR
Bradt
TRAVEL TAKEN SERIOUSLY
LEBANON
PAUL DOYLE
Bradt
TRAVEL TAKEN SERIOUSLY
SAUDI ARABIA
GRACE EDWARDS
Bradt
TRAVEL TAKEN SERIOUSLY
SRI LANKA
PHILIP BRIGGS
UPDATED BY NANCY CHUANG
Bradt
TRAVEL TAKEN SERIOUSLY
Bradt GUIDES
TRAVEL TAKEN SERIOUSLY
bradtguides.com/shop
BradtGuides
@BradtGuides
@bradtguides

5

Roseau Valley and Morne Trois Pitons National Park

The **Roseau Valley** stretches eastwards from the capital, through the crowded suburb of Bath Estate, and then all the way to the villages of **Trafalgar** and **Wotten Waven**. On the southern ridge at a height of 460m is the farming community of **Morne Prosper**. On the northeastern ridge, at a height of 600m, is the community of **Laudat**.

Morne Trois Pitons National Park was established in 1975, and in 1997 it was designated a UNESCO World Heritage Site. It's approximately 7,000ha in size and contains a high concentration of volcanoes – one of them active. The park's vegetation zones include deciduous and semi-deciduous forest, secondary and mature rainforest, montane forest, and elfin woodland at the summits of the *mornes*. Volcanic activity can be seen within the park. The **Valley of Desolation**, the island's only active volcano, is a turbulent landscape of steaming fumaroles, hot-water rivers and cascades, bubbling mud and a thin crust of rocks and boulders that have been stained by the chemicals and gases released from the magma chamber below. **Boiling Lake** (page 119) is a flooded fumarole with both a diameter and a depth of around 60m.

Of the volcanoes within the park boundary, it's the broad, three-peaked **Morne Trois Pitons** itself, at 1,342m, that's the highest. To the south are the peaks of **Morne Micotrin** (1,221m), **Morne Watt** (1,224m) and **Morne Anglais** (1,123m).

In addition to Boiling Lake, Morne Trois Pitons National Park has two other large freshwater lakes. At an elevation of 853m, the 2ha **Boeri Lake** (page 123) is Dominica's highest mountain lake. A short distance beyond Boeri Lake, though difficult to access, are two much smaller lakes. Located close to Boeri Lake at a slightly lower altitude of 762m, is the 4ha **Freshwater Lake** (page 125). Within the park are several waterfalls that are worth visiting. The tallest is **Middleham Falls** (page 126), which can be found to the west of Morne Micotrin. Perhaps the least visible, especially for the non-swimmer, are the waterfalls located within the water-filled **Ti Tou Gorge**. The stunning **Cathedral Canyon** (page 117) is home to another reasonably accessible waterfall, a little further down the river gorge.

Morne Trois Pitons National Park's main habitat is rainforest. Common vegetation includes trees such as *chatanier* (*Sloanea dentata, Sloanea caribaea* and *Sloanea berteriana*), *gommier* (*Dacryodes excelsa*), *mang blanc* (*Symphonia globulifera*), *karapit* (*Amanoa caribaea*), *maho cochon* (*Sterculia caribaea*) and *bwa bandé* (*Richeria grandis*). There's an abundance of tree ferns and epiphytes such as bird's nest anthuriums, orchids and bromeliads. In the more exposed montane forest, the vegetation is shorter. *Palmiste moutan* (mountain palm)

DON'T MISS

There's a lot to see and do in the Roseau Valley and Morne Trois Pitons National Park. If your time is limited, here are three things you should try to include in your trip:

The Boiling Lake hike If you're in reasonable shape and enjoy a good walk then Dominica's best hiking trail ought to be top of your to-do list. Go with an experienced, recommended guide – it really helps, and the journey is usually more interesting.

Trafalgar Falls Go on a day when no cruise ships are calling, and it will feel like you have these magnificent waterfalls all to yourself. It's really worth getting up to the Father Falls, where there's a great hot- and cold-water cascade and pool. Guides at the visitor centre can show you the way for a very reasonable fee.

Hot springs at Wotten Waven There are several creatively designed, volcanically heated pools in Wotten Waven. Go at dusk so you can enjoy the surroundings and then soak under the stars.

and a wide variety of ferns are common. At the summits of the *mornes*, mossy covered, low-growing elfin woodland is dominated by plants such as the *kaklen* (*Clusia mangle*), *z'ailes mouch* (*Asplundia rigida*) and *kwé-kwé* (*Miconia mirablis*). Fumarole vegetation is found in the Valley of Desolation. Plants able to withstand hot and sulphurous gases include *kaklen*, bromeliads and grasses.

GETTING THERE AND AWAY

Within 30 minutes of leaving the capital you can be setting off on a hike, climbing a waterfall or soaking in a hot spring. The natural attractions and trailheads of the Roseau Valley and Morne Trois Pitons National Park are very accessible. This means that on cruise ship days things can get a little busy, so it's worth planning for this if you'd rather avoid the crowds. The CruiseDig website (**w** cruisedig.com) has a reasonably reliable cruise schedule for Roseau. If you can't avoid the cruise ships, head up the valley in the afternoon – most shore excursions take place in the morning.

BY BUS AND PRIVATE TAXI Catch a bus to the Roseau Valley from King George V Street near the Astaphans store. Public buses will usually only take you as far as the village of Trafalgar and Laudat, so if you're heading to the waterfalls or the hiking trails, you'll have to complete the journey on foot. If you book a taxi from your hotel, you'll be taken all the way. If you're in Roseau, you can usually find a private taxi near the tourist information building or around Fort Young Hotel. Alternatively, you could try hitching a ride as there are usually other travellers heading in your direction.

BY CAR From downtown Roseau, head east along King George V Street and at the junction with Bath Road (with the Police Headquarters to your left), go straight across on to Valley Road. The route passes the Botanic Gardens and then crosses a bridge over the Roseau River. Beyond the crowded residential suburb of Bath Estate, the road continues eastwards into the Roseau Valley. The Valley Road forks just beyond Bath Estate near the settlement of Fond Cani. The road to the right goes to Wotten Waven and Morne Prosper. The road to the left heads towards Trafalgar and Laudat. The junction is clearly signposted. Note that if you're heading to Wotten Waven, the best route is to head towards Trafalgar and the waterfalls and, just beyond Trafalgar village, take a right-hand turn (follow the signs). This is because the main road to Wotten Waven suffered a huge landslide in 2015 and it hasn't been possible to recover the road safely. There's now a diversion off the Morne Prosper road, but the route is narrow and rough.

Continuing towards Trafalgar, there's a second fork. The road to the left goes up to Laudat, Ti Tou Gorge, Freshwater Lake, the Boeri Lake Trail, the Boiling Lake Trail, Morne Micotrin and the Chemin L'Etang Trail. The fork to the right goes to Trafalgar and Wotten Waven. The junction is well signposted.

Pass through the village of Trafalgar and continue straight to the end of the road to get to the waterfalls. Turn right beyond Trafalgar village to get to the hot springs of Wotten Waven.

If you're heading up to Laudat, stick to the main road all the way and use your horn on the numerous blind corners. You'll pass a sign on your left, with a steep turning and a narrow road that goes down to the Middleham Falls trailhead (in all likelihood there'll also be a sign for the Sanctuary Rainforest Eco Retreat and Spa – under construction at the time of writing; page 114). A little further on is a junction where you may meet a park warden checking site passes. The concrete road straight ahead goes to Freshwater Lake, the Boeri Lake Trail, Morne Micotrin and the Chemin L'Etang Trail. The road to the right goes to Laudat village and, before it, a left-hand turn-off to Ti Tou Gorge and the Boiling Lake trailhead. If you're heading for one of these, keep going to the left of the hydro plant and balancing tank until you come to a dead end. Park up around here and walk. It's also worth mentioning that the road to Laudat is also where there will eventually be (in theory at least) the entrance to the cable car (page 116). If so, this road is going to be busy one day.

If you're heading for Morne Micotrin, Freshwater Lake, Chemin L'Etang and Boeri Lake, follow the concrete road at the Laudat junction all the way into Morne Trois Pitons National Park. This road eventually splits with a left-hand fork going to the Boeri Lake and Chemin L'Etang trailheads, and the right-hand road going to the Freshwater Lake visitor centre and car park. See page 127 for the exact whereabouts of the Morne Micotrin trailhead.

WHERE TO STAY *Map, page 112*

By and large, accommodation options in the Roseau Valley are commensurate with the kind of travellers to whom Dominica is perfectly suited – adventurous, nature-loving travellers who like to hike and explore. As usual, the online booking sites have lots of options, especially for budget travellers. Here's a selection of those I like:

Aura Villa, Cottage & Apartment Shawford; ☎ 767 235 7955; e auradominicanow@gmail.com; w auradominica.com. Located just off the road to Trafalgar, Aura offers an assortment of accommodation options. The 3-bed villa has a huge open balcony space with hammocks, seating, dining table & wonderful forest & mountain views, & there's Wi-Fi & a fully equipped kitchen & lounge area with TV. The master bedroom has AC, others have fans. The artistically designed & beautiful 2-bed Bauhinia Cottage is the pick of the accommodation. Located in Aura's expansive gardens, each bedroom has private WC & there's a shared outdoor shower. There's Wi-Fi, & a large open veranda with hammocks & day beds. The 1-bed SC apt is part of the main villa building but has its own entrance. It has a fully equipped kitchen, living area, Wi-Fi, &

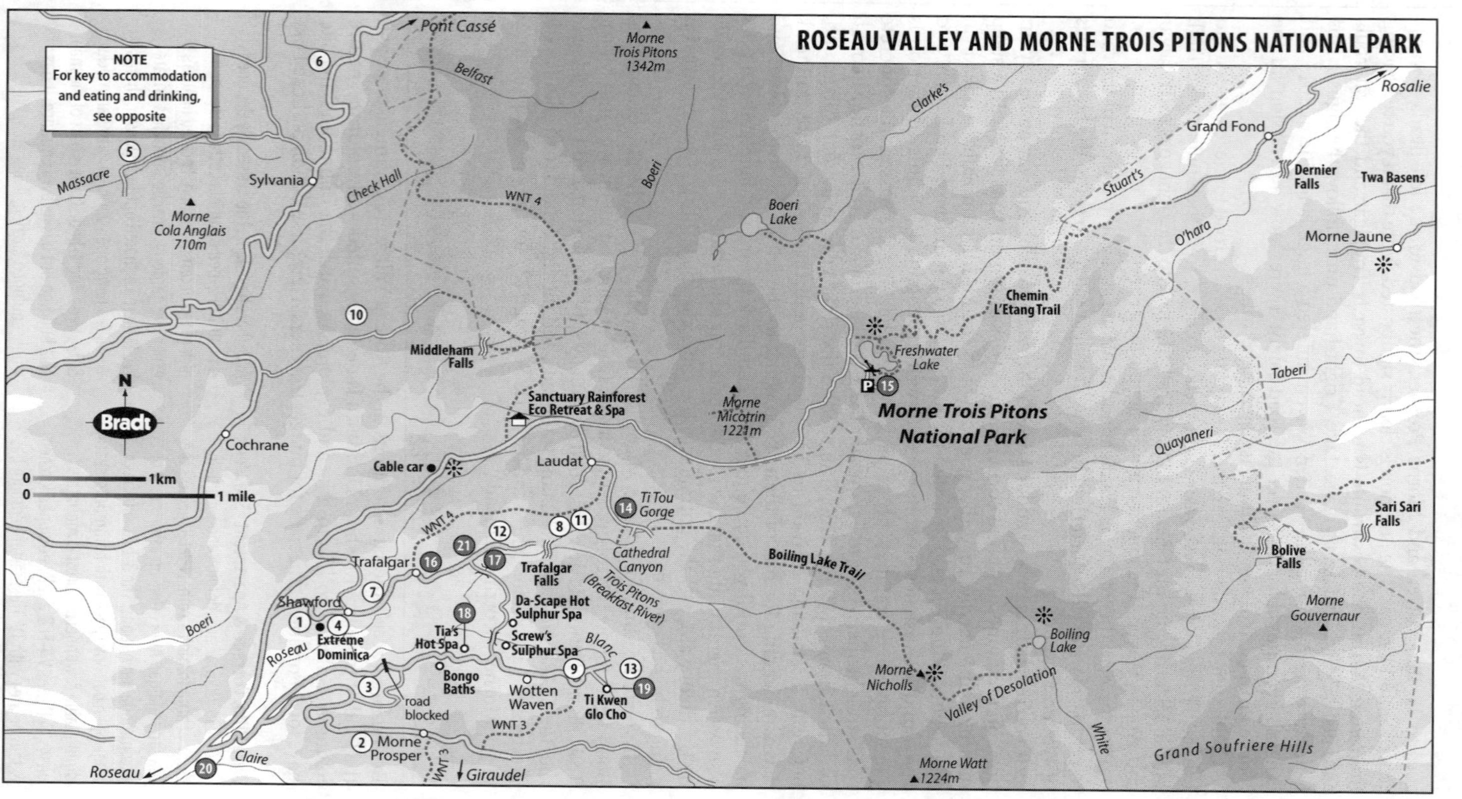
ROSEAU VALLEY AND MORNE TROIS PITONS NATIONAL PARK
NOTE
For key to accommodation and eating and drinking, see opposite
Bradt
N
0 1km
0 1 mile
Morne Trois Pitons National Park
Rosalie
Twa Basens
Morne Jaune
Dernier Falls
Grand Fond
O'hara
Stuart's
Taberi
Sari Sari Falls
Bolive Falls
Morne Gouvernaur
Grand Soufriere Hills
Quayaneri
White
Boiling Lake
Valley of Desolation
Morne Watt 1224m
Morne Nicholls
Chemin L'Etang Trail
Freshwater Lake
Clarke's
Boeri Lake
Morne Micotrin 1221m
Boiling Lake Trail
Morne Trois Pitons 1342m
Boeri
Ti Tou Gorge
Cathedral Canyon
Trois Pitons (Breakfast River)
Blanc
Ti Kwen Glo Cho
Laudat
Sanctuary Rainforest Eco Retreat & Spa
WNT 4
Belfast
Pont Cassé
Check Hall
Middleham Falls
Cable car
Trafalgar Falls
Da-Scape Hot Sulphur Spa
Screw's Sulphur Spa
Wotten Waven
WNT 3
Giraudel
Tia's Hot Spa
Bongo Baths
road blocked
Morne Prosper
Trafalgar
Shawford
Extreme Dominica
Roseau
Claire
Sylvania
Cochrane
Morne Cola Anglais 710m
Massacre
Boeri
1 2 3 4 5 6 7 8 9 10 11 12 13 14 15 16 17 18 19 20 21
P

veranda with hammock. This is good-value budget accommodation in a great location. Villa **$$$$**, Cottage **$$$**, Apt **$**

Cocoa Cottage (4 rooms, 1 suite, 1 treehouse) Shawford; ☎ 767 316 8746; e cocoa.cottage.dominica@gmail.com; w cocoacottagedominica.com. This is stylish yet laid-back accommodation on the road to Trafalgar that would suit independent travelling couples or a group of friends. The main cottage has 4 lovely rooms, each with private bathroom & views of the garden. The Honeymoon Suite is standalone accommodation with en-suite bathroom & private veranda. Sleeping as many as 6, the fabulous open-sided SC treehouse is ideal for a travelling family. It's close to nature & private. Cocoa Cottage's communal lounge & dining area are great for making new friends & exchanging travel tales, tips & advice. B/fast & dinner can be prepared for guests on request. A great option for hikers, divers & canyoneers. **$$–$$$**

Papillote Wilderness Retreat (2 suites, 2 rooms) Trafalgar; ☎ 767 295 9564; e papillote@cwdom.dm; w papillote.dm. Location is the big attraction of Papillote, which was established in 1969 as an 'eco-inn'. It's set in mature tropical gardens with volcanically heated pools & waterfalls (page 118), & Trafalgar Falls, hiking trails & the hot springs of Wotten Waven are all nearby. The 2-bed SC suites have kitchen, en-suite bathroom with 'volcanic hot tub', Wi-Fi & large, shared veranda with garden & forest views. The smaller garden rooms have en-suite bathroom & Wi-Fi. Simple, no-frills accommodation – a good option for nature lovers & hikers travelling on a budget. **$–$$**

ROSEAU VALLEY AND MORNE TROIS PITONS NATIONAL PARK

For listings, see from page 111

Where to stay

1 Aura Villa, Cottage & Apartment
2 Bluemoon Studio
3 Chez Ophelia Cottage Apartments
4 Cocoa Cottage
5 Crescent Moon Cabins
6 D-Smart Farm
7 Firefly Cabin at D'Auchamps
8 Kai Morne Macak
9 Le Petit Paradis
10 Mountain Caapi Cottage
11 Nature's Cabin
12 Papillote Wilderness Retreat
13 Roots Cabin

Where to eat and drink

14 Café Mon Plezi
15 Freshwater Lake Facility
Le Petit Paradis (see 9)
16 Munch & Brunch
17 River Rock Café & Bar
18 Tia's Bamboo Restaurant & Bar
19 Ti Kwen Glo Cho
20 Vado's Hot Spot
21 Water Bar

Bluemoon Studio Morne Prosper; w bluemoonstudiodominica.com. This small self-contained studio attached to the owner's cottage sleeps 2 & has private bathroom, fully equipped galley-style kitchen, Wi-Fi, TV, AC & fans. Located in the elevated farming village of Morne Prosper, the studio has off-road parking & a small porch looking out on to gardens with mountain views. This is a good budget option for a travelling couple or someone travelling to Dominica for work. **$**

Chez Ophelia Cottage Apartments (10 apts) Copthall; ☎ 767 616 8000; e chezophelia@cwdom.dm; w chezophelia.com. Located on the old road to Wotten Waven (now a dead end), this is simple & affordable SC accommodation for budget travellers. Apts are split across 5 cottages so 2 can be connected if travelling with friends or family. Each apt has a private bathroom, cooking facilities, porch & Wi-Fi. There's a communal dining area where b/fast & dinner can be prepared with prior reservations. Owned & managed by 'Dominica's Lady of Song', Ophelia Marie. Another good budget traveller option in the Roseau Valley. **$**

Firefly Cabin at D'Auchamps Shawford; ☎ 767 285 2117; bookings via w airbnb.com. Firefly is a popular 1-bed SC cabin located in a garden & organic farm just off the main road to Trafalgar. In addition to an equipped kitchen, the cabin has 2 porches & bathroom with shower. Although the owner lives on the property, the cabin is private & enjoys great mountain views. Ideal for hikers & outdoor lovers travelling on a budget. **$**

Kai Morne Macak Laudat; bookings via w airbnb.com. This secluded 1-bed open-plan mountain cabin enjoys extraordinary views of Dominica's Morne Trois Pitons National Park. It has a bathroom, fully equipped kitchen, Wi-Fi & spacious veranda with hammock. It's owned by Nahjie of Just Go Dominica, meaning you also get an experienced island & hiking guide living nearby. **$**

Le Petit Paradis (5 apts, 1 dorm) Wotten Waven; ☎ 767 276 2761; e lepetitparadis20@hotmail.com; w lepetitparadisdominica.com.

SANCTUARY RAINFOREST ECO RESORT & SPA

Under construction at the time of writing, Sanctuary Rainforest is a CBI-funded hotel development that's located right at the Middleham Falls trailhead (Laudat end). Time will tell, of course, but unlike many of the other resorts under development, this one seems to have a design that's a bit more appropriate for Dominica. Although aimed at a luxury market, the unit designs are rather Hobbit-like, partially submerged into the landscape. For information: w rainforestecoresort.com.

This is good budget accommodation in Wotten Waven village, close to hot springs & a short drive to Trafalgar. Apts have en-suite bathroom & Wi-Fi. Some have cooking facilities. Dorm-style accommodation has 4 rooms, each sleeping 2. Rooms have private bathrooms. In the garden there are 'hammock shacks' & areas to pitch a tent if you're hiking or on a rock-bottom travel budget. The large open-sided bamboo restaurant serves Creole-style b/fast, lunch & dinner daily. There's a taxi & tour service & laundry. For WNT through-hikers, Le Petit Paradis is conveniently at the junction of segments 3 & 4. **$**

Nature's Cabin Laudat; bookings via w airbnb.com. This is a simple but comfortable 1-bed mountain cabin that enjoys fabulous views of Morne Trois Pitons National Park from its veranda. The cabin has a bathroom, kitchenette & Wi-Fi. Access is via steps. **$**

Roots Cabin Wotten Waven; bookings via w airbnb.com. Set in forest & garden surroundings, this is a rustic, open-plan 1-bed cabin constructed from wood, bamboo & recycled materials. It has an indoor & outdoor kitchen, bathroom & shower, large living space & access to nearby rivers. **$**

WHERE TO EAT AND DRINK *Map, page 112*

The **Sanctuary Rainforest Eco Resort** has a bar and restaurant in its conceptual design, so, if the project is completed, you can probably expect a high standard of dining. There's a great restaurant space at **Papillote Wilderness Retreat**, but at the time of writing it's not open. Look out for something perhaps happening here in due course. There are several small bars and snackettes in Trafalgar village that offer good-value local lunches at the time of writing and the singular **Water Bar** on the main road to the waterfall is an interesting though sometimes rather touristy place to stop for a drink. **Ti Kwen Glo Cho** (page 118) – my pick of the hot springs – also has a rustic bar that's a nice place to hang out after a soak.

RESTAURANTS

Le Petit Paradis Wotten Waven; 767 276 2761; lunch & dinner daily; advance reservation usually required. Joan's colourful, open-sided restaurant is spacious, traditional & enjoys great views. It's important you call ahead – it's hard for them to offer a full menu to walk-ins. The food is traditional Creole & Caribbean. Joan makes her own rum punch, named Bullet, that's worth a try. **$**

River Rock Café & Bar Trafalgar; 767 225 0815; lunch daily; dinner by advance reservation. Enjoying great valley & river views, River Rock's covered deck is a great spot for a cold beer or rum punch, local lunch, sandwiches & more. Find it on the road to Trafalgar Falls. **$**

Tia's Bamboo Restaurant & Bar Wotten Waven; 767 275 7870; lunch daily; dinner by reservation. Located within Tia's Hot Spa, this snug Creole restaurant & bar serves traditional fare & occasional w/end specials. **$**

NOTEWORTHY BARS, CAFÉS AND SNACKETTES

There are quite a few bars & snackettes in & around the Roseau Valley. They tend to come & go over time, but here are some that you could check out.

Café Mon Plezi Laudat. Located on the road to Ti Tou Gorge & the Boiling Lake trailhead, this bar & snackette sells drinks & local eats. You can also buy a site pass here if you don't have one.

Freshwater Lake Facility Wotten Waven. If you're hiking either Freshwater or Boeri Lake, perhaps Middleham Falls, this is a lovely spot for a drink & a light bite. Sandwiches, soup, local specialities or maybe a pot of hot coffee or tea after a rainy lake hike – it's a proper hiker's pit stop.

Munch & Brunch Trafalgar. Located just off the road to Trafalgar Falls, this tiny snackette is good for local dishes & light bites.

Vado's Hot Spot Copthall. This is a snackette in the Copthall area on the main road to Trafalgar & Laudat. Look for the bright red container. There's a nice seating area with good views of the river valley. Food is traditional & simple – try the fried *balao*. It's a great spot to stop off for a cold drink & a cheap bite to eat after your adventures.

WHAT TO SEE AND DO

VILLAGES OF THE ROSEAU VALLEY Following the 1805 **Battle of Trafalgar** between the British and the French fleets, the estate at the head of the Roseau Valley was named in honour of Nelson's famous victory by the English landowners who had settled there. The estate produced coffee and sugar through the labour of enslaved workers. After their emancipation in 1838, these workers established a settlement and grew vegetables and *ground provisions*, supplying fresh produce to the townspeople of Roseau. This became **Trafalgar village**. At the head of the valley, above the village, are the famous twin waterfalls, also called Trafalgar (page 119). Nearby is a hydro-electric plant that uses water that runs down from Freshwater Lake, via Ti Tou Gorge and the waterfalls. The cascading water and rapids that descend from the falls below the village and along the valley floor become the Roseau River. During Tropical Storm Erika in August 2015 the river tore into the land, expanding its banks and flooding low-lying areas. The shanty village of Silver Lake was almost entirely swept away along with riverside dwellings and gardens of Copthall and Bath Estate. If you're on this river or exploring the waterfalls during periods of unsettled weather, you should always take note of conditions.

Trafalgar village is compact and rather steep with a handful of good local bars and snackettes. The **Water Bar** on the road to the falls, along with **River Rock Café** (see opposite) are favourites with visitors.

The village of **Wotten Waven** is in the opposite corner of the Roseau Valley and is connected to Trafalgar by a road that crosses the valley floor and the accessible volcanically active fumaroles of the River Blanc (touristy on cruise days). In addition to the volcanic activity in these parts, note the tall river reeds that give Dominica's capital its name. Where Trafalgar is famous for its twin waterfall, Wotten Waven is known for its numerous hot springs.

The village of **Morne Prosper** is perched atop a ridge on the southern side of the Roseau Valley. It's predominantly a farming community. If you have time to head up there, you can enjoy great views across the farmlands and *mornes* from the back of the village. There's an old and largely abandoned route to the main Boiling

PRACTICALITIES

Given their proximity to the capital, the villages of the Roseau Valley have no supermarkets or petrol stations of their own. If you need **site passes**, the visitor centre at Trafalgar Falls is your best bet though you can also get them at Café Mon Plezi near Ti Tou Gorge.

DOMINICA GEOTHERMAL ENERGY PROJECT

Dominica is in the process of building geothermal wells, a power plant and a transmission network that, in the first instance, will reduce the country's reliance on diesel to fuel its main power station at Fond Cole. Ultimately, the whole country and potentially some island neighbours may be using this much cleaner form of energy. The heart of the project is Laudat and the Roseau Valley, where test wells and surveys have been carried out over the last few years. The project is run by the Dominica Geothermal Development Company Ltd, which is wholly owned by the government of Dominica. Travellers exploring the Laudat and Roseau Valley areas may see evidence of this project in the form of the construction of the geothermal power plant, well heads and piping, as well as occasional heavy vehicles on the roads. For information on this project visit w geodominica.dm.

Lake Trail that emerges near the Valley of Desolation from Morne Prosper. When the Wai'tukubuli National Trail was established, this old route was opened as an optional diversion. The consensus since is that's it's just way too difficult to both navigate safely and maintain properly (when I eventually emerged from this trail after getting lost and stuck in swampy ravines, I was covered from head to foot in thick volcanic mud), so scratch this hike from your list for the time being.

Laudat is Dominica's highest village and came about as a stayover point when the Chemin L'Etang track (page 124) was the principal route across between east and west coasts. People would walk either from Rosalie or Roseau with their loads and then overnight near Freshwater Lake. Today Laudat is a quiet place, rural and mostly engaged in farming. This may change when construction of the new Sanctuary resort is complete (page 114). It's known for being the main gateway to the natural attractions and hiking trails of Morne Trois Pitons National Park.

CABLE CAR TO BOILING LAKE At the time of writing, a cable car is being constructed that will theoretically run from Baiac, near Laudat, over Trafalgar Falls to a ridge beyond Boiling Lake, where there'll be a restaurant and viewing platforms. There are many factors that make the construction of a cable car to an active volcanic region rather daunting, as anyone who hikes there will testify, and it's thought it will need large passenger numbers for it to be operationally viable (a reminder of a similar endeavour is the once-popular Rainforest Aerial Tram that's now abandoned and is a forest ruin). If it's completed, the new cable car ride should offer extraordinary views of the Roseau Valley and Morne Trois Pitons National Park. Access will be off the road to Laudat, so you should expect heavy tour bus traffic in this area during the cruise ship season.

✷ CANYONING Dominica's most popular and dramatic canyoning trips take place in and around the Roseau Valley. They begin near Ti Tou Gorge and follow the same river through a spectacular continuation of the gorge to an exit point near the stunning Cathedral Canyon (see opposite). The journey includes rappelling down several waterfalls, leaping into deep pools and negotiating the river while all the time looking up to see the trees of the forest above. For the more adventurous, Cathedral Canyon need not be the exit point at all. Continue the journey down river until reaching the top of Trafalgar's Father Falls, which you then rappel down.

Whether you're a complete novice or a seasoned professional, canyoning in Dominica is an exhilarating and memorable experience. I recommend it. For more information about what canyoning entails, as well as details of canyoning guides, see page 71.

CATHEDRAL CANYON Canyoneers named this canyon, so I'm not sure if it's considered official and will stick, but I hope so. It's a beautiful place. If you take a canyoning trip from the Ti Tou Gorge area with one of Dominica's canyoning guides (page 71), then Cathedral Canyon is where you end up before exiting the river gorge and heading back up to your starting point. Thanks to a local landowner, Mr Rolle, it's now also possible to access the canyon via a forest track. It takes 20–30 minutes, depending on your level of ability. It's steep and the terrain is quite tricky – over rocks and boulders and along a fast-flowing stream. There's also a step-assisted boulder climb at the end, made of rebar stuck into the rocks (it's sturdier than it sounds). Once in the main river, you must wade and swim upstream (left – if you go right, you'll end up getting stuck at the top of Trafalgar's Father Falls, which is also a canyoning trip). There's a dry gravel bed inside Cathedral Canyon where you can get out of the water.

To get there, head to Ti Tou Gorge and the Boiling Lake trailhead. Before you reach the parking area, look for the trail on the right, just before the bridge. Use the car park and walk back to the trail. At the time of writing, Mr Rolle was in the process of putting up signage and a bar/ticket office. He charges US$5. You'll need swimming gear, surf shoes or trainers that you don't mind getting wet, and a waterproof bag to keep all your valuables dry when you swim into the gorge. Keep a change of clothes in your car or just head to Ti Tou Gorge afterwards (page 118). Be careful on your way down the trail as it's easy to slip or turn an ankle.

HOT SPRINGS

The relatively shallow magma layer in this region has provided local entrepreneurs with an opportunity to design and create pools that are fed by volcanically heated freshwater springs. The hot water is rich in minerals, especially sulphur, which is said to have positive benefits to the body, including the detoxification of skin cells and the soothing of joint and muscle pain. Whether true or not, the pools are a treat, especially after a long hike. Most of the hot springs are in the village of Wotten Waven and many are works of art, fashioned in local stone and set in tropical gardens with water piped along bamboo channels. These natural and often rather artistic settings add to the feeling of wellness that the hot springs are meant – and marketed – to provide. Entry fees are similar, usually US$10 for visitors.

Bongo Baths Wotten Waven; ☎ 767 295 2233. At the time of writing, the only way to enjoy this charming hot-water spa was by prior reservation – but it was changing ownership, so things may end up being different. Find it along the approach to Wotten Waven on the road to/from Morne Prosper & Bath Estate or, if you're coming from Trafalgar, drive all the way through Wotten Waven & find it on the left beyond Tia's.

Da-Scape Hot Sulphur Spa Wotten Waven; ☎ 767 616 6800. Located just off the link road between Wotten Waven & Trafalgar, Da-Scape has a combination of small indoor & screened-in outdoor hot-water pools set in garden surroundings.

Papillote Tropical Gardens Trafalgar; ☎ 767 295 0564. Papillote Wilderness Retreat (page 113) is known for its immaculate & mature tropical gardens. Hidden within them are several small hot-water pools.

Screw's Sulphur Spa Wotten Waven; ☎ 767 440 4478. After his large & popular hot spa was destroyed by Hurricane Maria, the affable & enigmatic Screw has created a new spa near the bridge spanning the volcanically active River Blanc. At the time of writing he has 2 pools, but, knowing his passion for design, it's likely things will develop.

Ti Kwen Glo Cho Wotten Waven; ☎ 767 315 3489. Set in beautiful garden surroundings, Ti Kwen has hot-water pools & traditional bathtubs. There's a waterfall, a volcanic mud pool, changing facilities & a rustic wooden bar serving refreshments. Massage is also available. Follow the signs up from the village junction.

Tia's Hot Spa Wotten Waven; ☎ 767 448 1998, 767 225 4823. Riverside hot pools are located at the foot of colourful tropical gardens. There are also enclosed private pools, one of which has wheelchair access. Rustic cottages, restaurant & bar are also on site. Well signposted, Tia's is on the main road close to the village junction.

PAPILLOTE TROPICAL GARDENS (w papillote.dm/gardens) First started in 1967, and then substantially repaired following successive extreme weather events, Papillote has long been Dominica's best-known private tropical garden. It's loaded with rainforest plants and flowers, and there are natural hot springs and pools and a couple of waterfalls. The garden attracts hummingbirds, butterflies, stick insects and more and has been a draw for plant and nature lovers for many years. An accompanied or self-guided walk takes in a variety of tropical flora including tree ferns, bromeliads, orchids, heliconias, gingers, breadfruit and calabash trees, jade vines and rare aroids. The streams, terraced walkways and rest areas all complement this garden beautifully. Check the website for opening times, bookings and prices. Papillote Tropical Gardens are part of Papillote Wilderness Retreat (page 113).

TI TOU GORGE There's a deep and narrow river gorge between Freshwater Lake and Trafalgar Falls with an opening near Laudat, making it accessible to swimmers. Known as Ti Tou (patois for small throat), it's a popular attraction, especially during the cruise ship season and at weekends.

Because of several incidents in the past, including drownings, it's now mandatory to use a floatation device when swimming up the gorge. You can either bring your own or rent one. There's a narrow opening in the gorge and, by swimming upstream into it, you can reach a small waterfall. The gorge walls are tall and smooth, and the river is cold and deep with few places shallow enough to touch the bottom. It's about a 5-minute swim (or float) upstream to the small waterfall – longer than that if you must negotiate your way past other visitors and avoid the tour guides who like to jump down from the cliff above. There's an artificial shallow pool at the mouth of the gorge that has volcanically heated (though rather lukewarm) water piped to it. Like most of the attractions in this area, it's a good idea to either visit on a day when there are no cruise ships, or aim for the late afternoon when most excursions have been and gone. For film lovers, Ti Tou Gorge was a set location for the film *Pirates of the Caribbean* (the scene where they are dropped into a river gorge inside a spherical cage).

It's important not to swim into the gorge either during or immediately after heavy rains as it can flash flood. If you see brown water and leaf debris on the surface, don't go in. There's no entrance fee, nor do you need a site pass for Ti Tou Gorge. There are basic bathroom and changing facilities as well as vendors selling drinks and snacks (try the homemade coconut cheese and coconut tablet). At the time of writing, there's also the Ti Tou Gorge Restaurant & Bar that says it's open from 09.00 to 18.00 every day – though I suspect these hours may only apply during the high season. Still, it's a nice addition if it's open. Ti Tou Gorge is also the start and finish of the Boiling Lake Trail (see below).

A public bus will only get you as far as the village of Laudat – you'll have to walk the rest of the way (about 20 minutes). If you're driving, turn right at the junction with the road to Freshwater and Boeri lakes and then turn left towards the bottom of the hill. You'll pass the Café Mon Plezi and a power plant and balancing tank before reaching the car park. It's possible to drive right up to the gorge but I'd advise against it as it's often used by tour buses. It's a better idea to park up and walk the final stretch.

✷ **TRAFALGAR FALLS** (Site pass required) The Father Falls, with a drop of around 85m, and the Mother Falls, with a drop of around 40m, make up Trafalgar Falls. As you face them, the Father Falls are on the left-hand side and the Mother Falls on the right. From the visitor centre, it's an easy 15-minute walk up and down steps to the viewing platform.

The adventurous may wish to go a little further than this. From the platform, it's fun to walk down to the boulders and then investigate the rivers and pools. More interesting (and recommended) is the climb up to the Father Falls where there's a volcanically heated stream that merges with the river to form a hot- and cold-water cascade and pool. The waterfall pool itself, right at the top, is also glorious – perhaps one of Dominica's best. It's prudent to get a guide to go up with you (at the time of writing about EC$20 pp) as the easiest route isn't obvious. Essentially, you negotiate the boulders on the left-hand side of the river, along the margins where rocks meet bush, for most of the way to the hot- and cold-water cascade. From there, swim and traverse across to the right-hand side to take the flatter and easier route to the top pool. While it's possible to make it across to the Mother Falls, there's no pool to speak of as it's completely masked by the volume of water thundering down on to the rocks.

The river that feeds the Father Falls comes from Freshwater Lake via Ti Tou Gorge, and that feeding the Mother Falls is the Breakfast River, which you must cross when hiking to the Valley of Desolation and Boiling Lake.

The Trafalgar Falls visitor centre has a large car park with souvenir stalls, toilet and changing facilities, snack bar and an informative and well-presented interpretation room with information about volcanic activity as well as examples of flowers and birds that may be seen in the area. It also serves as the entrance to the waterfall trail and where a forestry officer will ask for site passes (you can buy site passes here). If you're planning on climbing up to the waterfalls then experienced and certified guides can usually be engaged here – depending on how busy things are.

HIKING TRAILS

✷ **BOILING LAKE (FROM TI TOU GORGE)** Without doubt, this is Dominica's signature hiking trail, and it's also my personal favourite. It's a there-and-back, challenging day-hike through rainforest, up and down a small mountain, and across an active volcanic caldera. For most people, it usually takes 3–4 hours each way. You ought to be in reasonable physical condition to take on this hike. There are lots of steps – some rather steep – there are a few small rivers to cross, there are some vertiginous sections, and there's a bit of climbing using rocks, rope and roots. The steps make the trail tough on your knees, especially on the return leg when you're tired and the climbs feel a little steeper. I recommend a guide for this trail. Although it's a well-beaten path, the Valley of Desolation

VOLCANIC ACTIVITY

Dominica has nine volcanic centres with one of them active. They are: Morne Diablotin, Morne Aux Diables, Morne Trois Pitons, Morne Micotrin, Morne Watt, Morne Anglais, Morne Plat Pays, Grand Soufiere Hills and Valley of Desolation. The island has a history of large, explosive eruptions, including what is believed to have been the biggest in the Caribbean in the last 200,000 years, which generated about 58km^3 of material. It produced pyroclastic (volcanic lava) flow deposits over 200m thick in central Dominica and blanketed nearby Caribbean islands and the Caribbean Sea in ash.

Dominica's volcanic landscape is made up of a series of domes that form a 'spine' down the island. Scientists believe that beneath them is a series of magma chambers that lie at different depths and have different effects on the visible landscape. At Morne Aux Diables, for example, the fumarole of Cold Soufriere (page 194) is, well, cold, whereas those at Wotten Waven and in the Valley of Desolation are piping hot. This is because the magma chambers in Morne Trois Pitons National Park are closer to the surface so the hot gases they produce don't have time to cool down.

The main gases that are released from magma chambers are carbon dioxide, sulphates and hydrogen sulphide, the last being the gas that has the 'rotten eggs' smell. When this gas dissolves in water it becomes a weak hydrosulphuric acid which, although initially clear, develops a cloudy white colour as it reacts with oxygen dissolved in the water. If metal ions are present, the reaction with hydrogen sulphide creates a dark colour.

Fumaroles are gas vents rising from the magma chamber that superheat any ground water or streams they meet to create steam and bubbling mud. Look around the mouth of fumaroles (carefully does it) and you'll see the yellowy

can be disorientating on the way back (people I've hiked with tend to get a bit confused when I ask them which way they would go), and a guide offers help and assurance, especially when things get a bit sketchy. You must have a site pass for this trail – the Café Mon Plezi on the way to Ti Tou Gorge sells them, but don't count on it always being open early enough. It's more prudent to buy a weekly pass when you go somewhere like Trafalgar Falls. At the time of writing, most of the trail is in good shape, though there are a few sections that need attention. The most obvious being the last part of the descent into the Valley of Desolation from Morne Nicholls where erosion and weather have destroyed the rather rudimentary, though helpful, wooden steps that had been there for years. It may get fixed but be prepared for a bit of a wet and slippery rock scramble here. It's the nature of the terrain and the high and exposed habitat that make some areas rather changeable and vulnerable to weather. Having said that, a wet and slippery rock scramble is also part of the Boiling Lake adventure. Note that there's no shelter anywhere on this trail and it often rains, sometimes heavily, so it's worth carrying a rain jacket and having your camera and other valuables stashed in waterproof or ziplock bags.

Dominica's Boiling Lake is a freshwater-filled volcanic crater in the heart of Morne Trois Pitons National Park. Two streams run into the crater and a large fumarole at its centre superheats the ground water, forcing it up above its natural level. This force, combined with hot hydrogen sulphide gas bubbling to the surface, brings the middle of the lake to a rolling boil. Just about every published narrative deposits of precipitated sulphur, which some consider effective in the treatment of skin disorders – one of the reasons why hot volcanic spas are lauded by wellness practitioners.

The road between Wotten Waven and Trafalgar crosses the Roseau River and the smaller River Blanc. From the River Blanc bridge crossing you can see at least two active fumaroles. This is where the hot gases have escaped the magma chamber, breached the surface and superheated the riverbank, forcing up boiling water and steam. A trek up the River Blanc reveals more fumaroles as well as hot-water pools.

Boiling Lake is a crater that sits above an extremely large and deep fumarole. Gases rise from a magma chamber and superheat the ground water, turning it into steam and forcing it up to the surface where it condenses to water and is trapped within the crater. The lake is also fed by two streams and spills out on its eastern lip to form the White River. This activity is largely consistent but there have been episodes when activity has subsided resulting in no steam being forced to the surface and the lake's level settling to that of the surrounding water table, thus 'emptying' the lake. Boiling Lake is at a higher level than the surrounding water table thanks to the superheated steam that forces it up, and so when it empties due to rare lulls in volcanic activity or a blockage in the fumarole itself, the water is simply finding its natural level.

As a footnote, the volcanic activity in this area is in the process of being exploited as an energy source. Test wells have provided data and encouragement needed for the government and private investors to begin the construction of a geothermal energy plant that, in the first instance, aims to satisfy around three-quarters of Dominica's electricity needs (page 116).

– including all the destination marketing speak – describes Boiling Lake as the second largest of its kind in the world, behind Frying Pan Lake and the connected Inferno Crater Lake in the Waimangu Volcanic Rift Valley on New Zealand's North Island. The lake is viewable from a natural ledge on the western edge of the crater, and this viewing point is reached via a hiking trail from the village of Laudat. As mentioned, every now and then an extreme weather event adds its mark to the trail – usually in the form of landslide and erosion. Guides who walk the trail regularly should be credited for much of its maintenance, often figuring out workarounds where trees have fallen or land slippage has occurred. Some of these guides hike the trail several times a week and have intimate knowledge of its many nuances. While the lake is certainly impressive, it's really the walk itself that makes this activity so rewarding. By the time you read this, however, there may be a cable car service to Boiling Lake – or perhaps the ruins of an abandoned or unfinished one (page 116). Who knows, maybe you can hike to the lake, head up to the restaurant for fish and chips and a beer, then take the cable car back. Times are changing, though the island, thankfully, remains unmoved by it all.

Though Amerindians no doubt came across it earlier, the first recorded sighting of Boiling Lake was in 1870, when a magistrate from the east coast village of La Plaine, Mr Edmund Watt, attempted to find an alternative route across the interior of the island. After several days spent in the depths of the forest he finally arrived at the village of Laudat and reported sighting a boiling volcanic crater. It was the age of discovery and adventure, and Englishmen like Watt would have been keen to make their mark, even on a small Caribbean island (which may have been considered a colonial backwater in terms of postings and prestige). Mr Watt was later accompanied by Dr H A A Nicholls and several porters and bush cutters to the location of his sighting, along roughly the same route that the main hiking trail follows today. The mountains of Morne Watt and Morne Nicholls were named by the two men after themselves.

The Nicholls–Watt route, the primary trail that's used to access the lake today, begins at Ti Tou Gorge and climbs up to Morne Nicholls before descending into the Valley of Desolation and then on to the lake itself. The Valley of Desolation is Dominica's only active volcano and is a wide valley, or caldera, containing volcanically heated streams, bubbling mud and scores of fumaroles. Touch the ground in some places and it's hot. The fumarole vegetation in the valley consists of lichens, mosses, bromeliads and *kaklen* (*Clusia mangle*). Subjected as they are to sulphurous gases and a heady concoction of heat and chemistry, the rocks of the valley are daubed in whites, browns, yellows and oranges, and the rivers and pools are shades of white, blue and black.

The Boiling Lake trailhead is at Ti Tou Gorge. Look for the stone steps (there may be a sign). From the steps it's a steady climb along a wide, rocky and sometimes sodden track through thick rainforest. You may hear the calls of jaco parrots, tremblers and the mountain whistler (rufous-throated solitaire). Once across a stream and then up the side of a ridge, it's a steep descent down to the Breakfast River following a series of switchbacks. The Breakfast River is roughly a third of the way to Boiling Lake. Unless there's been heavy rain, the river water is fine to drink and it's one of few places to top up your supply. The Breakfast River comes to an end at Trafalgar's 'Mother Falls' where it joins the 'Father' and becomes the Roseau River.

From the Breakfast River it's a steep climb up to a narrow ridge. Crossing this ridge may be tricky if you're not good with heights as there are vertiginous drops on either side. Once across, it's another abrupt climb, this time to the top of Morne Nicholls. There's a circular clearing atop this *morne* from where – if the cloud ceiling is high and the thicket low enough – you can enjoy fabulous 360-degree views of Dominica's coast and interior, including several other *mornes* and swathes of forest. It's exposed here and you'll certainly feel chilly if the weather is inclement.

After recovering from the ascent, it's now a precipitous descent into the Valley of Desolation. The mud steps and track can be swampy here after rains, so it's important to take your time going down. A narrow cliff path leads to the top of what used to be rough wooden steps which, at the time of writing, have been washed away leaving a tricky rock scramble. Take care as it's steep, wet and slippery. You'll emerge on to a rock face where a stream flows into the valley. Take care climbing down and across to the trail on the far bank. At the end of this narrow path, clamber down the final set of boulders to the valley floor. You're now about two-thirds of the way to the lake. Take time to look up at Morne Watt, the magnificent volcano that rises high above the Valley of Desolation.

The route across the Valley of Desolation follows the course of the stream which, by the time it reaches the far side, will have been heated by the caldera. If you've decided to walk the trail without a guide, it's worth turning around before you get too far across so that you can memorise where you've come from – maybe snap a photo – as it may help you on the return leg when you're tired, perhaps a little disorientated, and the surrounding landscape gives nothing away.

The Valley of Desolation is an amazing place with – in my view – an inappropriate name. Instead of being dark and desolate, the valley is colourful, dynamic and animated, and a perfect reminder of how the island came to exist in the first place. The valley floor is alive with active fumaroles. Some are violent emissions of hot water, gases and steam. Others are only noticeable as tiny bubbles rising from the muddy bed of the stream and nearby pools. Be careful where you walk and don't get too close to any of these volcanically active vents – they're unpredictable and extremely hot. Notice the ground, the stones, rocks and boulders that are all stained in different colours by gases and chemical deposits, the pools of inky black water, and the soupy grey mud.

At the far side of this section of the Valley of Desolation, the trail follows the stream and then ascends the right-hand bank via a vertiginous ledge. The narrow track meanders through woodland along the high bank. Look out for the accessible warm water pools and cascades that are fabulous places to enjoy a warm bath on the return leg.

A tricky climb down another rock face precedes a series of wooden steps that bring you up a forest-covered hillside where it's easy-going until you reach the second section of the valley. Skirt the exposed hillside, following a faint track down through the multi-coloured rocks towards a fast-flowing warm-water river. Use the rocks and boulders to get across the river and then climb up a steep, rocky escarpment to a plateau. The clear path leads around a final valley section to Boiling Lake itself.

Two things are important here: don't get too close to the edge (there's not much supporting it) and don't climb down to the shoreline (it's swampy and hot and you'll sink). Wait for the steam to clear and enjoy the view over the lake. On the far side, you may notice a lip where the lake water overflows. This is the White River, which leads to Victoria Falls (page 172) and the Atlantic coast near Delices.

The Boiling Lake Trail is a wonderful hike that's made interesting and scenic by the three main habitats you walk through: rainforest, montane thicket and fumarole vegetation. The rainforest walk between Ti Tou Gorge and the Breakfast River is lush and has myriad interesting trees and plants. Look for the *gommier*, *chatanier* and *bois bandé* trees as well as the elephant ear anthuriums, the wax flowers and the different varieties of bromeliads. The montane thicket up to and around Morne Nicholls is dense with low-growing trees and ferns, with *kaklen* dominating much of the landscape as you near the summit. *Kaklen* is also prevalent throughout the forest section of the Valley of Desolation. When looking out from the high ridges and the small plateau on Morne Nicholls, notice the mountain palms peeking through the forest all around the steep hillsides. In the Valley of Desolation itself, it's always amazing to see plants, grasses and even flowers thriving in such a hostile environment. For more details of Dominica's plants and habitats, see page 5.

BOERI LAKE This is an easy to moderate there-and-back hike that should take no more than an hour each way. You must have a site pass. Although the path is well beaten and straightforward, the second half of the trail is over rocky terrain that's usually slippery. Take your time and watch your footing as there's certainly the potential for a fall or a twisted ankle. There are also a couple of shallow river crossings at the midway point.

At an elevation of 853m, Boeri Lake is Dominica's highest mountain lake. It's a 2ha crater lake that's sandwiched between the peaks of Morne Micotrin and Morne Trois Pitons. Boeri is thought to be around 40m deep and is noticeably devoid of subsurface vegetation or aquatic life. Surrounded by large boulders and upper montane thicket, overlooked by the cloud-covered summit of Morne Micotrin, and with the only sound coming from a lonesome mountain whistler (rufous-throated solitaire), the lake is exquisitely, perhaps even eerily, serene.

There are two more lakes beyond Boeri. Both are smaller and, without a sharp machete, rather inaccessible.

To get to Boeri Lake, head to Laudat and at the main junction, take the fork to the left (there's a sign). Follow the concrete road into the national park and, upon reaching Freshwater Lake, take the left-hand fork. The trailhead is at the end of this road and is signposted.

The trail is easy to follow. From the sign, follow it uphill for around 20 minutes until the wooden steps give way to a level path of rocks and boulders. Just before reaching this point, if the weather is clear, there should be fine views across to Freshwater Lake in the south and the village of Grand Fond in the east. Head down the hill and then take great care over the rocky path; this walk is often wet underfoot and these stones can be slippery. Cross over the narrow and shallow Clarke's River twice as it snakes across the path (if there have been heavy rains, the trail can become flooded around here) then finally an outlet for Boeri Lake itself. Negotiate a further rocky path that leads up and then downhill to the lake.

It's a spooky place to swim – so silent and so deep – but I like to do it if the weather is warm enough. Often it isn't. Cloud hangs over the forest, sometimes low over the lake itself, thick enough to mask the shoreline. I was once swimming when this happened to me – bear it in mind! Also bear in mind that, according to legend, there's supposed to be a Loch Ness style monster lurking in this lake…

On the road between Freshwater Lake and the Boeri Lake trailhead is a warm-water spring – look for the pipes. It's quite a nice place to warm up again after a chilly Boeri hike. Head to the Freshwater Lake Facility for drinks and something to eat.

CHEMIN L'ETANG This trail is largely unmarked and can be confusing in places, so a guide is a good idea. Some of it is quite steep and often rather overgrown. There's also a river crossing. You should allow about 4 hours for a one-way trip, either heading uphill from Grand Fond or downhill from Freshwater Lake.

The Chemin L'Etang Trail was used to cross between the east and west coasts of the island before roads were built. Together with rough sea routes, this path joined Roseau to Rosalie and was an important method of cross-island transportation for people and their produce. Meaning 'lake road', the Chemin L'Etang Trail passes Freshwater Lake in what is now Morne Trois Pitons National Park at an elevation of 762m. Originally people would have walked from the mouth of the Rosalie River up to the lake, then down the Roseau Valley to the capital, and vice versa. The village of Laudat was created by people who needed to overnight on the journey. Thanks to road access, today's Chemin L'Etang Trail is considerably shorter and more forgiving than that, with one end at the village of Grand Fond and the other at Freshwater Lake itself. Unfortunately, this heritage doesn't seem to carry much weight as the trail is irregularly maintained and, these days, has become a far less beaten path. If your hiking time is limited on the island, you should probably skip it, but if you're here for a while, it's a nice cross-island walk with a lot of history to it. No site pass is required.

The trailhead at the Freshwater Lake end is just off the Freshwater Lake Circular Trail (see opposite). Enter the Freshwater Lake Trail from the road that runs to the Boeri Lake trailhead and follow it for about 10 minutes. You'll reach a small clearing and junction; straight on is the continuation of the Freshwater Lake Trail, left is Chemin L'Etang. If you're walking it in reverse, the trailhead at Grand Fond is right at the end of the paved road at the top of the village. Follow the wide track to the right of the building and then right again as it transitions to rough vehicle track. Here's a brief description from the Freshwater Lake end of the trail, which is the easier of the two ways to walk it.

The first part of this track is steep and narrow. That's largely because it had to be cut anew across a landslide several years ago. There's a lot of tall grass and, if it hasn't been maintained, the route can be a little sketchy as it winds its way downhill in a series of narrow and steep switchbacks. Take care not to slide where it may have eroded. Eventually, the track widens and becomes a little easier as it follows the route of the utility poles east and downwards along the contours of the wide valley. On your right, look for a tall cascading waterfall called Ravine Dejeuner, where there are several small pools. The trail narrows again as it hugs the side of the valley and heads downhill. Cross a tributary of the Stuart's River – itself a tributary of the Rosalie River – on to a wider path that follows the riverbank and eventually brings you to the top of Grand Fond village.

✷ THE FRESHWATER LAKE CIRCULAR TRAIL What this hike lacks in longevity, it makes up for in beauty. Whether enshrouded in mist and drizzle, or clear and sunny with fabulous views of the dormant volcanoes of Morne Trois Pitons National Park and the east and west coasts, this is a scenic and atmospheric hike on any day of the week. If you're just walking, there's no real need for a guide, but if you're interested in the plants and flowers of this thriving montane habitat, you could learn a lot from someone with expertise in that area (page 77). It usually takes around an hour to complete this loop and you must have a site pass (you can buy one from the Freshwater Lake Facility). If you're not especially fond of high places, you ought to know that there are a couple of high and narrow, rather exposed ridges. There's also a steep descent down some rather impermanent wooden steps.

Freshwater Lake is located at the base of Morne Micotrin. On clear days, there are great views of the surrounding *mornes*: Nicholls, Trois Pitons, Watt, John and Anglais. A broad crater lake, it has a surface area of approximately 4ha and is at an elevation of 762m above sea level. In the dry season, the level can drop significantly. This area receives some of Dominica's highest rainfall, however – almost 900cm a year – making it just about the wettest place on the island. It's often cloaked in cloud and can be subject to strong easterly winds that can make the walk along some of the taller, exposed ridges a little shaky. Sometimes it can feel rather more like a Scottish loch than a Caribbean lake. But don't let this put you off. Although clear day views are indeed awesome, there's something very beautiful about Freshwater Lake and its vegetation when it's soaked in the mist.

Due to its weather and location, the area around the lake is a combination of upper montane thicket and cloudforest. The vegetation is low growing, consisting of ferns, mosses, *kaklen* (*Clusia mangle*) and mountain palms. Bromeliads, colourful gingers, heliconias and orchids can also be found growing around the trail. The lake itself is home to tilapia, a tropical freshwater fish species belonging to the cichlid family, that were introduced some time ago. As they are located so close to each other, I often combine the Freshwater Lake loop with the Boeri Lake Trail.

To get to the lake, drive up to Laudat and, at the top junction, take a left. Follow the narrow, paved road into the national park and, where it forks, head right to the Freshwater Lake Facility and car park. If you don't have a rental car, you must either hire a private taxi, hitch a ride or walk from the top junction. Public buses don't stop at the lake.

I always walk the loop in an anticlockwise direction. This means that you descend rather than ascend the steepest parts. It also works best if you wish to go on to Boeri Lake.

The trailhead is beyond the facility and across the dam wall. It's a clear path (and usually well maintained) that winds its way around the lake and up and down the peaks and ridges along the way. From the top of these ridges there are views of the lake and the village of Grand Fond, with Rosalie Bay and the Atlantic Ocean beyond it to the east. On a clear day it's even possible to see the French island of Marie-Galante further to the northeast.

You'll make a gradual ascent to the top of a ridge around the eastern margin of the lake (the peak behind the lake is Morne Micotrin). There's a steep descent down some mud and log steps. A rope railing had recently been installed at the time of writing but I'm rather sceptical about its potential longevity as the posts don't seem to have been set deep enough. There's no shame in shuffling down the steps on your backside – especially if this descent is wet and muddy. If it's clear, there are great views of the surrounding *mornes*. In front of you is Morne Micotrin and a little to the right, beyond it, is Morne Trois Pitons. To the left you'll see two prominent volcanoes: Morne Anglais to the west, facing the Caribbean, and the magnificent Morne Watt a little further to the east. To the east of Morne Watt, though out of sight, lies the Valley of Desolation and Boiling Lake.

After a flat ridge, there's a steepish climb up to the next peak on the circuit. If it's windy, this section can be a little sketchy: it's narrow and exposed. After descending again, you reach a small clearing by the lake's edge. There's a trail junction here. The loop trail is straight ahead. The track to the right is the Chemin L'Etang Trail to the village of Grand Fond. The trail emerges on the paved road that links Freshwater Lake to Boeri Lake. To the right is the Boeri Lake trailhead and to the left is the Freshwater Lake Facility and car park. There's a nice little snackette at the facility where a hot coffee or tea on a cold and rainy day really hits the spot.

MIDDLEHAM FALLS In terms of difficulty, the there-and-back route between Laudat and the waterfall is easy to moderate and takes about an hour each way. It's a well-beaten path that's easy to follow. It has some steep climbs and descents via wooden steps, and it can be a little swampy in the rainy season. There's a short section where you must negotiate a few rocks and boulders and there's a shallow river crossing right at the beginning of the walk. The trail terminates at the wooden viewing platform, but it's also possible to climb down boulders to the waterfall pool. A guide isn't essential on this trail but would certainly be of value if you happened to slip and fall, so do consider it, based on your confidence and ability. You must have a site pass for this trail.

When plans were being developed to create Morne Trois Pitons National Park in the 1970s, the then-owner of the Middleham Estate, Mr John Archbold, an American millionaire, donated the land in its entirety to the World Wildlife Fund in an effort to encourage the formation of the park. The estate covered more than 400ha and was transferred to the government of Dominica when the national park was created in 1975. The rainforest vegetation in this area includes fine specimens of the buttress-rooted *chatanier* tree, *gommiers*, tree ferns, epiphytes and bromeliads. Jaco parrots, one of two endemic Amazonians, also inhabit this region and are frequently heard if not actually sighted.

The main trail to the waterfall runs all the way between the villages of Cochrane and Laudat, and WNT Segment 4 also connects Middleham Falls with Pont Cassé and Sylvania. The most common route used by visitors is the trail from Laudat.

The route from Cochrane is less frequently walked and you're unlikely to encounter other hikers. It's a lovely, peaceful forest trail, less steep than the route from Laudat, but with a handful of trickier river gulley crossings. Finding the trailhead is also a little more challenging. From the top of the village of Cochrane, you must turn right and then left at the next junction, following a rough feeder road until you reach a small clearing where you can park. Because fewer people walk it, the track from Cochrane is inevitably less well maintained. Whether walking from Cochrane, Laudat, Sylvania or Pont Cassé, all routes meet at the waterfall trail junction.

Just before you reach the main Laudat junction, there's a sign for the Middleham Falls Trail on the left. Take care when turning into this narrow road – there may either be construction or resort vehicles emerging. Follow the road right to the end. There are toilets at the parking area if you need them. No doubt that by the time you read this, there'll also be a sign for the Sanctuary Rainforest Eco Resort which, at the time of writing, is being constructed at the Middleham Falls trailhead (page 114). Quite how this will all pan out is anybody's guess, but I'm assuming the trailhead and facilities will be preserved, as will access.

Walk up a wide track towards the Providence River, which you must cross. After crossing the river, the trail climbs – often rather steeply – via steps through lush rainforest to the top of a ridge where it's flat and easy-going to the trail junction. En route, you'll see large *gommier* and *chatanier* trees. If it's been raining, the plateau can be somewhat boggy though there are logs to walk on. You can often hear, but not always see, jaco parrots along this stretch. Also listen out for the mountain whistler (rufous-throated solitaire) – it's lonesome call sounds like a squeaky bicycle wheel. The trail from Laudat is easy to follow and there are no spurs until you reach the signposted four-way junction. Straight on is Cochrane, right is the continuation of WNT Segment 4 to Pont Cassé and Sylvania, and left is the trail down to the waterfall.

It takes about 15–20 minutes to reach the waterfall-viewing platform from the trail junction. There are a few obstacles to negotiate along the way. You must descend some steep wooden steps (don't put too much of your weight on the handrail). Also, when you're down the steps, look out for a turning on your right – over a boulder and then across a rocky riverbed (there's a wooden step by the boulder). Take your time through this wet river section (there's no avoiding getting wet feet). From here it's a short downhill stretch to the viewing platform.

To get down to the pool, go through the gap in the platform and then take your time negotiating the boulders to the bottom. The water in the pool is cold, so do think about whether you want to jump or ease yourself in.

MORNE MICOTRIN At 1,221m, Morne Micotrin is Dominica's fourth-highest mountain after Morne Diablotin, Morne Trois Pitons and Morne Watt (which is inaccessible to hikers). It's located close to and immediately south of Morne Trois Pitons. Morne Micotrin is also known as Morne Macaque, which is a confusing name as there are no monkeys in Dominica. Perhaps there once were, though there are no records to support this. It's also been suggested that the mountain is so named because you must be able to climb like a monkey to reach the top. Well, if you take it on, you'll see for yourself that it is rather steep in places (I've taken friends who made the entire descent on their backsides).

The climb is both technically and physically demanding. There are some large boulders to negotiate but one of the main challenges is avoiding concealed holes. Micotrin is thought to be a volcano that collapsed in on itself and there are places where rocks and boulders that fell together left gaps between them. These deep holes are often masked by grass and other vegetation, making the upper part of the mountain a rather sketchy climb. A hiking pole may be useful for prodding the ground if you're not sure. I have a theory that there's a lake hidden beneath all those collapsed boulders. Where else does all the water come from that perpetually fills the stream and the warm-water springs along the road to the Boeri Lake trailhead? Maybe it's even a warm-water lake.

Despite the boulder and hole hazards, Morne Micotrin is a fun and rewarding mountain to climb. Unlike the others, it is very open, especially towards the top, where rocky crags and ferns make the terrain seem more like the highlands of Scotland than the tropics – just like Freshwater Lake on a misty day. This is an offbeat trail and there's no site pass requirement. If you're not hiring a guide, do let someone know where you're heading.

To get to the trailhead, follow the same directions to Freshwater Lake but look out for a metal ladder on the left-hand side, propped against the steep embankment halfway between the steel bridge and the road junction that separates Freshwater Lake from the Boeri Lake trailhead. This trail is also a maintenance track for the communications tower near the summit.

At the top of the ladder, the track goes immediately to your left where you'll find a wide path ahead of you. The terrain here is a little tricky with lots of loose scree, so be careful with your footing. The first hour or so is simply a straight uphill slog and there are not many views through the trees. After that it becomes more interesting. Wonderful vistas appear, including a bird's-eye view of Freshwater Lake. From now on the climb is much more open, there are some large boulders to negotiate, and you must look out for those troublesome holes. It is more a climb than a hike at this point, and the route can be difficult to follow, but the open surroundings more than make up for your growing tiredness and paranoia about slipping down a dark fissure, never to be seen again.

As you get near the top, the more beaten path leads straight up to the communications mast and (sad to say) lots of discarded materials, but the actual peak of the mountain is off to the left along a far more rugged track (in fact, it may well be completely overgrown). The rocky peak to the left is a much nicer place to sit and enjoy the view, if you can find it. And be careful of more holes!

MORNE TROIS PITONS I've written this account based on memory as, at the time of writing, the trail hasn't been cleared or rehabilitated since Hurricane Maria in 2017. A guide friend tried and failed to clear and climb it, so we're now all waiting on the Forestry and Parks Division to allocate time and resources to it. I've included it here because it used to be a great mountain trail with fabulous views and I'm hoping that within the lifetime of this edition, it will be again. So, the best I can do is give you a taste of how it was.

At 1,342m, Morne Trois Pitons is the second-tallest mountain in Dominica. Named after its three-peaked summit, this magnificent volcano dominates the southern landscape and includes three main vegetation types: rainforest, montane thicket and cloudforest, or elfin woodland. It's also possible to see all four species of hummingbird on this hike, especially as you get closer to the summit.

It's a strenuous climb to the first summit of Morne Trois Pitons, but worth the effort if the weather is good and the skies are clear. It used to be possible to continue to the middle summit (adding another 2 hours to the hike), though I doubt this stretch will ever be cleared.

The trail used to be easy to follow and there were no spurs. In a couple of places towards the summit it was steep and the ascent involved climbing up and over rocks, tree roots and branches. There were also three places where you had to scale short but steep slopes using ropes. Morne Trois Pitons can be cold and wet at the top, regardless of the weather below, so it's worth taking a rainproof jacket and having fresh clothes to put on when you're back down again. You must also have a site pass.

The trailhead is located a short distance along the road from Pont Cassé to Castle Bruce and Rosalie. If it's open again, look for it on the right. The first half of the climb was a steady but steep ascent through thick rainforest and there were no views to speak of. About halfway up, the habitat transitions to montane thicket and that's also when the views began to appear. This was also where there were the three short, rope-assisted rock sections. Once at the top of these rocks, the terrain flattens somewhat, and the views are wonderful. From here, it was a gradual climb through low-growing montane thicket and *kaklen* clusters to the first peak.

WNT SEGMENT 4: WOTTEN WAVEN TO PONT CASSÉ Most of this segment is a lovely forest hike, though, due to a bridge collapsing in the 2017 hurricane, there's a difficult rope-assisted descent and ascent of a deep river gorge near trail end at Pont Cassé. Fortunately, there's an exit to the village of Sylvania before you reach that point and, until the WNT is properly rehabilitated, I recommend you take it – unless you're with an experienced trail guide. Allow 5 hours from Trafalgar to Sylvania and 6 hours to Pont Cassé. If you plan on hiking all the way to Pont Cassé without a guide, I'd urge you to let someone know, just in case you get into difficulty in the river gorge.

The segment begins in the village of Wotten Waven (though if you're not through-hiking, you may prefer to begin in Trafalgar to cut out the paved road section between the two villages) and follows Trafalgar's back roads to a steep and often rather muddy forest path. When you reach the top, you're in the village of Laudat. On the way up, there are nice views of the Roseau Valley and the waterfalls. From the outskirts of Laudat, the trail meets a small road junction (left for the trail, right to Ti Tou Gorge) and then follows the main road up and out of the village and all the way to the signposted Middleham Falls trailhead (see page 126 for Middleham Falls Trail description).

At the main junction on the Middleham Falls Trail (left to the falls, straight on to Cochrane), take the trail to the right and follow it across the former Middleham Estate, now part of Morne Trois Pitons National Park. This is a lovely forest trail – one of my favourites – crossing several streams and going up and over a small hill until it eventually meets another junction. Despite the hurricane, the forest is thick and there are tall *gommier* and *chatanier* trees. It's also a good place to hear and perhaps even catch sight of jaco parrots. As the landscape is mostly flat, it can be quite wet and muddy in places.

Straight on at the trail junction is Sylvania (if you don't fancy the rope climb in the forthcoming river gorge, you could exit here and meet the main road between Pont Cassé and Roseau where you can catch a bus without too much waiting) or turn right and follow the trail on a long and steep uphill climb. From the peak, it's a rope-assisted downhill scramble to the top of a deep river gorge. There used to be a bridge here, but now there are more ropes and it's not easy at all. Using the ropes, you must climb down to the bottom and then back up the other side. Before you do so, be sure you can see the location of the climb back up and ascertain that ropes are in place. Assuming you make it (!) there's a second, though much easier, river gulley to negotiate before the trail ends at the Pont Cassé traffic island. Plenty of buses pass this way – especially on the route between Roseau and Marigot.

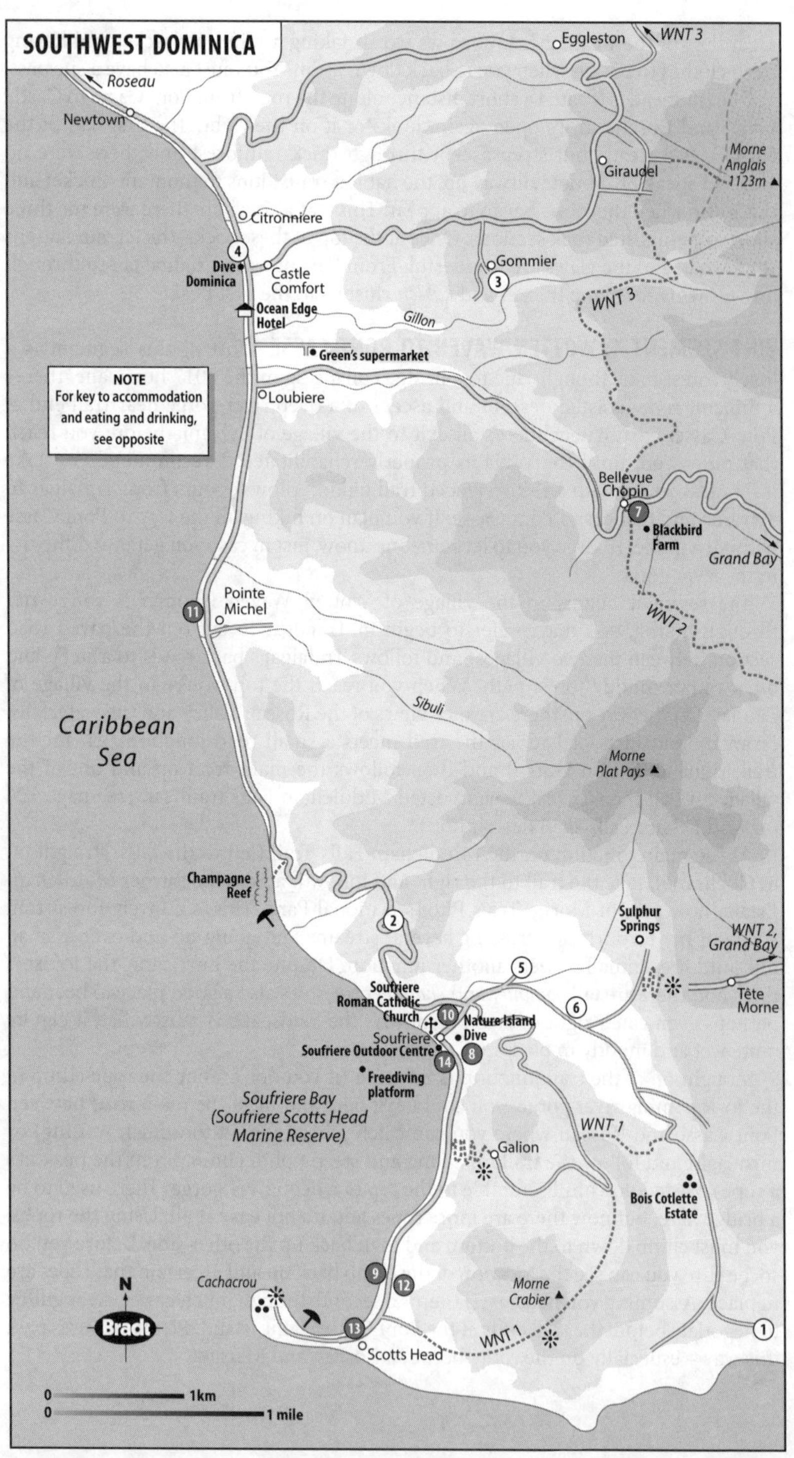
SOUTHWEST DOMINICA
Roseau
Newtown
Eggleston
WNT 3
Giraudel
Morne Anglais 1123m
Citronniere
Gommier
Dive Dominica
Castle Comfort
Ocean Edge Hotel
Gillon
Green's supermarket
NOTE
For key to accommodation and eating and drinking, see opposite
Loubiere
Bellevue Chopin
Blackbird Farm
Grand Bay
Pointe Michel
WNT 2
Sibuli
Caribbean Sea
Morne Plat Pays
Champagne Reef
Sulphur Springs
WNT 2, Grand Bay
Tête Morne
Soufriere Roman Catholic Church
Nature Island Dive
Soufriere
Soufriere Outdoor Centre
Freediving platform
Soufriere Bay (Soufriere Scotts Head Marine Reserve)
WNT 1
Galion
Bois Cotlette Estate
Cachacrou
Morne Crabier
Scotts Head
N
Bradt
0 1km
0 1 mile

6

The South

In August 2015, Tropical Storm Erika dropped around 30cm of rain in 12 hours. The south coast of Dominica was one of the hardest hit places. The vertiginous slopes of the Foundland volcano became saturated and slid down into the surrounding communities in deadly waves of mud and boulders the size of vehicles. Rivers became unimaginable torrents ripping away the landscape. Homes, businesses and lives were lost. Such was the scale of the calamity that few would have believed that an even bigger storm was to hit just two years later. Suffering worst from Erika were the south coast communities of Petite Savanne and Dubique, both of which had to be evacuated and largely remain that way today. In Delices, the Jungle Bay resort was abandoned to landslide, and the road connecting Delices with Petite Savanne was obliterated. Though a rough track has since been cut, the engineering consensus is that it's still too dangerous to attempt to reinstate the road – though there has certainly been talk of it.

Travellers rarely make the journey down to Dominica's southern coastline. This is unfortunate as the communities in and around the Grand Bay area are scenic and – in the form of music, dance, farming, fishing and *patois* – brimming with cultural heritage. The coastal villages of Stowe and Fond St Jean in particular are picturesque and certainly worth the journey.

The story is much different in the southwest, where the photogenic Soufriere Bay is becoming a magnet for watersports enthusiasts and marine researchers, and two prestigious resorts – the new Jungle Bay and Coulibri Ridge – are noteworthy places to stay.

GETTING THERE AND AWAY

BY BUS Buses run frequently between Roseau and Soufriere as well as between Roseau and Grand Bay. They're a little less frequent between Roseau, Giraudel and Eggleston, running mostly in the early morning and late afternoon. See page 52 for Roseau bus stops and fares.

BY CAR The road to the two mountain villages of **Giraudel** and **Eggleston** is a loop with both ends located on the coastal road south of Roseau. The road to Eggleston (look for a turning marked 'Kaibel' in Citronnier) is very narrow

SOUTHWEST DOMINICA

For listings, see from page 132

Where to stay

1 Coulibri Ridge
2 Jungle Bay
3 Kai Merle
4 Ocean's Edge Lodge
5 Rodney's Wellness Retreat
6 Soufriere Guest House

Where to eat and drink

7 Bellevue Chopin bus stop
8 Bottom Time
Calabash Restaurant & Bar (see 2)
9 Chez Wen Cuisine
Kanawa (see 5)
10 La Belle
Ocean's Edge (see 4)
11 Pointe Michel main road
12 Roger's Bar
13 Scotts Head snackettes
14 Weefee's Kubuli Snack Shack

DON'T MISS

The southwest offers the opportunity to see how the underwater environment mirrors that of the land. Go deep and go high – though not in the same day.

Scuba-diving The dive sites of the Soufriere Scotts Head Marine Reserve are healthy and dramatic – and those around the tip of Cachacrou even more so. If you've never been diving before, the bay is a good place to learn.
Cachacrou It's a short walk but well worth it for the view. Head up to the viewpoint on Cachacrou and then treat yourself to a swim and a seafood lunch.
Morne Anglais The best mountain hike of them all – and perhaps also the easiest – with stunning views from the top.

and winding with steep drops so, if you're nervous on the roads here, it's probably better to head up there via the Giraudel road which begins behind the Rubis petrol station in Castle Comfort.

To get to **Pointe Michel**, **Soufriere** and **Scotts Head**, take the southern coastal road from Roseau that passes Fort Young, the State House and the House of Assembly and follow it all the way to Soufriere without turning off. When you arrive in Soufriere, there's a junction with no signage. The road immediately to the left goes to the remains of Soufriere Sulphur Springs (page 143), the road next to it goes up to Galion, the road ahead goes into the back of the village, and the road to the right goes down through the village and continues along the coast to Scotts Head.

To get to **Bellevue Chopin**, **Grand Bay**, **Fond St Jean** and **Petit Savanne**, take the southern coastal road out of Roseau through Newtown and Castle Comfort. Immediately over the small bridge in Loubiere is a wide road to the left. This goes to Grand Bay via Bellevue Chopin and Pichelin. Upon reaching the Grand Bay junction, the road to the left goes east along the south coast past the Geneva Estate, Dubique, Stowe, Fond St Jean and eventually to what's left of Petite Savanne. The road to the right goes to Grand Bay village and on to Tête Morne.

WHERE TO STAY *Map, page 130, unless otherwise stated*

Accommodation listed here is selective. If you're travelling independently on a budget or in a large group, I urge you to get online and spend time browsing w airbnb.com and w booking.com because there are scores of private rooms, apartments and homes listed for Scotts Head, Soufriere, Pointe Michel and Giraudel. I think they're all worth considering. One of the great developments over the years has been the ability of Dominicans to make an income by letting their property and it's lovely to see that there are now so many good options for travellers with different tastes and budgets. Have a look at **Mathew's Miracle View** (**$**) in Eggleston, **Yellow Door Escape** (**$**) in Giraudel, **Diamond View Cottages** (**$**) in Castle Comfort, **Sibouli Lodge** (**$**) in Pointe Michel and the unique **Lower Love** (**$**) eco lodge near Soufriere.

Coulibri Ridge (14 suites) Soufriere; 767 255 9200; e info@coulibriridge.com; w coulibriridge.com. It's hard to know where to begin with Coulibri Ridge – & I've written extensively about it. In a class of its own as far as visionary design for a sustainable high-end resort project goes, Coulibri Ridge combines complete off-grid living with luxurious design concepts that are envisaged to have minimal impact on the environment. All 14 accommodation options are spacious, fully equipped to a high standard with AC, Wi-Fi, en-suite bathrooms, living areas & private terraces that enjoy fabulous views – either of ocean, mountains or both. Some suites have private pools & the resort has communal pools for those that don't. There are 2 dining rooms, gym, yoga pavilion, meeting rooms & business areas, spacious outdoor terraces, 200 acres of forested gardens & daily guided excursions. **$$$$$**

Jungle Bay (31 villa suites, 58 villa rooms) Soufriere; 767 235 0025; e info@junglebaydominica.com; w junglebaydominica.com. Having switched location from Delices following Tropical Storm Erika in 2015, Jungle Bay has been redesigned & rebuilt on Morne Acouma, overlooking Soufriere Bay. All accommodations are spacious & thoughtfully designed with a mix of ocean & garden views. Suites can accommodate 2 adults & 2 children; rooms 2 adults. All have en-suite bathrooms, AC & Wi-Fi. The large, alfresco Calabash Restaurant & Bar enjoys fabulous views of Soufriere Bay & serves b/fast, lunch & dinner. The menu is varied with vegetarian & vegan options. Amenities & services include spa, yoga & a range of inclusive packages such as dive, wellness, adventure & wedding. **$$$$–$$$$$**

Kai Merle Giraudel; bookings via w airbnb.com. Perched on the hillside below Giraudel, this is a lovely 3-bed home with fabulous views. The house is completely fitted out with everything you need & would perfectly suit a travelling family. There are expansive terraces, large gardens & a swimming pool. A housekeeper lives on site in a self-contained apt. **$$**

Ocean's Edge Lodge (14 rooms) Castle Comfort; 767 235 3417; w oceans-edge-lodge-restaurant-bar-corp.business.site (or via w booking.com). Located – as you might expect – on the water's edge, this lodge used to be called Castle Comfort Dive Lodge & was an integral part of Dive Dominica. Now the lodge & restaurant are managed by another company. The rooms haven't changed much, however. They are functional & clean, with en-suite bathroom & Wi-Fi. Some rooms have sea view. Dive Dominica & the popular Ocean Edge Restaurant & Bar are located downstairs. **$$**

Rodney's Wellness Retreat (2 cottages & camping) Soufriere; 767 616 7077; e relax@rodneyswellness.com; w rodneyswellness.com. Located in the Kanawa district behind the village of Soufriere, Rodney's offers budget accommodation in the form of 1-bed cottages & camping. The cottages have en-suite bathroom. For camping, either pitch your own tent or rent one. Cottage & camping grounds are set in large gardens with a communal pool, restaurant & bar. Rather bizarrely, there's a bit of a Mayan theme going on (the Mayans were in Mesoamerica, not hereabouts). There are hot springs nearby & co-owner Bevin is an experienced hiking guide. **$**

Soufriere Guest House (5 rooms, 2 dorms) Soufriere; 767 275 5454; e info@soufrieregueshouse.com; w soufrieregueshouse.com. This is budget accommodation in the form of private rooms & dorm-style rooms. Private rooms have private bathrooms, dorm-style rooms with bunks have shared bathrooms. Dorms sleep 4–5 people. There's Wi-Fi throughout, a communal kitchen, a large, covered terrace with hammocks, & yoga gear. It's popular & friendly accommodation for outdoor- & adventure-loving travellers – especially those who are into watersports (particularly freediving) & hiking. The guesthouse is a short walk from the village on the Sulphur Springs road. **$**

OCEAN EDGE HOTEL

Ocean Edge is a CBI-funded hotel development that, at the time of writing, is in progress on reclaimed waterfront land in Castle Comfort. According to the online prospectus, it will have 27 oceanfront rooms (Caribbean Sea), three executive suites and two restaurants when it's complete. It will also have jetty and mooring facilities. Judging by the mention of 'games room with slot machines', one could perhaps infer that the developers may also have their sights set on a casino.

WHERE TO EAT AND DRINK

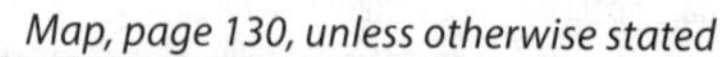

Map, page 130, unless otherwise stated

RESTAURANTS

Calabash Restaurant & Bar Jungle Bay, Soufriere; 767 235 0025; b/fast, lunch & dinner daily. Described as a 'farm-to-table' & 'boat-to-plate' dining experience, the popular Calabash Restaurant at Jungle Bay serves a range of Caribbean-inspired dishes. The restaurant is spacious & airy with great views of Soufriere Bay. Vegetarian & vegan dishes are usually available. It's a good idea to book ahead, especially during the peak season. **$$**

Chez Wen Cuisine Scotts Head; 767 615 5452; lunch & dinner daily. A popular place to eat in Scotts Head, Chez Wen has been in operation for many years. The menu is mostly local with a focus on seafood, but there's a good selection of international food too. The lobster is good here, as is the octopus, crayfish & catch of the day. Sit outside on the deck to enjoy views of the bay. Chez Wen can get very busy on Sun. **$–$$**

Kanawa Restaurant Rodney's Wellness Retreat, Soufriere; 767 235 3417; noon–22.00 Tue–Sun. Alfresco dining in the retreat's pleasant garden restaurant is predominantly Caribbean-style cooking. It's authentic & the ingredients are fresh & locally sourced. Call ahead as opening times vary. **$–$$**

Ocean's Edge Castle Comfort; 767 612 4789; lunch & dinner daily. Located at Dive Dominica, Ocean's Edge deck restaurant offers waterside, alfresco dining. Food is predominantly international with burgers, wraps, pasta etc, but there's also a good selection of seafood – the snapper & lobster are great. This is good value, unfussy dining with lovely sea views. It's popular, so make reservations for dinner during busy holiday periods. **$–$$**

Roger's Bar Scotts Head; 767 235 1839; from morning to midnight daily. Located on the main village road, Roger's serves traditional fish meals, sandwiches, burgers, bakes & good codfish *ackras*. If they have it, try the fried *balao* (halfbeak). **$**

NOTEWORTHY BARS, CAFÉS AND SNACKETTES

Local bars & snackettes do come & go. At the time of writing, these were worth a mention.

Bellevue Chopin bus stop There are some good snackettes around the main bus stop at Bellevue Chopin. One saltfish bake was so good that I immediately went back for another!

Bottom Time Soufriere. Located within Nature Island Dive; drop in for coffee, a smoothie or a lionfish sandwich.

La Belle Soufriere. Easy to miss, La Belle is located on the right-hand side of the road from the main village junction down to the waterfront. It's truly unique. A creative collection of curios & antiques have been fashioned by its talented owner, Mr Boyce, to create a lovely stone garden & bar. Likely, he'll have to go to the local shop for your beers, but don't let that deter you because the place is fabulous.

Pointe Michel main road On the north side of the village, along the main road, there's a string of snackettes & bars – most are good.

Riverside Shop [map, page 138] Bagatelle. If you're exploring the south coast, head up to the top of Bagatelle & enjoy a snack & a beer at this little riverside shop.

Scotts Head snackettes Just before you get to the fishing boats on the Cachacrou isthmus, there's a colourful building containing several snackettes. Try Rose's bakes.

Weefee's Kubuli Snack Shack Soufriere. Located on the waterfront by the Soufriere jetty, Weefee's is a container bar & garden serving drinks & local snacks from morning until evening.

EXPLORING THE REGION

The south coast is thought to be where European settlers first gained a permanent foothold in Dominica – although the La Soye archaeology project (page 18) suggests Europeans (perhaps the Dutch) may have established a small trading post on Woodford Hill Bay from the 1600s. Despite an agreement between Britain and France stating that the island should remain in the possession of the indigenous Kalinago, prospectors from Martinique soon began to venture across the channel

PRACTICALITIES

In Wallhouse, just off the main coastal highway between Castle Comfort and Loubiere, **Green's supermarket** is well stocked with basic food and drink as well as toiletry items. There are **petrol stations** on the main road in Castle Comfort.

to start up small lumber enterprises in the area now known as Grand Bay. Land pressure on other islands, the need to grow and produce food, and general fortune seeking meant that the agreement was probably always doomed. These settlers lived alongside the indigenous people for a time and soon spread around the coast to the Kalinago settlement of Sairi, now known as Roseau.

The influence of France and the French islands has always been especially strong in the south; indeed, it was with the co-operation of villagers from La Pointe (now Pointe Michel) that the French were able to mount an invasion in 1805, sacking Roseau and forcing the outnumbered British to retreat all the way to Fort Shirley at the Cabrits. Today people from Grand Bay, Pointe Michel and the tiny hamlets around manage to maintain Creole traditions, especially in the form of the patois language, music and dance. Farming and fishing also play an important part in the life of these southern villages. Fond St Jean, Stowe, Soufriere and Scotts Head are noted for their fishermen, and Bellevue Chopin is known for its hillside farming.

Eggleston and **Giraudel** are small mountain villages located at an elevation of around 450–500m on the western slopes of Morne Anglais. Looking down on Roseau and the Caribbean Sea, the height of the villages usually means temperatures are a little lower than down on the coast and they both enjoy panoramic views of coast and mountains. The two villages are noted for their annual flower show – usually, though not always, in May – taking place at Giraudel's Flower Show Site.

The original Kalinago name for **Pointe Michel** was Sibouli, the name of a fish species that was presumably caught in abundance in the area. The early 18th-century French settlers who arrived from Martinique named the area La Pointe and several estates growing coffee, sugar and limes were established on the hillside of Morne Plat Pays and Morne Canot behind the village.

The Pointe Michel of today is a lively community of farmers, fishermen, and diaspora returnees. The coastal road and new sea defence on the northern end of the village are home to several bars and snackettes. The road through the village is very narrow, so take care when driving through – especially if buses are coming at you. Standing at the centre of the village above the cemetery, and looking out across the sea, is the Roman Catholic Church of St Luke.

Soufriere is a coastal village located between Pointe Michel and Scotts Head. Soufriere Bay, home to the **Soufriere Scotts Head Marine Reserve**, is a submerged crater formed by the eruption of a large volcano millions of years ago. The volcanically active hot springs and sulphur deposits are testament to this formation and are also what give the village its name.

Soufriere's Roman Catholic Church of St Mark is perhaps one of the most photographed landmarks in the south – despite the ugly buildings and containers that have been erected around it. Completed in 1880, the interior walls of the church are decorated with murals depicting simple village life. On either side of the altar there are colourfully painted scenes of villagers dancing the *bélé* and men fishing from small wooden boats. Along the sides of the church are wooden louvre windows and decorated arches. Outside are the convent and presbytery buildings, and at the foot of the cliffs, where the church grounds meet the shoreline, is a cave/grotto where it's believed Dominica's original Amerindian settlers may have sheltered (artefacts have been discovered here). Above the cave is a shrine and in front of it an altar for open-air services.

On the shore in front of the church is a small area known as **Bubble Beach**. A submerged fumarole in the shallows beyond the beach warms up the sea. Rocks and sandbags have been used to create a makeshift spa. If you'd like to use it, you're expected to make a voluntary contribution that goes towards its upkeep. Bubble Beach also has a snackette and bar, sun lounger rentals, and even massage services. Look out for the simple *pwi pwi* fishing rafts that are used to catch fish from inshore waters. Though most fishermen have boats these days, you'll still see *pwi pwi* rafts being used in the bay by those who don't.

Before colonists created estates in the area, Soufriere Bay and the hillsides around were the home of Amerindians. In the 1970s, archaeological excavations at several sites around Soufriere uncovered artefacts dating back to the earliest Amerindian settlers – Morne Acouma, where the Jungle Bay resort is now located, is one of them. Carved *zemi* stones and conch shells depicting nature spirits were also found in this area, though sadly taken to France. In more recent times, archaeological work by researchers specialising in colonial sites has discovered interesting artefacts from sites on Morne Patates as well as around Bois Cotlette (see below) that help to describe the lives of the enslaved and their interaction with Maroons (page 209).

In the heart of the village are the ruins of Rose's lime factory. Established in Scotland in the 1860s, the L Rose and Lime Company, manufacturer of Rose's Lime Juice Cordial and lime marmalade, was a prominent business in Dominica in the early part of the 20th century. Several estates in the west of the island were purchased by the company to produce lime products, including Bath Estate, Picard Estate, St Aroment Estate, Canefield Estate and, in 1950, Soufriere Estate. Economic and social circumstances forced the company to withdraw from Dominica in the late 1970s and the estates were either sold off or presented to the Dominican government.

Every July, Soufriere hosts the denouement of Dominica's annual **Dive Fest**. Traditional Kalinago canoe races are held here on the final Sunday of the festival. Anyone can take part but be prepared to get wet – capsizing is common, even encouraged. The prize is usually a crate of beer and there's plenty of street food and music into the night.

BOIS COTLETTE ESTATE

Bois Cotlette is one of the oldest surviving French plantation estates in Dominica. Some preservation work has restored the planter's house and some of the factory buildings where coffee, sugar and limes were once processed. There's also a stone windmill tower, though it's somewhat doubtful that there would ever have been enough wind power to drive the machine works – some of which are scattered around the property. Instead, the estate's machinery was probably driven by tethered cattle. Unfortunately, the estate is privately rather than state owned and so visits in the form of cruise excursion-style tours are by appointment only. Note, at the time of writing, Bois Cotlette was closed to visitors. Check the website for updates: **w** boiscotlette.com. Bois Cotlette is located on the road to the Coulibri Ridge resort so, if you're heading that way, you can catch a glimpse of the estate en route.

The village of **Scotts Head** is named after Colonel George Scott, who was lieutenant governor of Dominica from 1764 to 1767. Scott was part of the British invasion force that captured Dominica from the French in 1761 and was responsible for the construction of some of the island's military installations, including a fortification on the prominent isthmus beyond the village. This headland also bears his name, as well as the original Kalinago one, **Cachacrou**, whose literal meaning is thought to be 'that which is being eaten' – presumably by the surrounding swells of the convergence of Atlantic Ocean and Caribbean Sea. Scott's fortifications on top of Cachacrou have mostly slipped down the cliffs beneath the waves, though some ruins have been rehabilitated to create a wonderful viewpoint over Soufriere Bay.

Predominantly a fishing village, Scotts Head received a severe battering from Hurricane Maria in 2017, when sea surge was as high as first-floor verandas, and many buildings were damaged. Much of this is still evident and, at the time of writing, villagers still await the construction of a long-promised sea defence. At the southern end of the village, towards the Cachacrou isthmus, there's a colourfully painted building that houses snackettes, and next to it are structures where fishermen keep their boats, nets and fishing tackle. It's common to see fishermen attending to outboard motors and fishing nets or building fish traps.

In the corner of the bay, beneath the Cachacrou headland, is a small, sheltered beach that's good for bathing and snorkelling (the dive site buoy marks the spot where the coral reef plummets down a drop-off). There's also a nice walk up to the Cachacrou viewpoint (page 141).

Inland, the village of **Bellevue Chopin** is perched on a ridge between the peaks of Morne Anglais, Morne Canot and Morne Eloi. It's predominantly a farming village that's grown through housing projects that were undertaken in the wake of Hurricane Maria to house some of the displaced from the evacuated village of Petite Savanne. There's a great view down to Roseau from the bus stop and snackettes at the main village junction.

The sprawling community of **Grand Bay** stretches between Pointe Tanama and Carib Point and is surrounded by the peaks of Morne Vert and Morne Plat Pays to the west, Morne Anglais to the north and Foundland to the east. The Amerindian settlers who arrived in the bay are thought to have named the area Bericoua, a name which survives today though is often written 'Berekua'. This is also the area where the first recorded French settlers arrived from the neighbouring island of Martinique and set up small plantations and timber works. Records tell us that a man by the name of Jeannot Rolle came from Martinique and established the first significant plantation here. He invited Jesuits to the area and erected a large stone cross, known as **La Belle Croix**, which can still be seen standing in the cemetery today.

Often referred to as **Grand Bay Village** or **South City**, the main community of Berekua is on the western edge of the bay. When approaching from Roseau via Bellevue Chopin, a right turn at the main village junction takes you into the heart of Grand Bay Village. The road passes through a residential area before joining the main thoroughfare of Lallay. Once somewhat notorious for its raucous nature, this is the lively main street of Grand Bay Village and is lined with small shops, bars and snackettes.

The Lallay road runs from the seafront all the way up through Grand Bay Village to **Tête Morne**. The road is steep, narrow and has lots of hairpin bends so take care and use your horn on blind corners if driving up there. As you enter the hillside community of Tête Morne, there are nice views across the valley as well as down to the bay below. There's a track from Tête Morne down to Soufriere (WNT Segment 2, page 146).

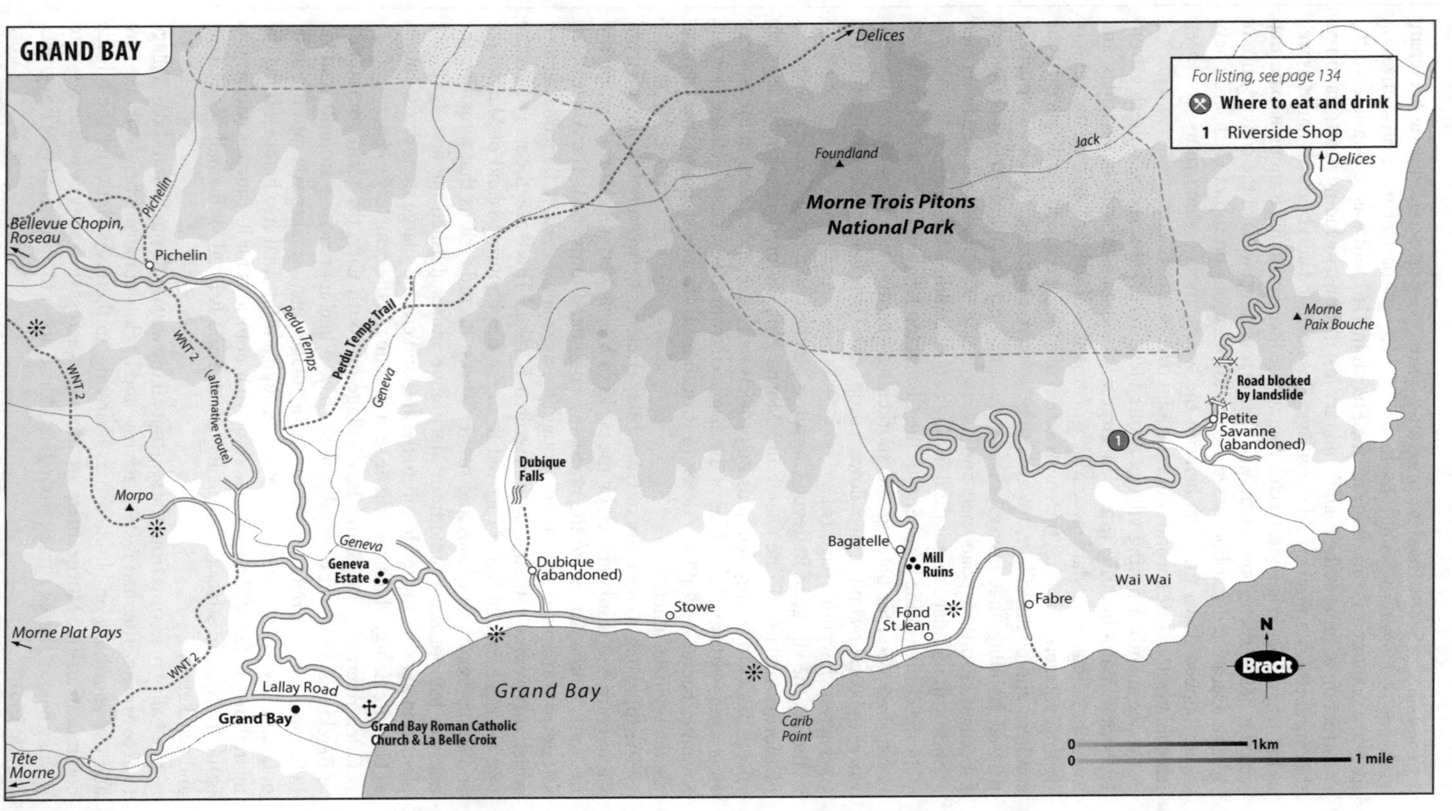
GRAND BAY
For listing, see page 134
Where to eat and drink
1 Riverside Shop
Delices
Delices
Jack
Foundland
Morne Trois Pitons
National Park
Morne
Paix Bouche
Road blocked
by landslide
Petite
Savanne
(abandoned)
Bellevue Chopin,
Roseau
Pichelin
Pichelin
Perdu Temps
Perdu Temps Trail
Geneva
WNT 2
WNT 2
(alternative route)
Morpo
Dubique
Falls
Geneva
Geneva
Estate
Dubique
(abandoned)
Bagatelle
Mill
Ruins
Wai Wai
Fabre
Stowe
Fond
St Jean
Morne Plat Pays
WNT 2
Lallay Road
Grand Bay
Grand Bay
Grand Bay Roman Catholic
Church & La Belle Croix
Carib
Point
Tête
Morne
N
Bradt
0
1km
0
1 mile

At the foot of the Lallay road where it meets the sea is the ruined Grand Bay Roman Catholic Church – also a victim of Hurricane Maria. The church was beautiful, built from stone with a bright, galvanised-steel roof. Tall stone arch windows were opened to let in the Atlantic breeze and above them were modern stained-glass windows decorated in a kaleidoscope of abstract colour. The ruined church is situated beneath the cemetery, within which stands the 18th-century La Belle Croix, and a tall stone bell tower that stands proud on the hill above.

At the heart of the Grand Bay area, between the village and the Geneva River, is the **Geneva Estate**. Once a large estate originally owned by Jesuits and then by a family of Swiss Huguenots who named it after their home town, it produced sugar, rum and molasses. In the early 19th century it was sold to the Lockharts, the family of novelist Jean Rhys's mother. In her 1966 novel, *Wide Sargasso Sea*, the Geneva Estate features as 'Coulibri' and, just as with the estate of the book, Geneva has experienced periods of uprising, arson and violence in each of the last three centuries. Today the estate is owned jointly by the state and by private holdings and is the location of the Geneva Heritage Park, which seems to spark rather sporadically into life from time to time. It is worth looking out for if you are in this area, as there are plans to rehabilitate it once again. There's a short trail around the ruins of the estate with informative signs. If clear, it merits the walk, with the highlight being the ruins of the sugar factory with its water wheel.

Also within the grounds of the former Geneva Estate is **The Coal Pot**, a local cottage industry producing a number of agri-products that include soaps, shampoo, oils and even coffee.

Heading east along the Grand Bay coast, you reach a narrow road to the abandoned village of **Dubique**. Now in ruins, though often with signs of life where people have returned to what's left of their homes and gardens, Dubique was a victim of landslides and flooding from Tropical Storm Erika in 2015. Its former residents now live in one of the many housing estates that have been constructed in the Grand Bay and Bellevue Chopin area. Up in the hills beyond the ruined village is a series of narrow cascades known collectively as the **Dubique Falls**.

BAY LEAF PRODUCTS

The leaves of the bay tree, or *bois d'Inde*, are strongly scented and used to season foods, aromatise Bay Rum and produce an essential oil. The organic manufacture of bay oil and its distillation to bay rum has traditionally been one of the prime income sources for the farmers of Dominica's southeast. The production method begins with the harvest of bay leaves – this is essentially coppicing plantations of small bay trees periodically throughout the year. The leaves are transported to large bay sheds and then boiled in water in a large vat. Bay oil rises to the surface and is siphoned off and decanted into bottles. The owner of the bay shed charges a small fee for this service. Some of the oil remains in this basic, unrefined form, and some is distilled to create bay rum. Dominica's bay sector looks rather basic with its ramshackle sheds and old vats and stills but is in fact well organised via a co-operative that purchases the oil from bay farmers and then sells it on the international market. If Dominica had a bay oil refinery, it could generate far more income than it currently receives for its unrefined oil. You'll find bay oil and bay rum on the shelves in pharmacies as well as the Zeb Kweyol shop in Roseau's Old Market (page 98).

If your time on the island is limited, this will not make it on to your must-see list, but if you do have time and feel like heading up there, you should recruit a guide to go with you as the trail is rough. To the east of Dubique is the coastal community of **Stowe**. Once a large estate that produced sugar and rum, Stowe was also the site of a gun placement defending one of the few accessible landing places in the bay. The stretch of coastline between Stowe and Carib Point is scenic, with lovely views to the south across the Martinique Channel and to the rugged Morne Fous across the bay to the west.

To the east, between Carib Point and Point Retireau, is the small fishing community of **Fond St Jean**. It's a quaint village with a scenic approach. The village has a long tradition of fishing and is one of the south's main sources of fresh fish caught by intrepid fishermen using hand lines from small boats in the choppy seas of the Martinique Channel. Boats used to be hauled up on to the shoreline of the village but are now kept at Stowe where there's a Fisheries building and makeshift harbour.

The narrow road to Fond St Jean runs alongside a terracotta-coloured cliff face that's been shaped by weather and sea and is usually decorated with tropical plants. The road enters the village and passes a village shop (good for a beer and a bake) and a couple of bars before winding its way steeply up to **Fabre**, from where there are great views of Fond St Jean and the coastline all the way westwards to Point des Fous. This area is picturesque, with steep hills, deep valleys and lush greenery. The hillsides are dotted with bay trees. At the end of the road is a small coconut-lined rocky beach. The isolated valley beyond Fabre is called **Wai Wai**, a former Kalinago settlement.

Bagatelle is a village above Fond St Jean. Midway through the village is a small road that runs down to some houses above the Malabuka River, ending at the ruins of an old mill. Fittingly, the road is called the **Bagatelle Old Mill Road** and the ruins

PETITE SAVANNE AND TROPICAL STORM ERIKA

Beyond Bagatelle, the narrow road winds around the steep slopes of the southern coastline until it reaches the small village of Petite Savanne. In August 2015, this area experienced terrible destruction from Tropical Storm Erika. Countless landslides tore down the steep mountainsides, ripping away sections of road, utilities and homes – some with people trapped inside them.

The government decided the village had to be evacuated and that the land, the roads and the homes that had survived were considered too dangerous to inhabit. As they had been cut off, villagers made their way down the slopes to the shoreline where they were collected by boats and taken to Roseau and given temporary shelter and housing. Now most of the former residents of Petite Savanne live in the housing developments at Bellevue Chopin. Those who still have homes in the village go back there regularly to clean, tidy, fix up the garden. But no-one really knows what the future holds.

At the time of writing, it's possible to drive to the western outskirts of the village but then you must walk to get any further into what remains of the community. Following the route of the road, there's a track connecting Petite Savanne with Delices but it's not yet motorable (there's talk of this road being rehabilitated). Until the road has been repaired and the area declared safe again, I'd advise against journeying beyond the Riverside Shop at the top of Bagatelle village.

are worth visiting if the gates are open and someone is there to seek permission from first.

The **Riverside Shop** is on the road out of Bagatelle. Until the Petite Savanne road is repaired, this is a good place for refreshments before turning around and heading back to Grand Bay.

WHAT TO SEE AND DO

BLACKBIRD FARM (Bellevue Chopin; ☎ 767 265 4700; e theblackbirdfarm@gmail.com; w theblackbirdfarms.com) This is a women-owned organic farm on the scenic hillsides of Bellevue Chopin. Growing a wide variety of produce as well as raising livestock, Blackbird Farm is a commercial enterprise that, at the time of writing, is considering opening to visitors by appointment. If you're interested, get in touch to see if they can accommodate you.

✷ **CACHACROU VIEWPOINT** The Cachacrou isthmus (geographically, a tombolo) marks the southwestern tip of Dominica. Its name has Kalinago origins and is thought to translate to 'that which is being eaten', which may refer to the narrow spit of land connecting the village of Scotts Head to this distinctive headland. On the south side of the isthmus is the Atlantic Ocean and the French island of Martinique, to the north is Soufriere Bay and the Caribbean Sea.

During the island's colonial times, the Cachacrou headland was the location of a military lookout and gun battery. Most of it has slipped away down into the sea, though bits of it remain and have been partially reconstructed to create a viewpoint, with cannon. The view is worth the walk, though it's also possible to drive up the concrete road to the top. It takes about 15–20 minutes to walk up the hill to the viewpoint. Prickly pear cacti decorate the margins of the road and there are informative signs along the way that describe both history and vista. At the communications tower you may notice a large white cross – a shrine to lost mariners that was in situ before the telecoms company arrived and rather spoiled things.

If you're feeling particularly adventurous, it's possible to scramble to the summit of the headland. Climb the concrete steps next to the comms tower and then follow a rough trace to the top. Be careful – it's dry and crumbly terrain.

FREEDIVING Soufriere Bay is ideal for freediving – it's sheltered and deep close to the shore – and a permanent freediving platform is afloat just off the village of Soufriere, where freediving operations are based. If you've never tried freediving before, you can learn how to do it by taking a lesson or a course, and each year there are local and international freediving competitions here. For information and bookings contact **Blue Element** (w blueelementfreediving.com) and/or **Deep Dominica** (w deepdominica.com).

KAYAKING The sheltered Soufriere Bay and west coast make for easy and interesting kayaking. While hotels and dive shops may help with kayak rental, it's worth contacting the **Soufriere Outdoor Centre** (☎ 767 616 4848). Their office is located on the waterfront in Soufriere (between the Marine Reserve office and the bridge to the church) and they offer rentals, lessons and guided kayaking trips around the bay – from Pointe Guignard to Cachacrou, with optional snorkelling and cook-outs. The adventurous can book a place on the 60km **Waitukubuli Sea Trail**, devised by the operators, using TRAK portable kayaks.

✱ SCUBA-DIVING Operators in the south offer daily boat-diving tours of sites within the marine reserve, as well as to more advanced sites on the Atlantic side of Scotts Head. Popular dive sites in the southwest are usually along and around wall and pinnacle formations. The sheltered conditions of the bay mean there's little current which is good for photography and less experienced divers. Some of the more dramatic dive sites are around the more exposed western and southern formations of Cachacrou. The marine reserve has healthy reefs with diverse aquatic life that includes frogfish, seahorses, turtles and rays, and large schools of barracuda patrol the drop-off at Scotts Head (see page 83 for descriptions of some of the dive sites).

Dive site tours are led by qualified divemasters or dive instructors. In addition to basic dive rates, operators in this area must also charge a Marine Reserve Fee of US$2 per diver (see page 85 for dive operators).

SNORKELLING **Champagne Reef** at the southern tip of the marine reserve is the most popular snorkelling site in Dominica. The reason for this, and for the name, is because of the accessible active fumaroles that lie in shallow water, venting gaseous bubbles from the seabed. Avoid it on cruise ship days when bait balls of snorkellers on guided excursions crowd the reef. To get there, either go with a reputable dive operator or drive to and park up at the access point on the west coast highway, about a mile south of Pointe Michel village (there's a big sign). At the bottom of the steps there are huts and cabins on the beach that are occupied by seasonal businesses that offer everything from rum punch and cold beer to whale watching, snorkelling and scuba-diving.

STONY CORAL TISSUE LOSS DISEASE (SCTLD)

SCTLD is an aggressive pathogen that, so far, affects over 20 coral species. It was first recorded in Florida in 2014. Its cause is unknown, but it's thought to travel via ocean currents as well as in the waste and ballast water discharged by commercial shipping. The disease has spread rapidly from Florida throughout the Caribbean. SCTLD attacks important reef-building corals by eating their soft tissue, resulting in large patches of dead coral regions that are then populated by algae.

Many Caribbean islands have been slow to react to the disease or even acknowledge that it exists. Turning a blind eye or a deaf ear to the problem will not help tourism, however. Collective acknowledgement of the disease, study, dedicated local resources and the enforcement of rules and restrictions on cruise and commercial shipping are required. So far, this has not happened.

Currently, the only known short-term treatment of the spread of the pathogen is to apply antibiotic paste to infected corals. But this is not without risk as the impact on other reef inhabitants or the long-term implications of antibiotics on what is already a fragile and interdependent marine ecosystem is unknown. In Dominica, this activity is being undertaken in the Soufriere Scotts Head Marine Reserve and has predominantly been funded by Resilient Dominica (REZDM; w rezdm.org). It has been acknowledged, however, that regardless of the potential side effects, the antibiotic treatment is not sustainable. The focus currently is more on identification, study, recording and information sharing with regional SCTLD programmes.

The reef system is at the southern end of this sand-and-stone beach. To find the fumaroles, snorkel in the shallow waters around the rocky outcrop and you'll see them – likely closer to the shore than you imagined. From the bubbles, head directly out to deeper water to find the coral reef and drop-off. Because of the number of people visiting this site, it's important to try to protect the aquatic life here as much as possible. You can do this by not standing on the reef, whacking it with your fins (especially the vulnerable tube sponges and elkhorn coral), or touching anything (sea urchins and fireworms will certainly spoil your holiday).

There's actually the scattered remains of a shipwreck here – in the form of encrusted cannons and chains – though you'll probably need a guide to point it out to you as it's difficult to spot. If you're an experienced snorkeller, consider coming to Champagne Reef at night if there's a full moon, when corals open and expand, and critters emerge from their hideouts.

Cachacrou is also good for snorkelling. Start on the small, sheltered beach in the corner of the bay and head to the dive site mooring buoy. From there, work your way along the top of the wall and around the headland to a small beach on the western point. The formation is interesting and dramatic, and there's lots of life – including large barracudas.

At **Soufriere**, walk north along the beach from Bubbles Spa to the outcrop, climb over it to a small shingle beach and then snorkel around the headland. Dive sites in this area include Soufriere Pinnacles, La Sorciere and L'Abym and, while scuba-diving is the best way to appreciate them, they have shallow formations that you can enjoy as a snorkeller. This area is a good place to see hawksbill turtles.

SOUFRIERE SULPHUR SPRINGS Soufriere Sulphur Springs used to be a government-run eco-site. Extreme weather events changed all that and the site has largely been destroyed and, for some reason, never repaired. Frankly, it was never the most attractive hot spring on the island and those of Wotten Waven were and still are much better options. However, one of the pools still functions and, at the time of writing, is run by an operator called **Bambooze Sulphur Baths** (☎ 767 265 6694). To get there, take the first left at the main Soufriere village junction if you're coming from the direction of Roseau, and follow the rough road past the school and savannah until you reach a second junction where you'll see a sign for Coulibri Ridge pointing right. Go left and drive all the way to the end. At the large, weed-covered car park, follow the track to the left (there are signs) to the sulphur bath. Another option is to walk beyond the bath to the river and then follow the track upstream to a more natural series of shallow, warm-water pools.

HIKING TRAILS

✷ MORNE ANGLAIS This is my favourite mountain trail, though perhaps I'm a little biased as I live on its slopes and can hike it from my garden! I recommend it because it's not too strenuous and there are fantastic views from the top. You don't need a site pass for this one and, though you could probably figure out the route by yourself, a guide is certainly a prudent idea. Take plenty of water as there are no springs or rivers on this trail. Allow up to 3 hours to get up, and a little less for the journey back down. In the wet season, it can be muddy near the top and there's often razor grass. If you don't mind hiking in long trousers and sleeves, then they'll give you some protection. There are one or two vertiginous spots but nothing too troublesome for those with little affinity for high places. One of these days, I'll paint some trail markings.

Finding the trailhead is tricky because it's off a village back road and there's no sign. Head up to Giraudel from the main road at Castle Comfort (not from Eggleston). It's a steep road and it will take about 15–20 minutes to reach the village. When you pass the small council office (left) and the primary school (right), you'll be on a straight road that runs in a north–south direction through the village. Pass the small shop, a couple of bars and the Flower Show Site and, just before the road reaches a T-junction, at a sign that says Pawadis, take the steep concrete road to the right, opposite the small bar (the road has a metal drainage grate). Drive all the way up to the top of this road until it curves to the right. This is known as the village back road. When you reach the second small road on your left – almost immediately after the curve to the right – park up somewhere by the junction. You'll know if you've found the correct side road because if you walk up it a short distance, you should see the main village water tank on your right. If you've located the correct road, walk right to the end. It's steep and narrow. It's possible to drive up it but parking at the top is a little tricky. You should be able to see a communications tower up ahead of you.

When you get to the end of this road, you'll see a chain-link fence surrounding what used to be a concrete water catchment. Now it's home to weeds, the occasional grazing goat and the communications tower (complete with non-stop generator). There's a track – likely overgrown – that runs up the left-hand side of the fence. Follow it right to the top and be careful not to snag yourself on erroneous barbed wire. Beyond this old catchment, the trail now wanders uphill on a faint but visible trail through the forest until it reaches a large, open pasture. Walk up the pasture, heading for the top right-hand corner. Before you get there, remember to turn around and enjoy the view.

After leaving the pasture, the trail is straightforward and easy to follow through the forest and eventually along a narrow ridge. There are several viewpoints along the way: one to the south with a view to Bellevue Chopin and Grand Bay; one to the north with a view of Morne Micotrin and, if you look carefully, Freshwater Lake.

As you get closer to the top, the trail goes downhill for a short section. This part is a little tricky because it's steep and narrow, and you must do a little climbing using tree roots to help. After heading back up again, you'll come across an area where *kaklen* trees were downed by a storm. There are workarounds to the left and right that end up in the same place. The final stretch can be muddy and there's often razor grass around. Head through the tall grass to the summit and please don't sit on the solar panels that are used by local ham radio enthusiasts. It used to be possible to reach the second peak, but the trail has now gone and it's way too dangerous to try. Enjoy the amazing views of east, south and west coasts.

GALION LOOP This is a lovely, offbeat loop hike with great sea and mountain views along the way. It usually takes about 2 hours to complete and is a dry and exposed walk, so be sure to carry plenty of water. Other than the steady and occasionally rather steep climb at the beginning of the walk, there's little to trouble hikers on this route. There's no site pass requirement and you don't need a guide.

The walk begins along the shoreline about 1km south of Soufriere. Look for a small stone building with a galvanised steel roof and a wide track running up behind it. The main road is wide here, so there's ample room to park safely if you're coming by car.

The track winds its way up the steep coastal hillside to the tiny village of Galion via a series of switchbacks. This track and its drystone walls were part of former estate lands, and the route is commonly used as a shortcut linking Galion to the coastal road below. Pause for breath and enjoy lovely views of Soufriere Bay as you climb. It takes about 30–45 minutes to reach Galion.

Follow the main road through and then out the village. If you look around, you'll see the clear definition of a volcanic crater – with you in the middle – and from time to time you can see gas venting from the southern slopes. If you know your trees, there are cashews lining the road beyond the village. Head up the hill and, at the junction with a farm track and a tottering WNT shelter, continue along the main road, exiting the crater and walking along the eastern margins of Morne Patates.

After about 1.5km from the WNT shelter, beyond a couple of houses, you should see a WNT sign and track on the right. Here, you can either follow the track or continue along the road to Soufriere. Both routes enjoy nice views. If you're following the track, turn left when you reach a junction with a concrete road (Bois Cotlette is to the right – page 136). This narrow road follows pastureland until it reaches another junction. Soufriere village is to the left, the Sulphur Springs (page 143) and WNT Segment 2 (page 146) are to the right. If you opt for the road, simply follow it around Morne Patates all the way back to Soufriere. It's nice to combine this walk with lunch and a swim at either Soufriere or Scotts Head.

PERDU TEMPS (FROM GRAND BAY TO DELICES) This used to be a fabulous, though challenging, hike but, as much of it follows rivers around the base of the Foundland volcano, it was badly impacted by Tropical Storm Erika in 2015 and then Hurricane Maria in 2017. Add to this the fact that this trail was always offbeat and never properly maintained, and you end up with what is today a difficult and even more obscure hike. I'm including it because I'm optimistic that it may be rehabilitated. If you want to hike it, you must find a guide who knows it. This could be a challenge – try KHATTS for starters. You must allow at least 6 hours to complete the hike.

The Perdu Temps is a historic trail that links Grand Bay and Delices. It follows the Geneva River and then the Jack River around the former Perdu Temps Estate and Foundland volcano. In Delices, it emerges at the White River in Zion Valley near the trailhead for Victoria Falls.

On the road to Grand Bay, south of Pichelin village, there used to be a small settlement called Perdu Temps. In 1979, Hurricane David forced the abandonment of the settlement, much as Tropical Storm Erika did to the inhabitants of Dubique and Petite Savanne on the south coast. Serious flooding and landslides have long been a problem in these parts, and still are. Even if you do find a guide, you shouldn't attempt this hike in the wet season. The trail starts where Perdu Temps was once located. At the time of writing, there's no trailhead sign.

The hike involves several river crossings, beginning with the Perdu Temps River itself shortly after setting off. Upon reaching the Geneva River, the route follows the riverbank upstream and through forest, making further river crossings until the trail reaches the Jack River. From here it's a little easier though the river exit to a trail on the northern bank isn't at all obvious. Look out for the impressive Jack Falls to the north. (Jack Falls is accessible, but there's no pool.) The riverbank trail ends at the White River which you must cross to exit.

You'll end up on the land of Moses James and his family – known as Zion Valley (page 167). The trail to Victoria Falls (page 172) is upstream to the left and the access road out of the valley to the main road at Delices is straight ahead.

WNT SEGMENT 1: SCOTTS HEAD TO SOUFRIERE The first segment of the WNT is a challenging hike straight up Morne Crabier and then straight down the other side.

It's steep, slippery and – in one area – quite dangerous. It begins in the village of Scotts Head at the Cachacrou isthmus and ends at Soufriere Sulphur Springs where Segment 2 begins. At the time of writing, although it's a clear track, it needs rehabilitation work to make it less risky. Allow 4 hours to complete it.

From Cachacrou, a right-hand turn just before Chez Wen and Roger's (good local eateries) takes you steeply uphill to the top of the village. Once there, take a right and then a left, following a rough vehicle track up the mountain slope. Follow the rough trail through dry coastal woodland to a steep ridge. This is the tricky bit. Not only is the ridge steep, but you must also negotiate loose scree. At the time of writing, this part of the trail is sketchy to say the least and you must take great care not to slide if taking it on.

If you make it beyond the scree, you'll reach Crabier Plateau: an area of lush pastureland, planted rather incongruously on the side of this small mountain, and more resembling the Yorkshire countryside than the eastern Caribbean. It's a lovely place to rest and catch your breath while enjoying the fabulous views down to the Cachacrou isthmus. When ready, head up to the left-hand corner of this valley and make your way around some ruined buildings – part of a former coffee estate. A short but steep section takes you up to a small tree-covered plateau at the top of the mountain.

Walk straight across the top, past the shelter, and begin a steep descent down the other side of Morne Crabier to a small glade with a wide, grass-covered track that becomes a stony feeder road. Follow it all the way to the main paved road between Soufriere and Galion. Turn right on to this road and walk uphill for about 1.5km. The trail resumes on the right-hand side. It's a wide track that runs downhill to the concrete road that connects Coulibri Ridge and Bois Cotlette with Soufriere village. There are good views across the valley to the sulphur-scarred hillside beyond Soufriere.

Turning left along the paved road, follow it all the way to the next junction where a right turn brings you to the start of Segment 2 and a left turn takes you into Soufriere village.

If you're walking the segment before it's been rehabilitated (there's a pretty good chance of this) and you don't fancy the high scree section, an alternative is to walk to Galion village and pick up the segment from there (page 144). I think even if you're through-hiking, this is a good option.

WNT SEGMENT 2: SOUFRIERE TO BELLEVUE CHOPIN At the time of writing, Segment 2 needed some post-hurricane rehabilitation, though mostly due to erosion and overgrown vegetation. Allow 5–6 hours to complete it.

The segment links the fishing village of Soufriere to the high farming community of Bellevue Chopin. A section of the trail from the heights of Morpo to Bellevue Chopin is said to have been cut by enslaved workers who were forced to create a route from the inland estates to the southern coastline where produce could be loaded aboard ships. The trail also takes in areas of volcanic activity and hillside farmlands. Even when in good condition, this segment is challenging because it has some steep climbs and several vertiginous sections. It's important to carry sufficient drinking water, too; aside from a standpipe in Tête Morne, this is a dry trail.

The hike begins at what's left of Soufriere Sulphur Springs. Follow the narrow forest track to the right of the car park, alongside the active volcanic mountainside and climb up to the village of Tête Morne via a series of switchbacks. Be careful with areas of trail erosion. After enjoying the views of Soufriere Bay, pass over the ridge and walk down through Tête Morne village. You should pick up trail blazes on the left after the stone cross.

The trail follows a back road lined with bay trees, before heading left at the bottom and then into dry forest and glades, before descending steeply down a narrow ridge. This section is quite tricky – especially if you're not too fond of heights. At the bottom, pass a gulley and farmland before arriving at a paved road. Follow the WNT blazes along a maze of narrow farm roads and tracks before heading up a long, steep road to the top of a peak called Morpo. This is a tough climb, especially if it's hot and sunny because there's no shade. The hillside is worked by farmers and enjoys great views down to the Grand Bay coastline.

Some hikers like to take an optional path to Pichelin instead of walking up to Morpo (this alternate route is marked on some WNT material). If you choose this path, you'll still have to climb a long hill to get to Bellevue Chopin – although you could catch a bus, I guess. It's a tough slog to the top of Morpo, but I think it's worth it for the views of Grand Bay as you get higher up the hill.

At the top of Morpo, pick up the trail again as it heads into forest. It's tricky along this stretch, and often overgrown. The trail is undulating and narrow, clinging to the hillside with steep drops down to the right. Eventually, it turns a bend and passes through a cleft into a scenic woodland trail. This section is recorded as being cut by enslaved workers to shift produce from the estates. Beyond this point, there are great views of Dominica's mountainous interior with Morne Anglais directly ahead. To the right of Morne Anglais are Morne John, Morne Watt, and then Foundland.

Emerging at a clearing where *tarrish* (volcanic stone) was once quarried, it's a broad and rather overgrown track all the way downhill to the village of Bellevue Chopin. Here, at the main road, you can get a local bite and a drink from one of the snackettes, catch a bus to Roseau or continue onward to WNT Segment 3.

WNT SEGMENT 3: BELLEVUE CHOPIN TO WOTTEN WAVEN This long trail connects Bellevue Chopin with Wotten Waven and passes through the villages of Giraudel and Morne Prosper. Rather unfortunately, a sprawling housing estate has been constructed where the trailhead used to be, so now you must pass all the way through the estate and out the other side to get on to the trail proper. Once out the other side, it's a pleasant walk that follows a feeder road past several homes and farms before it turns at a junction into the forest. Between Bellevue Chopin and Giraudel, it's a pleasant and largely unchallenging forest walk. The trail narrows on the approach to Giraudel, and erosion has made some parts a little tricky, but it's not too bad. The toughest challenge on this segment is the climb up to Morne Prosper. It's a short but exposed cliff climb that's steep and narrow in places. If you don't like heights, you may find this part of the segment a little unsettling. It's a long walk between Bellevue Chopin and Wotten Waven and you should allow at least 7 hours. You can bail out at Giraudel and Morne Prosper where buses can bring you into Roseau.

Beyond the housing estate and access road at Bellevue Chopin, the undulating forest track crosses a couple of dry creeks and passes through an area where cocoa was once farmed – the trees are now wild – before climbing up towards the village of Giraudel. Some of the trail along this stretch is tricky, especially where it narrows. There are good views back towards Morne Canot and Morne Plat Pays.

At Giraudel, the trail follows the main road through and then out the village. Giraudel has a small shop and several bars if you need supplies and refreshment. Beyond Giraudel, the trail turns off the main road and follows a rough feeder road uphill for a distance. There's a fork – often easy to miss if not properly marked – where a left turn brings you back around and down a bamboo-lined road that ends at gated private property. Just before the gate, look for a forest track on your right.

The next stretch is steep as the trail heads sharply down into the River Claire valley that sits between Giraudel and Morne Prosper. When you meet the river, look across to the other side – slightly downstream – for the continuation of the trail. There used to be a bridge here and the trail has shifted a little since.

Once across the river, the trail climbs steeply up a cliffside where you must use a rather narrow and often slippery 'staircase' of rocks to ascend. You must be cautious here. It's not a great place for those with no love of heights. However, once you get beyond the rocks, the going gets a little easier until you reach the top of the ridge and the farming village of Morne Prosper. There are great views back across to Giraudel and Morne Anglais.

The track emerges on the main village road where you take a right turn and follow it out of the village to the farmlands beyond. At a trail junction, there's an old trail to the Valley of Desolation that I urge you to ignore! This is an extremely difficult track that's not properly marked or maintained, and can be a complete mud fest in the wet season as it passes through several gullies in the foothills of Morne Watt. So, instead, follow the much easier trail downhill to Wotten Waven where it emerges in the village near Le Petit Paradis guesthouse and restaurant. You know you're getting close to the village when you can smell the sulphur. Wotten Waven is known for its hot springs (page 117), which may be just the ticket by the time you arrive. Segment 3 continues along the link road from Wotten Waven to Trafalgar where it ends and Segment 4 begins.

7

The Kalinago Territory and the East

Dominica's east coast is home to the fascinating Kalinago Territory, where you can learn about the lives and heritage of the island's indigenous people at sites such as Kalinago Barana Auté and Kalinago Touna Auté. There's also a lovely walk along Horseback Ridge that offers great views of the Territory. In the less visited southeast, there are two of Dominica's best waterfalls – Victoria and Sari Sari – both of which can be reached via short but tricky river trails. Finally, the black-sand beaches at Rosalie and Bout Sable are known for the annual visit and hatching of giant leatherback turtles.

THE KALINAGO

The Kalinago were the indigenous people of Dominica and surrounding islands when Europeans arrived at the end of the 15th century, and their descendants live here today. They used to be referred to as Caribs, but this name is rarely used nowadays. Much has been written by academics on pre-Columbian Caribbean migration and settlement of people – often with conflicting views – based on stone and ceramic artefacts that have been unearthed at sites around the region. With due respect to their expertise, we really don't know anything for certain.

DON'T MISS

Tourism has become important to the Kalinago people. Even the purchase of a small basket will help to put dinner on the table or buy the kids new shoes. Go there, enjoy learning about the culture and maybe even take a scenic walk.

Kalinago Barana Auté The 'model village' in the village of Crayfish River is an important and interesting site, especially if you take a tour with one of the Kalinago guides who work there.
Horseback Ridge Either take a drive or take a walk up and down Horseback Ridge to enjoy fabulous views of the Territory.
Victoria Falls One of Dominica's most impressive waterfalls, Victoria is reached via a lovely hike along and across the White River. It's possible to combine Victoria Falls with either the Glassy Trail or Sari Sari Falls to make a day of it.

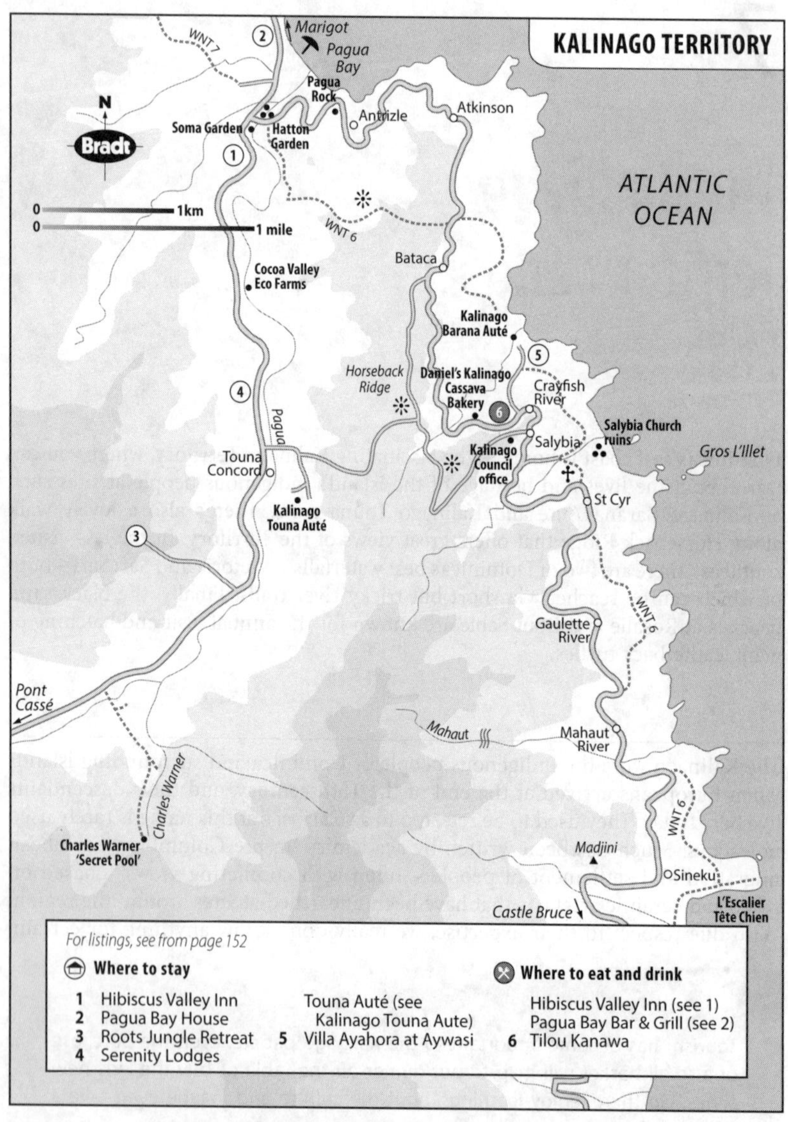

It's generally assumed that from around 5000BC, people from the South American continent began to arrive at the islands. Whether they worked their way up the island chain, down the chain, across the Caribbean Sea, or a combination of all these things is the subject of much discussion among academics. The picture is probably a messy one, with migrations of different people from different places all happening over several thousand years. Some people would probably have been displaced, others may have been subsumed into different societies, and new cultures and variations in language would have developed. In Dominica, it's assumed that early hunter-gatherers (referred to by archaeologists and anthropologists as Ortiroid people) were here first. Exactly who they were is not known – indeed, perhaps they were not just one but several different migratory

South American groups. Then came an Arawakan-speaking people usually referred to as the Igneri, who, after a long period of occupation, were displaced and had their society consumed by a more dominant group called the Kalinago. It's thought the Kalinago probably arrived and dominated just a century before the Europeans turned up.

The only documentation of post-Columbian Kalinago society was penned by Europeans and so we must bear that in mind when reading historic accounts. Perspectives would have been personal, perhaps skewed, and based solely on interactions with small groups. According to such European accounts, the Kalinago were war-faring people who were much feared by the Taino people of the Greater Antilles. This fighting spirit also appears in later accounts of Kalinago resistance to European colonisers. The Kalinago attacked ships from their canoes and raided European settlements on neighbouring islands. Over time, perhaps as resources became scarcer and movement more dangerous, the Kalinago formed transient allegiances with Europeans who were also in conflict with each other, sometimes allied with the French against the British, sometimes the other way around. It was probably all a matter of survival and, against great odds, survive they did. We don't know how many indigenous people occupied the islands when the Europeans arrived and it's probably safe to assume that their numbers were adversely impacted by European diseases such as influenza and smallpox in much the same way as populations were devastated on the South American mainland.

Though the first non-Kalinago settlers were interested in logging and growing food for export back to the French islands, land for growing sugarcane became an increasingly valuable commodity in the region and, though the British and the French had agreed to leave Dominica to the Kalinago, it was inevitable that fortune seekers would eventually arrive, establishing small sugarcane estates and claiming more and more land as their own. Consequently, the Kalinago who were left were pushed further into the more remote reaches of the island.

CANOE BUILDING

The Kalinago and their predecessors were master canoe builders, carving out vessels from single tree trunks, usually *gommier* (*Dacryodes excelsa*), and using them to catch fish, to migrate between islands and for inter-island trade. Unfortunately, the art of canoe building is no longer as strong as it once was, though there are still one or two builders in the Kalinago Territory who are trying to keep the tradition alive.

The method of creating a canoe has changed a little with the introduction of modern tools, but the process itself is still very much the same. The hull of the canoe is carved out from a large *gommier* tree – either in the forest, or after it has been dragged out to the workshop, depending on how big it is. Sometimes fire is used to speed up the hollowing-out process, together with simple hand tools. In former times, sharp volcanic rock would have been the cutting tool of choice. Hot rocks and steam are also used to stretch out the canoe, with tree branches acting as props. The bordage along the top of the canoe is also made from the *gommier* tree and is sealed using soft *gommier* sap blended with black sand to produce a tough, water-resistant sealant and resin that the builders refer to as *putty*. The ribs, bow and rowlock pins are usually made from white cedar. As a finishing touch, canoes are painted in bright colours according to the wishes of the customer.

In 1903, Crown Colony administrator Hesketh Bell secured a reservation for the Kalinago on the east coast. Bell is said to have been a curious man with a particular affinity for the Kalinago. Whatever his personal motivations, his legacy has endured and perhaps been key to helping to preserve a Kalinago population, identity and cultural heritage, however tenuous. The land he set aside became known as the Carib Reserve and, nowadays, the Kalinago Territory.

Contemporary Kalinago life is often a hand-to-mouth existence, and many people live in conditions of poverty. An income from small-scale agriculture, fishing, tourism and short-term construction work is supported by traditional indigenous crafts such as basket weaving. Nowadays, there's also a conscious and tangible effort among some Kalinago people that's aimed at reclaiming their cultural identity, re-examining their history, and connecting with networks of other indigenous people in the Caribbean and the Americas.

GETTING THERE AND AWAY

BY BUS Buses run to all places along the east coast from bus stops in Roseau (page 52). Please remember that they tend to stop running in the early evening and that you should be prepared for longer waits in more remote places such as Saint Sauveur, Petite Soufriere and Delices.

BY CAR To get to the Kalinago Territory by car you can either approach it from the north at Hatton Garden junction or from the south near Castle Bruce. Alternatively, you can take the small but convenient access road that joins Touna Concord with Salybia and Bataca.

To get to the rest of the east coast from Roseau, head to Pont Cassé and take the third exit at the traffic island. Turn left at the next junction for Castle Bruce and continue straight ahead to Rosalie, La Plaine and Delices. To get to Good Hope and Saint Sauveur, you must take the road that runs south next to the playing field at Castle Bruce. The road ends at the village of Petite Soufriere.

WHERE TO STAY *Map, page 150, unless otherwise stated*

There's a range of accommodation options in the east – from luxury hotel suites and villas to forest cabins and camping. Here are some suggestions:

Pagua Bay House (6 rooms) Hatton Garden; ☎767 445 8888; **e** paguabayhouse@gmail.com; **w** paguabayhouse.com. Located on the Atlantic Ocean coastline of Pagua Bay – a little south of Marigot – accommodation comprises cabanas & suites, all furnished in style, with en-suite bathrooms & terrace with ocean views. Pagua Bay's open-sided restaurant & bar with lounge & pool area enjoys similar sweeping ocean views. Pagua Bay is also very handy for the airport. **$$$$**

Rosalie Bay Eco Resort & Spa [map, page 160] (28 rooms & suites) Rosalie; ☎767 446 1010; **e** info@rosaliebaydominica.com; **w** rosaliebaydominica.com. Located at the mouth of the Rosalie River & powered by wind & solar energy, Rosalie Bay Eco Resort & Spa prides itself on being environmentally friendly & supportive of local farmers, fishermen & artisans. Rooms & suites vary in size & view – overlooking ocean, garden or river – but all are stylishly designed with private bathrooms, Wi-Fi & veranda. The resort has a restaurant & bar, spa & gym. Wedding packages, seasonal giant leatherback turtle watching & island-wide excursions are available. **$$$$**

Banana Lama Eco Villa & Cottages [map, page 157] (3 cottages) Newfoundland Estate, Rosalie; ☎767 245 1912; **e** bananalamaecovilla@mailbox.as; **w** bananalamaecovilla.com. Owned & managed by the lovely Melissa & Andy, Banana Lama's riverside cottages are a peaceful & relaxing

Cocoa Valley Eco Farms provides one of several fascinating farm and garden tours on offer across the island PAGE 162 — above left (PC)

Crab back, a traditional Creole dish made with black crab PAGE 57 — top right (CS)

Kanki is a traditional Kalinago dish made from sweetened and spiced cassava PAGE 154 — above right (CS)

Fresh fruits, vegetables and *ground provisions* are grown islandwide PAGE 56 — right (CS)

Produce for sale at Roseau's New Market PAGE 62 — below (CS)

above (PD) The annual World Creole Music Festival takes place during the last week of October PAGE 63

left (WAA) The Waitukubuli Artist Association is noted for its exhibitions and street art PAGE 32

below (PC) The colourful costume parade is an intrinsic part of Roseau's annual Carnival celebration PAGE 31

Kalinago craft includes masks carved from giant tree ferns (*Cyathea arborea*) PAGE 156 above (both PC)

Traditional canoes at Kalinago Barana Auté in Crayfish River PAGE 162 below (PC)

above left (PC) The *bwa kwaib* (*Sabinea carinalis*) is Dominica's national flower PAGE 6

above right (SS) The sisserou (*Amazona imperialis*), Dominica's national bird PAGE 7

upper left (CS) Torch ginger (*Etlingera elatior*) is one of many ginger species grown on the island PAGE 6

lower left (CS) Purple-throated Carib (*Eulampis jugularis*), one of four hummingbirds recorded in Dominica PAGE 7

bottom left (PC) The agouti (*Dasyprocta leporina*) is a land mammal that was originally brought to Dominica by Amerindian settlers PAGE 8

bottom right (PC) The Dominican boa constrictor (*Boa nebulosa*), or *tête chien* PAGE 9

The hawksbill turtle (*Eretmochelys imbriocota*) is the most common of the four turtle species observed in the waters around Dominica PAGE 12 above (OL/D)

The longlure frogfish (*Antennarius multiocellatus*) is one of the more unusual fish species found around Dominica PAGE 11 right (OL/D)

Blackbar soldierfish (*Myripristis jacobus*) at Scotts Head Pinnacle in the Soufriere Scotts Head Marine Reserve PAGE 83 below left (DSa/S)

Sperm whales (*Physeter macrocephallus*) can be seen all year round PAGE 12 below right (AM)

above (DDA) River tubing is a popular group activity on the Pagua River PAGE 82

below left (DSa/S) Scuba-diving in the Soufriere Scotts Head Marine Reserve PAGE 82

below right (ED) Canyoning below Ti Tou Gorge – the waterfalls, pools and rock formations in the canyons are quite breathtaking PAGE 71

A guided boat trip on the Indian River is a relaxing way to see birdlife and mangrove forest PAGE 194 above (DP/S)

Traditional organic farmers grow wholesome food and medicinal plants PAGE 74 below left (PC)

Hiking through primary rainforest on Segment 8 of the Wai'tukubuli National Trail PAGE 222 below right (PC)

above (RG/S) Roseau is Dominica's diminutive yet bustling capital PAGE 90

accommodation choice. Entirely off-grid, each 1-bed cottage is self-contained with private bathroom, Wi-Fi & balcony with hammocks overlooking garden & river. If you don't fancy cooking, you can order meals & enjoy them with your hosts in the villa or have them delivered to your cottage. Access to Banana Lama is by feeder road & zipline. This is due to bridges collapsing in severe weather & not yet being replaced. It's been so long, however, that ziplines have become an established & enjoyable feature of the Banana Lama experience. **$$$**

Citrus Creek Plantation [map, page 160] (1 villa, 4 cottages) Taberi, La Plaine; ☎ 767 613 3113; e citruscreekplantation@gmail.com; w citruscreekplantation.com. Set in 200 acres of riverside valley & developing food forest, accommodation is constructed from wood & river stone in traditional style & forms part of a solar-powered 'eco-village'. The 2-bed villa & 1-bed cottages are fully self-contained & enjoy private access to the Taberi River. The Riverside Bar & Restaurant is open for dinner by reservation. Long term rental stays & land & cottage sales are available. **$$$**

Villa Ayahora at Aywasi Crayfish River, Kalinago Territory; bookings via w airbnb.com. This beautiful Kalinago-owned 2-bed villa is on the road to the Kalinago Barana Auté (KBA). Creatively designed & constructed primarily from local woods, the villa enjoys fabulous ocean views. Rooms have en-suite bathrooms, & there are spacious living & dining areas, fully equipped kitchen, wrap-around veranda & outdoor shower. There's also a tropical fruit garden & ocean pool. The villa is located on WNT Segment 6 & is a short walk from the KBA. **$$$**

Roots Jungle Retreat (4 cabins) Concord; ☎ 767 295 8895; e rootsjungleretreat@gmail.com; w rootsjungle.com. One of Dominica's more remote accommodation options, Roots Jungle Retreat is about a 30–40min drive up a rough track (4x4 essential) off the main highway near the community of Concord. Managed & run by a lovely family, it's perfect for anyone who wishes to get away from the world for a while (though Wi-Fi is available!). The rustic but comfortable off-grid wooden cabins are suitable for couples & small families. Each has private bathroom & veranda space with forest & garden views. There's a covered deck dining & kitchen area where meals can be prepared for you on request. The surrounding area has a river with bathing pool & forest trails. **$$**

Hibiscus Valley Inn (12 rooms) Concord; ☎ 767 276 3694; e hibiscusvalleyinn@gmail.com; w hibiscusvalley.com. Located a few steps from the Pagua River, Hibiscus Valley Inn has 8 rustic 'nature bungalow rooms' set in its floral gardens & 4 'semi-deluxe rooms' in the main lodge building. The bungalows are colourful though basic. Each has private bathroom & covered porch. Some have additional beds for families. The 'semi-deluxe room' is standard hotel-style accommodation with AC & en-suite bathroom. There's a restaurant serving good local & international fare (usually by reservation) & the associated Hibiscus Eco Tours company offers a wide range of island experiences, including river tubing. **$–$$**

3 Rivers Eco Lodge [map, page 157] Newfoundland Estate, Rosalie; ☎ 767 616 1886; e info@3riversdominica.com; w 3riversdominica.com. 3 Rivers offers tent (pitch your own or rent), dorm & 1-bed cottage accommodation. There's also a small restaurant where meals can be prepared by reservation. A good option for budget travellers, backpackers & campers. Access is via zipline. **$**

Serenity Lodges (3 rooms) Concord; ☎ 767 225 5881; e serenitylodgesdominica@gmail.com; w serenitylodgesdominica.com. This is a friendly & welcoming family-run guesthouse located close to the river in forest & garden surroundings. Each 1-bed room has private bathroom & veranda with either garden or mountain view. B/fast & dinner can be prepared on request. Tour packages & taxi services are also available. **$**

Tete Canal Cottages [map, page 160] La Plaine; ☎ 767 265 2702; e tetecanalcottages@gmail.com; w tetecanalcottages.com. This is off-grid cottage accommodation located inland from La Plaine in forest & river surroundings (4x4 required). Creatively designed, wooden 1-bed SC cottages would perfectly suit budget travellers looking for a complete escape to nature. No Wi-Fi. **$**

Touna Auté Touna Concord, Kalinago Territory; ☎ 767 285 1830; e onenicepeople@gmail.com. For an original Kalinago experience, consider staying with former Chief Irvince & his lovely family. He has a wooden cabin rental & pitches for camping. It's basic living, but authentic, friendly, educational & scenic. **$**

WHERE TO EAT AND DRINK *Map, page 150, unless otherwise stated*

There are several roadside snackettes in the Kalinago Territory that are good for fried chicken and stuffed bakes. For an idea of Kalinago cuisine, try the **KBA** and **Tilou Kanawa** and look out for anyone selling *kanki* (see below) by the roadside. If **Daniel's Cassava Bakery** (page 164) is open, then cassava bread should also be on your list of things to try. Otherwise, here's a selection of good places to eat and drink in the east.

Hibiscus Valley Inn Concord; 767 276 3694; b/fast, lunch & dinner daily. The rustic veranda restaurant at Hibiscus Valley Inn serves a combination of traditional Caribbean & international dishes. Vegetarian options are available. Calling ahead is recommended. $–$$

Islet View [map, page 157] Castle Bruce; 767 276 9581; b/fast, lunch & dinner daily. Rudy's Islet View is known for its great views, its diverse collection of infused rums & rum punches, & its great Caribbean cooking. Dine out on the deck & enjoy views of St David's Bay & the twin islets. Try the Creole b/fast on Sat & Rudy's exceptional homemade plantain chips. $–$$

Pagua Bay Bar & Grill Pagua Bay House, Hatton Garden; 767 275 9701; 07.00–21.00 daily (subject to change). International fare is served in the open-sided restaurant, enjoying fabulous ocean views. For lunch there are tacos, burgers, sandwiches & salads. For dinner opt for steak, pasta, ribs or seafood. There's also food to go. Calling ahead is advised. $–$$

Riverside Café [map, page 160] Citrus Creek Plantation, Taberi, La Plaine; 767 613 3113; call as hours subject to change. As the name suggests, this open-sided restaurant enjoys a lovely riverside setting. Food is local with a heavy hint of France. Opening times change frequently, according to demand & season, so it's often not possible to simply turn up. Therefore, call first. $–$$

Zamaan Restaurant & Leatherback Pool Bar [map, page 160] Rosalie Bay Eco Resort & Spa, Rosalie; 767 446 1010; b/fast, lunch & dinner daily. A wide variety of international cuisine is on offer here – from pizza, burgers & gourmet sandwiches by the pool to lionfish, shrimp & steak in the main restaurant. Vegetarian options are offered. $–$$

Kalinago Barana Auté (KBA) [map, page 164] Crayfish River; lunch daily. An integral part of the Kalinago Barana Auté experience (page 162), the small open-sided restaurant is located near the craft & basket-weaving huts. Here you can sample a combination of traditional Kalinago & Creole fare. A great idea, therefore, is to plan your KBA tour experience in the morning so you can finish here for lunch. $

The Lunchbox [map, page 160] La Plaine; 767 225 4404; 09.00–21.00 Mon–Sat. Located on the main road in La Plaine, The Lunchbox, as the name suggests, is a popular spot for a traditional Creole lunch, though you can get other light bites throughout the day. $

Tilou Kanawa Salybia, Kalinago Territory; 767 295 4375; 18.00–22.30 Wed–Fri, 12.30–22.30 Sat–Sun. Meaning 'little canoe', Tilou Kanawa is a

KANKI

Kanki is a traditional Kalinago dish made from cassava roots (*Manihot esculenta*). The roots are peeled and grated then soaked in water before being strained through muslin. The water is left to settle in a bowl until a starchy residue has collected at the bottom. The excess water is poured away, and the starchy residue mixed up with the grated cassava, sugar and a variety of spices until it becomes sticky. Portions of the mixture are wrapped in banana leaves and tied up with string before being boiled in a pot of water. After around 15 minutes the *kanki* is ready to serve. *Kanki* is occasionally sold roadside in the Territory. Also check out the restaurant at Kalinago Barana Auté (page 162).

PRACTICALITIES

There are small shops selling essential items in Bataca, Salybia, Castle Bruce and La Plaine. Riviere Cyrique and Delices have **petrol stations**.

Kalinago-run restaurant & bar on the main road in the village of Salybia. From the deck restaurant, there are great views of the coast. Often in the evenings Tilou is more of a bar than restaurant, so perhaps head there on Sat or Sun lunchtime for some interesting dishes that combine international with traditional Kalinago cooking. Try the cassava taco. $

EXPLORING THE REGION

THE KALINAGO TERRITORY The Kalinago Territory covers 1,530ha on Dominica's east coast, from the village of Bataca in the north to the village of Sineku in the south. It was established in 1903 by Dominica's first Crown Colony administrator, Hesketh Bell, who governed Dominica between 1899 and 1905. The semi-autonomous Kalinago Territory is administered by the Kalinago Council, which is headed up by the Kalinago Chief. Both council and chief are elected by residents of the Kalinago Territory every five years. The Kalinago Territory and its people are also represented in government at ministerial level.

By law, the Kalinago Territory is communally owned. No one person can buy or sell part of the territory nor use it as collateral at a bank for a loan. This is often cited as a hindrance to both personal and business development and for this reason some are calling for statutory modifications or specific financial allowances to be enacted for Dominica's indigenous people. A form of Kalinago bank or credit union is apparently in the works. Any Kalinago resident may stake a claim to a vacant portion of land, however, and so long as no-one else has already claimed it, and the Kalinago Council approves the claim, then that resident may build a house there and work the land. Any land which has been left untended for more than a year may theoretically be claimed by someone else, subject to approval by the Kalinago Council. Sometimes there may be a transfer cost, the value of which is determined by the Kalinago Council.

There are eight hamlets within the Kalinago Territory: Bataca, Salybia, Touna Concord, Crayfish River, Mahaut River, St Cyr, Sineku and Gaulette River. In many ways these hamlets resemble any other rural settlement in Dominica, consisting of small houses of wood and concrete, flower gardens and vegetable plots. But there's a feeling that things are a little different here. There are always people walking the main road between the villages (the bus service is irregular, and they can save a few dollars by walking) and along the roadside you'll see stalls selling traditional *larouma* basketwork and various other handcrafted gifts made from coconut and calabash husks. Inland, beyond the villages, much of the Territory is uninhabited, stretching from Sineku westwards across a high ridge and up to the banks of the Pagua River in the area of Charles Warner.

The administrative centre of the Kalinago Territory is **Salybia**, which is home to the Kalinago Council, the community centre and the main police station. Heading north through Salybia there's a road to the right that goes down to the Salybia Catholic Church, which was built in 1991. Its steeply pitched roof and the anchor poles that are driven deep into the ground are designed to protect the church from hurricanes. Both the exterior and interior have murals depicting Kalinago life and the arrival of Europeans. The church altar is a small hand-carved canoe.

TREE FERN CARVINGS

You may come across hand-carved masks made from a dark, fibrous material. This is actually the bottom of a tree fern trunk (known locally as *fwigè* or *fougère*) that has been split, had the core carved out, and then been shaped into two separate masks (which come in various types). There are several very competent exponents of this craft in Dominica, some of whom are Kalinago. One such person is Israel Joseph, who has a small and packed roadside shop in Mahaut River. He makes high-quality masks, plant holders, bird feeders, wood carvings and reliefs. Israel's wife, Victoria, is an accomplished *larouma* basket weaver.

Continue down the path towards the Atlantic coast and you'll discover the original Salybia Church in an area that was once a settlement called St Marie.

Located in Salybia Bay are two islets referred to as either the Salybia Isles or Petit L'Ilet and Gros L'Ilet. According to Kalinago legend, each islet was once a ship that was used to transport the spirits of dead Kalinago out to sea. It's said that on at least one of the islets there is a large steel anchor chain emerging from the rock down to the ocean floor.

On a high ridge overlooking the hamlet of **Bataca** and the Pagua River Valley is **Pagua Rock**. This volcanic rock formation, some 20m in height, is said to be the home of a benevolent spirit and the steps leading up to it were once used by locals seeking good fortune, which could be found in the form of charms on the top of the rock itself. According to legend, if you're very lucky, you may find a small white flower that only blooms on one day of the year. If it is in bloom, you should rub it into the palm of your hand and then point your palm at any person you wish to command. Upon calling their name, that person will do as you wish. There's a catch, however. The rock has several cracks and if you were ever to catch sight of the spirit living within, you could be sure someone you knew was going to die.

This story is typical of the Kalinago myths and legends that form part of the culture as well as the landscape. Historically, the Kalinago would attribute spirits to everything from the weather to the natural environment and their understanding of plants and their practical and medicinal applications is still knowledge that's handed down. Though, as with all things, the lifestyle of the modern world competes for attention in this mind space.

EAST COAST VILLAGES Amerindians arrived on the black sandy shores of **Castle Bruce** some 2,000 years ago and built a settlement there. They named it **Kouanari** and probably lived off fish and shellfish caught from the bay and the brackish water of the lagoon at the mouth of the river. On the fertile land of red soil, they would have planted cassava and other root crops until the Europeans turned up and changed their existence here forever.

When the French and British settled in this area, the flat and fertile lands stretching inland from the bay became sugarcane and coffee plantations. In 1761, when the British captured Dominica from the French, the bay was named St David's Bay and Royal Engineer Captain James Bruce, who built some of the island's fortifications at the time, purchased 600ha of the river valley and named the area after himself. Bruce imported over 150 enslaved Africans to work his plantations. After emancipation in 1838, the estate was abandoned and the liberated workers began to settle in the valley and further to the north in the area of the former Richmond and Senhouse Estates. A sprawling village eventually began to develop up the hillside overlooking the bay. Access to Roseau was by ship or on foot and horse across the interior – more or less along the route that's now Segment 5 of the Wai'tukubuli National Trail.

The people of Castle Bruce have depended on fishing and agriculture for their living ever since the estates broke up and free people began tending to their own smallholdings. The predominant crop for a long time was the banana and the region was badly impacted by the end of the lucrative trade with Europe. Many farmers gave up their farms and others were forced to rethink, diversifying into

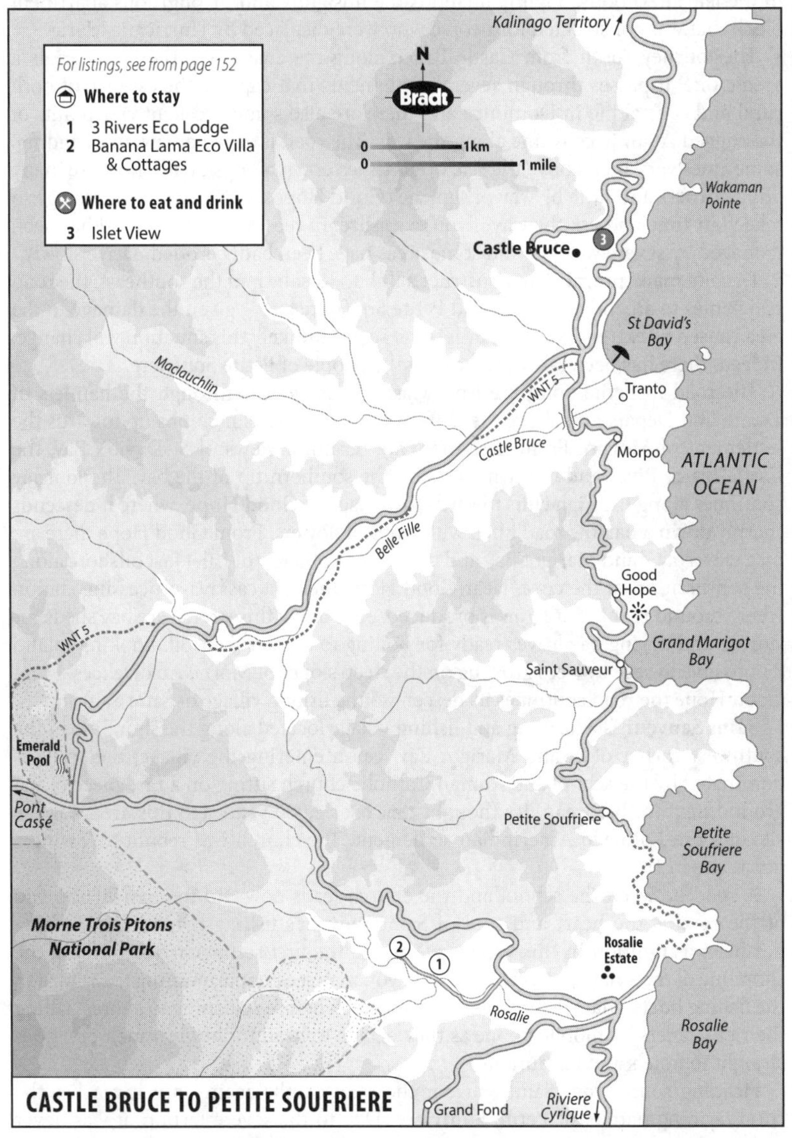

CASTLE BRUCE TO PETITE SOUFRIERE

smaller scale, higher value crops that they could sell to neighbouring islands as well as the domestic market.

Castle Bruce is a patchwork of homes perched along steep slopes overlooking the ocean. The area was badly impacted by Hurricane Maria in 2017 and there are still several broken and abandoned buildings. The quaint Roman Catholic church stands at the centre of the village.

The beach along St David's Bay is natural and wild. Smooth driftwood of all shapes and sizes litters the black sandy shoreline all the way to the mouth of the river. At the southern end of the bay are two islets and at the mouth of the Castle Bruce River is a brackish water lagoon where local families are often seen bathing in the late afternoons. Slightly inland is the unsightly and incongruous apartment block that was constructed for people who were displaced by Hurricane Maria.

The journey south from Castle Bruce along the coast to Petite Soufriere is a scenic one. It passes through several settlements that capture the essence of both rural and coastal life in Dominica and there are also some excellent viewpoints of the rugged Atlantic coastline along the way. The road is very narrow and winding, sometimes very high above the sea, other times down alongside it. There are many blind corners and little by way of signage (Good Hope can be a little confusing) so take your time and ask the way if you're unsure. In recent times, the road has been damaged by severe weather and some areas have been badly eroded. Drive slowly.

Despite many promises to construct a link to Rosalie and the southeast, the road still comes to an end a little beyond Petite Soufriere and – given the damage to the area caused by extreme weather events – it seems unlikely this situation will change. Indeed, there has been talk of relocating the people of Petite Soufriere.

The road to Petite Soufriere from Castle Bruce passes through the hamlets of Tranto and Depaix and above the cliffs of Pointe Zicac, as it climbs up towards the settlement of **Morpo**. From here there are beautiful views of St David's Bay, the Castle Bruce River and the twin islets on the southern tip of the bay. The journey continues along the high cliffs towards the village of **Good Hope**, where it descends sharply down a narrow road lined with tropical flowers. From Good Hope there are nice views of Grand Marigot Bay and the pointed outcrop of L'Ilet just offshore along the southern tip of the cove. Near Good Hope there's a cassava-processing station where ground manioc or *farine* is produced. Also along this stretch are bay sheds for storing and drying bay leaves ready for boiling to extract their oil. Looking inland it's possible to see bay trees growing on the steep slopes of Morne Aux Delices. From Good Hope the road continues its descent to the fishing village of Saint Sauveur.

Saint Sauveur is a farming and fishing village located along the shoreline in the southwest corner of Grand Marigot Bay. Upon entering the village, the scene is dominated by the school and Roman Catholic church sitting on a rare piece of flat ground next to the ocean. It's thought that over 2,000 years ago this area was the site of a pre-Kalinago Amerindian settlement. The church was rebuilt following a hurricane in 1916.

A road between the school and the church leads down to the bay. At the end of the road is the heart and soul of Saint Sauveur's fishing community. Fishing has been a tradition in this village ever since the first settlers arrived. Along the shoreline of the small, protected harbour, you may see people awaiting the return of the fishing boats. Many fishermen sell their catch before returning to shore. Calling their customers by mobile phone as they decide to head for home, much of it goes straight to hotels and restaurants.

Heading south from Saint Sauveur the road climbs again until it reaches the rural farming hamlet of **Petite Soufriere**. Due to the severe terrain, it was never

SARGASSUM

The **Great Atlantic Sargassum Belt** is a mass of sargassum seaweed in the tropical Atlantic Ocean that stretches from West Africa to the Gulf of Mexico. Sargassum is a genus of seaweed that floats in large masses on the ocean surface, never attaching to the sea floor like most seaweeds. These huge mats of sargassum provide a home and a source of food to a wide variety of fishes and other marine creatures. In recent years, large blooms and mats of sargassum have drifted into the Caribbean and washed ashore. This isn't great news for the Caribbean tourism industry, especially for those islands that rely on their beaches and beachside resorts. When the sargassum washes ashore, it dies quickly and then rots, expelling hydrogen sulphide, an unpleasant odour that can be extremely strong where there are large concentrations of weed. Sargassum usually appears in spring, though there are no hard-and-fast rules about this, and scientists are still trying to determine why there are large blooms and how wind and currents move these huge floating mats around. The shoreline and bays on Dominica's east coast are especially impacted from time to time, though the west coast has not been immune to it either. At the time of writing, there's an interesting independent website called w sargassummonitoring.com that you may wish to check out.

part of a working estate but instead developed as a peasant farming community. Today you may see the villagers of Petite Soufriere tending to their root crops on the vertiginous slopes above the ocean. You may also see the scars of landslides that make this a rather perilous place to live in these times of climate change and extreme weather events.

The Rosalie River is formed by the convergence of several other rivers (the Clarke's River, the Cacao River, the Stuart's River and several smaller tributaries) that find their source deep within Morne Trois Pitons National Park. It's along this river that one of Dominica's largest estates was once located. Covering an area of over 840ha, the Rosalie Estate produced sugar, limes, cocoa, bananas and coconuts. In the 1780s, during a period of conflict with bands of well-organised Maroons (enslaved Africans who had escaped captivity), the estate was attacked and plundered. Chief Balla, one of the most prominent Maroon leaders of the time, led an assault in which several estate workers were killed, including the manager, and much of the estate was burned down. This action led to a greater intensity and focus by Governor George Robert Ainslie to capture and kill Dominica's bands of marauding Maroons. Thanks to tip-offs from captives, several leaders were taken, including Balla, who was shot and then exposed on the iron frame of a gibbet, taking, it's said, a week to die.

Today, the ruins of the estate buildings can still be seen near to the river mouth, including those of an aqueduct and sugar works. The church has been restored and is now the Rosalie Diocesan Centre. From the rough track that passes the ruins, there's a trail that follows the coast northwards and emerges at the village of Petite Soufriere. A link road was promised and planned, but it never materialised.

Immediately to the south of the Rosalie River bridge, opposite the Rosalie Bay Eco Resort, is a road that runs steeply up into the interior and the elevated village of **Grand Fond**. At a height of around 400m, the small settlement lies on a narrow ridge with deep river valleys to the north and south. The village is part of the original **Chemin L'Etang Trail** (page 124) that climbs up above the Stuart's River valley to

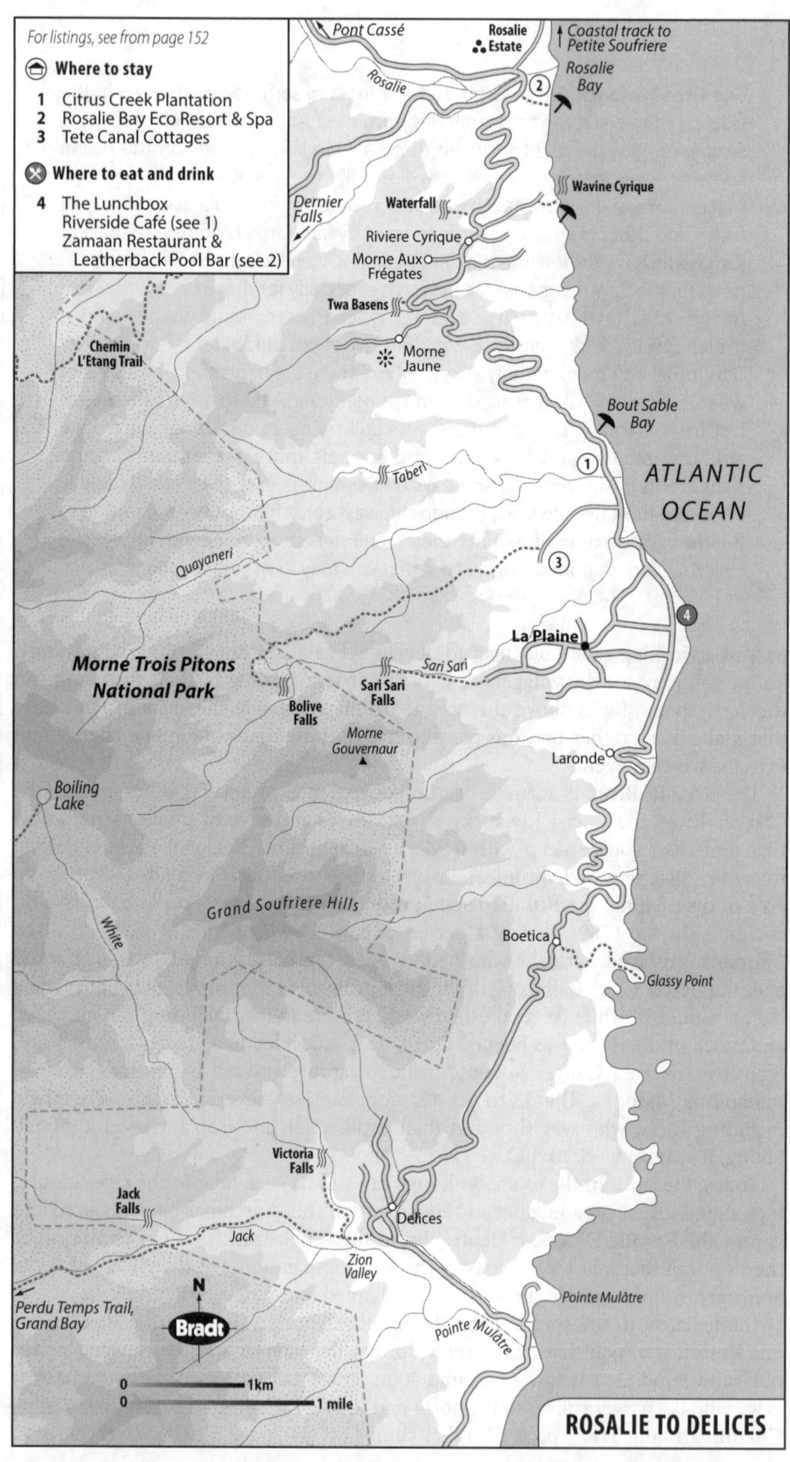
For listings, see from page 152
Where to stay
1 Citrus Creek Plantation
2 Rosalie Bay Eco Resort & Spa
3 Tete Canal Cottages
Where to eat and drink
4 The Lunchbox
Riverside Café (see 1)
Zamaan Restaurant &
Leatherback Pool Bar (see 2)
Pont Cassé
Rosalie Estate
Coastal track to Petite Soufriere
Rosalie Bay
Rosalie
Wavine Cyrique
Dernier Falls
Waterfall
Riviere Cyrique
Morne Aux Frégates
Twa Basens
Chemin L'Etang Trail
Morne Jaune
Bout Sable Bay
ATLANTIC OCEAN
Taberi
Quayaneri
La Plaine
Morne Trois Pitons National Park
Sari Sari
Sari Sari Falls
Bolive Falls
Morne Gouvernaur
Laronde
Boiling Lake
Grand Soufriere Hills
White
Boetica
Glassy Point
Victoria Falls
Jack Falls
Delices
Jack
Zion Valley
Perdu Temps Trail, Grand Bay
N
Bradt
Pointe Mulâtre
Pointe Mulâtre
0 1km
0 1 mile
ROSALIE TO DELICES

Freshwater Lake and then – now by paved road – down through the Roseau Valley to the capital. The road up to Grand Fond has some scenic views of the interior and the deep river valley on the south side of the ridge. As buses rarely reach Grand Fond, expect plenty of people to ask you for a ride up to the village if you're driving.

From the Rosalie River bridge, the road along the southeast coast twists and turns through the small communities of **Riviere Cyrique** and **Morne Aux Frégates**. There are a number of interesting, though off-the-beaten-path natural features in this area, including a hidden waterfall on the northern outskirts of Riviere Cyrique and **Twa Basens** river pools (page 167) on the northern outskirts. The oft-photographed waterfall at Wavine Cyrique has been out of bounds for some time. The cliff climb was always tricky but since the storms it's now considered too dangerous by most guides.

The road south of Riviere Cyrique to La Plaine passes a road up to the mountain community of **Morne Jaune**, from where there are more great views, and also the former **Taberi Estate**. Once a large sugar and lime estate, Taberi got its name from the Kalinago word *taboui*, meaning 'house' or 'meeting place'. Also in this area, along the shoreline, is the rugged **Bout Sable Bay**. This bay of smooth pebbles and dark volcanic sand is a recognised turtle nesting site where, at certain times of the year, giant leatherbacks can be seen returning to lay their eggs (page 166).

South of Bout Sable Bay is the village of **La Plaine**, which gets its name from the gently sloping area of flat land upon which it is built. The original Kalinago settlement here was called Koulirou. The brightly painted Roman Catholic church with small bell tower, galvanised roof and arched windows stands at the centre of the village near the school. Predominantly residential, La Plaine is where you'll find the **Sari Sari Falls** trailhead (page 171).

To the south of La Plaine is a small village called **Boetica**, also once a Kalinago settlement. Opposite the Roman Catholic church is the start of the **Glassy Pool Trail** (page 168).

The quiet farming village of **Delices** is located at the southeastern tip of Dominica. At the end of a long stretch of road from Boetica there's a junction by a bus stop. From the north, the road straight ahead goes to the upper part of the village and beyond to the beautiful coastal farmlands of the Belvedere Estate. The small Roman Catholic cemetery in this area, located on a high narrow ridge, is one of the most beautiful places of rest you could ever imagine. The main road to the right runs down to the lower village and then past arrowroot, bay and banana plantations to Victoria, where you'll find the trailhead for **Victoria Falls** (page 172). The road meets the Atlantic coast again at Point Mulâtre Bay (this is where the White River from Boiling Lake eventually meets the ocean). Until the through-road to Petite Savanne is fixed, you should consider the Point Mulâtre bridge journey's end along this coast.

PAGUA RIVER VALLEY The Pagua River is one of Dominica's longest waterways and runs northeastwards from the area of Gleau Gommier in the Central Forest Reserve, all the way to the east coast, where it meets the Atlantic Ocean at Pagua Bay just south of Douglas-Charles Airport. The river also marks the western boundary of the Kalinago Territory. It's a picturesque river with several accessible bathing pools.

Both river and road pass through the small village of **Touna Concord** on the northern edge of the Central Forest Reserve. The name of this village is rather confusing. Essentially, it's split across the Pagua River. On the south side of the river is the Kalinago Territory, where the settlement is referred to as Touna. On the north side of the river, it's called Concord. From the main road, heading east, there's a right turn along a narrow concrete road and bridge. This road will take you over Horseback Ridge to the Kalinago villages of Salybia and Bataca. It will also bring you to **Kalinago Touna Auté** (page 164), where you can experience a little of contemporary Kalinago life. About a mile to the south of Touna Concord is the start of the **Charles Warner 'Secret Pool'** trail (page 167).

To the north of Concord, where the Pagua River meets the sea, is an area called **Hatton Garden**. As the name suggests, this was once a British-owned estate that produced sugar, rum and limes. It had a water wheel and around 200 enslaved workers. Some of the estate ruins can be seen by the roadside. When you emerge from the interior to meet the Atlantic Ocean at Hatton Garden, you are greeted by the wide Pagua Bay. At the junction before the bridge, the road to the right goes south along the coast through the Kalinago Territory and the road straight ahead follows the coast to Marigot, Douglas-Charles Airport and the beaches and villages of the northeast.

On the northern edge of Pagua Bay is Marigot and on the southern edge are the villages of **Antrizle** and **Atkinson**. The original Kalinago name for this area was Warawa, but it was renamed in the 1760s after William Atkinson, a British landowner in the area. Atkinson is a small farming community overlooking the bay on the northern boundary of the Kalinago Territory. Right next to Atkinson, Antrizle has a wonderful, secluded cove and beach.

WHAT TO SEE AND DO

✷ COCOA VALLEY ECO FARMS (Touna Concord; ☎ 767 276 1234; tour fee US$25 pp; 24hr advance notice required) Join Kenny and his family on a tour of their 'all natural' farm in the Kalinago Territory near Touna Concord. With an extensive knowledge of plants and soil composition, this family farming team grow produce in a thoughtful and interconnected way, placing high value on small numbers of heirloom varieties rather than hybrids that are grown in bulk for rapid commercial cultivation. All composts and bug sprays used are made only with what's grown on the farm – nothing comes in from the outside. The largest banana plants and banana bunches I've ever seen are here, along with other interesting plant species. The enthusiasm and knowledge of Kenny and his young family is wonderful, and a tour of the farm a real treat. After your walk, try some of the creative cooking that the family prepare with produce from their farm. Look for the sign on the main road near Serenity Lodges, and then wade across a shallow section of the Pagua River to get here.

✷ KALINAGO BARANA AUTĖ (🕘 09.00–17.00 Mon–Fri, 10.00–16.00 Sat–Sun; entry fee US$10) Kalinago Barana Auté (KBA) translates to 'Kalinago village by the sea'. Located down a very steep, paved road in the hamlet of Crayfish River, the village is well signposted from the main road and therefore easy to find.

This showcase village was opened in April 2006. It's a representation of a pre-Columbian Amerindian village and attempts to recreate and promote greater awareness of Kalinago culture, tradition and former way of life. Without doubt, the best way to experience the KBA is in the company of one of the Kalinago guides that work there. They are paid a salary, so there's no additional charge for guide services (though they do appreciate tips, of course).

A circular trail begins at the reception centre where you pay the entrance fee and – if available – hire a guide. Take time to enjoy the exceptional and informative displays in the interpretation room.

Passing through a tall, thatched archway there are craft stalls on the left where Kalinago women weave *larouma* basketware. On the right are toilets and refreshment facilities (the food is good here). The **Old Mapou Tree Trail**, or Binalecaall Mapou Wêwê, takes you to the cliff edge where there's a viewpoint, or Barana Neupatae, over the rugged Atlantic coastline. Curving back inland, the path crosses the Crayfish River before heading back to the coast again. There are further viewpoints of the rugged coastline as well as the **Isulukati Waterfall** as it cascades down the smooth rocks, through a pool and on into the sea. The pool beneath the falls is known locally as Basin Bleau and is a nice place to bathe. Signs along the route point out plants and trees that have been traditionally used by the Kalinago for both herbal medicine and shelter construction.

The trail then ascends and passes several thatched huts called *ajoupas* and *mwenas*. On the way back towards the Crayfish River, it meets the impressive Karbet. Traditionally, a *karbet* was a large, thatched hut that was in the centre of an Amerindian village, with the smaller *ajoupa* huts surrounding it. The word *karbet* is said to be a French term that was used to describe this structure. The original Kalinago word was *taboui* but sadly it has been lost over the years. Supposedly, only Amerindian men were allowed in the *karbet*, which would probably have been around 20m long and 10m wide. It was thought to have been a place where they kept their weapons and slept in hammocks strung up between the beams. The women and children of the village probably slept in *ajoupas*, but nothing is known for certain and there were likely many variations to living style and community rules. The replica *karbet* in the KBA is used for presentations of Kalinago culture as well as for dance performances by groups such as the Carina Cultural Group and the Karifuna Cultural Group – usually on cruise ship days.

BASKETWORK

The Kalinago are excellent basket weavers. Their beautiful products can be purchased from stalls and craft shops around the island. Traditionally, basketwork would have been used to carry food, store clothing and supplies, and to catch fish and crustaceans. Today a variety of wares is available, including beautifully shaped baskets, bottles, mats and 'finger traps'.

They are usually made from the ***larouma*** reed (*Ischosiphon arouma*), which was probably brought by Amerindians from the Amazon River basin several thousand years ago and planted as a crop. The Kalinago word for the reed was *oualloman*, but it underwent a transition to French Creole and became *l'arouman*. It's a tall reed which, after harvesting, is split and the pith removed. The strips of reed are laid out in the sun to dry and turn a reddish brown. Some reeds are coloured black by covering them in mud and leaving them for a few days. White reeds are created simply by using the underside of the reddish-brown reeds that have been left out in the sun. Some baskets were traditionally lined with the leaves of the *z'ailes mouches* (*Caludovica insignis*) plant, which is found growing in the rainforest and provides a natural waterproofing.

Traditionally, *larouma* baskets are made by Kalinago women and you can see some of them at work at the Kalinago Barana Auté (KBA). Kalinago basketwork is sold at the KBA, at a number of roadside stalls and craft shops throughout the Kalinago Territory, and in gift shops and boutiques in Roseau. The sale of basketware is an important source of income for Kalinago families.

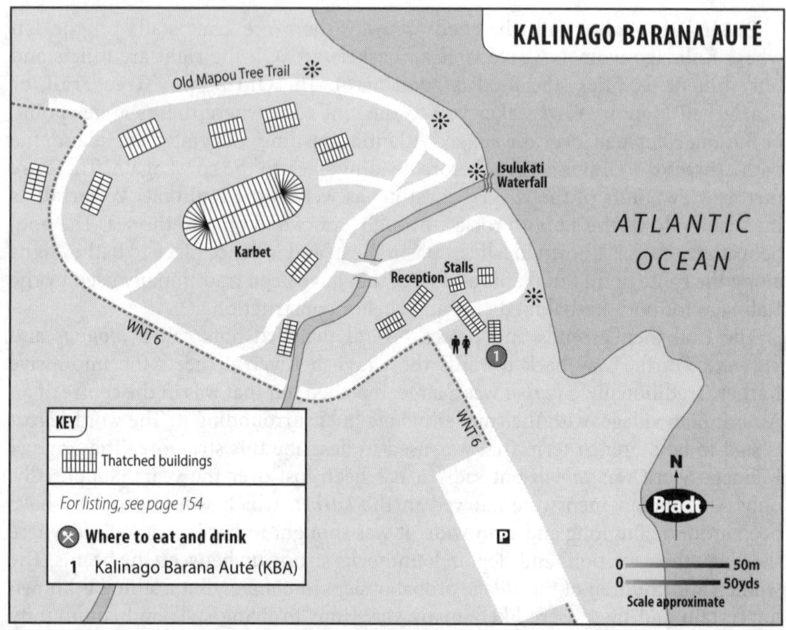

The old coastal road brings you back across the Crayfish River to the reception building. The basketwork crafts sold at the gift shops are great value for money and unique souvenirs of your visit. Try to support them if you can – every basket sold puts food on the family table.

DANIEL'S KALINAGO CASSAVA BAKERY Cassava (*Manihot esculenta*) was brought to the island by Amerindian settlers. It's extensively cultivated in many subtropical regions of the world, where it's a food staple for both humans and animals. Also called **manioc**, the root must be cooked thoroughly to rid it of its toxins. It's high in starch content but is quite bereft of protein and other nutrients. It can be cooked in many ways: as puddings (*tapioca*) or sweet cakes (*kanki*), but it's commonly used as a flour to make a basic bread. Daniel's Cassava Bakery in Crayfish River is functional as well as a visitor attraction. If it's open and operating when you're there, call in and try some (opening times are not fixed and are also subject to cassava being harvested).

KALINAGO TOUNA AUTĖ Meaning 'Kalinago village by the water, or river', Touna is the smallest of the Kalinago Territory's communities. The village is often called Touna Concord (half of the village is in the Territory, the other half – Concord – isn't). Some years ago, former chief and village elder Irvince Auguiste came up with the idea of showing travellers contemporary and traditional Kalinago village life. Despite suffering badly from Hurricane Maria in 2017, Irvince and his family are back on their feet and the Kalinago Touna Auté experience has been revived.

Irvince will walk you around his property, showing and explaining different trees and plants; he may also cook cassava bread over an open fire, and take you into the village or down to the river. You may even get lunch. The tour is on the cruise ship schedule, so if you'd like a less scripted and more informal experience, I'd suggest sending him a WhatsApp message or email (767 285 1830; e onenicepeople@gmail.com). If you like, you can camp on the family property, and they also have simple accommodation that they rent out. This is an interesting experience that offers an opportunity to find out about Kalinago life – both past and present – in Dominica.

L'ESCALIER TÊTE CHIEN L'Escalier Tête Chien is an impressive lava dyke at the foot of the coastal cliffs in Sineku. Such dykes are created by lava forcing its way up through cracks in a volcanic landscape and then hardening to form impermeable rock. As the rocks and earth around the dyke wear away with weather, and in this case ocean, the dyke is revealed as a prominent and permanent geological feature.

That's how science explains it. According to Kalinago legend, L'Escalier Tête Chien was formed by a giant snake (the local name for boa constrictor is *tête chien*) climbing up the volcanic coastline from the abyss, churning up the rock along the way. Upon reaching the top of the cliff, the snake then made its way to a mountain called **Madjini** that overlooks the community of Sineku, where it now resides in a large, hidden cave. The lava dyke is therefore the boa's staircase (*l'escalier*) and the snake itself is said to be one of three gods residing in the Kalinago Territory. The other two are a giant centipede in St Cyr and a smaller snake spirit hidden within the Pagua Rock area near Hatton Garden. Legend has it that if you take a carved canoe paddle, some tobacco and a rooster to the snake god in his hidden cave at Madjini, the spirit of a man will appear and grant you a wish.

The track to L'Escalier Tête Chien has some interesting plants that have several medicinal uses in the Kalinago Territory. There are also several types of bromeliad along the way as well as an endemic grass known locally as *bartad lapit*, which has a white powdery substance on its underside. According to the Kalinago, this powder may be used as an antiseptic, traditionally for the severed umbilical cord of a newborn baby.

At the main junction of the coastal road in Sineku, there's a sign for L'Escalier Tête Chien. There's also a ruined building and a bar where, unfortunately, local men hang out with the sole intention, it seems, of relieving tourists of their money – purporting to be guides. They're not and, if you feel uncomfortable here, it's wiser to spend your day doing something else than getting into a situation. No matter how often this problem is flagged, it never seems to go away. For this reason, I urge you to visit L'Escalier Tête Chien with a guide.

From the junction, follow the narrow, paved road through an unfortunately sited housing estate to the end – it's not far and you can easily walk it from the main highway. The road transitions to a grassy track along a ridge that works its way down towards the ocean; it's a pleasant walk and the track is usually well maintained. At the end of the track (a 10-minute walk), there's a viewpoint that

KALINAGO CULTURAL GROUPS

The **Karifuna Cultural Group** and the **Carina Cultural Group** are dedicated to preserving and teaching the cultural heritage and traditions of the Kalinago people. You may see them performing at the Kalinago Barana Auté and in the village of Concord on cruise ship days, as well as at cultural events throughout the year. The groups also travel abroad occasionally, promoting and developing relationships with people sympathetic to or with a common interest in the promotion and preservation of Kalinago cultural heritage.

overlooks the formation. There's also a rough track down if you wish to get a closer look. The terrain is loose, so take care. Also, be especially wary of the ocean as powerful waves often consume the lava dyke.

✷ **SOMA GARDEN** (Concord; ☎767 277 6062; tour fee US$25 pp with discounts for large groups; 24hr advance notice required, groups preferred) Vaughan Green is a self-declared 'fruit fiend' and I challenge you to find anyone with more enthusiasm for the subject. Take a tour of the expansive Soma Garden with him and you'll likely end up feeling the same way. Vaughan's knowledge is extensive and his enthusiasm infectious. The 37-year-old fruit farm – now his personal project – was originally part of the sprawling Hatton Garden estate and grew sugarcane then coconuts for *copra* (page 191) and latterly avocado and pineapple. The farm still grows large quantities of pineapples – but selective varieties rather than mass production hybrids. The full story of Soma Garden is best told by Vaughan on his 90-minute tour, on which you can expect to see more varieties of exotic and local fruit trees in one place that you ever thought possible. There's also a chance to sample fruits as well as bathe in the river – the farm's access to Pagua River pools is awesome.

TURTLE WATCHING At certain times of the year, it's possible to see endangered giant leatherback turtles coming ashore to lay their eggs (March/April), and then baby turtles returning to the sea (September/October). Turtles arrive at night, but organised releases of young turtles usually take place during the day.

Head for Rosalie before nightfall, giving yourself time to set up a tent on the beach (I know, it isn't strictly allowed but it's 'unofficially accepted' when it comes to turtle watching). There is a defined and well-maintained **Nature Trail** with access to the expansive black sands of Rosalie Bay beach a short distance to the south of the Rosalie Bay Resort. Look for the sign and rather attractive wooden hut (known as The Ark). It's a nice track (in the daytime, great fun for kids) that follows a stream to the beach. It also incorporates a small **campground**.

At the height of the season when turtles come ashore, the beach is patrolled through the night, and if you're a guest of Rosalie Bay Eco Resort, you can ask for a phone call to alert you if turtles come ashore. Bring a flashlight or headlamp with a red filter as this gives you light without confusing the turtles.

Be sure to view these creatures as unobtrusively and respectfully as possible. There is a period after digging and laying eggs when the turtle rests; this is the

POTTERY

Some of the best examples of Amerindian pottery that have been unearthed at archaeological sites across the region pre-date the Kalinago. Often described as Cayo and Saladoid, the early pottery artefacts discovered are well made (usually coil pottery) and are often decorated with representations of animals or spirits – usually referred to as adornments. Later Amerindian pottery tends to be less ornate and more functional. Objects such as the *canalli*, which was used to ferment *ouicou*, a beer made from cassava, is one such example. Pottery is a skill that is dying out and rarely practised today. Pottery fragments have been discovered at sites around Dominica, including most recently Woodford Hill Beach at the La Soye archaeological site, where evidence suggests interaction between the Kalinago and Europeans (page 18). The KBA has examples of more contemporary Kalinago pottery.

TÉWÉ VAVAL

Vaval is the spirit of Carnival and Téwé Vaval is the symbolic burial or burning of an effigy representing the spirit of Carnival that takes place on Ash Wednesday. In the west-coast village of Dublanc and in Bataca in the Kalinago Territory, these effigies are paraded through the streets before being burned at sunset. This ritual symbolises the end of Carnival and the beginning of the Lent period. These days, instead of marking the end of festivities, Vaval appears to be a good excuse to make the Carnival jump-ups last one more day (for those who still have any strength left, that is). I'd suggest resisting the urge to make a drunken leap across the flames – it may spoil your holiday, and more.

time for a photograph or two, but patrolling wardens will advise you. For information about Dominica's turtles and turtle watching, you could get in touch with Dominica's Sea Turtles Conservation Organisation (DomSeTCO; 767 265 0908; e info@domsetco.org; w domsetco.org) or contact local turtle-watching tour services (767 277 1608; e mynettoti@gmail.com).

TWA BASENS This is a series of three pools and cascades located on a shallow river near the village of Riviere Cyrique. The first pool is very accessible and follows a short, though often soggy, walk along the riverbank. The pools above it require a tricky climb up each cascade. All three pools are excellent spots for a refreshing river bathe.

Twa Basens is unmarked, so finding it can be a little challenging. However, at the time of writing, a flash flood had cleared the debris from the river and Twa Basens could be seen from the road. The flood offered an opportunity for the local community to open up the pools as a more accessible feature. So, this access description may change. To find it, look on the south side of Riviere Cyrique village; before you reach the turning for Morne Jaune, there's a sharp hairpin (curving left if you're heading south), that crosses a small river. On the north side of the concrete bridge barrier, there's a track that follows the river inland and upstream. Follow the stream for about 5 minutes to the first pool and cascade. The track crosses the stream and runs along the left-hand side of the first pool right up to the cascade – which you must then climb if you wish to go up to the two higher cascades and pools. It is slippery but not too high. I like the second and third pools best.

ZION VALLEY AND THE RASTA WAY OF LIFE If you're hiking the Victoria Falls Trail (page 172), you'll start in Zion Valley which is home to Moses James (page 20) and his family. Although they were hit hard by the hurricane, anyone interested in learning more about the Rasta way of life is welcome here. From time to time, they cook simple Ital food (page 58), and there are spots along the river where – with their permission and for a small fee – you may pitch a tent. Moses doesn't move too loosely these days thanks to his bullet wounds, but he's a fascinating person to chat with and his knowledge of plants and herbs is impressive (he's written a book about it). You'll usually find Moses sitting on a bench beneath a large mango tree.

HIKING TRAILS

✷ CHARLES WARNER 'SECRET POOL' This pleasant hour-long walk from the Pagua River into the Kalinago Territory ends up at a delightful river pool and cascade on the Charles Warner River. There's a shallow river crossing at the beginning with a steep climb up the far bank, and there are several short sections of carved mud steps, but, overall, the trail isn't especially demanding. You'll need swimming gear for the pool as well as a change of clothes at the end.

The trail is named after the river which, in turn, is named after Charles Warner, a British landowner who was a descendant of Sir Thomas Warner and relative of Kalinago Chief Thomas 'Indian' Warner who was murdered by his half-brother in the infamous massacre of 1764 (page 214). Charles Warner owned several properties in Dominica. His main estate was in the parish of St Paul on the west coast between Mahaut and Layou, and is now called Warner village.

There's no sign for the trailhead (well, it's a secret, right?), so it's a little tricky to find. It's marked by a pale-blue painted 'X' on a utility pole on the road between Hatton Garden and the Central Forest Reserve. If you're coming from the east, look for it on the left a couple of miles beyond Hibiscus Valley Inn. From the west, look for it on the right, about a mile beyond the sign for Roots Jungle Retreat. There's a small parking area from where you can clearly see the trail.

Head down to the river – it can be a little swampy – and cross to the other side. The trail continues behind the large boulder and is a steepish climb up the bank. At the time of writing, it was a little confusing at the top of the bank. A new trail, the 'Canoe Trail', was being developed by a Kalinago group immediately to the left (where there's also a canoe). The Charles Warner Trail is straight on, though it may be that the farmer wishes you to go along the bank to the right and then climb some steps on your left. Assuming things are as they were when I walked it, go straight ahead from the river and pick up the trail 20m or so further on. It's a beaten path through the grass and trees.

From here, it's a clear and distinct trail across country. You may notice a spur to the left further on but stick to the right all the way. The verges of the track are bushy but also filled with wildflowers, heliconias and large *z'alies mouches (Caludovica insignis)* – a palm-like plant with two large leaf lobes (like large insect wings) that were used by the indigenous people for thatching and waterproofing.

You'll ascend several banks with steps carved into the mud before reaching denser forest with the Charles Warner River now running down on your left. Continue along the track – careful where it's eroding – until you reach the pool and cascade.

GLASSY POOL As an acrophobic, this is one of my least favourite trails (I especially dislike like high, eroding cliff tracks), but I'll include it for all the more level-

KALINAGO CANOE TRAIL

At the time of writing a new trail in the Kalinago Territory is being developed (I'm not sure what its name will be, so have nicknamed it the 'Canoe Trail'). The aim is to create a path through the more remote forested areas of the Territory while at the same time educating hikers about the tradition of canoe building. The development of this trail is being funded by a Kalinago-based non-government organisation (NGO). You may see a bit of it if you walk the Charles Warner Secret Pool trail. Once across the Pagua River, an immediate left (rather than straight ahead) brings you on to the track that's in development. My understanding is that it's likely to be a rather strenuous forest and hillside walk with some steep and muddy slopes. It may be something to look out for when you're on the island.

DERNIER FALLS AND WAVINE CYRIQUE

Both victims of Hurricane Maria in 2017, Dernier Falls and Wavine Cyrique were inaccessible at the time of writing, but I'm mentioning them because they may be rehabilitated during the lifetime of this edition. Dernier Falls is set inside a cavern and was accessible via a steep track from the village of Grand Fond. Wavine Cyrique is a waterfall that tumbles from a cliff into the sea and was accessible via a rather hair-raising climb from the village of Riviere Cyrique. Both waterfalls were worth the effort of getting to see them, so if access has been fixed, try to go if you have time to do so.

The trail down to Dernier Falls was signposted towards the top of Grand Fond village. It was a short but steep trail, taking about 20–30 minutes to get to the bottom. Once there, you walk a short distance upstream (right) to the cavern and waterfall.

The trail to Wavine Cyrique was also signposted from the main road on a tight corner in the village of Riviere Cyrique. The trailhead is at the end of the narrow and paved village road. Parking here was tricky, though possible. The short and scenic downhill track followed the spine of a ridge for about 20 minutes before coming to an end at the cliff. Then all you would see was the end of a rope! The climb down was via rope, tree roots and rope ladder. Following the hurricane, the trees are no longer there and, though someone did install a rope ladder, I know of no guides who will take people there – it's considered way too exposed and dangerous. But this may change and, if it does, try to fit Wavine Cyrique into your schedule as it's always been a rather iconic waterfall.

headed people out there. Regardless of my irrational fear of heights, I'm not especially convinced the destination is worth the walk, but you decide. The track was eroded and damaged by hurricane and it seems like it's been patched up on the cheap rather than repaired properly. For this reason, at the time of writing, it's more than a little sketchy in places – especially for people like me. From the village of Boetica, it's an otherwise unchallenging hour-long walk through coastal woodland and around the cliffside to a wave-swept coastal formation that's home to saltwater pools. Don't go in bad weather and rough seas, or if your time on the island is especially limited.

The trail is signposted opposite the Roman Catholic chapel in the village of Boetica. It passes close to a small house and then alongside a small banana grove before heading into forest habitat. It's a narrow track that works its way around the coast and has some nice views. It can be a little tricky to follow when it reaches a gulley and stream – follow it down, taking care on the loose rocks until you pick up the track again on the right. There are several hair-raising moments around narrow and vertiginous cliff sections as well as across a precarious ridge that leads to the craggy outcrop that contains the pools. The large pool is vulnerable to high surf and tidal surges, so please use common sense if you choose to bathe in it. Also, as you make your way down to the pool, be aware that volcanic rock formations can have sharp edges.

✷ HORSEBACK RIDGE LOOP This is a walk I invented and have done a few times with friends who have enjoyed it. It's a pleasant and relaxing way of exploring the Kalinago Territory on foot. There's some great scenery and you'll meet plenty of

BOLIVE (BOLI) FALLS

Keen hikers may come across references to the Bolive or Boli Falls. Honestly, if your time is limited, you should pass on it. The trail is very long (3 hours each way), usually very muddy and in places quite steep and overgrown; and the 'reward' at the end is a little disappointing. Bolive is a three-tier cascading waterfall which you never really see from any decent vantage point – there's simply too much forest. Instead, the trail brings you to the middle pool, which is very lovely, but I'm not sure it's worth the walk. So I'd say Bolive is only for the ardent hiker who has done everything else and has plenty of time to spare. The trailhead is unmarked beside a farmer's field in the community of Carse O Gowrie, between Taberi and La Plaine. You'll definitely need a local guide.

Kalinago people. It takes around 3–4 hours to walk the paved loop – depending on how often you pause for photographs, conversations, drinks, saltfish bakes and craft stalls, of course.

Park up by the Salybia Police Station and Kalinago Barana Auté turning and take the Horseback Ridge road (a little to the north of the police station and just about opposite Tilou Kanawa bar and restaurant). It's a steepish walk but the views are wonderful. Pass a few houses and then some small *gardens* (farm holdings) until you get to the top. When you reach a fork, turn right. The paved road heads left and then steeply down to the village of Touna Concord. Instead of going that way, take the rough track (it eventually becomes paved again) to the right. This road follows the ridge all the way down to the village of Bataca. Again, the views across the farmlands and villages of the Territory are awesome. There are usually plenty of jaco parrots flying around here too.

In Bataca, you'll emerge on the main road again. Head right and follow the road through the villages of Bataca and Crayfish River, back to Salybia. Optional diversions include the cassava bakery (page 164) and the Kalinago Barana Auté (page 162). Do the walk on a Saturday or Sunday and have cassava tacos for lunch at Tilou Kanawa (page 154) when you return to your starting point.

ROSALIE TO PETITE SOUFRIERE There was once a well-beaten village track connecting Rosalie and Petite Soufriere. Then, the authorities decided the track should be a road and began construction only to be halted by an immovable object in the form of a huge rock formation that, it turned out, could not be blasted away with dynamite. So, the project was abandoned. After that, landslides and erosion from extreme weather battered and smothered what was left of road and track. But needs must, and people began walking the route again, forging a new path through the mess that man and hurricane had left behind. I walked it again and, frankly, it's a bit rough and probably shouldn't make your must-do list, but, if you have the time, freedom and inclination to walk some of these historic traces, I think it's worth including. I suggest taking a bus to Rosalie, walking the trail to Petite Soufriere, and then getting a ride to Castle Bruce from where you can catch a bus back to Pont Cassé and Roseau. It takes about 2 hours to walk from Rosalie to Petite Soufriere. The trail, clearly, is rough, and there are a couple of short cliff sections that are a little challenging if you don't like heights. Beyond that, it's a pleasant walk with lovely views, and probably the only way you'd ever visit the remote community of Petite Soufriere, itself the victim of landslides and extreme weather in recent times.

Rosalie was a large sugarcane estate in colonial times and the ruins of an aqueduct and factory are still visible from the main road, just before the bridge that crosses the Rosalie River. The wide track that runs alongside the ruins is where the walk begins.

Follow the rough track past the Diocesan Retreat Centre to where the first fragment of concrete road begins. It's a steep uphill climb around the back of a cliffside home and the road is rubble strewn. As it levels out beyond the house, you'll meet a large landslide where the route seems to end. Walk a short distance up the landslide and pick up the track on the right. From here, it's easy to see the beaten path through the coastal scrub and occasionally along concrete road remnants. There are good views to the south across the expansive Rosalie Bay.

Eventually you'll reach the rock formation that halted the road project. It's hard to believe that any survey carried out before work began would have ever considered this a movable object. Take care on the narrow path around the rock. There's a section of boulders that you must negotiate a little further along the track, but from here on in, it's a clear path around the coast. Enjoy the views of Petite Soufriere and the northern coastline as you make your way to the village itself. The village was impacted by Hurricane Maria in 2017 and again by a deluge that caused several landslides in 2022. There have been discussions about possibly abandoning the village – most of it is perched precariously on steep hillsides that are vulnerable to landslides – and rehousing its residents. The coastline that takes in the villages Petite Soufriere, San Saveur and Good Hope is very scenic and rarely visited by travellers.

✷ **SARI SARI FALLS** This is a tall horsetail waterfall on the Sari Sari River, inland from the village of La Plaine. Somewhat offbeat, it's probably one of Dominica's least visited waterfalls. The reason for this is perhaps twofold: firstly, the trail is steep and eroded, and often subject to land slippage, and secondly, because you do feel rather entrapped once you're down in the river, negotiating its boulders and cascades. The Sari Sari does flash flood in the rainy season and people have lost their lives here. Having said that, it's quite a short hike – about an hour each way – but I urge you to get a guide if you don't have much experience of this kind of terrain. It's not always easy to pick up the forest trail sections – including the exit point – when you're down in the river and you could easily find yourself a bit stuck looking for it. This hike is quite tough on your knees; it's steep in places and there are lots of boulders to clamber over down in the river.

Drive right through the village of La Plaine and find the signposted trailhead at the very end of the Balizier back road. You may need to ask for directions as La Plaine is a sprawling village with several back roads. Drive along the rough vehicle track and park up near the water tank. At the time of writing, a lack of signage beyond this point made things a little awkward. Walk to the end of the wide track and continue along it as it curves to the right. Now look for a beaten path through the grassy field on your right. It runs across the field towards the trees and then passes through bush before dropping steeply down to the river. This is a tricky descent (the climb back up even trickier).

When you meet the river, you must head upstream for about 5–10 minutes and look for the continuation of the forest trail on the right. Follow it until it meets the river again. Walk upstream and look for the trail – this time on the left-hand bank. This section climbs and then runs high above the river before descending sharply once again. There was a landslide along this stretch and so it can be muddy and slippery. The rest of the hike is in the river, and you must now negotiate boulders, cascades and pools. The river terrain changes but, at the time of writing, I found it easier to stick to the right-hand side up to the corner, where you get to see the waterfall, and then switch to the left to reach the pool (if you want to go that far).

If you're hiking without a guide, make a note of, or leave a marker at, each of the places where the forest track meets the river, so that you can find them again on the return leg. Also, be sure to tell someone where you're going.

✷ VICTORIA FALLS Victoria is my favourite Dominica waterfall. It's on the White River near the village of Delices and is usually less than an hour of trail walking, river crossing and boulder climbing. Like all river hikes, it's imperative that you keep a watchful eye on the weather and don't go during or after heavy rainfall. The route is well beaten and quite easy to follow to the point where you get a view of the waterfall. To get to the base of the waterfall, you must find a route over boulders and cascades, then climb up and over a steep bank.

Look for a Victoria Falls sign in the village of Delices. Either park near the sign or drive down the rough access road. You'll need a 4x4. Park up at the bottom and pay the fee (in this case, US$5 or EC$15). This area is home to the James family and their patriarch Moses who is a near legendary Rastafarian figure in Dominica. His story is interesting and tragic, yet it's always told with a feeling of optimism and positivity. Moses was arrested, beaten, imprisoned and then shot during the time of the Dread Act (page 20) that made it lawful for the police to shoot people with dreadlocks. This area is referred to as Zion Valley and, in addition to his home, there's a Rasta Café that's occasionally open and serving basic *ital* food. As with all genuine Rastas, living close to and in harmony with nature is a way of life, and that's how it has been here in the valley for a long time.

If you don't have a guide but would like one, ask if one of Moses's sons is available. If not, look for the beaten path along the right-hand bank, heading upstream from the parking area. Follow it for a short distance to the river where you must cross to the other side. Pick up the trail again, up and over the bank and through an area of wild bush until you return to the river. Cross again and follow the track through the woodland of the river margin. When you meet the river again, make your way up the right-hand side until the waterfall comes into view. If you'd like to reach the base of the waterfall, you must head for the high bank that you'll see up on the left near the waterfall. So, work your way carefully across pools and cascades and over the boulders to get there. The river terrain changes, of course, but at the time of writing, I walked for a short distance along the right-hand side of the river before crossing to the left and sticking mostly to that side all the way to the bank. It's tricky and often quite slippery. Using the dug-out footsteps, climb up and over the bank and then work your way down to the waterfall pool. The source of the White River is Boiling Lake, hence the discolouration of the water.

WNT SEGMENT 6: CASTLE BRUCE TO HATTON GARDEN This hiking route passes through most of the Kalinago Territory's villages and takes in cultural sites such as L'Escalier Tête Chien and Kalinago Barana Auté (KBA). A lot of it is along the main road through the Territory. Some offroad sections can be steep, muddy and slippery – and not especially interesting, sadly. I usually miss out a couple of them when I walk this segment as the villages offer more interest than the bush. My feeling is that these little diversions were probably added just to get hikers off the main road, but they add little to the journey. The segment joins Castle Bruce with Hatton Garden, near Pagua Bay, and you should allow around 6 hours to complete it. There's nothing too troubling along the way. You're likely to get some unwanted attention as you near L'Escalier Tête Chien in Sineku (page 165), and the tracks over and down the back of Horseback Ridge are a little steep. KBA is a good pit stop for lunch and a drink.

The segment officially begins on the former Richmond Estate, to the north of Castle Bruce and south of the Kalinago Territory. After leaving the main road, the route heads downhill through farmland and coastal woodland. It crosses the Aratouri Ravine and continues downhill towards the shoreline at Raymond Bay. Before meeting the coast, the trail begins to climb, crossing the Madjini River, and then through littoral woodland before meeting the main road just south of Sineku.

At the main Sineku junction, the route heads right towards L'Escalier Tête Chien and then cuts north through rather swampy and overgrown coastal grass and woodland, before climbing up to the road again at Mahaut River. This stretch is one I usually miss out, preferring instead to follow the main road.

At the village of Mahaut River, the route passes the roadside craft shop and home of Israel and Victoria Joseph. Israel carves tree ferns (known locally as *fougère*, or *fwigè*) into masks, plant holders and reliefs (page 156). His work is excellent. Victoria makes traditional *larouma* basketware.

A second offroad diversion leaves the main road at Mahaut River and follows a wide track over a bridge and then up to the back of Sineku Primary School and the Mahaut River Church. Dodging the main road for a while longer, the track takes you through thickets of bamboo, across another stream and then back up to the road. Again, you may want to miss this bit out and stay on the main road through to Mahaut River.

Back on the main highway (or continuing, if you didn't leave it), look for a sign by a bus stop in Gaulette River. The segment follows a paved vehicle track downhill to a playing field where it transitions to a narrow trail with coastal views of Pointe Belair and Gros L'Ilet. After crossing a river, you're directed back uphill to the main road. Again, I've never been too sure about this little diversion either! The next one is worth it, however.

Walk along the main road from St Cyr to the Salybia Primary School where the trail runs down to the sea and has nice views. It passes a memorial to the 'Carib War' (see below) and then heads through coastal woodland and across the Salybia River before turning uphill past the half-hidden ruins of the original Salybia Roman Catholic Church. Eventually, the trail emerges on the steep road to the Kalinago Barana Auté, where you could take a tour, have a rest and grab a bite to eat.

If you're continuing the walk, the trail winds around the KBA and works its way across country and over the Buluku River before rejoining the main road in

THE 'CARIB WAR'

On 19 September 1930, a rather heavy-handed attempt by armed policemen to search for and confiscate contraband – smuggled rum and tobacco – turned into a pitched battle with local people. The police retaliated by firing their weapons, killing two Kalinago and injuring two others. Incensed, the Kalinago beat the policemen, who somehow managed to escape. The Crown Colony Administrator escalated the furore when he decided to call on a nearby British naval vessel, HMS *Delhi*, to lend assistance. The *Delhi* arrived firing flares across the coastline to frighten the Kalinago and landing marines to round up those who were suspected of being the troublemakers. The incident became known as the 'Carib Uprising' or the 'Carib War'.

Bataca. A left turn on to the main highway and then a right turn in the village takes you up a steep road to Horseback Ridge. Through farmlands and sharply down the other side (it's slippery), the trail reaches the Pagua River. Follow it downstream towards the coast where the rough river track meets the main road at Hatton Garden. A right turn takes you back towards the Kalinago Territory via Antrizle and Atkinson; a left turn takes you to the junction with the main road to Marigot and the airport. If you're through-hiking, you'll pick up Segment 7 to the right, just after the junction.

8

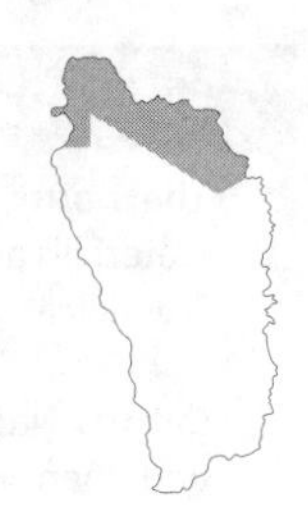

Cabrits National Park and the North

There's great diversity in the north of Dominica. The coastline has some of the island's prettiest beaches and coves as well as otherworldly rock formations and vertiginous cliffs. Portsmouth is Dominica's second town, Marigot is one of its largest villages, and the Indian River is the island's only navigable waterway. Cabrits National Park is home to what remains of Dominica's largest colonial garrison and is surrounded by pristine coral reefs. On its south side is a large natural anchorage that was used by Sir Francis Drake to provision his ship with supplies that were transported in canoes by the indigenous Kalinago of the bay area they called Ouyuhayo. The Portsmouth and Calibishie areas have become popular with travellers and there's a wide selection of accommodation options and good places to eat. Calibishie also has a large expat community.

GETTING THERE AND AWAY

BY CAR The journey along the west coast road between Roseau and Portsmouth takes about an hour. On arrival in Portsmouth, there's a three-way junction on the southern edge of town. The road ahead goes through the town and on to Purple Turtle Beach, Cabrits National Park, Douglas Bay and the villages of the northwest, where you can connect to a link road that takes you over Morne Aux Diables to Pennville. The road to the right links the west coast with Bornes, Vieille Case, Calibishie and the northeast coast.

To get to Marigot and Douglas-Charles Airport from Roseau, take the Imperial Road through the interior, passing Pont Cassé and the Central Forest Reserve, emerging at the Atlantic coastline via Concord and Hatton Garden. Heading north along the coastal road, you pass through the sprawling hillside community of Marigot. Douglas-Charles Airport is just a little further along the coast. The journey between Roseau and the airport takes about an hour. From Portsmouth, it takes about 30 minutes to reach Calibishie and then a further 20 minutes to get to Douglas-Charles Airport. Note that, at the time of writing, construction of the new international airport had commenced, meaning traffic can sometimes get held up around the Wesley area.

BY BUS See page 52 for information about buses in Roseau and Portsmouth. Buses run frequently – and often at speed – along the west coast highway between Roseau and Portsmouth. There's also a good service between Portsmouth, Calibishie and the northeast.

BY CRUISE SHIP From time to time, small cruise ships call at Portsmouth. The cruise ship terminal is in Cabrits National Park, on Prince Rupert Bay. If you're a

DON'T MISS

The north of Dominica is very scenic, with tall mountains, lush forest, waterfalls and lovely beaches. There's also volcanic activity, heritage sites and Dominica's only navigable river.

Cabrits National Park Explore the restored Fort Shirley garrison buildings and then walk the Cabrits forest trails to find atmospheric ruins in the embrace of tree roots and vines. Get to the top of the East Cabrit Trail to enjoy fabulous views.

Indian River Hire a boat guide and enjoy a sedate ride along the Indian River. Your guide will point out bird and other animal life along the way and there's a bush bar and *Pirates of the Caribbean* set location to add further interest to the journey.

Red Rocks The otherworldly coastal formations at Pointe Baptiste are unusual and beautiful. Go early morning or late afternoon when the low light reflects a broader palette of colours.

fan of cruise ship travel and plan on coming to Dominica, I think it may be an idea to find one that calls at Portsmouth as it's less busy in the north than, say, in the Roseau Valley on cruise ship days. The Fort Shirley garrison and Cabrits National Park trails are also right there, where you step ashore. You can easily walk into Portsmouth from the terminal – it's about 30 minutes on foot and there's Purple Turtle Beach and several bars along the way. Other accessible attractions in the north include the Indian River, Cold Soufriere, Bwa Nef Falls and the Syndicate Falls and Nature Trail.

BY FERRY Some high-speed ferry journeys between Dominica and the French islands also call at the Cabrits terminal. Check with the ferry operators for schedules and details (page 43).

BY PRIVATE OR CHARTER BOAT Although Dominica still doesn't have a proper marina, Prince Rupert Bay is undoubtedly the island's most popular anchorage. The bay is serviced by the Portsmouth Association of Yacht Services (PAYS). These services include customs and immigration clearance, fuel and water, water taxi services, mooring and provisioning, garbage collection and disposal, and laundry. Some PAYS members are also certified tour guides. To get in touch: **t** 767 317 9098; **e** dominicapays@gmail.com; VHF channel 16.

WHERE TO STAY

In addition to the places that I've selected opposite, there's self-catering accommodation galore, it seems, in the former student apartments at Picard. Since Ross University School of Medicine pulled out of Dominica following Hurricane Maria in 2017, student accommodation has mostly been empty and Picard rather a ghost town. Some of the flats have been let as long-term housing, others appear on booking sites as inexpensive holiday lets. And there's loads of it. I think some of it's a bit of a gamble, and if a new school comes along – regularly promised by the government – this situation may not last. But you may want to check it out if your funds are limited, or if you're looking for something long-term. If empty student digs are not your thing, there's some great holiday accommodation in the north. It's worth checking **w** airbnb.com and similar for cottage, apartment and villa accommodation in the Toucari and Calibishie areas – there's plenty to choose from across a range of budgets and they are lovely places to stay.

I've split my selected listings into the northwest and northeast. Please consider them curated rather than comprehensive.

NORTHWEST *Map, page 184, unless otherwise stated*

InterContinental Dominica Cabrits Resort & Spa (150 rooms) Portsmouth; ☎ 767 445 1000; **w** ihg.com/intercontinental/hotels/us/en/portsmouth/dompr/hoteldetail. Formerly the CBI-funded Kempinski Cabrits Resort & before that protected national park land, this hotel resort is located on the southern margins of Douglas Bay. In appearance a uniform Caribbean beach resort with restaurant (serving 'culinary creations'), spa, fitness centre, pools & swim-up bar, though this one is pitched at the luxury end of the tourism market. Apparently, there's also a shoeshine service which obviously none of us can do without on holiday. Rooms & suites have varying levels of luxury, views, private pools, outdoor bathtubs & other must-haves. **$$$$$**

Secret Bay (20 villas) Tibay, Portsmouth; ☎ 767 445 4444; **e** info@secretbay.dm; **w** secretbay.dm. Without doubt Dominica's most luxurious accommodation option, Secret Bay's hardwood villas are exquisite in design & their furnishings are sumptuous. Guest services are tailored & personal, & resort amenities include a restaurant, beach bar, infinity lap pool, sunset & garden decks, gym, spa, & watersports hut. The manicured grounds are spacious & each villa feels private. Access to the newer & larger hillside villas is via funicular. An art centre, bar & micro-brewery are planned. **$$$$$**

Manicou River [map, page 186] (2 cottages) Savanne Paille, Portsmouth; ☎ 767 616 9343; **e** info@manicouriver.com; **w** manicouriver.com. Set on a forested mountainside with sweeping views of Douglas Bay & Cabrits National Park, Manicou River has handcrafted 1-bed wooden cottages with en-suite bathroom, fully equipped kitchen & open-sided lounge/verandas enjoying those magnificent views. Completely off-grid, but with Wi-Fi, the cottages are rustic yet stylish, & also have sufficient space to feel private. Manicou River has an open-sided bar & bistro serving b/fast, lunch & dinner by reservation. The property is steep, so bring good shoes for walking about. **$$$$**

Picard Beach Cottages (18 cottages) Picard; ☎ 767 445 5131; **e** picardbeach@gmail.com; **w** picardbeachcottages.dm. Beach- or garden-facing 1-bed SC hardwood cottages have en-suite bathroom, AC, kitchenette & private veranda. This is an established accommodation option that's right on the beach. **$$$–$$$$**

Coconut Cottage [map, page 186] Toucari; bookings via **w** airbnb.com. This is a spacious wooden cottage built with a nod to time-honoured Caribbean architectural style. Combining traditional with modern, it has 2 bedrooms, bathroom, fully equipped kitchen, lounge area, Wi-Fi, TV & large veranda with great views of Toucari Bay. **$$$**

ANICHI RESORT & SPA

Anichi Resort & Spa is a rather sprawling CBI-funded hotel development on the fringes of Coconut Beach in Picard. At the time of writing, it had been under construction for quite some time and seemed to be progressing very slowly. If it's completed, according to the website it will be part of Marriott International's Autograph Collection, which sounds like it's going to be quite pricey (why are all the CBI hotel developments aimed at the luxury end of the tourism market, I wonder?). The promotional blurb talks of 128 'sophisticated rooms' that will 'subtly woo onlookers'. So, there you go. That sounds like an interesting challenge. Anyway, here's the website: **w** anichidevelopment.com.

Savanne Paille Holiday Homes [map, page 186] Savanne Paille, Portsmouth; 767 315 9916; e mauricechaplais@gmail.com; w accommodationdominica.com. This is a large & amply furnished plantation style house set in expansive tropical gardens with Caribbean Sea views. Accommodation is split into the upstairs main house (3 beds with private bathrooms) & the downstairs apt (2 beds with private bathroom). Kitchens are fully equipped, & there are spacious living & dining areas, Wi-Fi, ceiling fans & verandas with great views. A b/fast package is also available. **$$$**

Hotel The Champs (5 rooms) Picard; 767 613 0929; e info@hotelthechamps.com; w hotelthechamps.com. Perched on the hillside above the sprawl of Picard's former student accommodation & enjoying great sea views, rooms have en-suite bathroom, AC, Wi-Fi & either access to veranda or poolside deck/garden area. There's an open-sided veranda restaurant serving b/fast, lunch & dinner. B/fast inc. **$$–$$$**

Belle View Bungalow [map, page 186] Savanne Paille, Portsmouth; 767 275 8424; e nature100percent@me.com; bookings via w airbnb.com. This family-run 1-bed open-sided hillside bungalow enjoys spectacular views of Cabrits National Park, Prince Rupert Bay & Douglas Bay. It has a bedroom, fully equipped kitchen, private bathroom, mosquito nets, Wi-Fi & additional bunk-style dbl bed. **$$**

Hideaways of Tibay Heights (2 cottages) Tibay, Portsmouth; 767 285 7480; e info@hideawaysdominica.com; w hideawaysdominica.com. Hideaways is located on a wooded hillside near Picard & has 2 artfully designed treehouse-style cottages (one with 2 beds, the other with 1). Both have en-suite bathrooms, Wi-Fi, fully equipped kitchens & great sea views. One cottage has an open-sided lounge with views all around. There's a large garden for guests to enjoy, with dining pergola & fire pit. **$$**

Mango Garden Cottages [map, page 186] (1 villa, 2 studios) Savanne Paille, Portsmouth; 767 277 1371; e info@mangogarden.dm; w mangogarden.dm. Great-value accommodation with helpful & knowledgeable hosts (Eddison is a tour guide), Mango Garden has a standalone 2-bed villa with en-suite bathrooms, fully equipped kitchen, dining area & veranda. The next-door cottage comprises 2 SC 1-bed studios each with en-suite bathroom, kitchen/dining area & private veranda. There's Wi-Fi throughout, guests can enjoy seasonal fruits from the garden, b/fast & dinner can be prepared by request, & there's a laundry service available. **$–$$**

Lilly's Guesthouse Brandy, Portsmouth; 767 317 4723; w lillysguesthouse.com (or book via w airbnb.com). Rustic 1-bed treehouse accommodation with private bathroom & outdoor shower, no Wi-Fi & electricity some of the time. The organic garden is amid the forest & there are hammocks to chill on. The beauty of Lilly's Guesthouse is the feeling of being close to nature & Lilly himself is a fabulous host. He can take you out for a tour or fishing on his boat, or maybe to the local market. Obviously too basic for many, but this is an authentic Dominica experience. **$**

NORTHEAST *Map, page 190, unless otherwise stated*

Villa Passiflora & Cottage Calibishie; 767 245 3468; e parkneur@comcast.net; w villapassiflora.com. The attractive 3-bed villa has an open, Caribbean design with traditional louvre windows, spacious verandas & infinity pool. Each bedroom has a private bathroom & the master suite has an adjoining study. There's a large, fully equipped kitchen, lounge & dining area. The standalone, spacious cottage is of similar design & has fully equipped kitchen, private bathroom, living area & verandas. Villa **$$$$$**, cottage **$$**

Villa Vista Calibishie; 767 235 5760; e villavistadominica@yahoo.com; w villavistadominica.com. Located above Hodges Bay & with great views, this is a Mediterranean-style 3-bed villa with separate 1-bed apt. The upper-floor master suite has en-suite bathroom, large private veranda, spa room & jacuzzi. Ground-floor rooms have shared bathroom. There's a living room, fully equipped kitchen & large veranda with infinity pool. The 1-bed SC apt has bathroom, kitchenette, porch & private garden access. A trail down to Hodges Bay runs alongside the property. **$$$$**

Wanderlust Caribbean (5 suites & apts) Calibishie; 767 295 0890; e info@wanderlustcaribbean.com; w wanderlustcaribbean.com. I think I can safely say that, at the time of writing, there's no place like Wanderlust. Although many hotels offer activities, packages or a tour desk, Wanderlust is specifically geared towards outdoor adventure enthusiasts & exclusively offers a range of all-inclusive accommodation & activity packages. They'll do pretty much everything you read about in this guidebook & they're great people to boot. Suites & apts are 1 & 2 bed & are fully kitted out with all you need, including kitchens & verandas with ocean views. Committed to working with local people & the community, this is a fabulous option for responsible adventure travellers who would like their activities organised for them by people who know how to do it. Check out the website. **$$$$**

Pointe Baptiste Estate & Chocolate Cottage Pointe Baptiste; 767 225 5378; e manager@pointebaptiste.com; w pointebaptiste.com. Set in expansive private coastal grounds that include a chocolate factory, the 1930s-built colonial-style estate house is full of history with guests including Noel Coward, Somerset Maugham, Princess Margaret & Mick Jagger. Replete with antique furniture, it has 3 bedrooms, kitchen, lounge, library & large veranda. There's daily housekeeping & meals can be prepared on request. The lovely, modern 1-bed Chocolate Cottage sits above the chocolate factory & has private bathroom, kitchenette & windows you can throw open to enjoy expansive coast & mountain views. Estate house **$$$$**, Chocolate Cottage **$**

Atlantique View [map, page 186] (35 rooms) Anse de Mai; 767 277 5061; e atlantiqueviewresort@yahoo.com; w atlantiqueviewresort.com. This hotel is located on a hillside above the coastal village of Anse de Mai. It has 1- & 2-bed rooms & suites with en-suite bathroom, Wi-Fi, TV & balcony with either garden or ocean view. Facilities include bar & restaurant & swimming pools. **$$$**

Sea Cliff Eco-Cottages (5 cottages) Calibishie; 646 427 1808; e seacliffdominica@gmail.com; w seacliffdominica.com. Enjoying great views of Hodges Bay, the 5 solar-powered SC cottages are set in large coastal gardens & have a mix of 1 & 2 beds, private bathroom, kitchenette & veranda (the Luxe cottage has an oversized wraparound deck). All are airy & spacious, with Wi-Fi & ocean & mountain views. **$$–$$$**

Classique International [map, page 188] (7 rooms & suites) Marigot; book via w booking.com. Located close to the airport, this pleasant family-run guesthouse offers a combination of rooms & suites all with private bathroom & Wi-Fi. There's a balcony restaurant & pleasant garden surroundings. **$$**

Veranda View Guesthouse (2 rooms) Calibishie; 767 445 8900; e verandaviewdominica@gmail.com; book via w booking.com. Located in the village of Calibishie, the sheltered waters of the bay are just 1 step from the delightful beach garden & porch. The colourful 1st-floor 1-bed rooms enjoy ocean views from private verandas. Each has kitchenette & Wi-Fi. Owner Hermien lives on the ground floor. **$**

WHERE TO EAT AND DRINK

NORTHWEST *Map, page 184, unless otherwise stated*

Restaurants

In addition to the places listed below, you can also dine by advance reservation at **Secret Bay** & the **Intercontinental Cabrits Resort & Spa** (page 177).

Keepin' It Real [map, page 186] Toucari; 767 225 7657; lunch & dinner Tue–Sun. Considered by many to be one of Dominica's best restaurants. Seafood – especially lobster – is the speciality here, though it's all good. In a lovely location along Toucari Bay, it's popular, so call ahead. **$$**

Manicou River [map, page 186] Savanne Paille, Portsmouth; 767 616 9343; b/fast, lunch & dinner daily by reservation. Manicou River's bar & bistro serves a daily set menu of Caribbean fusion dishes by reservation only. The open-sided hillside restaurant enjoys fabulous views of the Cabrits & Douglas Bay. **$$**

The Almond Deck [map, page 186] Toucari; 767 615 0808; lunch & dinner Tue–Sun. This creatively designed restaurant & bar is located waterside on Toucari Bay. It has a varied menu with seafood pasta, kebabs & tacos all specialities. Popular with trendy locals, it often hosts events & DJs at w/ends. **$–$$**

Bell Hall Beach Spot Bell Hall, Portsmouth; 767 235 5909; lunch & dinner Wed–Mon. This spacious, open-sided bar & restaurant is located opposite Bell Hall Beach on Douglas Bay & offers a range of international fare – from burgers & fries to catch of the day. An occasional events venue, the Beach Spot is busy at w/ends. $–$$

The Champs Restaurant Bell Hall, Picard; 767 613 0929; 17.00–21.00 Thu–Sat. Enjoy Caribbean Sea sunsets from the restaurant deck at The Champs. A la carte cuisine is international & casual with fine dining on Sat. On Fri enjoy pizza. Vegetarian options available. $–$$

Iguana Cafe Glanvillea, Portsmouth; 767 315 0471; lunch & dinner daily. Delicious seafood dishes with a Rasta twist are served at this lovely, wooden, waterside eatery in Glanvillea, on the southern margins of Portsmouth. $–$$

Madiba Beach Café Lagon, Portsmouth; 767 225 5428; 16.00–22.00 Tue–Sat. As the name suggests, Madiba is located on the margins of Purple Turtle Beach in Lagon, Portsmouth. It's a small, wooden, open-sided restaurant, where seafood – especially catch of the day – is the speciality, though you can get other eats such as burgers & salads. $–$$

Roots Rock Bell Hall, Portsmouth; 767 277 7328; lunch & dinner Tue–Sun. This small roadside restaurant opposite Bell Hall Beach on Douglas Bay offers a limited but high standard of cooking with grilled lobster & fish the 2 specialities. Good value in a scenic setting. $–$$

Maford House Café Portsmouth; 767 277 7778; b/fast & lunch Mon–Sat. Located near the main bus stop on the southern edge of Portsmouth, Maford House Café has a beach beer garden out back where you can enjoy all-day b/fast, fish & chips, burgers & more in the shade of almond trees. $

Purple Turtle Restaurant Lagon, Portsmouth; 767 445 5296; 11.00–21.30 Wed–Mon. Thanks to its location on Purple Turtle Beach, this long-established eatery is popular with locals & travellers. Serving simple Caribbean & international dishes such as fish & fries, its standard fare is enhanced by lovely views of the bay. $

Noteworthy bars, cafés and snackettes

Miss Olive Shop Portsmouth. Serving simple light bites – from bakes to burgers.

Peter's BBQ Lagon, Portsmouth. One of Portsmouth's hottest Fri night BBQ spots.

Sea Bird Bar & Grill Purple Turtle Beach, Portsmouth. Popular bar, music venue & cheap eats spot located right on the beach. Try the *braf* & beer combo.

Water's Edge Portsmouth. Fast casual dining including fish, chicken & burgers.

NORTHEAST *Map, page 190, unless otherwise stated*

Restaurants

Poz Restaurant, Bar & Pool Calibishie; 767 612 5176; dinner Thu–Tue. Owner Troy offers a selection of Creole & international cooking in his intimate poolside restaurant on the outskirts of Calibishie. Call in advance. $$

Rainbow Restaurant by Caribbean Flavor Cuisine Calibishie; 767 716 7381; lunch & dinner Tue–Sun. Enjoy waterside dining at this open-sided restaurant that serves a range of Caribbean & international dishes, including tacos, shrimp & catch of the day. Located on the main road in Calibishie. $–$$

Red Rock Cuisine Pointe Baptiste; 767 315 6027; lunch & dinner daily. This rustic bar & restaurant is located at the Red Rock trailhead (& where you pay your access fee). Here you can enjoy Caribbean & international snacks & meals – from sandwiches & salads to pizza & lobster. $–$$

Unique Sea View Restaurant Calibishie; 767 315 3360; lunch & dinner daily. On the main road in Calibishie, chef Jahcall prepares a range of great French & Caribbean dishes that include lobster (served on banana leaf), crayfish & catch of the day as well as Jamaican jerk chicken & curried chicken & pineapple. Turn up or call ahead. $–$$

Coral Reef Bar & Restaurant Calibishie; 767 445 7432; lunch & dinner daily. Hidden behind the Coral Reef supermarket on the Calibishie main road, this long-established eatery offers enjoyable waterside dining. Serving a range of Caribbean & international dishes, the food is unfussy & good value. $

Noteworthy bars, cafés and snackettes

Big Tuff Bar Calibishie. A lively drinks & music spot on the main road in Calibishie.

Mer's Snackette [map, page 186] Paix Bouche. Good food matched by glorious views on clear days.

✷ **CABRITS NATIONAL PARK** (Site pass required & sold at the visitor centre's bar) The 525ha Cabrits National Park was established in 1986. The twin peaks of the Cabrits are thought to have been formed from the same volcano that collapsed and eroded over time. East Cabrit is 140m above sea level and West Cabrit stands at a height of 171m. Located within the park, and its most prominent feature, is the partially restored 18th-century **Fort Shirley garrison**. The park is connected to the mainland by Dominica's largest wetland, the Cabrits Swamp, and it also includes some 421ha of marine environment. The name 'Cabrits' is derived from the French word *cabri*, meaning 'young goat'. It's said goats were brought here for food and allowed to roam freely around the headland.

In 1990, the government of Dominica established a cruise ship berth at the Cabrits on the site of the dockyard that would have served Fort Shirley garrison some 200 years before.

On arriving at Cabrits National Park there's car parking on the left along the waterside, just before the gate and jetty terminal. Beyond this is the visitor centre, which houses an exhibition room and a snackette where you can get reasonably priced local dishes and drinks as well as a visitor pass if you need one. The exhibition room (at the time of writing, somewhat neglected) has information about the geological formation of the Cabrits as well as the history of the garrison.

The stone archway and path in front of the visitor centre forms the entrance to the park and leads uphill to the restored main garrison and the woodland trails. The trails are pleasant walks through the forested park and include several interesting and atmospheric garrison ruins. They also have excellent views of the surrounding area.

The Cabrits habitat is dry coastal woodland. Trees found here include teak (*Tectona grandis*), the silk cotton tree (*Ceiba occidentalis*), the bay tree (*Pimenta racemosa*), the naked Indian tree (*Bursera simaruba*), the mahogany (*Swietenia mahogani*) and the savonnet (*Lauchocarpus latifolus*). In the grassy area above the Fort Shirley powder magazine, you can see Dominica's national flower, the *bwa kwaib* (*Sabinea carinalis*).

PRACTICALITIES

In terms of shopping, Dominica's second town of Portsmouth is limited. Most commercial businesses are along Bay Street and consist of hardware stores, minimarts and small eateries. There's a branch of the **National Bank of Dominica**, with **ATM**, near the Indian River. Before Ross University School of Medicine moved out of Picard to Barbados, there was more diverse shopping in that area – including a large supermarket – but the area has fallen into decline. A return of students (promised by the government) will undoubtedly help to breathe some life back into both Picard and Portsmouth.

There are also **ATMs** in Calibishie and Marigot, both of which also have small shops selling the essentials, along with the ever present 'variety stores'. If you're driving, there are **petrol stations** in Portsmouth near the Indian River and National Bank of Dominica, in Calibishie, and in Marigot. **Site passes** can be bought at the Indian River, Syndicate and Cabrits National Park visitor centres.

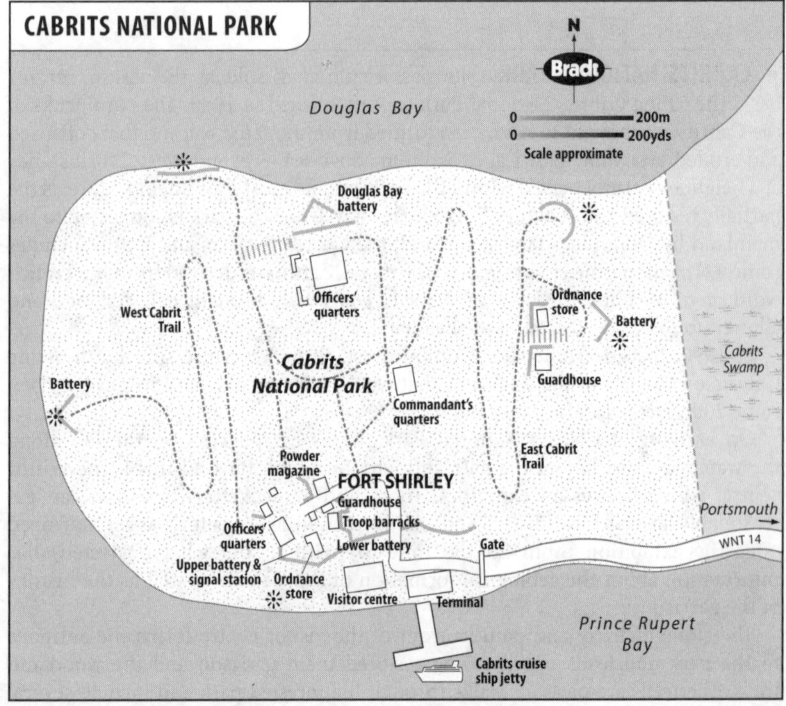

The Fort Shirley garrison Despite the fact that Portsmouth was no longer an appropriate location for the island's capital, the natural harbour of Prince Rupert Bay still needed defending from invaders. British Governor Sir Thomas Shirley began the task of constructing a military garrison on the headland of the Cabrits, based on the plans of Captain James Bruce, who designed many of the island's fortifications at the time. The forest was cleared from the area, and a fully functional and impressive 80ha military stronghold of over 50 buildings was created.

Other than witnessing the Battle of the Saints in 1782, the fort experienced no military conflict. Due to its location next to a large swamp, many of the troops stationed there fell ill and died from malaria and other fevers. The garrison's problems were compounded by the escalating costs of defending an island that was producing little by way of income. The solution was to create regiments of enslaved Africans and Creoles who were more accustomed to the testing climate and who were also considerably cheaper. These troops formed what became known as the Black West India Regiments, or the 'Black Regiments'.

In 1802, soldiers of the 8th West India Regiment staged a revolt at the Fort Shirley garrison. Their commander-in-chief was Governor Andrew James Cochrane, who took it upon himself to use the regiment to work his private estates without pay. On 9 April the regiment took over Fort Shirley for several days, though troop reinforcements and attack from HMS *Magnificent* resulted in many deaths. Those who survived fled into the forest where they joined up with bands of Maroons.

In 1805, French forces attacked Dominica from the south and a fierce battle raged off Roseau. The French fleet gained ground in La Pointe (Pointe Michel) and cannon fire from Fort Young resulted in flames drifting on the wind towards the town. Roseau was burned to the ground and the remaining British troops under

Governor Sir George Prevost retreated to the garrison at Fort Shirley. Prevost refused to surrender and the French, perhaps no longer relishing the prospect of further fighting and knowing the garrison would be a formidable challenge, withdrew from Dominica with their loot.

After the end of hostilities with the French, the requirement for military fortifications diminished and in 1854 the garrison of Fort Shirley was abandoned to nature. In 1983, restoration began under the professional guidance of historian Dr Lennox Honychurch.

From the clearing above the visitor centre, walk up the stone path to the fort. The entrance passes between two stone buildings. On your left is the **guardhouse** and on your right the **powder magazine**. The guardhouse has small windows through which guards would have been able to observe and fire at intruders entering the fort. The powder magazine now displays some of the region's artefacts. To the left of the guardhouse are the **troop barracks**, beyond which is the restored **lower battery**, with seven cannons pointing out across Prince Rupert Bay. At the rear of the lower battery is the **ordnance store**, where you can see cannonballs, grapeshot and ordnance tools.

The garrison is thought to have had 35 cannons in all and 17 of them can still be found here. The cannons were 32-pounders, each with a range of around 2.4km and accuracy to 1.2km.

Continue up the path past the bottle palms to the upper section of the fort. This area is dominated by the restored **officers' quarters**. Beneath the large mango tree in front of the building is an iron pump. This is a **cistern**, one of three located in the garrison that would have provided the troops with fresh drinking water collected from rooftops and a water catchment. To the left of the officers' quarters is the **upper battery** and **signal station** with cannons pointing out across the bay.

These days, with an ever-increasing emphasis on festivals, Fort Shirley has become a venue for wedding receptions and music events such as the annual Jazz 'n Creole (page 63).

PORTSMOUTH AND PICARD The broad and beautiful bay that stretches from the Cabrits headland south to Morne Espagnol was called **Ouyuhayo** by the Amerindian settlers who lived there and then later **Grand Anse** by the French. Today it's named after Prince Rupert of the Rhine, a Royalist commander during the English Civil War (1642–51) who is said to have taken refuge here in 1652. Following defeat by the Parliamentarians of Oliver Cromwell, the man he named 'Ironside' at the 1644 Battle of Marston Moor, Rupert took to piracy, attacking English shipping first in the Mediterranean and later in the West Indies.

Prince Rupert Bay was a natural harbour for ships, both military and commercial, and in 1765 the area along its eastern shoreline was laid out by the British as the island's capital. As it was to be a major seaport, it was named Portsmouth after the English naval town. Unfortunately, large swamplands both to the north and to the south of this developing settlement resulted in too many cases of malaria and yellow fever for this to be a practical plan. Just three years later the project was abandoned and the settlement of Roseau in the south was made Dominica's capital instead.

To the east of Portsmouth is a large sports and events field called **Benjamin's Park** and beyond that there is a grid of residential housing. To the north of the town is the district of **Lagon** (also **Lagoon**). Prince Rupert Bay is a popular anchorage for visiting yachts and cruisers, and the small bars, snackettes and restaurants along the beaches at Lagon benefit from the arrival of these visitors. Although Dominica still doesn't have a proper marina, the **Portsmouth Association of Yacht Security (PAYS)**, located on Purple Turtle Beach, takes responsibility for the administration,

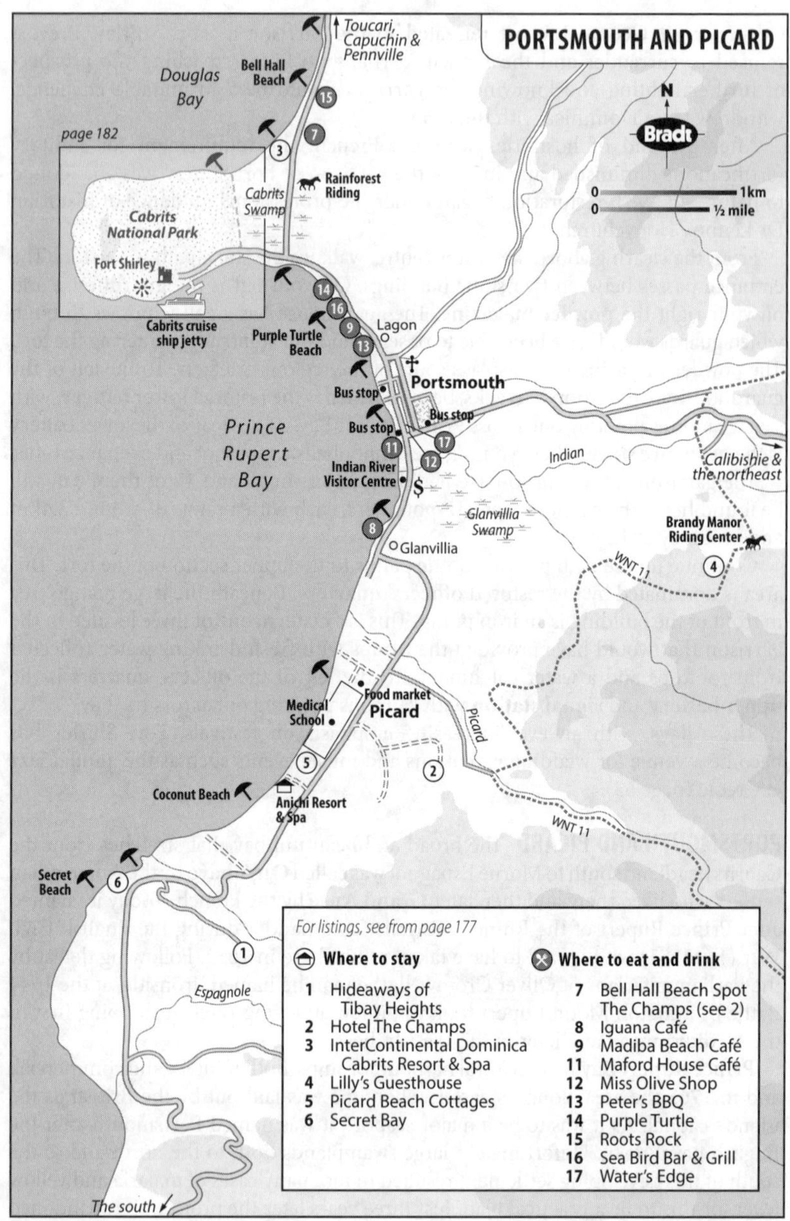

security and provisioning services of vessels opting to use Prince Rupert Bay as an anchorage.

A little to the south of Portsmouth, beside a long stretch of beach, is the once-thriving community of **Picard**. This area experienced a significant – and somewhat haphazard – expansion primarily due to a medical school that was located here. Following Tropical Storm Erika in 2015 and then Hurricane Maria in 2017, the medical school decided to relocate to Barbados and since then Picard has become rather a ghost town with many of the former student accommodation buildings either sitting empty or occupied by migrant workers from Haiti. The Government of Dominica has revealed several new medical schools over the years since, none of which have materialised. The latest is the newly established **American Canadian School of Medicine** (w acsom.edu.dm) which, at the time of writing, is slated to open its doors in late 2023.

Located next to the university campus is a small market area with stalls selling a selection of food and drinks. It is a good place to drop in for a take-away or to gather provisions for a hike or a picnic. To the south of the campus is the sprawling CBI-funded **Anichi Resort & Spa development** (page 177), located alongside the lovely **Coconut Beach**.

THE TOP END The northern tip of Dominica has rugged stretches of coastline with a mountainous interior. A narrow road winds along the west coast from Douglas Bay to the remote village of Capuchin. A road from the community of Savanne Paille cuts across the interior and passes through and across the Morne Aux Diables volcanic crater to the Delaford Estate and the elevated coastal community of Pennville. From here, the steep road meanders along the east coast through the village of Vieille Case down to Thibaud, where it joins the road that connects Calibishie and Marigot to Portsmouth.

To the north of the Cabrits is **Douglas Bay**, once called Malalia by Amerindian settlers, then renamed after Sir James Douglas, an 18th-century admiral of the British navy. With the twin peaks of the Cabrits to the south and the headland of Douglas Point to the north, this calm and tranquil bay is very picturesque. It also has a sandy beach (**Bell Hall Beach**). Beyond the tiny community of **Tanetane**, the road curves around the bay and offers a choice of routes. To the left, the road goes uphill through the hamlets of Savanne Paille, Morne A Louis and then down into the very pretty Toucari. The road to the right is the route across the Morne Aux Diables volcanic crater to Pennville.

Taking a left at this junction and ascending to Savanne Paille and Morne A Louis presents you with lovely views of Douglas Bay and the Cabrits. The narrow road then heads downhill into Toucari Bay. Take care and use your horn here as the road is steep and narrow with tight hairpin corners.

The sheltered bay at the village of **Toucari** is worth a visit. The bay serves as a natural harbour for sailboats and hidden beneath its waters is a reef formation of hard and soft corals, an abundance of aquatic life and a number of small caves and swim-throughs. The northern end of the bay is especially worth exploring as there's also a submerged fumarole – if you can find it. Skirting the bay side are several popular bars and restaurants, including the much touted Keepin' It Real (page 179). To the north, perched on the hillside above the road, is Toucari Roman Catholic Church, and beneath it on the opposite side of the road, the beachside cemetery.

The road north from Toucari hugs the west coast until it reaches the most northerly village of **Capuchin**. En route it passes through the hamlets of **Cottage**, **Cocoyer** and **Clifton**. In 1567, several Spanish treasure ships were wrecked in a storm off the coast of Capuchin. The Kalinago are said to have salvaged some of the valuable cargo and stashed it in a secret cave. Stories of this lost treasure are alive and well, though none of it has ever been found. North of Capuchin the road ends and becomes a dirt track. This track passes Capuchin Point, or Cape Melville, and arrives at the **Canna Heritage Park**. In addition to a gun battery placement, cannon and some stone ruins, there's evidence that this area was also once an Amerindian settlement as well as a missionary site of the Capuchin religious order. The track that

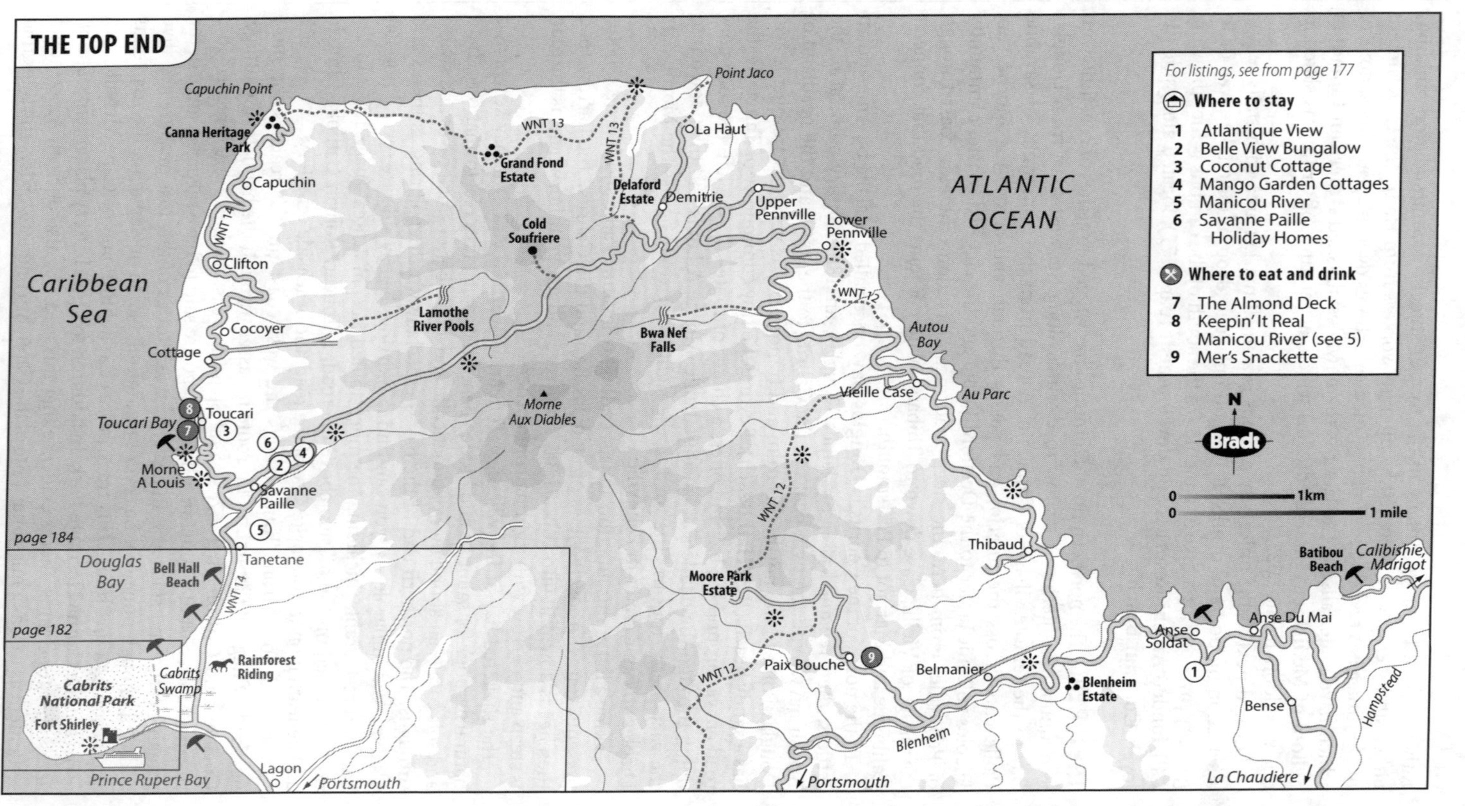
THE TOP END
For listings, see from page 177
Where to stay
1 Atlantique View
2 Belle View Bungalow
3 Coconut Cottage
4 Mango Garden Cottages
5 Manicou River
6 Savanne Paille Holiday Homes
Where to eat and drink
7 The Almond Deck
8 Keepin' It Real
Manicou River (see 5)
9 Mer's Snackette
ATLANTIC OCEAN
Caribbean Sea
Capuchin Point
Canna Heritage Park
Point Jaco
La Haut
WNT 13
Grand Fond Estate
Delaford Estate
Demitrie
Upper Pennville
Lower Pennville
Capuchin
WNT 14
Clifton
Cold Soufriere
Lamothe River Pools
Bwa Nef Falls
WNT 12
Cocoyer
Cottage
Autou Bay
Toucari
Toucari Bay
Morne Aux Diables
Vieille Case
Au Parc
Morne A Louis
Savanne Paille
Tanetane
page 184
page 182
Douglas Bay
Bell Hall Beach
Cabrits Swamp
Rainforest Riding
Cabrits National Park
Fort Shirley
Prince Rupert Bay
Lagon
Portsmouth
Moore Park Estate
Paix Bouche
Belmanier
Blenheim Estate
Blenheim
Thibaud
Batibou Beach
Calibishie, Marigot
Anse Soldat
Anse Du Mai
Bense
Hampstead
La Chaudiere
N
Bradt
0 1km
0 1 mile

runs eastwards from this point is the **Capuchin to Pennville Trail**, now Segment 13 of the Wai'tukubuli National Trail (page 201), a historic coastal track that ends at a small farming community on the former Delaford Estate, a little to the west of the village of Pennville. Segment 14 begins at Canna and runs all the way south along the coastal road to Cabrits National Park.

The road up the western slopes of Morne Aux Diables from Savanne Paille and Toucari has some spectacular views of Prince Rupert Bay and Portsmouth to the south, and the islands of Les Saintes to the northwest. Once over the ridge you enter a wide crater that was once part of a multi-domed volcano. At the base of the crater there's a sign for **Cold Soufriere** (page 194).

Following the road up and over the crater's eastern ridge, there are breathtaking panoramas of the Atlantic Ocean and Dominica's high and rugged eastern coastline.

Descending Morne Aux Diables through the farming community of Delaford Estate, you may notice two turnings to the left. The first is the eastern trailhead for the Capuchin to Pennville Trail, or Segment 13 of the Wai'tukubuli National Trail. The second turning goes to the tiny hamlet of **La Haut**, which is located at the very northeastern tip of Dominica. This area is also known as **Carib** because there was once an Amerindian village here.

On the lower slopes of Morne Aux Diables the winding road meets the village of **Pennville**. The village is in two parts: Upper Pennville and Lower Pennville. Located on the main road beyond Lower Pennville is the signposted trail to the **Bwa Nef Falls** (page 196).

In 1646, Father Raymond Breton, a French priest of the Dominican order, gave the island's first Christian service at the Amerindian village of Itassi in the *karbet* of Chief Kalamiena. Unfortunately for Father Breton, it was not for another hundred years that Christianity gained a firm footing in Dominica. A mural of his first Mass is painted on the wall of the parish hall at the top of the village, now called **Vieille Case**.

In November 2004, an earthquake 27km north of Dominica, measuring 6.3 on the Richter Scale, shook the island and caused damage to several buildings in the north, including the Vieille Case Catholic Church. The quake was followed by a series of aftershocks and torrential rains. This very unusual church – completed in 1869, constructed from volcanic rock and with a beautiful Spanish façade and shingle roof – unfortunately could not be saved. A new, more modern replacement has been erected.

Vieille Case is built on a steep slope overlooking the bay at **Autou**. This charming but rugged cove serves as a landing place for local fishermen and is accessed via a steep and narrow road at the bottom of the village. The road emerges at a small pasture where cows or horses may be grazing. On the left-hand side is a wide grassy path leading to the boat landing. Watch the waves rushing into the bay from the open ocean and imagine how tricky it must be both to set out and land at this point. At the end of the pasture is a narrow track leading out to a rocky volcanic outcrop, from where there are great views along the coast. There was once a rite-of-passage challenge for the children of Vieille Case called '*decouvé léglise*'. The children, usually young boys, had to swim out from the shore at Autou until they could see the roof of the church high up above the village.

Along the coast from Autou is a partially sheltered cove called **Au Parc** where gazebos and benches have been set up for bathing and picnics.

South of Au Parc is the small farming and fishing community of **Thibaud**, named after a French settler who purchased land from the Amerindians here in the 18th century. The school and playing field are located on the shoreline of Sandwich Bay.

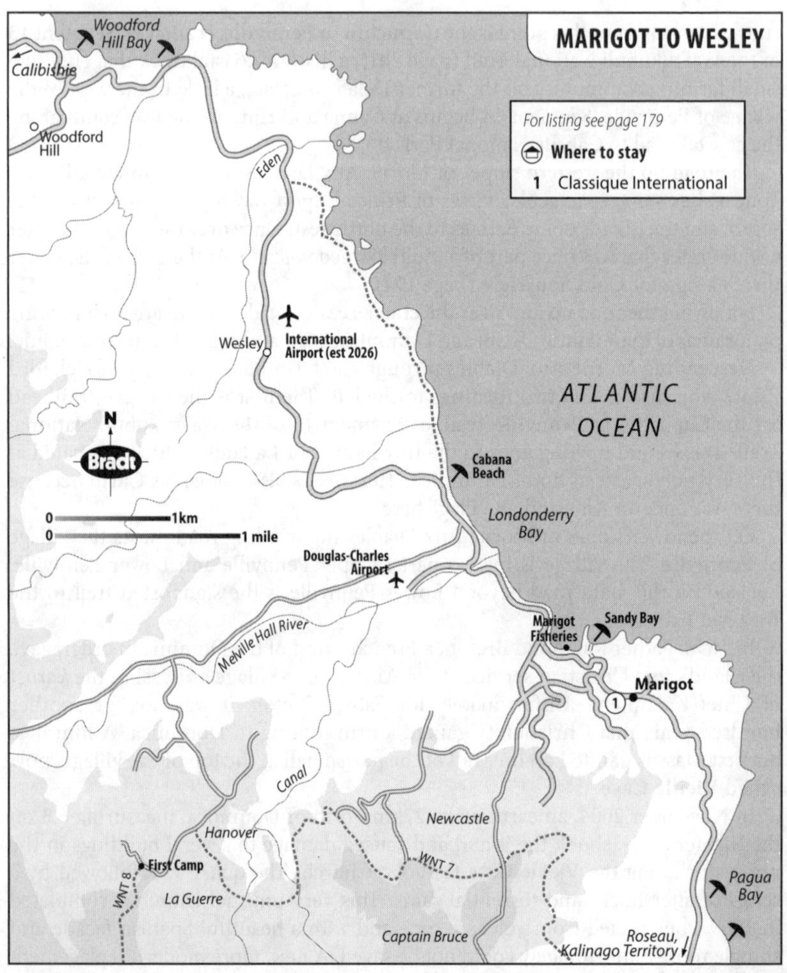

THE NORTHEAST COAST In the 1830s, British plantation owners in the northeast imported an enslaved workforce from other English-speaking islands such as Antigua. They also provided a base for Wesleyan missionaries who began to have a significant influence in the area. The settlements that developed around the estates following emancipation contrasted to those that emerged elsewhere on the island. Here it was a Methodist rather than a Roman Catholic community that did not speak in French Creole, but rather an English form of Creole known as *kockoy*.

The settlement that developed around the former estates of Charles Leatham, such as the Eden Estate, was known as Wesleyville and later simply as Wesley. A little to the south of Wesley is the village of Marigot, also a settlement that developed with significant English influence due to imported Leeward Islands enslaved labour. Marigot Bay was also a busy place for the trans-shipment of cargo. It had a jetty and a small fort for protection.

In the 20th century, the northeast was a major area of banana production and received significant economic benefit from this trade. When world trade rules were changed, the area was on the receiving end of a devastating reduction in demand for small island bananas. Unable to compete with the huge banana-producing companies of the Americas, the outlook in this area appeared quite bleak. Villages such as Woodford Hill and Wesley, places that had just begun to develop on the back of a banana boom, suffered a reversal of fortune and became run-down. Thanks to the assistance of The Fairtrade Foundation, the small island banana producers in the Caribbean received a fragile lifeline – though this has since stopped since the black sigatoka disease resulted in the cessation of transatlantic banana exports. The ridges and elevated tracts of land behind the villages of the northeast are covered in banana farms and, despite the challenges, bananas and plantains still remain an important source of income for the people of this area.

At the time of writing, construction of Dominica's long-awaited **international airport** has begun near Wesley (many families were relocated). The airport is scheduled to be completed in 2026.

The sprawling hillside village of **Marigot** developed around the plantation of John Weir, who brought in enslaved labourers from Antigua and the Leeward Islands. The modern village stretches from Pagua Bay to Douglas-Charles Airport and consists of several small districts, including one called Weirs after the former plantation owner. The main road runs through the heart of the village and is where most of the bars, shops and eateries are to be found.

Located on the southern edge of the village is an area called North End. In 1795, there was fighting in North End between the British and the French and in the mid 19th century there was a small Kalinago village here. As the village of Marigot expanded southwards, the Kalinago crossed the Pagua River and settled in what is now the Kalinago Territory.

The Marigot Fisheries complex on Marigot Bay was funded by Japan. You can buy fresh fish here most days of the week. North of Marigot is the expansive and dramatic Londonderry Bay, where **Douglas-Charles Airport** is located. Following the coast north of Wesley, you come to the banana-farming community of **Woodford Hill** – once the location of one of the island's largest sugar-producing estates. The area also had a harbour and a small fortification for protection. Woodford Hill has a large bay and lovely beach. This is also the site where archaeologists uncovered evidence of what was perhaps Dominica's earliest – though unrecorded – European settlement, known as La Soye (page 18).

Pointe Baptiste is home to an historic estate house and **chocolate factory** (page 195), black- and white-sand beaches, and the must-visit **Red Rocks** coastal formations (page 195).

Calibishie is a small coastal village with a pretty shoreline and great views across the sea to Les Saintes, Guadeloupe and Marie-Galante. A shallow reef extends beyond the light sand shoreline to breakers and the rock formation Port D'Enfer, or Hell's Gate. The formation was once a natural arch through which water surged from open ocean to calmer shore.

This area has experienced a consistent wave of overseas investment, with ocean-view lots developed and sold for guesthouses and second homes. The sandy beaches, panoramic ocean views, sea breeze and proximity to Douglas-Charles Airport have seen tourist accommodation and ancillary services both supplement and replace the banana as a source of local income. Check out accommodation websites such as Airbnb and you get the impression every household is offering a room to let.

To the back of the village are coconut palms and banana farms covering a series of tall ridges in a blanket of green. A network of farm access roads runs along these ridges and makes for a fun hike or drive. The roads are a little rough in places but

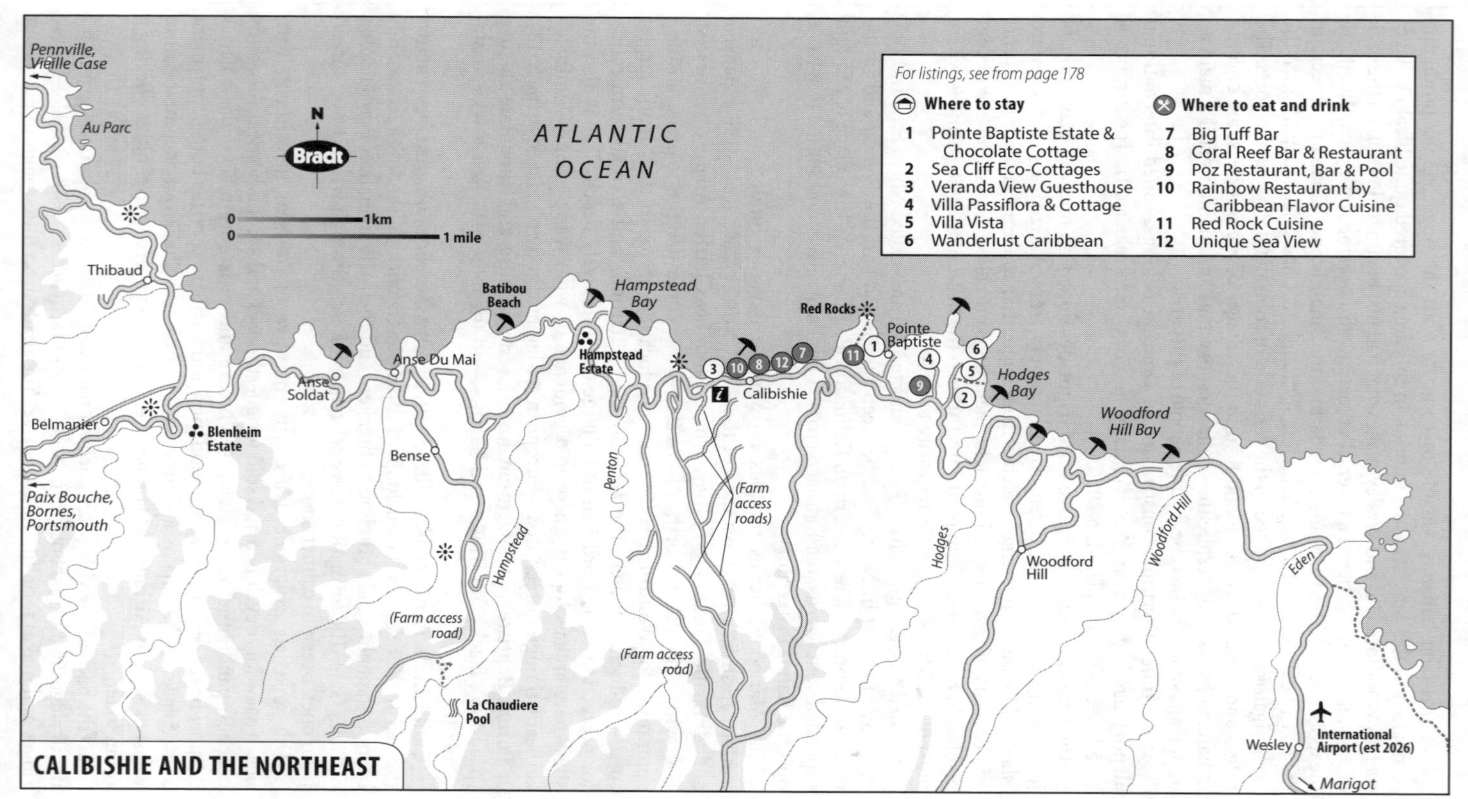

CALIBISHIE AND THE NORTHEAST
ATLANTIC OCEAN
For listings, see from page 178
Where to stay
1 Pointe Baptiste Estate & Chocolate Cottage
2 Sea Cliff Eco-Cottages
3 Veranda View Guesthouse
4 Villa Passiflora & Cottage
5 Villa Vista
6 Wanderlust Caribbean
Where to eat and drink
7 Big Tuff Bar
8 Coral Reef Bar & Restaurant
9 Poz Restaurant, Bar & Pool
10 Rainbow Restaurant by Caribbean Flavor Cuisine
11 Red Rock Cuisine
12 Unique Sea View
N
Bradt
0 1km
0 1 mile
Pennville, Vieille Case
Au Parc
Thibaud
Belmanier
Paix Bouche, Bornes, Portsmouth
Blenheim Estate
Anse Soldat
Anse Du Mai
Bense
Batibou Beach
Hampstead Estate
Hampstead Bay
Hampstead
La Chaudiere Pool
(Farm access road)
Penton
(Farm access road)
(Farm access roads)
Calibishie
Red Rocks
Pointe Baptiste
Hodges Bay
Hodges
Woodford Hill
Woodford Hill Bay
Woodford Hill
Eden
Wesley
International Airport (est 2026)
Marigot

the scenery is captivating, with views over the ocean to the north, and across the rainforest interior of the Northern Forest Reserve and Morne Diablotin National Park to the southwest.

The **Hampstead Estate** once produced sugar, limes, cocoa and coconuts. The ruined estate building and machine works can be seen on the apex of a bend between Calibishie and Bense, near a bridge that crosses the Hampstead River. The ruins consist of stone buildings, several items of heavy machinery and presses, as well as a waterwheel that was driven by water channelled from the river. Along the side and to the rear of the ruins is a track that follows the Hampstead River into the depths of the former estate, through plantations of coconut palms.

On the road from Calibishie, before reaching the Hampstead Estate ruins, there's a vehicle track that runs to **Hampstead Beach**. It takes about 15 minutes to walk down (there's a fee as the access road is private – page 192). It's a long and broad beach and was one of the iconic locations for the feature film *Pirates of the Caribbean: Dead Man's Chest*.

Beyond Hampstead Beach, heading away from Calibishie, you'll see what's left of a quaint Methodist church on the right-hand side of the road. Not far away is another (private) access road running down to **Batibou Beach** (page 192). Batibou is the original Kalinago name for the area.

To the west of Batibou Beach is the signposted road to **Bense**. This small farming village is perched on the spine of a narrow ridge that extends inland towards the foothills of Morne Diablotin. Beyond the village, the paved road transitions to dirt track and continues to the remote farming area of Ti Branches. En route, and probably much further along than you expect it to be, there's the signposted trailhead for **La Chaudiere Pool** (page 198).

Anse is the Creole word for bay and, to the west of the junction for Bense, along the coastal road, are the two fishing villages of **Anse Du Mai** and **Anse Soldat**.

Near the ruins of the former Blenheim Estate, is the road to Vieille Case and Pennville. A short distance to the west, at the next junction, is a road to the elevated

MAKING THE MOST OF COCONUTS

The flowering of the coconut palm produces *drupes*, which are large green fruit growing in bunches high in the tree. Each fruit is surrounded by a tough fibrous husk up to 15cm thick which is called the *pericarp*. Beneath this is a thin, hard brown kernel containing the *albumen*, or coconut milk, which transforms itself into a white flesh as the fruit matures. Young coconuts are often referred to as *jellies*, in reference to the soft, sweet jelly-like flesh that is beginning to form. The albumen of these young coconuts is often called coconut water and is a refreshing drink. You'll see pick-up trucks or makeshift roadside stalls selling jelly coconuts. Buy a jelly, drink the water, then eat the flesh. It's great refreshment after a hike and is said to be very healthy.

Mature coconuts are harvested, and their dried fibrous husks removed to extract the tough, thin shell of the kernel. This in turn is cracked in half to expose the white flesh of the coconut. Mature coconut flesh is either eaten as is or it's converted into products such as coconut milk. Further work involves thoroughly drying coconuts in the sun or in an oven. The dried flesh is then extracted from the kernel. Known as *copra*, the flesh can now be used to create coconut oil or as an ingredient in soaps, skin-care products, shampoos and so on. Low-grade copra can also be used as cattle feed.

hamlet of **Paix Bouche**, and above it **Moore Park**. Paix Bouche means 'shut your mouth' in reference, it's said, to walkers climbing up the steep hillside having to stop talking to save their breath. The road that runs straight up and through both hamlets continues beyond Moore Park, past a communications tower, and transitions to a farm track and part of Wai'tukubuli National Trail Segment 12 (page 200). Check out Mers' snackette at the top of Paix Bouche for fabulous views of Dominica's interior.

The road between Portsmouth and the east coast passes through the villages of Dos D'Ane and Bornes. In Bornes, you may see a colourful sign for **Indigo**, the unique gallery and studio of artist Marie Frederick (page 195). Also in Bornes is the delightful **Paradise Valley** (page 195) and **Brandy Manor** horseriding stable (page 194). In the Brandy Manor area (and the last stretch of Wai'tukubuli National Trail Segment 11) are the fragmented remains of a railway line. This line used to run from Brandy Ridge to the Indian River, transporting timber for the 1910 Forest Company Ltd. From here, the timber was taken by river to the coast. The company went bankrupt after operating for just three years and the rails were salvaged by construction workers for buildings in Portsmouth. The small steam train that transported the timber was sold overseas, though remains of discarded rolling stock can still be seen around Brandy Manor.

WHAT TO SEE AND DO

BEACHES Though it's known more for its greenery than it is for its sand, Dominica has some lovely beaches, bays and sheltered waters that are great spots for bathing and watersports. Some of the best are in the north. Here is a selection.

Batibou and Hampstead beaches Access to Batibou and Hampstead beaches is via private property and the owner has made it very clear through an abundance of signage that you must pay. The charge is US$5 for each. Taking its name from the Kalinago word for 'bay', Batibou is accessed via a vehicle track on the main coastal road from Blenheim to Calibishie. The road down to the beach is a comfortable 4x4 drive or a 20-minute walk. It's a lovely bay with a rather manicured beach that has the feel of a personal rather than public domain (Dominica's laws state that all beaches are public). There's a security guard, beach bar, tables and chairs, and even hammock rental. Hampstead is a much wilder, broader beach with less protection from the ocean. For film buffs, this is the spot where Captain Jack Sparrow is chased by cannibals to his ship, the *Black Pearl*, in *Pirates of the Caribbean*. The beach is signposted and is a short distance from the main road.

Bell Hall Beach on Douglas Bay This is a slight sliver of sand to the north of the InterContinental Dominica Cabrits Resort & Spa. The main attraction is the serene Douglas Bay. There's a picnic area and across the road are the Bell Hall Beach Spot and Roots Rock, two good places for food and drink.

Coconut Beach This lovely and often overlooked beach runs along the entire length of Picard (it's also sometimes referred to as Picard Beach). At the southern end is the garden boundary of the Secret Bay resort, complete with beached shipwreck. Centre stage is the more dissonant Anichi Resort & Spa (at the time of writing, a CBI project under construction), and the more established Picard Beach Cottages. At the northern end is the medical school campus. Access to Coconut Beach is alongside Anichi or Ti Bay Villas and Secret Bay.

Hodges Bay To the southeast of Calibishie and Pointe Baptiste is Hodges Bay. Infrequently visited, this is a fairly sheltered bay with a long beach and offshore islet (known locally as Treasure Island). To find it, look for the signs to Sea Cliff Eco Cottages and Wanderlust, and follow the road down towards the bottom. There's a signposted track on the right-hand side of Villa Vista that goes down to the beach. It's short but quite steep. At the bottom you must cross the mouth of the Hodges River to get to the beach proper. There's a track on Treasure Island that runs along its spine and goes right to the end. If you have a mask and snorkel, there's a large bank of sea fans between the shore and the islet that's worth exploring. Be careful of sea surge and cross-currents when you're swimming close to the islet.

Pointe Baptiste Beach There's a scenic white-sand beach near the village of Pointe Baptiste. Along the road to Pointe Baptiste Estate and Red Rocks, look for a wide track before a small shop on the right – just after the turning from the main road. It's tricky to drive down, so park up and walk for around 20 minutes to the beach.

Purple Turtle Beach To the north of Portsmouth and Lagon (also Lagoon), Purple Turtle is a lovely beach that's popular with locals at the weekends. The sea is sheltered and shallow making it great for kids, and there are several bars and restaurants along the margins.

Sandy Bay Completely off the beaten path, Sandy Bay has a lovely white-sand beach. In Marigot, next to My Father's Place Guest House and the small shop in front, there's a narrow track. Follow it downhill for about 10 minutes where it widens and reaches the beach, which is in two parts, separated by a rocky outcrop and cave. The inshore waters are protected by a reef system that is not bad for snorkelling, though you should stick to the inshore side of the formation. Despite being hidden away and somewhat offbeat, the beach is quite popular with local people at weekends.

Secret Beach The only way to get to the gorgeous Secret Beach is by sea. Rent a kayak or charter a boat from either the Indian River or Purple Turtle Beach to get there. There's also great snorkelling along and around the rocky headland.

Turtle Point Beach This is a lovely white-sand beach that's often overlooked by visitors. Find it to the west of Woodford Hill Beach via a short access road from the main road where it passes Woodford Hill village.

Woodford Hill Beach Also the location of the La Soye archaeology site (page 18), Woodford Hill Beach is lovely though sea bathing can be tricky as there's often a strong undertow. The beach is maintained by the village council and is patrolled by a security guard (it used to have a reputation for petty theft).

CALIBISHIE FARM ACCESS ROADS The farm access roads up to and along the ridges behind the village of Calibishie are accessible by car or on foot and have panoramic sea and mountain views. I recommend them as a pleasant walk for anyone staying in the Calibishie area. The network of narrow roads winds around the high ridges and loops back down to the village in several places. If you prefer to drive, you should have a 4x4 as the terrain is a little rough in places. Don't be surprised if some of the farmers you meet offer to sell you land; this is a popular area for overseas investors looking to build first or second homes and many locals have opted to cash in.

COLD SOUFRIERE Travelling on the Northern Link Road between Savanne Paille and Pennville takes you through and across the Morne Aux Diables volcanic crater. It's a visibly dramatic and atmospheric area – clearly a crater, and equally clearly part of a series of volcanic domes – that's often shrouded in mist. At the bottom of the basin is a sign and small wooden hut marking the trailhead for Cold Soufriere.

An easy 15-minute walk takes you along a country track and down a series of small steps to the active fumaroles in the heart of the crater. You reach a wooden viewing platform over the primeval terrain of stained rocks, mosses and bubbling pools. The area is surrounded by *kaklen* (*Clusia mangle*), which is a typical species of fumarole vegetation found at Dominica's volcanic sites and mountain peaks. The water is cold because the magma layer from where the hot gases are released is thought to be much lower down than those, say, in the Wotten Waven area. This means that by the time they reach the surface they have cooled down. This area is of particular scientific interest to geologists and volcanologists as some of the more recent volcanic swarms recorded in Dominica have come from the Morne Aux Diables volcanic centre. Although it's possible to explore the site, please do so carefully and resist the urge to etch your name into this natural formation. The stream that runs through Cold Soufriere becomes the Lamothe River (page 198).

HORSERIDING Whether you're a novice or a seasoned rider, enjoy the trails through semi-deciduous woodland and rainforest around Brandy Estate and Wai'tukubuli National Trail Segment 11 with **Brandy Manor Riding Center** (w brandymanor.wixsite.com/riding-center), which is located off the road between Portsmouth and Bornes. Trail rides can be from 30 minutes to 4 hours and cost up to US$85 per person. Riding lessons are also available and cost around US$20 per 30 minutes. Alternatively, contact **Rainforest Riding** (w rainforestriding.com) which is based opposite the InterContinental Dominica Cabrits Resort & Spa. Valerie Francis offers accompanied horseriding around the Cabrits National Park trails, on part of WNT Segment 14, and along Purple Turtle Beach. She can also teach you how to ride and has a training ring at her stables and farm. Accompanied riding tours cost up to US$100 and lessons US$20 per 30 minutes.

*** INDIAN RIVER BOAT TRIP** Boat tours along the Indian River begin at the visitor centre near the Indian River bridge to the south of Portsmouth. The colourful wooden row boats can carry up to eight passengers along a roughly 2km stretch of the Indian River, Dominica's only navigable waterway. It's a sedate, scenic and informative journey with your boat guide explaining the flora and fauna along the way. The river is lined with a type of mangrove that's known locally as the bloodwood tree because of its reddish sap. It has large buttress roots that weave their way across the banks like giant tendrils before disappearing beneath the water. You'll probably see shoals of mountain mullet and water birds such as kingfishers, herons, moorhens and coots. Iguanas can sometimes be seen lazing in the tree branches.

Fans of the *Pirates of the Caribbean* feature films will be interested to know that the Indian River was the location of the hideaway of Tia Dalma (Calypso) in *Dead Man's Chest*. Your riverboat guide will take you there before calling in for refreshments at the rustic bar that marks the furthest point upriver. Wander the colourful gardens and enjoy a rum punch before making the return journey. The standard fare is EC$50 per person and because the Indian River is a designated eco-site, you must either purchase or show a site pass.

INDIGO ART GALLERY Located in the northern village of Bornes, Indigo Art Gallery is the home and workplace of artist Marie Frederick. It's as much a masterpiece of design and originality as her Fauvist-style artwork. The gallery enjoys views of the forest canopy and her tropical garden, with birds regularly flying in and out enjoying fruits and other treats laid out or hanging for them. Marie was born in Deauville, France, but has been living in Dominica for many years after falling in love with the island. She finds her inspiration in daily village life, the natural environment and simple wooden *ti-kai* houses. Marie works in pen and ink, watercolour, acrylic and oil pastel. Her opening times vary and often depend on how she's feeling! If you're interested in seeing and perhaps buying some of her artwork, call or WhatsApp in advance (767 276 0402). Look for the colourful hand-painted Indigo Gallery signs along the roadside in Bornes and follow the signs along a rough vehicle track to her gallery and home.

✷ PARADISE VALLEY GARDENS & NURSERY The creation of local Dominican landscape gardener and stonemason Dian Douglas, Paradise Valley is a must-visit for gardening enthusiasts. Guided walks of the gardens are available at around EC$20 per person (it's wise to call or WhatsApp ahead 767 277 4671, 767 225 9199). Gently undulating pathways meander around the valley and through creative and colourful planting displays that also integrate antiques and other interesting objects of Dominica's history such as copper boiling pots, bells and machinery from former sugarcane estates. Dian has also designed and constructed a handful of delightful wooden cottages that he aims to rent as holiday lets at some point in the future (perhaps even by the time this book goes to print). There's also a large nursery area that's home to a wide variety of cultivated plants including hundreds of anthuriums. Paradise Valley is in the village of Bornes. Look for the sign and entrance on the apex of a bend near a church and a stone bus shelter – Dian's contribution to the village.

✷ RED ROCKS Pointe Baptiste village is located on the northeast coast, a short distance to the east of Calibishie. It's noted for its historic estate and chocolate factory, but especially for the Red Rocks, an unusual and beautiful coastal formation of smooth reddish earth that's been compacted and shaped by both ocean and weather. Best visited when the sun is low in the sky – to bring out the range of

POINTE BAPTISTE ESTATE CHOCOLATE FACTORY

Sited on the grounds of the historic Pointe Baptiste Estate, the chocolate factory (with a lovely rental cottage; page 179) is the manifestation of years of learning, investment and work by estate owner Alan Napier. Providing a market for Dominica's cocoa farmers, Alan's small business has evolved to become *the* Dominica chocolate factory and is open to visitors. Either learn something about the process or just taste and buy some of the chocolate – it's certainly worth stopping by, especially if the Red Rocks is on your holiday agenda. The chocolate factory is signposted from the main Pointe Baptiste road junction, a short distance to the east of Calibishie village.

colours that are not quite as visible in the harsh midday sun – the ochre hues of the formation reflect a gradual oxidation of iron over time.

As access is via part of the private property of the Pointe Baptiste Estate, there's a small visitor fee (US$2 pp) for trail maintenance that you pay at the bar and restaurant by the trailhead. Follow a short track through coastal scrub until you emerge at the formation.

To get there, take the road to Pointe Baptiste village from the main road near Calibishie and go straight on at the next junction (right is the chocolate factory and main estate). There's space to park at the end of the paved road.

WATERSPORTS In addition to its beaches, the north has several great places to kayak, paddleboard, snorkel and scuba dive (page 84). It's certainly worth asking at the PAYS centre on Purple Turtle Beach where you can also get boat rides, water taxi services, yacht provisioning and Indian River tours. Here are some of the operators who can also help.

Eddison Tours Savanne Paille; 767 225 3626; w eddisontours.dm. In addition to island, coast & Indian River tours, experienced guide Eddison also offers inshore fishing trips.

Island Dive Operation Purple Turtle Beach; 767 277 5673. This small scuba-diving operator offers daily boat diving at the Cabrits & Toucari Bay sites, as well as try-dives & tuition. Find the office near the PAYS centre on Purple Turtle Beach.

JC Ocean Adventures Cabrits National Park; 767 295 0757; w jcoceanadventures.com. Located within Cabrits National Park near the main reception building, JC Ocean Adventures offers boat diving, snorkelling, PADI dive tuition & whale-watching excursions.

Keepin' It Real Toucari Bay; 767 225 7657. Known more for its great food than its watersports, this restaurant on the bay front rents out paddleboards & snorkelling equipment.

Lilly's Guesthouse Brandy, Portsmouth; 767 317 4723; w lillysguesthouse.com. Boat builder & all-round nice guy, guesthouse owner Lilly also offer boat tours & inshore fishing trips.

HIKING TRAILS

BWA NEF FALLS Bwa Nef is an unusual waterfall, located within a tall and narrow cavern on the Celestin Brenner River between the villages of Pennville and Vieille Case. Access is via a steepish but easy-to-follow forest track (20–30 minutes) from the main road. It's partially private land and, if the farmer is around, he may expect a 'contribution'. Usually, US$5 or EC$10 per person is standard – certainly no more.

On a sharp curve between Lower Pennville and Vieille Case, there's a sign for Bwa Nef (oddly, it's been placed so you can only see it when coming from the north). There's an offroad parking area and the trailhead is easy to find. Beginning on the right-hand bank of the river, then crossing to the left, it's a clear though often steep uphill track. As you approach the waterfall, the track ends and there's a short section where you must negotiate the river and its rocks. The tall waterfall is inside the conical cavern. Check out the huge boulder hanging overhead.

CABANA BEACH AND CLIFFS Cabana Beach is a wild stretch of sand on the Atlantic Ocean coastline south of Wesley, north of Douglas-Charles Airport. This offbeat trail follows beaches, bays and high coastal formations to the former Eden Estate where a track brings you back to the main road. The trail is tricky to follow and is marked with sporadic red ribbons tied to bushes and trees. But it's a beaten path, still used, mostly by fishermen. As it's along high cliffs, those with an aversion to high places may find the walk somewhat challenging in places. Allow around 2 hours to reach Eden from Cabana, assuming you don't spend too much time searching for the elusive ribbons.

The highlight of this walk is the coastal cliff formation. Similar to the Red Rocks of Pointe Baptiste, yet far less visited, the cliffs are dramatic and beautiful.

The trail starts by the abandoned building on the windswept Cabana Beach. Head north, following the wide track and then beach around the rugged coastline. Although occasionally difficult to find, the ribbons and the paths essentially follow the route of the headland. Simply walk to the end of a beach or bay and look for the ribbon and the path at the far end. Some tracks are steep, climbing up the headland to the high cliffs where the trace is still visible, though often precariously close to the edge, so do take care. Along the highest cliff, there's a scary little section where you must negotiate a sharp curve and deep gully. You'll know it when you see it! Common sense prevails along this walk. Don't walk too close to the cliff edge, especially if it has been raining, as the compacted earth is smooth and slippery. After negotiating several bays, thickets of coastal scrub and high cliffs, you'll come to an area of flat grassland. Head west, away from the sea along the track (the ribbons tend to run out here and it's a little confusing) until you reach the main road. You're now north of Wesley and south of Woodford Hill.

CABRITS NATIONAL PARK TRAILS There's a network of easy walking trails around Cabrits National Park. Perhaps due to the restoration of the heart of the Fort Shirley garrison (page 182), the trails are often overlooked or even unknown. This is a shame as they're lovely walks with vine and tree root entangled ruins along the way. If you were to walk just one, I'd suggest East Cabrit as there are fabulous views from the former lookout station at the top. You need an eco-site pass for the Cabrits which you can buy at the snackette by the main entrance.

Douglas Bay battery Follow the signposted trail to the Douglas Bay battery from the wide clearing and stone footpath that leads up to the restored Fort Shirley garrison. After a short distance you'll reach a sign pointing to the commandant's quarters up a spur trail to the right. Take this trail up to the ruins of the **commandant's quarters**. From here, continue northwards along the main trail until you see the impressive ruins of the officers' quarters down to your left. Walk down to them and look around. Trees and vines embrace and weave themselves around the stone ruins. Three cannons lie abandoned beside the ruins of the defensive wall and a gateway leads to the remains of the battery. Take care when exploring the ruins as there are many sharp rocks and plenty of things that can trip you up. The woodland area to the south of these ruins was once a parade ground. Also in this area and at the foot of East Cabrit were stables, further troops' barracks and a cistern.

To the west of these ruins, heading steeply uphill, are some steps. Climb up to the top where you meet a wide path. Head to the right for 15–20 minutes around the northern edge of West Cabrit, along the partially restored ruins of a wall, until you come to the end of the path. There are nice views across Douglas Bay and along the coast towards Capuchin. To the north you can usually also see The Saints and Guadeloupe. Walk back along the same wide track all the way to Fort Shirley.

East Cabrit Trail This is a pleasant and interesting trail with panoramic views from the peak of East Cabrit. In the wide clearing below the Fort Shirley garrison, follow the signposted trail to the Douglas Bay battery. When you reach the sign pointing up to the commandant's quarters, follow it. At the ruin, the wide trail running north leads to the officers' quarters and the Douglas Bay battery (page 197), but there's also a narrow spur trail on the north side of the ruin that heads upwards through the trees. This is the East Cabrit Trail. It's an easy walk that gradually climbs up East Cabrit in a series of long but fairly gentle switchbacks. It takes around 30–45 minutes to reach the ruins of the East Cabrit guardhouse, ordnance store and powder magazine. Up the stone steps are the ruins of a battery position with views across to the east. Continue along the East Cabrit Trail until you reach the end at the remains of the lookout and battery emplacement. From here there are fabulous views from Douglas Bay to Prince Rupert Bay. Immediately below is the InterContinental Cabrits Resort & Spa, embraced by the wetlands of the Cabrits with its distinctive clumps of fern and sedge.

West Cabrit Trail From the top of the Fort Shirley garrison, behind the restored officers' quarters, a sign points to the start of the West Cabrit Trail. The track passes through dry coastal woodland and climbs gradually to the top of West Cabrit via a series of gentle switchbacks. Look out for the unusual naked Indian tree, known locally as *gòmyé wouj* (*Bursera simaruba*), and the savonnet (*Lauchocarpus latifolius*), which is the most common tree found growing on the Cabrits headland. After around 30–45 minutes of steady climbing, you reach the cannon emplacement of the West Cabrit battery. In addition to the lookout and gun battery, West Cabrit was also the location for a hospital and surgery, surgeons' quarters, further troops' barracks, artillery quarters and the commandant's house.

LA CHAUDIERE POOL Either a short walk or a hike, depending on where you begin, La Chaudiere is a deep river pool and cascade on the Hampstead River near the village of Bense. The narrow access road along the scenic Hampstead Ridge is a little sketchy in places – especially after heavy rain. You certainly need a 4x4 to get to the trailhead, but you may prefer to park up somewhere along this road and walk, turning it into a hike. To get to the access road, you must follow the main, paved road through the village of Bense. Drive straight through and at a bus stop junction near the end of the village, take a right. Here, you may encounter a handful of locals offering guide services. When you've negotiated the ridge (if driving, it's 20–30 minutes from village to trailhead), you'll reach a large sign indicating the trail. I like to walk along the access road because the views from the ridge are wonderful and, if concentrating on driving, you tend to miss them.

From the access road, you must follow a wide vehicle track downhill (you can drive down if you prefer). After around 20 minutes walking, there's a signposted trail to the left. Follow this well-maintained track down to the river. At the bottom, the river flowing from the right is a tributary of the Hampstead River which you must cross. Then, simply head upriver to La Chaudiere Pool.

The name La Chaudiere references a cooking pot. It's a very deep pool with tall sides of smooth rock and the powerful cascade creates an effervescence that resembles simmering water. People like to jump in from the sides. It's certainly deep enough, and if this is your thing, be sure to aim for the middle. La Chaudiere Pool is scenic and a nice place to hang out, perhaps with a picnic. Take care if climbing the rocks up along the sides as they're smooth and often quite slippery.

LAMOTHE RIVER POOLS This offbeat hike is along old estate tracks, forest trails and then up the Lamothe River. The land section is mostly easy-going. In the river, you must negotiate rocks and boulders, making your way upstream to river pools and cascades. Be prepared to get wet and take a change of clothes. Lightweight hiking shoes or old sneakers are fine for this. Alternatively, carry a pair of sturdy surf shoes to put on when you reach the river. If you'd like to go with a guide, I recommend contacting Mango Garden Cottages (page 178), Eddison Tours (page 71) or Nigel George (page 81). Allow 3–4 hours for the whole trip.

The Lamothe River begins in the vicinity of Cold Soufriere in the volcanic crater of Morne Aux Diables. It meanders down a valley between the communities of Cocoyer and Cottage through a former coffee and cocoa estate before reaching the sea in Lamothe Bay. You can enjoy this trip either as a there-and-back or a loop hike as there are two places where you can choose to start or finish: Cottage or Cocoyer. Both starting points are a little tricky to find (see map, page 186). If you're beginning from Cottage, park your vehicle near a large peach house where the road forks and then follow the overgrown track on the left. When it forks again (there's a track on the left heading back towards Cottage), stick to the right and keep going until you come across a spur on the left that crosses the river. Once across and up the far bank, there's a trail junction. To the left is the track to Cocoyer, to the right is the trail to the river pools. If you're starting in Cocoyer, simply follow the wide track from the main coastal road to this point. Both routes are a similar distance and should take about an hour on foot (a 4x4 will get you some of the way if you so choose). Now follow the narrow trail to a clearing of citrus and cotton trees and immediately head right. Follow a stream (it can be a little swampy) down to the river. From here, it's a river hike. Before heading upstream, remember this spot (take a photo) for the way back. Carefully negotiate the rocks and boulders to several lovely river pools and cascades. Either walk back the way you came or turn the hike into a loop.

WNT SEGMENT 7: HATTON GARDEN TO FIRST CAMP This segment runs between the former Hatton Garden Estate near Pagua Bay and the farmlands of Hanover on the forested hillsides to the southwest of Marigot. It passes through farmland, wet and dry forest habitats, and across several small rivers. It's quite a long walk in some remote areas of the island. Regions in this area carry names such as First Camp, Captain Bruce, La Guerre, Gregg and Newcastle that reflect a history of Maroon chiefs and colonialism. There are also some great views of the northeastern coastline as well as westwards across the volcanoes of the interior. From beginning to end, allow at least 6 hours to complete the segment and – if you're not through-hiking – a further 90 minutes down from the interior to the main coastal road.

The trail begins along a rough access road from Hatton Garden which you must follow to its end, crossing the Marechal River that has been running towards the ocean on your right-hand side. The forest trail climbs gradually and emerges into an open valley of mostly abandoned farmland. After crossing a couple of streams and climbing a hill where the grass is often high (sometimes too high), you pass through woodland and then emerge in another open valley where there are good views down to Pagua Bay and the east coast.

After more stretches through farmland and forest, the route climbs steeply up to a network of farm access roads where there are panoramic views to enjoy, especially by the time you reach the communications mast atop the ridge. Pass through and then exit a working citrus and banana farm before heading down into a wet gulley. Once across the Manitipo River, the habitat transitions to drier coastal forest where you reach a viewpoint over Douglas-Charles Airport. On a clear day, you can see the island of Marie-Galante.

Heading back inland, the trail begins an ascent and a long journey towards the interior through thick forest. The terrain can be challenging, and it can feel like rather an endless trudge along this difficult stretch. Eventually, there's a steep descent into a river valley where the trail meets a farm access road, more farmland, and then the Coffee River, which is a good spot to cool off and replenish your water supply. After fording the river, there's a short climb to a further farm access road junction. Heading left will take you deeper into the interior between remote farmsteads all the way to an area called First Camp which marks the beginning of Segment 8. Heading right gives you the option to bail out of the hike and begin a long walk down farm access roads that eventually emerge on the main road a little to the north of Douglas-Charles Airport.

WNT SEGMENT 11: SYNDICATE TO BORNES This is one of the longest WNT segments and you'll need all day for it if you're not through-hiking. It begins at the Syndicate Nature Trail visitor centre and ends in the village of Bornes. You can miss out a rather oddly circuitous ending of this segment (roughly 2 hours) by exiting on the main road at Brandy. I do recommend this, as do several guide friends. In addition to the segment being very long, there are several steep ascents and descents as well as stream and river crossings. Be prepared to spend much of the walk surrounded by thick forest. At the time of writing, this segment was clear though in need of repair and enhancement. Allow at least 6 hours to get to Brandy.

Setting off from the Syndicate visitor centre, Segment 11 begins as a long and wide forest track – part of a former logging road, complete with Timberjack ruin – that you follow for about an hour before turning off on to a narrow hiking trail. You'll be heading downhill, sometimes gradually, other times steeply enough to use roots and rope (if there) for support. After crossing a stream, a short uphill stretch rewards you with views of Prince Rupert Bay, Portsmouth and the twin peaks of the Cabrits.

The route leads to the banana farming plantations of Ross Castle where you must follow a farm access road before heading to and then crossing the Picard River. Beyond the river there's a series of seemingly endless ridges and gullies to negotiate – some rather steep – before you're rewarded with further views of the north and west.

Eventually, you come to a valley and more open surroundings before the trail emerges at an access road near Brandy Manor Riding Center. If you've had enough, you can bail out here by simply heading left and following the track to the main road between Portsmouth (left) and Bornes (right). Alternatively, walk along the access road until you see a WNT sign on the left. This section of the trail can be rather boggy, but it runs westwards along the route of a former railway line that joined Brandy Estate with the navigable section of the Indian River and was part of a short-lived timber business. The trail eventually crosses the river and the main highway, heading into woodland, and then reverses direction and heads eastwards back towards Bornes (hence my suggestion that this section is perhaps one you could skip). You'll emerge on a feeder road near Marie Frederick's Indigo Art Gallery, where WNT Segment 12 continues to the left and the main Portsmouth/Bornes road is down to the right.

WNT SEGMENT 12: BORNES TO PENNVILLE This segment runs from Bornes to Delaford Estate above Upper Penville. If you're just hiking this segment, then I suggest bailing out at Vieille Case as much of the final stretch is along the main road. This is a nice hiking trail with fabulous views south. On a clear day, most of Dominica's high *mornes* can be seen. The second part of the trail is along farm tracks and beaten paths, but the first cuts eastwards across countryside where it's often overgrown. At the time of writing, the segment was clear, but it was indeed very overgrown between Bornes and Moore Park. Allow 5 hours from Bornes to Vielle Case and a further 2 hours if you're heading all the way up to Delaford.

Starting near the Indigo Art Gallery in Bornes, follow the trail up a paved feeder road. It's a steep climb up towards Morne Destinee past farmlands of bananas, mangoes, avocados and coconuts, but the views from the top are great. From the paved road, the trail heads eastwards across a wide valley where there continue to be nice views, especially of the Atlantic coastline. Once through the Grand Riviere Valley and over a bridge, the trail joins a farm road. To the right is the village of Paix Bouche. Heading left through the farmlands of Moore Park, there's a steep climb up the spine of a ridge (often rather overgrown). Some of the best views on the island are to be enjoyed from here. When you reach the top, there's a sign pointing downhill to the right. This trail leads very steeply all the way down and through the village of Vieille Case.

Once through the village, you meet the main east coast road. To the left is Delaford, WNT Segment 13 and the Northern Link Road to Portsmouth. To the right is the road to Bornes and Calibishie. If you're not bailing out of the hike here, head left along the main road for about 1km until you pick up the trail on the right. Follow it down into a valley and across two small rivers before climbing steeply up along the high cliff coastline to Lower Pennville. There are great views of the east coast from this part of the track. Walk up the steep village road to meet the main coast road again. To the right is Delaford and WNT Segment 13, to the left is Bwa Nef Falls and Vieille Case.

WNT SEGMENT 13: PENNVILLE TO CAPUCHIN This segment follows the route of an historic path that runs along the northern coast, connecting east and west. It passes farmland, dry coastal woodland and the entangled ruins of Grand Fond, a former coffee growing estate. Weather events eroded the track in parts and there are a couple of sketchy spots that may challenge those with a dislike of high places. Allow at least 4 hours to complete the journey.

The start of the trail is on the Northern Link Road in an area called Delaford Estate, which is above the village of Pennville. The track meanders around the margins of worked and abandoned farmlands. It's narrow and sometimes a little rough, but easy to follow. Continue heading north above the Delaford River until you meet two trail junctions in an area called Resposoir Estate. At both junctions, Segment 13 continues to the left.

Now heading back inland, the trail follows the contours of the steep ridge and crosses a couple of streams before reaching the remnants of the Grand Fond Estate. Look for coconut palms, coffee trees and broken stone walls in an area of relatively flat but usually overgrown land. Climbing upwards and out of the Grand Fond Estate, the trail eventually meets the cliffs again at the former Seaman estate. A short walk beyond the cliffs brings you to the Taffia River. If you walk upriver, you'll find lovely pools. A short distance beyond the river is an extremely steep spur on the right. This goes down to more river pools and eventually the top of a waterfall that tumbles down on to the rugged coastline. Continuing along the trail, you reach the Canna Heritage Park at Capuchin where the segment ends. This area, settled by Amerindians and later by Capuchin monks, has a small cannon battery and views of Les Saintes and Guadeloupe.

WNT SEGMENT 14: CAPUCHIN TO CABRITS No doubt the most disappointing segment of the Wai'tukubuli National Trail, Segment 14 is a walk along the main coastal road from Capuchin to Cabrits National Park. I've included it here because it's designated a WNT segment but, unless you are through-hiking the whole thing, you may wish to prioritise some of Dominica's other more interesting hiking trails. If you are doing it, plan for around 4 hours.

From the Canna Heritage Park, there's a track that heads along and steeply down the cliff towards the Capuchin coastline. I suggest you skip this as it's not especially interesting and, in parts, is badly eroding. Instead, walk the main road towards Capuchin village and onwards to Clifton, Cocoyer, Cottage and Toucari (the detour to Lamothe Bay between Cocoyer and Cottage isn't worth it either). Walk down into Toucari where there are some (by this time very appealing) bars, restaurants and snackettes. It's a steep climb out of Toucari and up to Morne A Louis and Savanne Paille before dropping back down to sea level at Tanetane and eventually arriving at the Cabrits.

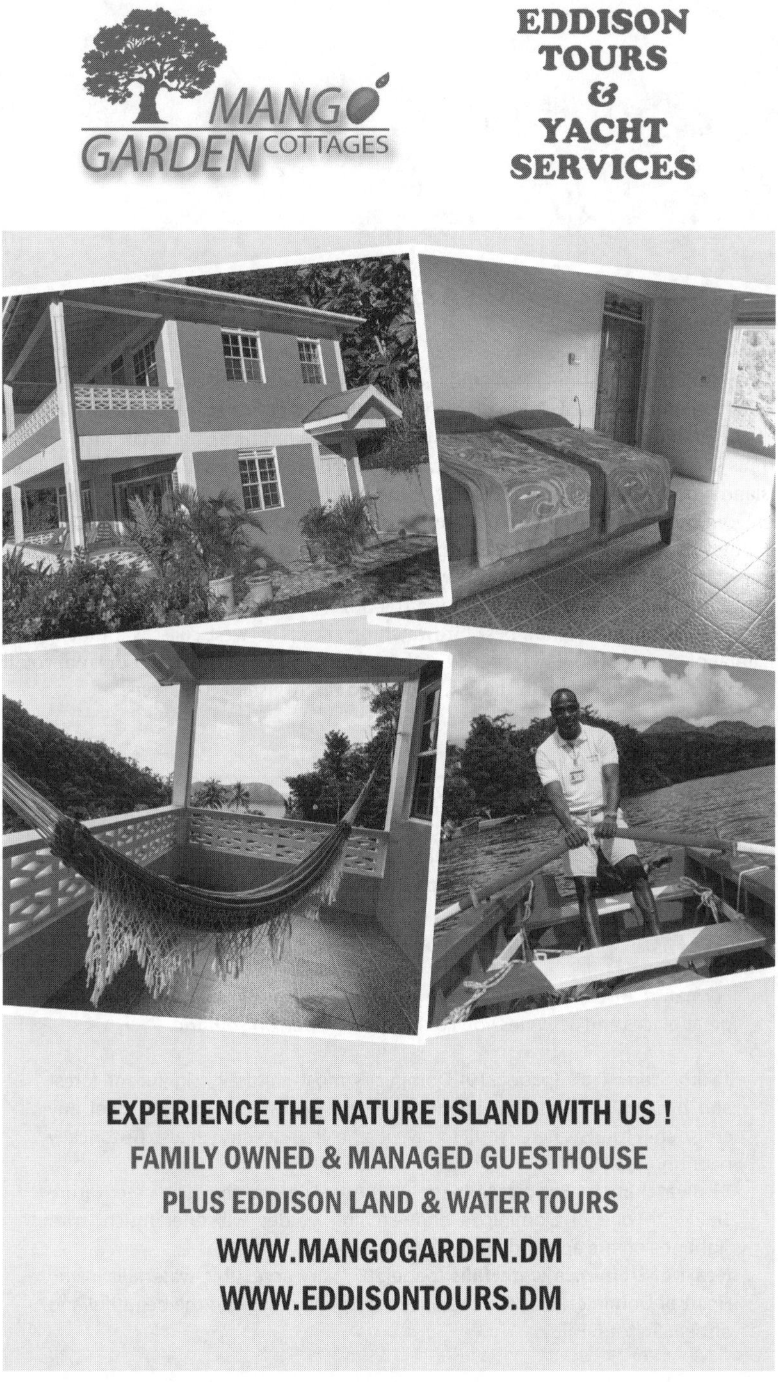
MANGO GARDEN COTTAGES
EDDISON TOURS & YACHT SERVICES
EXPERIENCE THE NATURE ISLAND WITH US !
FAMILY OWNED & MANAGED GUESTHOUSE
PLUS EDDISON LAND & WATER TOURS
WWW.MANGOGARDEN.DM
WWW.EDDISONTOURS.DM

9

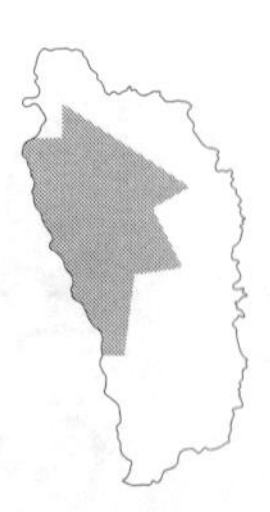

Heart of Dominica, Morne Diablotin National Park and the West

Morne Diablotin National Park and the Northern Forest Reserve contain some of the most remote and inaccessible places in Dominica. They're also the primary habitat of the endemic and endangered sisserou parrot, Dominica's national bird. Hiking trails such as the Morne Diablotin Trail and WNT segments 8 and 9 are three of the island's most challenging – testament to the extremity of these wild places. The Heart of Dominica is also enveloped by forest, ridges, valleys and rivers. This is also Maroon country, where former enslaved Africans such as Jacko (page 209) established near impenetrable encampments. For visitors, both places are full of accessible and harder-to-reach natural and cultural attractions. There are waterfalls, hiking trails, river pools and the island's best birdwatching sites. The west coast is a much drier habitat of coastal woodland, rugged cliffs and volcanic sand beaches. On land, you'll see endemic iguanas, and in the sea, you'll find rarely visited coral reefs.

GETTING THERE AND AWAY

BY CAR It takes about an hour to travel the west coast highway between Roseau and Portsmouth. It's a good road, and bridges that were damaged by Tropical Storm Erika and Hurricane Maria have been repaired. It does attract rather speedy and occasionally thoughtless driving, however, so it's important that you keep your

DON'T MISS

For nature lovers, there's so much to see and do in this area. Here are three great places and activities you could try to include on your trip.

Jacko Steps Trail (page 219) Dominica's most culturally significant forest and river trail still sits bewilderingly below the radar. You'll not meet any cruise ship tourists here (yet!), so give it a go. It's a scenic, yet also historically haunting, walk.

Birdwatching at Syndicate (page 215) A walk along the Syndicate Nature Trail with one of Dominica's birdwatching guides will offer much, with sightings of rare and endemic species assured.

Heart of Dominica waterfalls (page 207) Very accessible waterfalls in the Heart of Dominica include Emerald Pool, Spanny Falls and the beautiful and offbeat Soltoun Falls.

wits about you. With a couple of exceptions, the roads in and out of the Heart of Dominica are also in good condition. It's about 40 minutes by car between Roseau and Pont Cassé. The road up to Syndicate is perhaps the most challenging for visitors. It's narrow and often has tall grassy margins making visibility a little sketchy, especially around bends. Always use your horn and be aware that this road is regularly used by farmers and farm trucks as well as by visitors and occasional tour buses.

BY BUS Buses run frequently along the west coast highway between Roseau and Portsmouth and through the Heart of Dominica between Roseau and Marigot. The Layou Valley road between Layou and Pont Cassé isn't a recognised bus route and neither do public buses travel up to Syndicate and Morne Diablotin National Park. See page 52 for bus stop and fare details.

WHERE TO STAY *Map, page 212, unless otherwise stated*

The popular booking websites offer much and there are plenty of inexpensive choices for budget travellers. Here are some well-established accommodation options.

Harmony Villa [map, page 208] Pont Cassé; ☎+44 7470 446 502; e info@harmonyvilla.com; w harmonyvilla.com. This is a lovely 3-bed villa owned by artist Carla Armour. Each bedroom has en-suite bathroom, there's an open-plan kitchen, dining & lounge area with a long & wide veranda looking out on to the large gardens. Stylish & modern, yet with a nod to eclectic Caribbean design, this is a colourful & comfortable place to stay in the Heart of Dominica & would suit couples, families & groups of friends. **$$$$$**

Mango Island Lodges (6 rooms) St Joseph; ☎767 617 7963; e mangoislandlodges@yahoo.com; w mangoislandlodges.com. Describing itself as a boutique hotel, the eclectic rooms have private bathroom facilities, deck with sea view, AC & Wi-Fi. The Voyage Restaurant & Bar offers a range of international cuisine to guests only; there's also a pool & wellness area. Located on the hillside between St Joseph & Mero, Mango Island Lodges enjoys lovely coastal views & sunsets. **$$$–$$$$**

Tamarind Tree Hotel (15 rooms, 3 bungalows) Salisbury; ☎767 616 5258; e hotel@tamarindtreedominica.com; w tamarindtreedominica.com. Located cliffside on the west coast near Salisbury, ground-floor standard rooms have private bathroom, fridge, Wi-Fi & fan. Upper-floor superior rooms also have AC. The standalone 2-bed SC bungalows have fully equipped kitchen, living area & deck. Facilities for hotel & bungalow guests include restaurant, pool & tour desk. This is a long-established family-run accommodation with inclusive hike, dive & 'explorer' packages available. **$$–$$$**

Caribbean Sea View (3 apts) Mero; ☎767 276 4238; e info@caribbeanseaview.com; w caribbeanseaview.com. Located above the beach & village of Mero, Caribbean Sea View has nicely furnished 1-, 2- & 3-bed SC apts all with fully equipped kitchen, Wi-Fi, private bathrooms, living areas & large verandas with sea views. **$$**

Crescent Moon Cabins [map, page 112] (2 cabins) Riviere La Croix, Sylvania; ☎767 449 3449; e jeanviv@yahoo.com; w crescentmooncabins.com. Crescent Moon is lovely, family-run off-grid accommodation set in a forest, farm & garden location. The 2 1-bed cabins have private bathrooms, Wi-Fi & veranda with fabulous sea & mountain views. Professional chef Ron will cook b/fast, lunch & dinner on request with produce from the organic farm, & certified tour guide David has years of experience and would be happy to help you make the most of your stay. A great option for outdoor & nature-loving couples. **$$**

Mountain Caapi Cottage [map, page 112] (1 cottage) Cochrane; ☎767 275 2343; e jessica@earthbook.tv; bookings via w airbnb.com. Located on a secluded forested mountainside above the village of Cochrane, the self-contained cottage has 1 dbl & 2 sgl beds, kitchenette, Wi-Fi & veranda with great views. There's also a communal pool. Owners live on the property & also host wellness retreats & student groups. **$$**

TRANQUILITY BEACH

At the time of writing, Tranquility Beach (**w** tranquilitybeachdominica.com) is a CBI-funded hotel project with a Hilton Curio Collection badge. It's a contemporary upmarket design and, as with most of Dominica's CBI hotel developments, appears to be targeting the so-called 'eco-luxury' market. It will comprise condominium suites and villas located around a pool, restaurant, spa etc. It's located atop a low cliff with beach access on the mid-west coast.

Sunset Bay Club [map, page 211] (12 rooms) Coulibistrie; 767 446 6522; **e** sunset@cwdom.dm; **w** sunsetbayclubhotel.com. No-frills Belgian-owned & managed beachside accommodation, Sunset Bay Club has long been a popular option for budget travellers from mainland Europe. Each room has private bathroom, fan, mosquito net & Wi-Fi. There's a restaurant serving b/fast, lunch & dinner, dive shop, pool & sauna. **$$**

D-Smart Farm [map, page 112] Corona, Pont Cassé; 767 315 5128; **e** d-smartfarm@hotmail.com. Budget travellers have an opportunity to get close to nature at this family-run permaculture farm & forest campground near Pont Cassé. There's a simple A-frame wooden cabin as well as several 2-person tents on fixed pitches. Toilet & shower facilities are available. **$**

WHERE TO EAT AND DRINK *Map, page 212, unless otherwise stated*

This region doesn't offer a great variety of dining options, but those listed below are popular and of a high standard. There are several bars and snackettes along the beach at Mero (**Indee's**, **Merokai**, **Vena's** and **Connie's**) that are good for drinks and fast food (chicken, burgers, fries etc). Also, if you follow the Cuba road up above Mero (follow the sign for Campeche Villa), you'll discover a lovely bar called **Paradise** that has a deck overlooking the beach and sea. On the main road in Coulibistrie, there's a handy cluster of roadside bars and snackettes.

Lobster Palace [map, page 211] Sunset Bay Club, Coulibistrie; 767 235 6522; lunch & dinner daily. Crustaceans are the speciality here though you can also get catch of the day, chicken & vegetarian dishes. **$$–$$$**

Zeb Zepis Bistro [map, page 208] Pont Cassé; 767 316 3005; noon–15.00 Thu–Sun. Professional chef Eileen & her husband Jacques serve a range of excellent Caribbean/French fusion dishes from an ever-changing menu in the rainforest surroundings of the Heart of Dominica. The bistro is often busy so call ahead & make a reservation. **$$–$$$**

Tamarind Tree Restaurant Tamarind Tree Hotel, Salisbury; 767 616 5258; dinner Wed–Mon by reservation only. Tamarind Tree's clifftop restaurant has a changing dinner menu depending on what's fresh. It's high-quality cooking at an often-overlooked restaurant. **$$**

EXPLORING THE REGION

MORNE DIABLOTIN NATIONAL PARK When it was formed in 1977, the **Northern Forest Reserve** covered 8,900ha of mountains and rainforest. In January 2000, 3,335ha were taken from the reserve to form **Morne Diablotin National Park**, which was created primarily as a sanctuary to protect the natural habitat of Dominica's two endemic parrots, in particular its national bird, the **sisserou** (*Amazona imperialis*). Morne Diablotin gets its name from the French for the black-capped petrel (*Pterodroma hasitata*), a bird that used to inhabit the cliff faces of the mountain. The name translates to 'little devil' and was given because of its apparent demonic-sounding call. The petrel typically nests on high cliff faces, burrowing a hole or using natural clefts. Though rarely seen these days, experts believe the bird may be returning to the mountain.

The higher elevations of Morne Diablotin are cloaked in elfin woodland. Low-growing *kaklen* (*Clusia mangle*) dominates the terrain, growing in a dense, tangled blanket some 2–3m above the ground. The *palmiste moutan*, or mountain palm (*Prestoea montana*), pushes its way through the *kaklen*, together with other low-growing trees and ferns. The lower elevations give way to montane forest and then dense swathes of rainforest. Trees such as the *gommier* (*Dacryodes excelsa*) and several species of *chatanier* (*Sloanea dentata*, *Sloanea caribaea* and *Sloanea berteriana*) can be found here, their unmistakable buttress roots reaching out across the forest floor. Other trees known locally as the *mang blanc*, *mang wouj*, *bwa kanno* and *kwé kwé* can also be found in this habitat and have prop roots. The *karapit* (*Amanoa caribaea*) produces both buttress and prop roots and is one of the most abundant species of large tree growing in the rainforest.

Within Morne Diablotin National Park is the Syndicate Nature Trail, one of Dominica's most popular birdwatching trails (page 219). There's also a tough hiking trail to the 1,447m summit of Morne Diablotin (page 221). There's a visitor centre where you can buy eco-site passes and it also has an interpretation room where you can learn about the rainforest habitat, including the trees, animals and birds that may be seen within it.

HEART OF DOMINICA Established in 1952, the 410ha **Central Forest Reserve** is Dominica's oldest reserve. As the name suggests, it's located centrally, between Morne Trois Pitons National Park and the Northern Forest Reserve. It has a rich biodiversity and consists of dense tropical rainforest, rivers, streams and waterfalls.

Bisecting the Central Forest Reserve is the main artery for vehicle traffic passing between Douglas-Charles Airport, Marigot and the capital, Roseau. Located along this road is the village of **Bells**, a farming community to the south of the Central Forest Reserve and along the Layou River. There are several accessible natural attractions in this area as well as sites of historical interest. They include sections of the Layou River (see below), Emerald Pool (page 215), Spanny Falls (page 217), Jacko Falls (page 216), Soltoun Falls (page 217) and the historic Jacko Steps (page 219).

The **Layou River** is Dominica's longest waterway, originating in the heights of the Northern Forest Reserve around Mosquito Mountain, and meeting the Caribbean Sea south of St Joseph on the west coast. It's a naturally beautiful river that passes through deep gorges and wide expanses of rainforest. It's alive with mountain mullet and crayfish, and bird species such as herons and kingfishers.

WEST COAST VILLAGES Located along the shoreline between the communities of Picard and Dublanc, **Morne Espagnol** is a 365m conical peak. There's a

PRACTICALITIES

There are several minimarts selling essential items on the main road in Massacre and Mahaut and there's a fresh produce market in Mahaut on Saturdays. On the beach road in Mero, there's a tiny but incredibly well-stocked shop called **Sunset Sweet Treats** that sells everything from ice cream to over-the-counter medicines. There's a **petrol station** on the west coast highway between Mahaut and Layou and another in Coulibistrie.

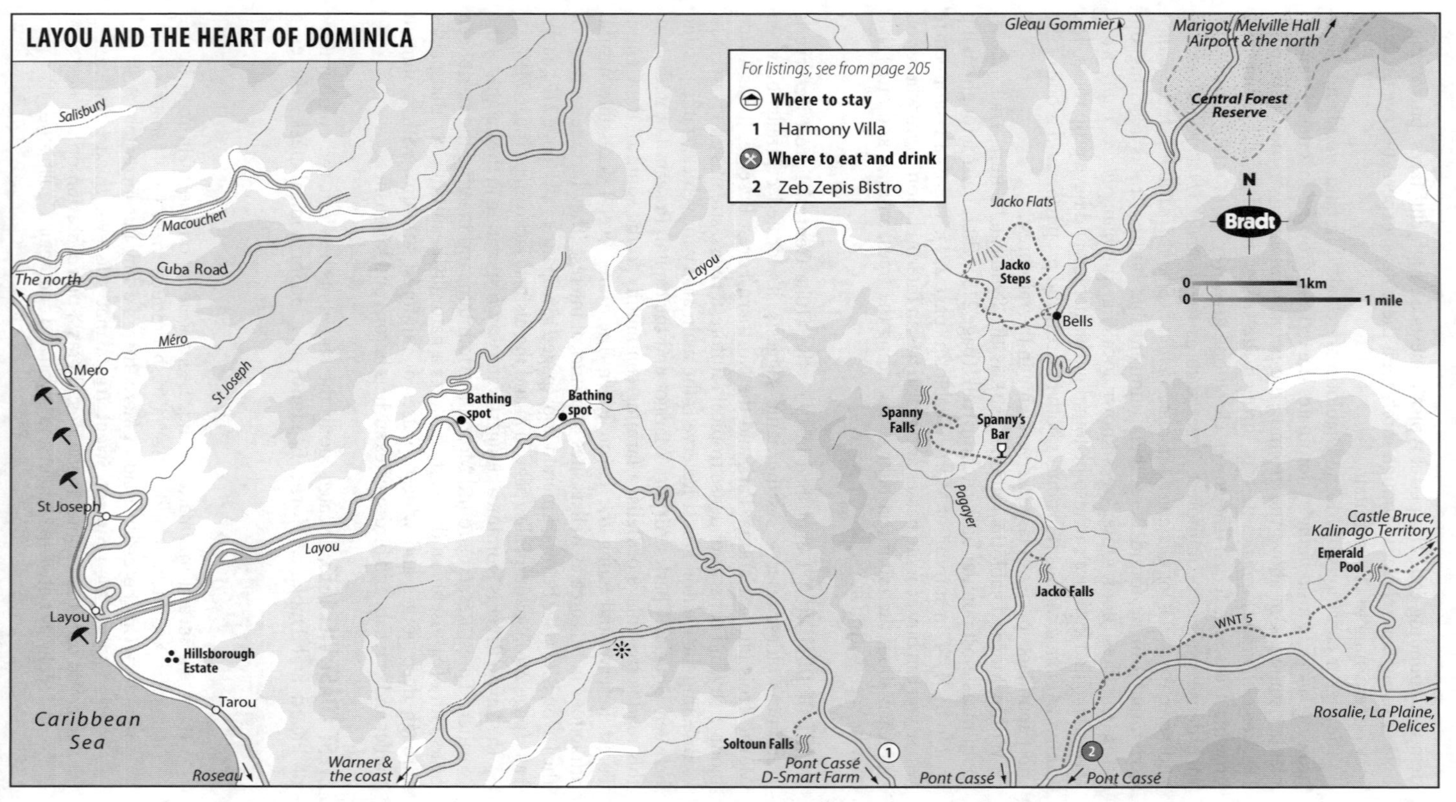
LAYOU AND THE HEART OF DOMINICA
For listings, see from page 205
Where to stay
1 Harmony Villa
Where to eat and drink
2 Zeb Zepis Bistro
Gleau Gommier
Marigot, Melville Hall Airport & the north
Central Forest Reserve
N
Bradt
0 1km
0 1 mile
Salisbury
Macoucheri
Cuba Road
The north
Layou
Jacko Flats
Jacko Steps
Bells
Méro
Mero
St Joseph
Bathing spot
Bathing spot
Spanny Falls
Spanny's Bar
Pagayer
St Joseph
Layou
Castle Bruce, Kalinago Territory
Emerald Pool
Jacko Falls
WNT 5
Layou
Hillsborough Estate
Tarou
Caribbean Sea
Roseau
Warner & the coast
Soltoun Falls
Pont Cassé D-Smart Farm
Pont Cassé
Pont Cassé
Rosalie, La Plaine, Delices

JACKO AND THE MAROONS

'Maroons' is a name given by colonists to the enslaved workers of the Caribbean who escaped captivity. Before the French settled on the island, bringing enslaved Africans to work their estates, it's thought that 'runaways' from other islands had already arrived in Dominica and were living in remote forest locations. Dominica had been left to the Kalinago by the British and French and was the last island to be colonised. It's quite plausible, though there's no evidence for it, that African people were living on this island for over 100 years before the Europeans eventually moved in.

The need for more land meant that colonisation of Dominica was inevitable and once Europeans had established an economic foothold here, the number of enslaved workers increased significantly. Although slavery arrived late in Dominica, it was no less brutal than elsewhere in the New World. Some of the captives managed to escape and banded together in camps in the island's interior. These Maroons, or *nègres marrons*, used the island's rugged terrain to their advantage, protected by tall peaks, deep ravines and dense rainforest, and their numbers grew. Having established a large and hidden network of forest camps and trails, the Maroon bands were led by a number of prominent chiefs including Robin, Hill, Quashie, Battrebois, Pharcelle, Clemence, Nico, Congo Ray, Moko, Zombie, Jacko, Goree Greg, Balla, Sandy, Juba, Elephant, Cicero, Soleil, Nicholas, Diano, Lewis and Jupiter. Areas of Dominica's interior where these chiefs had their camps still retain their names today.

By the late 18th century the number of camps and raids on estates meant that plantation owners demanded action from the authorities. In 1813, Major General George Robert Ainslie arrived to become Governor of Dominica. A violent, perhaps even psychopathic man who intended to make his mark, Ainslie was renowned for his brutality against runaway slaves and those who helped them, as manifested in the Maroon 'trials', public torture and executions that became the hallmark of his short reign. On 12 July 1814, Chief Jacko, who had spent upwards of 40 years as a Maroon leader, was shot and killed in a bloody battle with the Loyal Dominica Rangers, a militia of 'trusty slaves' who were offered the reward of freedom in exchange for killing a Maroon chief. His death marked the end of what became known as the Maroon wars.

communications mast on the summit and a rough and steep access track has been built to maintain it. A walk up to the top is a steep climb but the views are excellent. You'll also see lots of *bwa kwaib*, Dominica's national flower (page 6). If driving north to Picard and Portsmouth, the track can be found on the left-hand side once you are beside the mountain. Don't drive up. The access road is single lane, difficult and used by service vehicles.

The two villages of **Dublanc** and **Bioche** are situated between Colihaut and Picard to the south of Portsmouth. The road into Bioche follows the small river to the shoreline where fishermen land their catch. The village of Dublanc is also located on a river, the source of which is high up around Syndicate in the shadow of Morne Diablotin. Dublanc is a residential community with a small primary school and playing field located along its shoreline. A road loops through the village from the main coastal highway.

The French Roman Catholic priest Father Raymond Breton, who visited Dominica between 1642 and 1650 with the aim of converting the Kalinago to Christianity, built

SENSAY, BAN MAUVAIS AND *LA PEAU CABWIT*

The French and Creole term for Carnival is *masquerade*, and it's from this word that *mas* is derived, an abbreviated form which is used by Dominica's Festivals Committee and destination marketing office to brand the ever-growing Carnival period (you may come across the terms 'Mas Domnik', 'Real Mas' and 'Mas an Lawi'). Although Carnival is at heart a cultural event, it's influenced more and more by the tourism authorities – with mixed results. The new brand of Carnival has lost some of the history and tradition with many local people now prioritising the late-night street parties rather than the daytime costume parades.

Traditionally, this two-day festival before Lent features a combination of costume, music and dance with origins in West Africa and French Creole. Following emancipation in 1838, the festivities of *mas* moved to the streets of the capital, where bands from villages all around the island would come to celebrate. Each band had its own distinct style of music, dance and costume. One such costume is the *sensay*, which is a full dress of long strips of material with a headpiece that may include horns and a mask. The mask is of tribal origin and many demonic variations exist. The costumes of these groups, called *ban mauvais*, were deliberately intimidating, threatening terror with whips, sticks and batons. Today, one of Dominica's best-known and still active *ban mauvais* groups hails from the village of Colihaut.

During the Carnival season there's usually a *ban mauvais* parade accompanied by the drums of a *la peau cabwit* (goatskin drum) band through the streets of Roseau, and sometimes also in Colihaut itself. It's always atmospheric and stirring as the *sensay* dance their way through the streets accompanied by a cacophony of drums, horns and whistles. If you're visiting Dominica during Carnival, the best time to experience *ban mauvais* and *la peau cabwit* is at the *j'ouvert* (opening) parade in Roseau, from around 04.00 on Carnival Monday.

the first church on the island in a settlement at **Colihaut**. In 1795, Colihaut was the scene of a revolt when settlers who were sympathetic to the French attempted to aid an invasion from the north. Unfortunately for them, the invasion failed and the British military captured and deported a number of people from Dominica.

Colihaut is located at the foot of the Colihaut River valley. From the coastal highway heading north, the main part of the village is to the left, between the shore and the road, though residences have spread further up the valley to the right where you'll also see a large quarry. A narrow street lined with mango trees takes you alongside the river and into the heart of the village, where the Roman Catholic church dominates the small houses, convenience stores and bars. Built in 1950, the Church of St Peter is constructed from stone with large wooden louvre windows and a tall bell tower. On the north side of the church is a small garden and in front of the entrance gate a message of love has been tiled into the pavement.

Painted on a nearby wall is a mural of the *ban mauvais* parading through the streets in their *sensay* costumes accompanied by a band playing their *la peau cabwit* goatskin drums at Carnival time. A little further down the road is a traditional wooden house with large verandas featuring intricately carved, decorative fretwork, jalousie windows and large wooden hurricane shutters.

Like many coastal villages, **Coulibistrie** sits either side of a river (the Coulibistrie) that runs from the interior down through a deep valley and to the sea. In August 2015, Tropical Storm Erika turned the river into a torrent that brought destruction to this village and, for a long time afterwards, roads and houses were full of mud. It still has the appearance of a village yet to fully recover from the mess of the storm. The Coulibistrie Roman Catholic Church stands alongside the main coastal road opposite several lively bars and snackettes.

The name of the village of **Morne Raquette** is derived from the French word for prickly pear cactus, which grows wild in the area. The Kalinago word for the cactus is *bata* and the original name for the settlement below Morne Raquette was Batali, a name still given to the area today. The beach at Batali is predominantly used by local fishermen to store their boats and fish traps.

The village of Morne Raquette is a small community located high up on the slopes of Morne Jalousie, above Batali Bay and Coulibistrie. Access to the village is via a narrow road that joins the main coastal highway on the southern edge of Coulibistrie. The road is well signposted and is a steep climb. The village itself is pretty with excellent views of the Caribbean Sea. The road climbs up through the village and into dry coastal woodland and scrub that's dominated by the yellow blossoms of *kampech* trees (*Haematoxylum campechianum*) until it reaches the summit of the mountain. The views along the coast to the south are superb and it's possible to see the unmistakable shape of the Cachacrou isthmus when the weather is clear. If you're

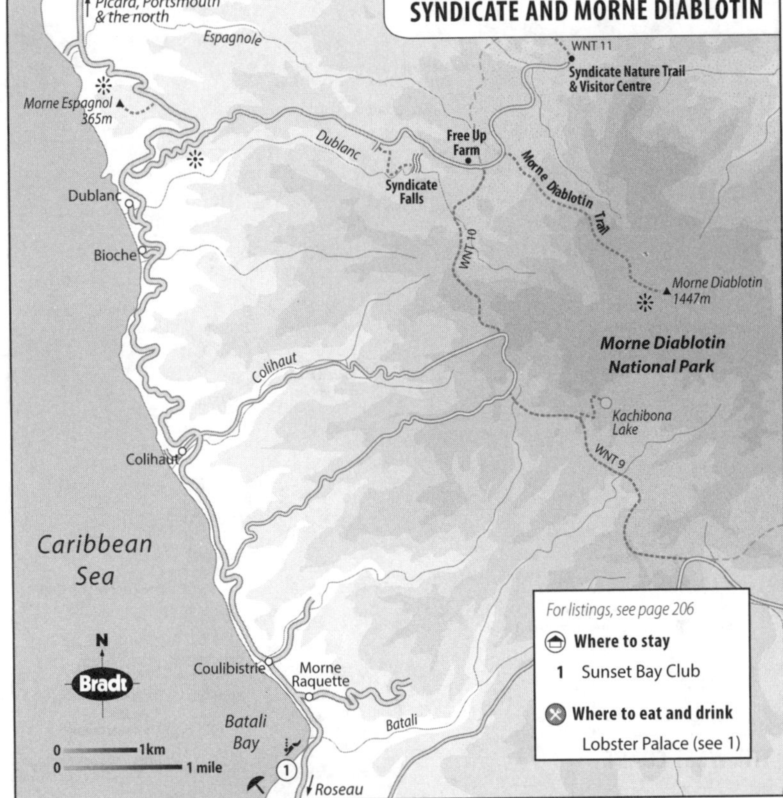

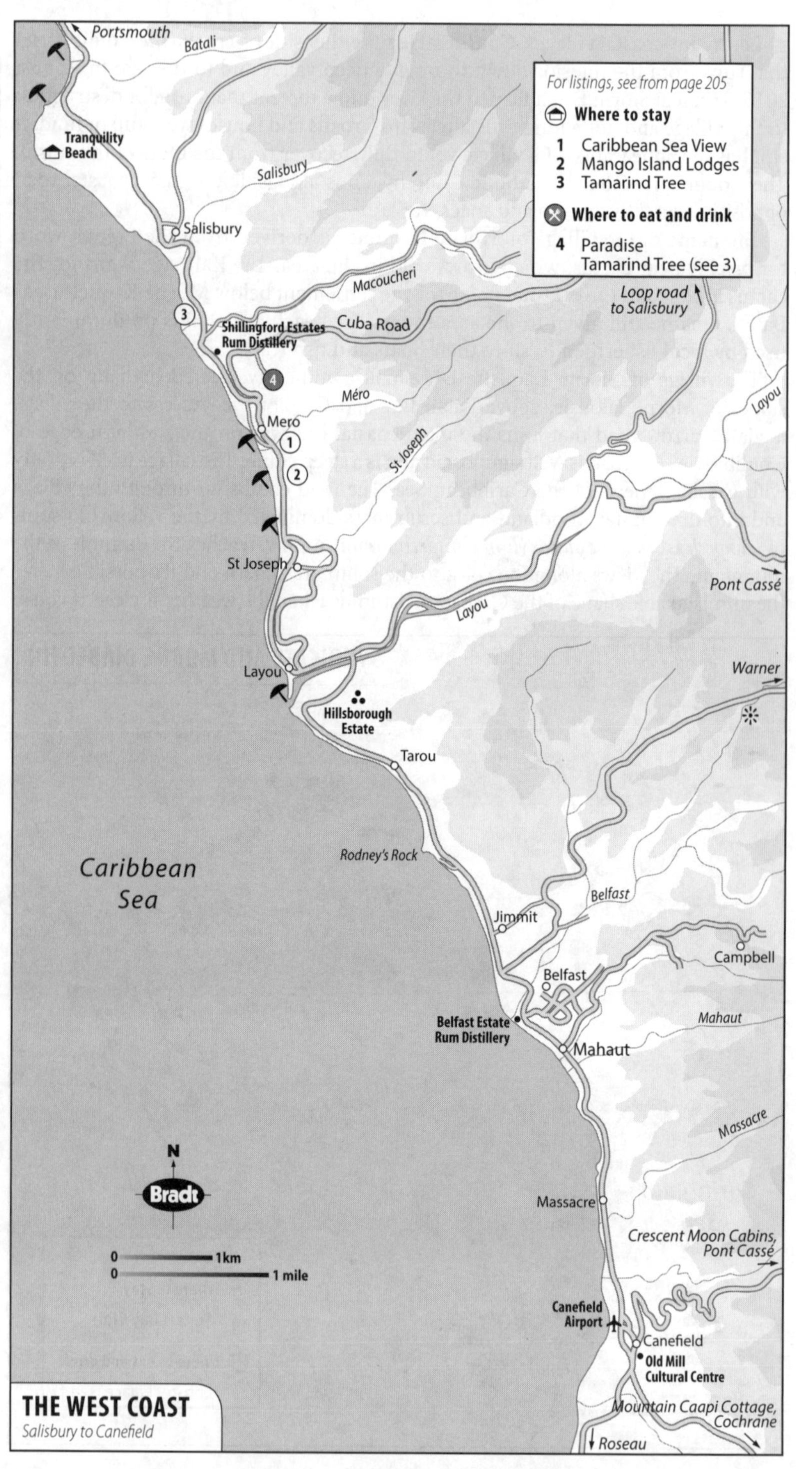

For listings, see from page 205
Where to stay
1 Caribbean Sea View
2 Mango Island Lodges
3 Tamarind Tree
Where to eat and drink
4 Paradise
Tamarind Tree (see 3)
Portsmouth
Batali
Tranquility Beach
Salisbury
Salisbury
Macoucheri
Loop road to Salisbury
Shillingford Estates Rum Distillery
Cuba Road
Méro
Mero
St Joseph
Layou
St Joseph
Pont Cassé
Layou
Layou
Hillsborough Estate
Warner
Tarou
Rodney's Rock
Caribbean Sea
Belfast
Jimmit
Campbell
Belfast
Belfast Estate Rum Distillery
Mahaut
Mahaut
Massacre
Massacre
Crescent Moon Cabins, Pont Cassé
Canefield Airport
Canefield
Old Mill Cultural Centre
Mountain Caapi Cottage, Cochrane
Roseau
N
Bradt
0 1km
0 1 mile
THE WEST COAST
Salisbury to Canefield

feeling adventurous you can drive this road, though it really requires a 4x4 vehicle because of its gradient and because the surface deteriorates in places. From the summit, the road descends a little and runs high along the side of the river valley. As it heads inland, the views of Dominica's interior are wonderful and, on a clear day, it's possible to see the peaks of several volcanoes as well as nearby Mosquito Mountain. The road continues through banana plantations and becomes part of the island's network of farm access roads. Consider parking up in a safe place and taking a walk.

Salisbury is a village that was once called Baroui, its original Kalinago name. The Kalinago settlement was in the area of the present Salisbury cemetery. The name Salisbury of course reflects the British influence on the island. Following emancipation, a settlement was established on the slopes of the Salisbury (or Baroui) River valley and now extends to the heights of Grande Savanne and along the southern ridge of the Batali River valley. Citrus crops, watermelons, pineapples and coffee are grown above the village, all the way up to Petit Macoucheri beneath the peak of Mosquito Mountain. The feeder roads up to these heights are used extensively by local farmers and make for a scenic walk into the interior, with impressive views from up above the river valleys. They also provide access points for National Trail segments 8, 9 and 10. Many of the people you may see hard at work in these remote fields are migrant workers from Haiti.

The Roman Catholic Church of St Theresa at Salisbury was built in 1929 and has since been renovated. It's a beautiful stone church standing above the main coastal highway to the south of the village. A rough vehicle track directly opposite, on the other side of the coastal highway, leads down to Salisbury beach, where the Salisbury fish landing site is located. There's a small concrete jetty and usually a scattering of fishing boats and fish traps. North of the jetty is a lovely and often overlooked beach.

The village of Salisbury is accessed via a signposted road that leaves the main highway and then turns sharply to the left. The road through the village heads straight up to the heights of the ridge above the river valley. On each side of the narrow road are houses, small convenience stores and several bars and snackettes. From the top of the village there are nice views down towards the sea and along the coast.

Macoucheri is home to the **Shillingford Estates Distillery**, which – before the storms of 2015 and 2017 – produced rum from sugarcane that it grew on its estate. The small distillery still produces Macoucheri Rum.

Mero is a seaside community between St Joseph and Salisbury. Look for a small one-way road off the west coast highway that runs in a crescent through the village and back out again. Residential areas of Mero extend to the inland side of the coastal road up towards the heights of a region called Cuba. The beach at Mero is a long and beautiful stretch of dark volcanic sand. It's a popular bathing and 'liming' spot for locals and visitors – especially at weekends and during the cruise ship season. Mero has several beach bars and snackettes as well as sun lounger rental. There's a Mero-based operator called **Jungle Carts & Jet Skis** (767 613 3273; w dominicafun.com) that, as the name suggests, rents out jet skis, dune buggies and sea scooters. They also run the floating Storm Island Water Park that you may see when you visit (pay by the hour). At the time of writing, it's a start-up and primarily aimed at the cruise ship season, so I suggest you contact them in advance for prices and availability if this is something that interests you.

The largely residential village of **St Joseph** is located just north of the Layou River. At the heart of the village is the large Roman Catholic church, built in the late 19th century and dedicated to Saint Gerard.

Tarou is a tiny fishing and farming community located along a small river valley beneath the dry scrubland slopes of Desjardin and Warner. In the summertime, the

THE BATTLE OF THE SAINTS

One of history's most famous naval battles was fought off the northwest coast of Dominica. In 1782, Admiral the Comte de Grasse set sail from Martinique with 35 warships and a plan to meet up with a Spanish fleet of 12 warships and together they would attack the British-held island of Jamaica. De Grasse was pursued by 36 ships of the British fleet that had set out from St Lucia under the command of Admiral James Rodney. On 12 April, the fleets lined up for battle off Les Îles des Saintes, a small group of islands between Guadeloupe and Dominica.

It's said that a sudden shift of wind allowed Rodney's flagship, *Formidable*, and several others to break the French line in two places, firing upon and scattering them as they did so. The resulting confusion and disorder of the French fleet ended in defeat and de Grasse surrendered on his flagship, *Ville de Paris*. No-one can be certain whether the manoeuvre to break the French line was deliberate or just pure luck, but it became a tactic that was repeated in later battles. The French and Spanish failed to capture Jamaica and Rodney was made a peer.

area is vulnerable to wildfires that scorch the dry bush along the slopes above the village. Its name is thought to be derived from the Kalinago name for a seabird that nests in the face of the nearby cliffs.

A little to the south of Tarou is Tarou Point, more popularly known as **Rodney's Rock**. A reminder of the island's volcanic history, this prominent lava formation is the source of a rather questionable legend. The story goes that when Admiral Rodney returned to Dominica following the British victory at the Battle of the Saints in 1782 (see above), the French who were occupying the island at the time used the rock to delay his continued pursuit of their retreating fleet. They placed lights on the rock and dressed it up to give the impression of a ship at anchor. In the darkness, Rodney is said to have been completely fooled and spent all night firing his cannon at this seemingly invincible foe.

Located further south along the west coast highway is the busy village of **Mahaut**. There's a small village market on Saturday mornings and fishermen sell their catch on the roadside throughout the week. The name 'Mahaut' is thought to be derived from the Kalinago word *maho*, which means a plant or tree bark that can be used to make rope. *Maho* was used extensively by the Kalinago for any type of work, tool or fixing that required the use of cordage.

Massacre, a small village of fishermen and farmers, is located between Canefield Airport and Mahaut. Above the road and framed by several flamboyant trees is the pretty Roman Catholic Church of St Ann. Built of stone and brightly painted, the church was constructed in 1921. The name of the village is said to have come from a French account of the 1764 massacre of Kalinago by British soldiers. Chief Thomas 'Indian' Warner, son of Sir Thomas Warner and a Kalinago woman, rose to prominence as a popular leader of the Amerindian people of this region. For several years, he led Kalinago fighters in conflict against the British occupying forces until his half-brother, Philip, offered a truce and invited the Kalinago to agree a treaty. During the celebrations of this new peace, Philip is said to have murdered his rebel half-brother as a signal to begin the massacre of the entire Kalinago settlement. There's a mural painted on a wall along the main coastal road in Massacre depicting the event.

WHAT TO SEE AND DO

✷ BIRDWATCHING The Syndicate Nature Trail (page 219) is located within Morne Diablotin National Park. It's naturally beautiful and is a very accessible introduction to Dominica's elevated rainforest environment. The forest-covered hillsides of Morne Diablotin and its surrounding ridges and peaks have become one of the last remaining habitats for the endangered sisserou parrot (*Amazonia imperialis*), an Amazonian species that's endemic to Dominica. This so far unspoilt and scenic habitat has become a draw for birdwatchers visiting the island and many species can be spotted here.

In addition to jaco and sisserou parrots, other sightings may include all four species of hummingbird that are found in Dominica – including the endemic blue-headed hummingbird (*Cyanophaia bicolor*) – the forest thrush (*Cichlerminia lherminieri*), the scaly-breasted thrasher (*Margarops fuscus*), the trembler (*Cinclocerthia rufcauda*), the plumbeous warbler (*Dendroica plumbea*) and many more.

The Layou River and the Pagua River are good places to find water birds such as the ringed and belted kingfisher (*Ceryle torquata* and *Ceryle alcyon*), the green-backed heron (*Butorides striatus*) and the least sandpiper (*Calidris minutilla*). Along the riverbanks you may see cattle egrets (*Bubulcus ibis*) and snowy egrets (*Egretta thula*). Other worthwhile places to go birding include WNT Segment 10 (which ends in the Syndicate area) and the Indian River. For bird enthusiasts who would like the company of an expert guide, see page 69. For more about Dominica's birds, see page 7.

D-SMART FARM (Corona, Pont Cassé; 767 315 5128; e d-smartfarm@hotmail.com) Dawn Francis and her family run a farm and campground in Corona near Pont Cassé. Popular with schools as an educational outing, the farm employs techniques such as permaculture and vermiculture, with Dawn growing all her produce organically. If this is of interest, please contact her in advance for more information and to book a visit.

EMERALD POOL Along with Trafalgar Falls in the Roseau Valley, Emerald Pool is one of Dominica's most visited natural attractions. It's a shore excursion for cruise

DIABLOTIN

Dominica's highest mountain, Morne Diablotin, is named after a rare sea bird, rather than anything more sinister (though there have been calls by some to change the name on religious grounds). The bird in question is the **black-capped petrel** (*Pterodroma hasitata*) which is considered to be one of the most endangered seabirds in the North Atlantic region. Endemic to the Antilles, it nests in small burrows in elevated areas such as forested cliffs. It's a nocturnal bird with an eerie-sounding mating call – two habits that gave it the moniker *Diablotin*, which is Spanish for 'little devil'. The namesake mountain of the north has been recorded as a nesting ground for the petrel though it hasn't been observed nesting there for many years. This may be due to predators, deforestation caused by hurricanes and storms, or simply because the species is nocturnal and nesting sites are incredibly difficult to access. In 2022, a black-capped petrel was observed in flight over Dominica, leading to speculation that it has returned. If true, Dominica and Hispaniola would be the only known nesting sites for this species.

ships and can get crowded during the high season. It's also popular with locals at weekends and on public holidays. But if you do manage to spend some time there alone, it's a lovely place to visit. Just within the Morne Trois Pitons National Park boundary, this is a designated eco-site and requires a pass (which you can buy here if you don't already have one).

The entrance to Emerald Pool is on the road to Castle Bruce from Pont Cassé, shortly after the Rosalie and La Plaine junction. There's a large car park, a permanent row of souvenir stalls and a visitor centre that houses a snack bar and an excellent interpretation room that's worth visiting before heading off on your short walk to the pool.

The clear and easy gravel path through the forest from the visitor centre ends in a viewpoint overlooking the pool before transitioning to a stone and concrete staircase. Take it steady if it's been raining. The steps bring you to a small wooden bridge and then a junction. To the right is Emerald Pool and to the left is a circular walk that brings you back to the visitor centre. Left is also part of WNT Segment 5 where it transects the Emerald Pool site.

The small waterfall and pool can be enjoyed from the viewing platform or up close from the rocks along the left-hand margin. The pool is deep enough for bathing, but I'd suggest resisting the temptation to jump in from the flat boulder by the tree – it's not really deep enough for that.

I recommend the loop walk back to the visitor centre rather than the same way you came. After the shallow uphill climb, it's an easy path that meanders through the forest and takes in a couple of viewpoints to the north and east.

✷ FREE UP FARM (☎ 767 614 3153; w freeupfarm.com) This is a 3ha permaculture farm that's owned, managed and developed by Aubrey and Lulu, who have dedicated their young lives to the subject. A continuously evolving project that aims to demonstrate how agriculture can be undertaken in a more sustainable way and in harmony with the environment, the farm has an extraordinary variety of fruits and vegetables, all of which are grown using a range of permaculture methods. It's located on the main Syndicate road beyond Syndicate Falls and visitors are welcome – but please call ahead. Aubrey and Lulu also welcome people who wish to share their expertise in the development of the project.

JACKO FALLS Just before you get to the village of Bells from Pont Cassé, you'll come across one of Dominica's most accessible waterfalls. Look for signage and wooden buildings selling fruit and souvenirs. The waterfall is located within a river gully that you can view from a platform at the top. If you wish, and are able, you can also go down to it. There are concrete steps leading to the river, the waterfall and the pool. Unless there are crowds of cruise ship tourists looking down on you, it is quite a nice place to visit. The surroundings are attractive; there's a cave, rainforest vegetation, moss-covered boulders, tropical flowers and birdlife. The waterfall is not especially tall but, like Emerald Pool, its draw is its ease of access. Expect a small entry fee.

LAYOU RIVER SWIMMING AND PICNICS The Layou is Dominica's longest river. It begins all the way up on Mosquito Mountain (see WNT Segment 8, page 222) and meets the sea on the mid-west coast at the aptly named Layou village to the south of St Joseph. It's possible to take a river tubing outing on the river (page 82) though you may have to tag along with a cruise ship tour to do so. Alternatively, there are two very nice spots where you can access the river to enjoy a swim and perhaps a picnic.

The first is a popular spot that's just off the refurbished road into the Layou Valley from the coast. You'll find this new road next to the bridge that spans the Layou on the west coast highway. Follow it for about 10 minutes along the river to the next bridge and park up somewhere nearby (there's a rustic roadside bar and snackette). Look for a track on the left, immediately after the bridge, and follow it for about 5 minutes past banana plants and cocoa trees. A short scramble down the bank brings you to a large riverside beach. Look across the river to a small bath that's been created on the far bank. This is full of volcanically heated water that runs down the steep bank and into the river. This spot is very popular with locals at the weekend.

The second access point is a little trickier to find. Follow the same road from the coast and drive a further 15 minutes or so beyond the bridge. Look for a small concrete bridge by a couple of houses (on the right). Just after the bridge, on the left, you should see a wide track. Park up somewhere along the main road and walk down the track for about 15 minutes. When you reach a junction, go left. This track should take you all the way down to the river where there are large boulders, pools and a small beach.

SCUBA-DIVING AND SNORKELLING Often overlooked, the mid-west coast has an expansive and pristine coral reef system. Barry's Dream, Lauro Reef, Brain Coral Reef, Nose Reef and Whale Shark Reef are all dramatic wall formations that are adorned with barrel sponges, hard and soft corals and a variety of marine life including seahorses, rays and the occasional nurse shark. At the time of writing, there's only one dive shop operating along this coast.

Sunset Bay Club Coulibistrie; 📞 767 446 6522; e sunset@cwdom.dm; w sunsetbayclubhotel.com. Sunset Bay Club operates a PADI dive shop & 2 small boats each capable of carrying up to 10 divers. Equipment rental, dive training & snorkelling trips are also available.

✷ **SOLTOUN (SOLTON) FALLS** A long time ago, my friends and I would cut through the forest and scramble down cliffside to get to these hidden waterfalls. I promised that I'd keep them out of the guidebook so that they would remain 'undiscovered'. Soon after, a local landowner decided to cash in and constructed a sign so large you could probably have seen it from space. Then came the hurricane and away flew the sign and Soltoun Falls (also written Solton and Sultan) reverted to an offbeat attraction that was once again rather tricky to find. The falls are still there, though the sign is much smaller. Pay EC$10 either to the landowner if he's there, or the neighbour if not, and follow the wide and rather unattractive track (there's lots of debris lying around) down to a trail. From there, it's a pleasant stroll through lovely forest surroundings. After about 10 minutes beyond the wide track, you'll meet a fork in the trail. Up to the left is one of the waterfalls and down to the right is the second. Both trails are a further 10 minutes' walking at most. These are lovely waterfalls, mysteriously though thankfully neglected by the tourist crowds. Be careful on the wooden steps and platform as they're in need of repair.

SPANNY FALLS Located near the rural village of Bells, this is a 'twin' pair of waterfalls that are separated by a steep ridge. Spanny is the name of the landowner as well as his roadside bar which marks the waterfall entrance on the main road (there's also a sign for the falls), and is where you should pay a 'voluntary contribution' of US$5 per person before you set off. Spanny's Bar is about a 15-minute drive along the airport road from the Pont Cassé junction. These days, the easily accessible first waterfall is on the cruise itinerary, so it's worth planning ahead. The second, less accessible waterfall, is not. Both waterfalls are reasonably tall and set in lush rainforest surroundings. The best time to visit them is in the wet season when the volume of the river above is affected by rain and the waterfalls are fuller, but they're worth a trip at any time of the year.

You can either park outside the bar or drive in at the entrance and along the wheel tracks for about 5 minutes to a small parking area. I like the walk, so I park at the bar, pay my fee and set off from there (be careful of road traffic). The short walk along the wheel tracks is lined with starburst clerodendrum trees which, when in bloom, are lovely. Beyond the small parking area, there's a clear and easy gravel track that meanders through the rainforest for about 15 minutes before reaching stone steps down to the first waterfall and pool. The path and steps have been designed to accommodate cruise ship visitors, so don't expect anything too taxing. The forest walk is pleasant, with several species of trees, ferns and epiphytes along its margins. If you've never experienced rainforest, here's an easy introduction.

The first waterfall has a viewing deck and stone path making access and photography easy. The pool is deep enough to bathe and there's a small cave where you can stash your gear if it rains. On the far side of the pool, to the right of the cave, you'll see a rope. This is the way to the second waterfall.

Carefully negotiate the boulders, river and fallen trees to the foot of the rope. Using a combination of rope and strong tree roots, look for the footholds in the rocks and the muddy ground and start to climb. Take your time – some areas are a little tricky – but there are foot and handholds if you look for them. The tree roots are very helpful but do check them first before trusting them with your full weight. At the top of the ridge, follow the track, again using the ropes to help you if needed. Pay attention to each step. Soon the second waterfall will come into view. The final approach is rather steep and tricky, with a rock face and then boulders to negotiate. Set amid a peaceful and lush rainforest, this harder-to-reach waterfall pool is also deep enough to bathe in.

SYNDICATE FALLS This is a lovely waterfall and pool at the end of a short forest and shallow river walk. As the track to the Dublanc River passes through private land, there's a US$5 access fee (and an additional US$5 for using the private car park). The walk is easy and takes no more than 30 minutes each way.

Follow the sign to Syndicate from the west coast highway and be alert for farm vehicles and tour buses as it's a narrow and winding road. Use your horn when approaching corners. It takes about 15–20 minutes to reach the sign for Syndicate Falls (on the right). Follow a rough vehicle track past a tropical flower plantation and then left and uphill to the gates of the private property. There's a sign and small parking area here. Alternatively, drive inside and use the private parking area.

Once inside, there's a reception building and bar where you pay your access fee. From there, follow the grassy track downhill to the river. Cross to the other side and take the narrow track along the right-hand riverbank until you can go no further. You should be able to see the continuation of the trail on the left-hand bank. Head upstream to the waterfall, negotiating a few rocks and small boulders to the pool.

You'll see what's left of a chain-link fence and metal posts. They were erected by the water company to prevent people from bathing in the waterfall pool when it was previously used as a water source for the coastal village of Dublanc. Raging floods carrying trees and boulders during Tropical Storm Erika in 2015 destroyed the fence and a different source is now used for the water supply. Unfortunately, no-one has thought it necessary to remove the remains of the fence and posts. Nevertheless, this is still a nice waterfall in a picturesque setting.

SYNDICATE NATURE TRAIL The Syndicate Nature Trail is a circular walk through the rainforest habitat of Morne Diablotin National Park. It's popular with bird enthusiasts as this area is a protected parrot habitat and has a wide variety of birdlife. The trail is an easy forest walk that takes about an hour to complete. If it's open, the visitor centre has an interpretation room, washroom facilities and a small snack bar. You can also buy your site pass here.

To get to Syndicate, look for a sign along the west coast highway, a little to the north of Dublanc. The narrow road climbs uphill and passes several farmsteads, many of them growing citrus and coffee. The road is long and narrow, and the margins are often quite overgrown, hampering visibility on bends. Use your horn liberally as you may well meet farmers' vehicles. Pass the sign for Syndicate Falls (on the right) and for the Morne Diablotin Trail, further along. Keep going right to the end of the road where you'll arrive at the visitor centre and car park. The length of the road may surprise you, but it's almost impossible to make a wrong turning. If you're walking up from the main road, allow at least an hour (public buses don't run to Syndicate).

The circular trail is lovely, with large examples of rainforest trees that managed to survive the hurricane. In fact, the trail shows remarkably few residual signs of the storm. There's a panoramic viewpoint towards a high plateau and conical peak across the deep Picard River valley where, in the early morning and late afternoon, you may well see parrots, including the sisserou. The best way to see these birds, however, is with an expert birding guide who will know exactly where and when to look (page 69). Consider combining the Syndicate Nature Trail with Syndicate Falls.

HIKING TRAILS

✷ **JACKO STEPS** This is either a there-and-back or a circular hike (usually depending on Layou River conditions) to one of Dominica's most important Maroon sites.

Jacko was a captive African who escaped and fled to the forest shortly after arriving in Dominica on a slave ship. With a group of other escapees, he established a camp on a high natural plateau above the Layou River near the present-day village of Bells. Due to his longevity, he achieved legendary status as one of Dominica's best-known Maroon chiefs. Jacko was eventually shot and killed at his camp by militia working for Governor Robert Ainslie in a bloody skirmish on 12 July 1814 (page 209).

Jacko Flats is the contemporary name given to the area atop the plateau where the camp was located, and Jacko Steps refers to a vertiginous staircase that was originally cut into the cliff by the camp's Maroons. The steps directly connected the high plateau to the Layou River. Although the steps were shaped and partially modified by an agriculturalist in later years, they remain a haunting reminder of colonialism, enslavement and the fighting spirit of Dominica's Maroons.

The trail is tricky, and you should do it with a guide (Eunice, the lovely lady who maintains the steps and lives nearby, is an option if you haven't planned ahead). You can either hike to the steps and back again, or you can make the return journey along the Layou River. Allow 3 hours for both options. Please note that walking along the Layou River should not be undertaken before, during or after heavy rains as water levels rise quickly and there's no obvious or easy exit from the river. Take a waterproof bag, a walking pole if you have one, and keep a set of dry clothes in your car to change into afterwards.

Look for the signposted trailhead on the road between Bells and the turn-off to Gleau Gommier. Follow the wide track downhill to the Layou River (flowing from right to left). Cross (it can be deep in places) and pick up the trail on the other side. Follow the well-beaten track uphill towards some small wooden buildings. This is the home of Eunice who, if you're lucky, may be able to guide you (for a well-deserved fee, of course).

The route continues from Eunice's house steeply uphill alongside a metal fence. At the top, the Flats begin. The trail meanders through the thick forest across the plateau – once the location of Jacko's camp – until it comes to the narrow spine of a high ridge. From here, the track heads downhill alongside thickets of bamboo, and you must take care with your footing – fallen leaves can be slippery and it's a long drop down. This track comes to an end at the top of Jacko Steps.

It's almost impossible for us to know what life was like in the camp, how many people lived here, where on the plateau it was exactly located, and how it was fortified. Archaeology would be a difficult undertaking here. The forest is thick, anything the Maroons constructed would have been made of wood, and this area was partially farmed for a while afterwards, so the land would have been disturbed. Severe weather events such as Hurricane Maria also altered the landscape, of course. So, we can only speculate and use the accounts of others to help us piece together fragments of what life was like here.

The steps are tall and steep and can also be leaf-strewn, though Eunice does her best to keep them clear. If they are leafy, then you must take great care not to slip and fall. The top half of the staircase has been cut within the steep bank of the cliff. The bottom half is far more exposed and eroding in places, with the river in view down below. The more modern blocks and hardware you occasionally come across on the steps were installed by a farmer who used to work the land here and who erected a pully system to carry produce across the river to the far side, where there's an agricultural area called Layou Park. (It's possible to get to Jacko Steps from a trail at Layou Park though the farm tracks there are rather labyrinthine, and nothing is signposted.)

Make your way down the steps to a stream in a deep gully known locally, and somewhat disconcertingly, as Fond Zombie. Once there, head left (downstream) where you'll meet the Layou River (flowing left to right). Turn left and walk upstream against the current, hugging the bank. The river changes with the seasons, so it's not easy for me to tell you where and when to cross. All you must do is keep heading against the current, crossing when you see dry banks where you can walk (usually on the right-hand side). There'll be a river joining the Layou on your right (the Pagoyer River – one of the waterfalls at Spanny; page 217) and there are usually rapids to negotiate here. Look out on the left bank for a waterfall that's partially hidden within a tall conical cave – it's known locally as Jacko's shower. Eventually, the river will turn sharply to the left (there's a small tributary flowing in from the right). Follow it around and you should see a wooden building and the Bells school across on the right. Keep going and you'll arrive at the point where you crossed the river at the beginning (alternatively, hop out of the river here). When you've dried off and changed, there's a roadside snackette near the Bells school that serves pretty good fried chicken and fish.

KACHIBONA LAKE I'd say Kachibona ought to be low on your hiking priority list, especially if you have limited time on the island, but its history and significance to the people of Colihaut, plus the fact that you may well see road signs or other references to it, means that it ought to get a mention here.

Maroon chief Pharcelle is said to have had one of his camps around Kachibona Lake. It's located on a high ridge beyond the Colihaut River and is protected by cliffs and dense forest. Unfortunately, the lake has suffered a series of landslides over the years that have reduced its size significantly – it's more a small and rather murky pond these days. But nature works wonders in Dominica and the people of Colihaut are proud of its legacy, so things may change for the better with time. The forest walk is tricky but pleasant, and the legacy of enslavement gives it historic context.

The trail follows WNT Segment 9 in reverse before heading off on a spur of its own. Although WNT Segment 9 is signposted and has painted trail blazes, there's not much to indicate you're on the right track once you follow the spur. It's not actually that far from the main trail – just 20 minutes or so – but the forest is thick, landslides are common, and it's easy to lose your bearings. So, if you really do want to see it, I'd urge you to get a guide.

Access the trailhead from the west coast highway. Drive up the farm access road that heads inland from the village of Colihaut and follow it up to the high farmlands of Colihaut Heights. The access road is narrow but paved and it will take about 30 minutes to reach the trail. You may see a WNT sign before you get to the shelter, which is for the start of Segment 10. Look a little further along for the end of Segment 9.

Follow the WNT blazes (sometimes they're hard to see when walking the trail in reverse) through the forest and then down to the Coulibistrie River which you must cross. Look for the continuation of the trail on the opposite bank before climbing down, so you know where to exit. Once out and up the other side, it's not far to the trail fork. Kachibona is to the left, WNT Segment 9 to the right. Here's where it can get tricky and why I recommend a guide. It should take about 20 minutes to get to the lake from the fork, but the forest is thick and can be disorientating, so take it slowly. A good tip on obscure trails is to stop every now and then and look back the way you came – maybe even take a quick photo – so you recognise things on the return leg. I know a guide who carries a bag of coloured ribbons which he ties to trees when in this kind of situation. A GPS app is also handy so you can track your route. In all, it will take about 90 minutes to reach Kachibona from the farm access road.

MORNE DIABLOTIN The hike to the 1,447m summit of Dominica's tallest mountain, Morne Diablotin, is a challenge. It involves a relentless uphill walk, a steep rock scramble and a lengthy climb through tree branches and roots that require upper- as well as lower-body strength. For the most part the route is clear and obvious, and, if you get a cloudless sky when you reach the top, the views across the island and beyond are spectacular. Even in the dry season, this can be a muddy hike and, as the summit is often windy and cloud-covered, it can also be rather cold. Bring something to keep you warm at the top and ensure you have a change of clothes standing by for when you return. Allow at least 3 hours to reach the summit and a similar time to get back down again. Although the trail is clear and easy to follow, you should consider hiring a guide to help you if you get stuck or tired. You'll need a site pass which you can buy from the Syndicate visitor centre – if it's open.

The signposted trailhead is near the end of the Syndicate road. The first hour or so is a steep climb through the rainforest habitat of the mountain's lower elevations. You'll see *chatanier* trees with their giant buttress roots, tall and straight *gommier* trees, *bwa mang* with their prop roots, giant tree ferns and an abundance of epiphytes. There's also a background of birdcall, often parrots.

You'll reach a section of boulders and steep mud scrambles as the habitat transitions to montane thicket and then as you attain the wetter cloudforest, the climb through, over, under and around *kaklen* (*Clusia mangle*) begins. Do take care when negotiating this part of the journey and look out for sharp branches where they have been cut by machete. The habitat is now very wet, muddy, and mossy. Take your time to avoid slipping and test the strength of branches before giving them your full weight. Eventually, you'll emerge from the *kaklen* at a rocky bluff known as Imray's View. This is where most hikers call it a day, though the actual peak is a further slog through the *kaklen* and mud of the summit ridge. After all the exertion, hopefully the clouds will part, and you'll be able to enjoy the views. Do take care on the descent as it's when most accidents and injuries happen due to fatigue.

WNT SEGMENT 5: PONT CASSÉ TO CASTLE BRUCE Segment 5 follows a historic route that's said to have originally been used by the indigenous Kalinago, then by Maroons, and in more recent times by people travelling on foot or horseback between Castle Bruce and Roseau before the road was built. The first half of the trail, between the start at Pont Cassé and the midway point where it transects Emerald Pool, is mostly flat. There are some swampy areas, especially in the wet season, as well as several small streams to cross, but, when both weather and trail condition are good, it's an easy walk. Beyond Emerald Pool, there's a short stretch of forest, then a long road section before the trail follows the right-hand banks of the L'Or and Belle Fille rivers. Before a series of destructive landslides in late 2022, the only tricky part was a rather high and narrow section around a cliff just beyond the area where the L'Or and Fond Figues rivers converge. After that, the trail follows the right-hand bank of the river for a stretch before it reaches a wide river crossing to the left-hand bank. Originally, a bridge was built spanning the river here, but Tropical Storm Erika swept it away in 2015. Since then, you've just had to manage it by yourself. It never really gets much tougher than thigh deep and is quite good fun (a walking pole really helps). Once across, the trail passes alongside some gardens and then meets the road again. A rather dreary 2km road section then leads to a turn-off into former farmlands that hug the left-hand margins of the river before finally meeting the coastal road. You're then asked to follow the main road through the sprawling coastal village of Castle Bruce where the segment ends just before it reaches the southern boundary of the Kalinago Territory.

Because of the 2022 landslides, the second half of this segment may eventually change somewhat, and, because of the extent of destruction, it may take a while before it's clear to walk again. This may mean lots more road walking.

WNT SEGMENT 8: FIRST CAMP TO PETITE MACOUCHERIE In my view, this is the most challenging hiking trail in Dominica. It crosses from east to west along the southern margins of the Northern Forest Reserve – undoubtedly some of the most remote areas on the island. Beginning in First Camp, itself at least 90 minutes' walk from the main east coast road, the trail passes through dense forest, across numerous rivers, then up and down Mosquito Mountain to Petite Macoucherie, another 90 minutes' walk from the main west coast road. You must allow up to 9 hours from First Camp to Petite Macoucherie. Depending on whether you've arranged drop-off and pick-up, are going with a guide, or plan on camping en route, you must also consider access to and from the start and end points of this segment. They are both at the end of long farm access roads. At the time of writing, Segment 8 had not been properly cleared following Hurricane Maria in 2017. Whether it's been rehabilitated or not when you go, common sense dictates a hiking guide, but if you're not taking one and are aiming to camp, then please do inform someone of your plans. I got lost for a little while in the middle of this segment, trying to figure out the route after the trail and the blazes had disappeared, and even with loads of Dominica hiking experience, the momentary disorientation in the thick forest was pretty scary.

From the farmlands above Hanover (see WNT Segment 7 on page 199), follow the trail along a ridge and into the forest to First Camp, so named because in 1964 it was used as a camp by the First Battalion of the Worcestershire Regiment who came to Dominica for jungle training. The rainforest gets thicker as you enter the Northern Forest Reserve, with large concentrations of *gommier* attracting riots of feeding jacos at canopy level. The trail is wide and easy to follow for a long stretch, though eventually the terrain becomes a little trickier and there are a couple of short-but-steep ascents and descents before you arrive at and then wade across a flooded area known as Gravel Gutter.

Continuing its meandering route through the forest, the trail eventually reaches the Melville Hall River. This can be a deep and fast-flowing river, especially after rainfall, so do take care crossing it. There now follows a series of river and stream crossings (take advantage of the water supply – you'll need it). Depending on time, energy and so forth, you must decide at this point whether you're continuing onwards, overnighting or bailing out, for what follows is a steep and challenging climb to the top of Mosquito Mountain (you're about two-thirds of the way when standing at the base of the mountain, near what's left of a wooden shelter). It's a strenuous climb to the top: steep, often muddy and wet, with little to help you. When you do make it to the summit, if the surrounding thicket isn't too high, there are good views from the partial clearing. To the northwest is Morne Diablotin.

From the top, follow the high, long and narrow ridge south for what feels like an eternity as it descends in stages rather than in one fell swoop. It's important to watch your footing here as it's a little snaggy with tree roots and slippery with erosion. Eventually the descent does get a lot steeper, and you'll emerge at a grassy area and rough farm access road. You're now in the remote farmlands of Petite Macoucherie. The road to the left is interrupted by a landslide, but there's a well-beaten track to get you across and back to pavement. This way leads down to Mero. Alternatively, follow the road to the right where you may well be able to get a ride with a farm vehicle down to Salisbury. If you're through-hiking, Segment 9 is also to the right.

WNT SEGMENT 9: PETITE MACOUCHERIE TO COLIHAUT HEIGHTS With countless steep, muddy ridges, deep river gullies, unstable and often changing terrain, Segment 9 is a serious challenge. The route is entirely in forest, skirting the Northern Forest Reserve and the peaks of Mosquito Mountain and Morne Diablotin. Allow at least 6 hours from the farmlands of Petite Machoucherie to those of Colihaut Heights. Also bear in mind that the walk between beginning and end points and the west coast highway takes at least 90 minutes. Segment 9 also passes a short spur trail to Kachibona Lake (page 220).

From the end of Segment 8, a roughly paved access road passes farmlands and enjoys fabulous views of Dominica's interior. After leaving the access road, follow the trail down past the farms and into the forest. Cross a river and climb. This is the first of countless ridges that you must climb on this segment. Once at the top, head steeply down the other side to the river at the bottom. Cross the river and repeat. Seriously, this is how it is for the next 4–5 hours. The forest is lovely, the rivers and streams too, but this is strenuous work, especially if it's muddy. One tip on this segment is to always find the continuation of the trail on the far side of a river before crossing. It's important to take your time at these crossings as this is where you can easily go wrong, looking for and missing the continuation of the trail.

Eventually, the ridges and gullies give way to a more continuous forest walk. You'll come across the spur trail to Kachibona Lake on your right. Beyond this spur, Segment 9 crosses its final river – the Coulibistrie – which is often the trickiest of all. Here, above all, work out where the trail is on the far side before crossing. Climb up and out of the Coulibistrie River valley and walk along much easier terrain to the end of the trail at Colihaut Heights. Head right and then downhill either for Segment 10 or to farmlands where you may be able to get a ride down to the west coast highway at Colihaut. Enjoy the views.

WNT SEGMENT 10: COLIHAUT HEIGHTS TO SYNDICATE Segment 10 is an easy and scenic walk from the farmlands of Colihaut Heights to those of Syndicate. Allow around 4 hours to complete the segment.

From the west coast highway junction in Colihaut, follow the farm access road uphill for around 20 minutes by car. The WNT sign is on the left. If you come to the WNT shelter and Kachibona sign at the end of WNT Segment 9, you've gone a bit too far. Backtrack for about half a mile and find the start of Segment 10 on the grassy apex of a bend.

The trail follows a wide track before transitioning to a narrow path. The route skirts the forest margins and there are occasional views down to the sea. Cross several streams – some areas can be a little boggy – and begin a gradual climb uphill along the bamboo- and begonia-lined trail. After about 2 hours, you'll meet a spur where you should head right. The trail has good signage and has been well cleared and maintained.

As you climb a series of switchbacks, you should hear and very possibly see jaco parrots – they are usually prolific around here. At the 3-hour mark, you'll meet a paved farm access road that will take you all the way to the Syndicate junction. To the left is Syndicate Falls, to the right is the Syndicate Nature Trail, visitor centre and Morne Diablotin trailhead.

If you're not walking there and back, the best way to do this segment is to pay someone to drop you off at the beginning and then thumb a lift or walk down to the west coast highway from Syndicate. I've seen people walking up the farm access road from Colihaut – also an option, though this will add a strenuous 90 minutes or more to the hike.

Appendix 1

ACCOMMODATION AT A GLANCE

Accommodation name	Location	Type	Price code	Page
3 Rivers Eco Lodge	Rosalie	SC	$	153
Atlantique View	Anse de Mai	H	$$$$	179
Aura Villa, Cottage & Apt	Shawford	SC	$–$$$$	111
Banana Lama Eco Villa & Cottages	Rosalie	SC	$$$	152
Belle View Bungalow	Savanne Paille, Portsmouth	SC	$$	178
Bluemoon Studio	Morne Prosper	SC	$	113
Caribbean Sea View	Mero	SC	$$	205
Charlotte Estate BnB	Newtown	H	$$$	95
Chez Ophelia Cottage Apartments	Copthall	H	$	113
Citrus Creek Plantation	La Plaine	SC	$$$	153
Classique International Guest House	Marigot	H	$$	179
Cocoa Cottage	Shawford	H	$$–$$$	113
Coconut Cottage	Toucari	SC	$$$	177
Coulibri Ridge	Soufriere	H/SC	$$$$$	132
Crescent Moon Cabins	Riviere La Croix	H	$$	205
D-Smart Farm	Pont Cassé	SC	$	206
Firefly Cabin at D'Auchamps	Shawford	SC	$	113
Fort Young Hotel	Roseau	H	$$$$–$$$$$	95
Harmony Villa	Pont Cassé	SC	$$$$$	205
Hibiscus Valley Inn	Concord	H	$–$$	153
Hideaways of Tibay Heights	Tibay, Picard	SC	$$	178
Hotel The Champs	Picard	H	$$–$$$	178
InterContinental Cabrits Resort & Spa	Portsmouth	H	$$$$$	177
Jungle Bay	Soufriere	H	$$$$–$$$$$	133
Kai Merle	Giraudel	SC	$$	133
Kai Morne Macak	Laudat	SC	$	113
La Flamboyant Hotel	Roseau	H	$$	95
Le Petit Paradis	Wotten Waven	H/SC	$	113
Lilly's Guesthouse	Brandy	H	$	178
Ma Bass Central Guesthouse	Roseau	H	$	96
Mango Garden Cottages	Savanne Paille, Portsmouth	SC	$–$$	178

Mango Island Lodges	St Joseph	H	$$$–$$$$	205
Manicou River	Portsmouth	H/SC	$$$$	177
Mountain Caapi Cottage	Cochrane	SC	$$	205
Nature's Cabin	Laudat	SC	$	114
Ocean Edge Lodge	Castle Comfort	H	$$	133
Pagua Bay House	Marigot	H	$$$$	152
Papillote Wilderness Retreat	Trafalgar	SC	$–$$	113
Picard Beach Cottages	Picard	H	$$$–$$$$	177
Pointe Baptiste Estate & Chocolate Cottage	Calibishie	SC	$–$$$$	179
Rodney's Wellness Retreat	Soufriere	SC	$	133
Roots Cabin	Wotten Waven	SC	$	114
Roots Jungle Retreat	Concord	H	$$	153
Rosalie Bay Eco Resort & Spa	Rosalie	H	$$$$	152
Rose St Gardens	Goodwill, Roseau	H	$–$$	96
Savanne Paille Holiday Homes	Savanne Paille, Portsmouth	SC	$$$	178
Sea Cliff Eco-Cottages	Calibishie	SC	$$–$$$	179
Secret Bay	Tibay, Picard	H/SC	$$$$$	177
Serenity Lodges	Concord	H	$	153
Soufriere Guest House	Soufriere	H/SC	$	133
St James Guesthouse	Goodwill, Roseau	H	$–$$	96
Sunset Bay Club	Coulibistrie	H	$$	206
Sutton Place Hotel	Roseau	H	$$$	95
Tamarind Tree Hotel	Salisbury	H/SC	$$–$$$	205
Tete Canal Cottages	La Plaine	SC	$	153
Touna Auté	Touna Concord	H	$	153
Veranda View Guesthouse	Calibishie	H	$	179
Villa Ayahora at Aywasi	Kalinago Territory	SC	$$$	153
Villa Passiflora & Cottage	Calibishie	SC	$$–$$$$$	178
Villa Vista	Calibishie	SC	$$$$	178
Wanderlust Caribbean	Calibishie	SC	$$$$	178

Appendix 2

ACTIVITIES AT A GLANCE

WHAT TO SEE AND DO

HIKING TRAILS

Appendix 3

FURTHER INFORMATION

If you have enjoyed Dominica and wish to pursue your interest, here's a selection of further reading options. The listings below are by no means comprehensive; they are just meant as a starting point for further research.

NON-FICTION

History and culture

Andre, Irving & Christian, Gabriel *Death By Fire* Pont Cassé Press, 2007; ISBN 978 0973734768

Bell, Stewart *Bayou of Pigs* Wiley, 2008; ISBN 978 0470153826

Boyd, Stanley A W *A Brief History of the Cathedral of Roseau* Roseau Public Library archives

Burton, Eileen *National Dress of Dominica* Paramount, 2003. Available from Dominica bookstores.

D'jamala Fontaine, Marcel *Dominica's Diksyonne, English Creole Dictionary* ISBN 1 85465074 2

Hauser, Mark W *Mapping Water in Dominica* University of Washington Press, 2021; ISBN 978 0295748719

Honychurch, Lennox *The Dominica Story* Macmillan, 1975; ISBN 0 333 62776 8

Honychurch, Lennox *Negre Mawon, The Fighting Maroons of Dominica* Island Heritage Initiatives, 2014

Jacob, Jeno J *Dominica's Folk Beliefs* 2008. Available from Dominica bookstores.

Keegan, William F & Hofman, Corinne L *The Caribbean Before Columbus* Oxford University Press, 2017; ISBN 978 0190605247

MacLean, Cathy & Mears, Karen *A Caribbean History, Hillsborough: a plantation in Dominica* Papillote Press, 2011; ISBN 978 0953222476

Pattullo, Polly *Your Time is Done Now: Slavery, Resistance and Defeat: the Maroon Trials of Dominica (1813–1814)* Papillote Press, 2015; ISBN 978 0957118775

Philogene Heron, Adom & Honychurch, Marica *Still Standing, The Ti Kais of Dominica* Papillote Press, 2022; ISBN 978 1838041588

Wilson, Samuel M *The Archaeology of the Caribbean* Cambridge University Press, 2007; ISBN 978 0521623339

Natural history

Adams, C Dennis *Caribbean Flora* Nelson Caribbean, 1976; ISBN 0 17 566186 3

Bannochie, Iris & Light, Marilyn *Gardening in the Caribbean* Macmillan, 1993; ISBN 0 333 56573 8

Evans, Peter G H & James, Arlington *A Guide to Geology, Climate and Habitats*. Available from Dominica bookstores and Forestry, Wildlife & Parks Division.

Evans, Peter *Birds of the Eastern Caribbean* Macmillan Caribbean, 2009; ISBN 978 0333521557

Evans, Peter G H & James, Arlington *Wildlife Checklists*. Available from Dominica bookstores and Forestry, Wildlife & Parks Division.

James, Arlington; Durand, Stephen; & Baptiste, Bertrand Jno *Dominica's Birds*. Available from Dominica bookstores and Forestry, Wildlife & Parks Division.

James, Arlington *Plants of Dominica's Southeast*. Available from Dominica bookstores and Forestry, Wildlife & Parks Division.

James, Arlington *Flora and Fauna of Cabrits National Park*. Available from Dominica bookstores and Forestry, Wildlife & Parks Division.

Lennox, G W & Seddon, S A *Flowers of the Caribbean* Macmillan, 1978; ISBN 0 333 26968 3

Lennox, G W & Seddon, S A *Trees of the Caribbean* Macmillan Caribbean, 1980; ISBN 978 0333287934

Malhotra, Anita & Thorpe, Roger S *Reptiles and Amphibians of the Eastern Caribbean* Macmillan Caribbean, 2007; ISBN 978 0333691410

Guides and travelogues

Bird, Jonathan *Dominica, Land of Water* Jonathan Bird Photography, 2004; ISBN 978 0972863414

Bond, James *Birds of the West Indies* Houghton Mifflin Harcourt, 1993; ISBN 978 0618002108

Bourne, M J; Seddon, S A; & Lennox, G W *Fruits and Vegetables of the Caribbean* Macmillan, 1988; ISBN 978 0333453117

Evans, P C H & Honychurch, Lennox *Dominica, Nature Island of the Caribbean* Hansib Publishing, 2009; ISBN 978 1906190255

Evans, Peter G H & James, Arlington *A Guide to Nature Sites*. Available from Dominica bookstores and Forestry, Wildlife & Parks Division.

Fermor, Patrick Leigh *The Traveller's Tree, A Journey Through the Caribbean Islands* John Murray Publishers Ltd, 2005; ISBN 978 0719566844

James, Arlington *An Illustrated Guide to Dominica's Botanic Gardens*. Available from Dominica bookstores and Forestry, Wildlife & Parks Division.

Kamyab, A *Dominica, A Tropical Paradise* AuthorHouse, 2009; ISBN 978 1438915678

Lawrence, Michael *Diving & Snorkelling Dominica* Lonely Planet, 1999; ISBN 0 86442764 6

Pattullo, Polly & Baptiste, Anne Jno *The Gardens of Dominica* Papillote Press, 1998; ISBN 0953222403

Pattullo, Polly *Roseau Valley Guide* Papillote Press, 2007. Available directly from the publisher, Papillotte Wilderness Retreat gift shop and Dominica bookstores.

Sullivan, Lynne M *Adventure Guide, Dominica & St Lucia* Hunter, 2005; ISBN 978 1588433930

Biographical

Higbie, Janet *Eugenia, the Caribbean's Iron Lady* Macmillan Caribbean, 1993; ISBN 978 0333572351

Kalinago People of Dominica *Yet We Survive* Papillote Press, 2007; ISBN 978 09532224 21

MacLean, Kathy Casimir *Black Man Listen, The Life of JR Ralph Casimir* Papillote Press, 2022; ISBN 9781838041526

Napier, Elma *Black And White Sands, a bohemian life in the colonial Caribbean* Papillote Press, 2009; ISBN 978 09532224 45

Paravisini-Gebert, Lizabeth *Phyllis Shand Allfrey, a Caribbean Life* Rutgers University Press, 1996; ISBN 0 813 52265

Pattullo, Polly & Sorhaindo, Celia, compiled by *Home Again, Stories of migration and return* Papillote Press, 2009; ISBN 978 09532224 52

Pizzichini, Lilian *The Blue Hour, a life of Jean Rhys* W W Norton & Company, 2009; ISBN 978 0393058031

FICTION

Novels and short stories

Aaron, Philbert *Decorated Broomsticks, a novel of political independence* Paramount, 2007; ISBN 978 97682121 84

Allfrey, Phyllis Shand *It Falls Into Place* Papillote Press, 2004; ISBN 978 0 9532224 14. Short stories.

Allfrey, Phyllis Shand *The Orchid House* Rutgers University Press, 1996; ISBN 978 0813523323

Brand, Pete *Harken's Caribbean Sea* Authorhouse, 2006; ISBN 978 1425947514

Bully, Alwin *The Cocoa Dancer* Papillote Press, 2021; ISBN 978 1838041564

Children of Atkinson School, Dominica *The Snake King of the Kalinago* Papillotte Press, 2010; ISBN 978 0 9532224 69

Christian, Gabriel *Rain on a Tin Roof* Pont Cassé Press, 1999; ISBN 978 0966845419

John, Marie-Elena *Unburnable* Harper Paperbacks, 2007; ISBN 978 0060837587

Kincaid, Jamaica *The Autobiography of My Mother* Plume, 1997; ISBN 978 0452274662

Lazare, Alick *Kalinago Blood* Abbott Press, 2013; ISBN 978 1458212641

Lazare, Alick *Pharcel, runaway slave* iUniverse, 2006; ISBN 978 0595395781

Rhys, Jean *Wide Sargasso Sea* W W Norton & Company, 1998; ISBN 978 0393960129

Shillingford, Christborne *Most Wanted, street stories from the Caribbean* Papillote Press, 2007; ISBN 978 0 9532224 38

Poetry and storytelling

Allfrey, Phyllis Shand *Love For An Island, collected poems* Papillote Press, 2014; ISBN 978 0957118751

Brumant, Lawrence *Ki Mannyè Donmnik Touvé Non'y (How Dominica Got its Name and Four Other Konts)*. Available from Dominica bookstores.

Cooke, Trish (illustrations by Caroline Binch) *Look Back!* Papillote Press, 2013; ISBN 978 095711872

Dominican Writers Guild *Words, Sound and Power, a collection of Dominican poetry.* Available from Dominica bookstores.

Grell, Jane Ulysses *Praise Songs* Papillote Press, 2013; ISBN 978 0957118744

John, Giftus *The Island Man Sings His Song* Writer's Showcase, 2001; ISBN 0595180906

John, Giftus *Mesyé Kwik! Kwak!* Virtualbookworm.com Publishing, 2005; ISBN 1589397649

Sorhaindo, Celia *Guabancex* Papillote Press, 2020: ISBN 978 1999776879

Sorhaindo, Celia *Radical Normalisation* Carcanet, 2022; ISBN 978 1800172395

Sorhaindo, Paula *Pulse Rock* Parnassus Publishing, 1993; ISBN 978 1871800401

Notes

Index

Page numbers in **bold** indicate major entries; those in *italic* to indicate maps

INDEX OF ADVERTISERS